TITANIC

About the Author

W. B. Bartlett is a writer and historian. He is the author of nine history books including *The Mongols: From Genghis Khan To Tamerlane* and *Islam's War Against the Crusaders*. He lives in Bournemouth.

Forthcoming from W. B. Bartlett:

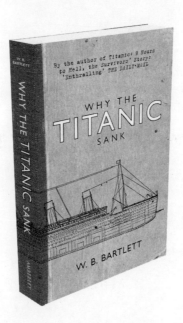

TITANIC

9 Hours to Hell,
the Survivors' Story

W.B. BARTLETT

AMBERLEY

Dedicated to my brother Darren

Cover illustrations: *Front & spine*: A drawing of the *Titanic* sinking by Henry Reuterdahl, prepared from material supplied by survivors of the wreck. © W.B. Bartlett. *Back cover*: *Titanic* survivors in lifeboat 12, the last to be picked by up *Carpathia* at about 8.30 a.m. © Jonathan Reeve JR2014f42 1912.

This edition first published 2011

Amberley Publishing
The Hill, Stroud
Gloucestershire, GL5 4EP

www.amberley-books.com

Copyright © W.B. Bartlett 2010, 2011

British Library Cataloguing in Publication Data.
A catalogue record for this book is available from the British Library.

ISBN 978 1 4456 0482 4
Typesetting and origination by Amberley Publishing
Printed in Great Britain

Contents

Acknowledgements

My sincere thanks to all who have helped with this book, especially Jonathan Reeve and the team at Amberley. Thanks too to family and friends who have lived with the *Titanic* for so long.

Prologue

And as the smart ship grew
In stature, grace and hue,
In shadowy silent distance
grew the iceberg too

THOMAS HARDY — *The Convergence of the Twain*

The impact of the *Titanic* story appears to show no sign of diminishing as time marches on. Some time in the next century the rusting hulk of the once-great ship will fade away to nothingness and will be no more than a geological anomaly, a lump of rogue iron with no shape or form, just a deposit, on the seabed. However, it is probable that the story itself will live on far longer than the ship because it is a classic tale of hubris, of fate, of pathos and of tragedy.

In the Middle Ages, the *Titanic* story might have been made up as a moral tale, a warning to rich and powerful mortals that however indestructible they might think themselves, there was something greater out there, a reminder of the old maxim that 'pride comes before a fall'. Back then they would have called it God but now, in a more secular world, we might name it Fate or even Nature. Whatever it is, it is more powerful than man.

Hundreds of publications have appeared on the great ship and this might prompt the question as to why another one should be written. The problem is that almost too much has been written about the *Titanic*, most books coming at the story from a particular angle in an attempt to be different. So much detail has been gone into that various *Titanic* sub-plots have become major stories in their own right, in particular the role of the nearby ship the *Californian* in the disaster.

Conspiracy theories too have made their inevitable appearance, such as the one that the *Titanic* was not the *Titanic* at all but her sister, the *Olympic*, damaged in a collision previously and sunk as part of an insurance scam. Highly convenient one might think that there happened to be an iceberg in the right place at the right time but a somewhat harsh judgement that 1,500 people had been condemned to death as a result.

The great danger of the level of detail available to researchers is that the simple story at the heart of it all can get lost. This book attempts to strip the story back to its basic level and to do so by relying in the main on the stories of eye-witnesses who saw everything close up. There is a wealth of such information around. Some survivors committed their stories to print. Over 100 witnesses were also interviewed in extensive Inquiries in the USA and Great Britain and the transcripts of these give hugely detailed records of the disaster and are in the main the sources of the material in this book.

In an attempt to give this account a narrative flow, I have deliberately avoided the use of footnotes. This is done out of a desire not to break up the storyline in any way. I have attempted to make it obvious in the text where quotations come from, or at least the individual they emanated from. There is in the storyline something of the quality of a saga and in my view this benefits from being told in a logical and sequenced way without the need for the reader to constantly cross-refer to footnotes.

Those who were there are the main sources used to describe these awe-inspiring events, with the aim of weaving their accounts together into a consistent narrative which tells the story in as straightforward a manner as possible. At the same time, it would be wrong to ignore the extra evidence that has come to light since the wreck itself was discovered in 1985, as this gives additional insights into some of the incidents of 14/15 April 1912. This too will be referred to at the appropriate places in the book.

The sequence followed in the book is broadly chronological. This is so that the reader might try and put themselves in the shoes of those who were present during the disaster, individuals who in the main had little idea when the iceberg was struck that the ship they were on was sinking and that it did not have enough lifeboats for over half of them. It is easy to think that the disaster must have been horrific looking back with our knowledge that the ship went down. How much worse then must the disaster have been when those involved in it only realized gradually that she was going to sink and that they were probably going to die, as if in slow motion?

It is important to note that the timings quoted in this book must of necessity be subject to some margin of error. Some specific examples will be mentioned when witnesses referred to individual events when there were differences of hours in their accounts. This does not mean that anyone was deliberately lying, in most cases there would be no reason for them to do so. It is just that when human beings are involved in great events, the memory can play tricks on them. However, I have tried to present events in a logical sequence. I do not claim to be perfect and there will no doubt be well-informed *Titanic* aficionados who will be able to pick holes in some of the timings. However, any errors present are there through human error (my own), not deliberate ignoring of the facts such as they are.

For a writer to state that he is not deliberately ignoring facts might seem like an odd thing to say, yet it must be recognized that there are certain features of the *Titanic* story that set it apart from many other historical events in terms of its historiography. The disaster was one that touched many people personally. In many ways, it still does. It inspires quite extraordinary partisanship and this is reflected in various commentaries on the disaster. This is because it is a tragedy that touches raw human emotions in a way that many other historical events do not.

It is not really because the *Titanic* was an event that, just about, happened within the timeframe of human memory which can of itself add to contentious expression. At the time of writing, the last *Titanic* survivor, Millvina Dean, has just passed on. She was just nine weeks old when the ship went down and remembered nothing of the event itself though of course she was more than aware of its repercussions on her life. No, this is not the reason for the partisanship.

The reason is far more the fact that it is easy for most people to identify as human beings with the roles of various actors in the drama. As a result, people *care* about the story far more than they do most others. This is in many ways laudable. It keeps the story alive and indeed helps it evolve. New findings from the wreck help expand our knowledge-base. Other findings also play their part; the reader will come across the amazing story of tragic baby Sidney Goodwin as one example.

Yet for some aspects of the tragedy it is virtually impossible to know the truth. Nowhere is a better example of this found than the part played in the drama by the *Californian*. This sub-plot of the disaster relies in the main on the stories of a small number of key witnesses especially from the ship itself. Yet most of them provided stories where key details were in direct contradiction of the accounts of other witnesses. To add to the confusion, some of these witnesses changed their stories over time (and then on occasion changed them back again).

In the absence of much in the way of incontrovertible forensic evidence, an observer's opinion is largely driven by the accounts of these contradictory eye-witnesses. Conclusions are arrived at by ignoring certain items of counter-evidence, implicitly judging that the statements of individual witnesses are wrong, deliberately or otherwise.

This is a dangerous position to be in. The observer makes a character judgment on individuals who are no longer alive, whose evidence only appears in a dry, dusty transcript with no real idea *how* it is given (watching someone give their evidence can give some extra insights into how reliable a witness is and how comfortable they feel with their story). The evidence available is also, crucially, in the main given without any form of cross-examination. No one was actually tried for their part in the disaster, with the exception of the White Star Line who were on the wrong end of a civil suit for their part in it and the avoidance of in-depth cross-examination leaves many a loose end to be tied up.

The point is this; it is impossible to know for certain what happened with the *Californian* in every detail. One can have an opinion for sure but that opinion must be subject to counter-argument; a counter-argument which can be fed with so-called facts from eye-witnesses. The end result is that there are some very-well prepared books about the *Californian* which assert that the ship was 5 miles away and on the scene, or 25 miles away and with one (and often more) ships between her and the *Titanic*. However, their conclusions can only be arrived at by either ignoring other counter-evidence or arguing its relevance and reliability away.

The story of the *Californian* is one that is subject to a considerable margin of error. It is merely the most extreme example of such a situation in the *Titanic* saga of which many other examples could be quoted: the actions of Captain E.J. Smith, what the band played when the ship went down, how Bruce Ismay, the White Star Chairman acted, how many people were in the lifeboats to give just a few random examples. Where possible I offer my answers to these questions in the account but, *mea culpa*, there are some where no definitive conclusion is possible.

These uncertainties in part are what make the story live on. In addition, the disaster is also highly relevant to anyone who gets on a ship even now. Many of the changes brought about by the disaster would almost certainly have happened anyway but the loss of the *Titanic* had a catalytic effect on legislation. Nowadays everyone in many jurisdictions supposedly has a place in a lifeboat, everyone has a lifeboat station (modern cruise passengers have to practise putting their lifebelts on and are often shown their boats before they even leave port), twenty-four hour round the clock radio operators are taken as a given. The tragedy drove all of these changes forward and, as is so often sadly the case, some good came out of an awful human disaster.

There is still much to be learnt and it is sadly still too often learnt painfully. When the ferry *Herald of Free Enterprise* turned turtle off Zeebrugge in 1987 she did so because water had poured through bow doors used for loading vehicles onto the ferry which had not been closed before sailing. It does not take a maritime expert to know that this cannot be good for a ship yet perhaps the most amazing fact about the whole tragedy in which nearly 200 people died was that there was no warning light on the bridge to say that the doors were still open; a simple enough measure, the absence of which had disastrous results. Ignoring the obvious was a feature of the *Titanic* too.

The *Herald* disaster also highlighted other issues, some resonant of the *Titanic*. The British Secretary of State for Transport noted that ferries frequently continued to sail with more passengers than their permitted maximum with all the implications of this in a crisis and the availability and accessibility of lifesaving equipment for all. The most extreme example of this was the foundering of the Philippine ferry the *Dona Paz* in 1987. The loss of life here was extraordinary but, because the ship was overcrowded and there were therefore not boats for everyone and proper passenger manifests had not been maintained, it is impossible to know how many were lost. However, most estimates suggest that over 4,000 people perished.

Of course the problem is, as the British publication *The Economist* noted on 26 June 2008: 'the rules governing shipping safety are comprehensive but they are often weakly enforced' (more so in some parts of the world than others it must be said). From time to time old lessons need to be learned by a new generation in a way that is painful and tragic. Yet the main conclusions about the *Titanic* were that no rules were broken in the disaster but that the rules themselves were deficient and in need of updating.

The *Titanic* disaster continues to exercise a fascination in a way that others do not, even though it has long been replaced as the worst shipping disaster in terms of life lost (it is not even clear that it was at the time; the steamboat *Sultana* blew up in 1865 near Memphis, Tennessee; some estimates suggest that 1,800 lives were lost, 300 more than perished on the *Titanic*). This is because the roll-call of death is not the main reason for our fascination; it is the human drama that keeps bringing us back to it of which that huge list of the lost is just a part.

Most people in the West have heard of the *Titanic* disaster, even children. New generations are introduced to the story in different ways. For me, it was as a child of around ten years of age watching *A Night to Remember* one Christmas via a small, grainy, black-and-white TV picture. I was at once hooked by the story and its elements of Greek tragedy. It was of course a romantic image, of heroic death, of stoicism in the face of adversity, which was not justified by the facts but the image created touched something deep inside because it was a life-and-death tale that affected everyone there, rich and poor, great and small, young and old. That person on the deck could have been me, you, everyman.

For many the story lives on, its longevity aided by Hollywood blockbusters and amazing underwater exploration and marine archaeology. Although the essential details might be a constant, new information is being unearthed all the time and so the tale continues to evolve. Neither is it just a collection of personal accounts of life and death, it is also a fascinating insight into a social structure that no longer exists (most would say, thank goodness for that) and it is therefore an important insight into wider historical issues. It raises questions about class structures, about gender (women and children first, or not?). It even gives insights into similarities and differences between the USA and Great Britain, then two great powers, back in 1912.

This is why I felt I had to write this book, to tell the story but also to give an insight into the history. No one, I trust, can fail to be touched at some level by the sheer gamut of human emotions in the tale, which remains as vivid and relevant as ever. This is what has driven me to write this book. I am absolutely convinced that such motivations will continue to inspire other authors for generations to come.

I
Arrival:
18 April 1912, NewYork & Washington

Night had fallen, throwing a dark blanket over the heaving crowds waiting; waiting to see loved ones that they had thought never to see again, waiting to have telegram messages of survival confirmed, waiting more often than not to have the last threads of hope cut once and for all. It was just four days since the first unbelievable news had come through that the great ship was in trouble. But no one could believe that the trouble was serious for, after all, she was a triumph of modern engineering, practically unsinkable, as safe as any vessel could be. Then came the reassurance; yes, the *Titanic* had struck an iceberg but she was alright and being towed to Halifax by the *Virginian* with all her passengers safe. But then more news had come in, disturbing, incomprehensible, beyond belief. The unthinkable had happened. The unsinkable had sunk.

As the bald facts emerged, a harrowing tale evolved. Of over 2,200 people onboard, just over 700 had survived. There had been insufficient lifeboat capacity for even half those sailing on her. There had been heart-rending scenes as wives bade a last farewell to husbands who bravely gave up their places in the boats so that others might live. The captain had been a true hero, calming everyone's nerves to the last and going down with his ship, demanding of all his fellow-victims that they must, first and foremost, 'Be British'. The passengers, stoically accepting their fate, sang a hymn of resignation accompanied by the band even as the ship slid down into the abysses of the ocean to her grave. Just four days, and the myths had already started to take shape.

There had been one hero above all others in this tragedy though. His name was Captain Arthur Rostron, skipper of the *Carpathia*. Receiving news that the *Titanic* was in trouble, he had turned his ship around and raced through a terrifying ice-field, shattering her personal best time in the process. Knowing that he was taking a great risk with his own safety and that of his crew and passengers, he had nevertheless deemed the risk necessary with so many souls at stake. Sadly, he had arrived only in time to pick up those who had found a place in the all too few lifeboats. That did not diminish his heroism and his reputation, almost alone among those involved in this catastrophe, had been secured for life by his actions.

It was his ship that was now eagerly awaited. The *Carpathia* had just passed the Statue of Liberty, that beacon of hope that was the symbolic traditional welcome to all those who came to America to find fame and fortune or merely to return home. The feelings of excitement that would normally be present at such a moment were on this occasion conspicuous by their absence. Many of the survivors on the *Carpathia* had lost loved ones on the *Titanic* and even those who had not were scarred by the nightmarish scenes they had witnessed.

Usually at the end of a trans-Atlantic crossing, the third-class passengers, 'steerage' as they were called at the time (the name had recently been officially dropped but was still in routine use in practice), would be put ashore at Ellis Island, there to be interrogated by customs officials to ensure that they were fit and proper persons to be accepted into the community of the United States of America. But in the circumstances, the normal formalities had been dropped. Steerage passengers would instead be quizzed by customs officials in New York itself. There were anyway a lot less of them than had been expected.

The *Carpathia* was not expected to dock until midnight but by 8.00 p.m. people with passes had started to be allowed onto the pier where she was due to tie up. Among the first to arrive was a delegation from the Stock Exchange complete with $5,000 in small bills to distribute to the needy. Religious representatives were there too: Miss Eva Booth from the Salvation Army, clerics from St Patrick's Cathedral, black-robed Sisters of Charity and a host of others. This was a time when spiritual consolation and practical help were needed in equal measure.

Mrs W.K. Vanderbilt had spent the day telephoning around her friends, organizing 100 limousines to ferry survivors around. Immigration Commissioner Williams had arranged for his staff to be at the pier when the *Carpathia* docked now the usual immigration rituals painstakingly observed at Ellis Island were to be dispensed with. His staff had been told to be sensitive. However, he suspected that some who had lost everything in the disaster would need to be sent back to their places of origin. Compassion had its place but sometimes one had to be cruel to be kind.

The Municipal Lodging House, with room for 700 people, had been prepared to put up any of the survivors for as long as they required accommodation. Twenty ambulances were on standby to transport any who might need it. Hospitals all over New York were prepared to deal with any casualties onboard. Charitable organizations were poised to help whoever needed it; the German Society of New York, the Irish Immigrant Society, the Italian Society, the Swedish Immigrants Society and the Young Men's Christian Association and many others.

The disaster had touched the heart of the city. Much of the help was needed and gratefully received. Some of it however was superfluous; there were simply fewer survivors than had been hoped for. The Red Cross had turned over all immediate relief work to the Women's Relief Committee, while the Salvation Army had arranged for fifty single men to be housed in accommodation in the city. Everyone it seemed wanted to do their bit to help those onboard the ship that was even now edging its way past the Statue of Liberty and down the Hudson River to Cunard Pier 54.

There was a huge amount of public interest in what was then a disaster of unparalleled magnitude. The crowds were enormous, some no doubt there out of genuine anxiety to find out the fate of loved ones, others out of curiosity, wanting to experience vicariously something of this titanic tragedy. Apart from anything else, it was a policing headache that the city could well do without.

There were some important political representatives in the throng. Major Blanton was there to enquire after the fate of Major Archibald Butt, reputedly at the insistence of President Taft, whose military attaché Butt was. Frantic wireless messages had been sent to the rescue ship *Carpathia* to enquire whether he was onboard or not. Harold Cottam, the wireless operator of the ship, had previously sent out a list of first and second-class survivors. Butt's name was not on it. However, the President hoped there had been a mistake, hence messages enquiring specifically about his fate. But Cottam had been overwhelmed by the volume of traffic and had been unable to answer any messages. Some however were later to impute different reasons for his silence.

To keep control of the multitudes, New York's Mayor Gaynor arrived with Police Commissioner Waldo to take charge of policing arrangements at the pier. Anticipating big crowds, large numbers of policemen had been deployed and they were much needed. The area around the pier was cordoned off and only those who had been issued with passes were allowed through. Coroners Feinberg and Holtzhauser were on standby in case there were any bodies aboard the *Carpathia,* along with an undertaker to treat the same with due dignity. Fortunately, these particular measures would be redundant.

Some could not wait for the *Carpathia* to dock to find out what had happened. During the day, the river had become a hive of activity, busy with a number of craft hoping to make early communication with the rescue ship. Some were carrying relatives of those onboard the *Titanic* who wanted to find out their fate as soon as they could, others housed opportunistic journalists hoping for a scoop. The sea was blowing up rough and there was a light fog, a gloomy pall to cloud the scene. The waiting seemed to go on and on but then, from out at sea, a shape at last loomed, the heroic *Carpathia* heaving into view, much earlier than expected.

As she drew closer, an unearthly hush descended on the scene. There was weeping, but quiet, dignified, not hysterical. A fleet of tugs were now shepherding the ship in. Flashlights started to light up the darkened sky, lightning flashes. The whole scene had a Wagnerian feel about it; Götterdämmerung, 'The Twilight of the Gods', would be particularly apt. A few silhouetted figures could be seen by the ship's rail but otherwise all appeared deserted, as if those on the *Carpathia* could not bear to face the world. An immigration inspection team drew up to the ship's side in a tug. A health official climbed aboard the *Carpathia* from her.

Now just a few minutes from stepping on dry land once more, a feeling perhaps he had thought never to experience again, Lawrence Beesley, a school teacher travelling on the *Titanic* in second-class, looked out from the rescue ship, pondering on his experiences, perhaps already thinking that he should commit them to print. He could not speak for all the passengers aboard, for there were in reality 2,200 different stories to tell but he suspected there might be some interest in the events of the night of 14/15 April among the general public. He was not wrong.

For those on the *Carpathia*, the sight of land coming into view again shortly before was a blessed relief that many had expected never to witness. It was a welcome sight, the first view of *terra firma* passengers like Beesley had seen for a week. Now the armada appeared. Tugs thronged the Hudson River, trying to negotiate the best position for newspaper photographers onboard to take a shot of a *Titanic* survivor. The flashes of magnesium bulbs from the tugs were supplemented by more distant explosions from those trying to take photographs from the shore. At last, the *Carpathia* made her way towards the Cunard pier where the *Titanic's* bedraggled survivors were expected to disembark.

The *Carpathia* was expected to dock at Cunard's Pier 54 but she first of all sailed past it. Instead she made her way to the White Star dock, which had been specially lengthened to receive the *Titanic* and her giant sister ships. How tragically ironic that the great ship would never once dock here. Instead, the *Carpathia* now lowered all that was left of her in a quiet and dignified manner. The lifeboats which she had brought back with her (thirteen had been rescued from the full complement of sixteen boats and four collapsibles) from the ice-ridden North Atlantic were returned to their rightful owners. It was an act more eloquent than any words could ever be, for in one poignant moment the full horror of the disaster that had occurred was symbolically affirmed in the eyes of the watching world.

Then the rescue ship sailed to her final destination, Pier 54. As she drew close, questions were shouted up from the shore. A buyer from the famous store Macys asked if Mr and Mrs Straus were aboard. No one answered; theirs would be one of the most poignant of all *Titanic* legends. At last, the giant hawsers that secured the ship were tied up and the gangplanks were lowered. A fenced area had been set up to protect the survivors when they finally stepped ashore, any minute now.

Crowds of reporters were ready to throng around them as they walked off the gangplank, wanting to know more about the myths that had already started to establish themselves. Did any of the officers commit suicide? Did passengers shoot each other? Had there been blind, uncontrollable panic aboard as the *Titanic's* fate became known to everyone aboard?

Passengers started to come ashore. The first of them were those who had been on the *Carpathia*, expecting to sail across to Europe and who were now returning to American shores much earlier than they had anticipated. They were smartly dressed though perhaps a trifle diffident about their moment in the news. Then, a few passengers more hesitant than these first arrivals started to tread cautiously down the gangplank. They were dressed in ill-fitting, unsuitable clothes but more than this their eyes, with their haunted looks, as if they had been witness to some apocalyptic vision, gave the game away. These were undoubtedly *Titanic* survivors.

Now they started to tentatively make their way onto the shore. Desperate families peered anxiously out at the ship, looking for loved ones who had been on the *Titanic* to appear, often in vain. Mr Allison from Montreal was there, looking for the family of four of his close relatives that had been onboard. Only one of them, eleven-month-old Hudson Allison, had survived. Hudson's father, (also Hudson), mother Bessie, and two-year-old sister, Helen, were gone forever. Bessie and Helen were both particularly unfortunate as they were first-class passengers and few other women and no other children from their privileged group had been lost.

Down the gangplank too came Mrs Madeleine Astor, the young widow of J.J. Astor, one of the richest men in America who had gone down with the *Titanic*. She made her way unaided onto the dockside, which must have come as a surprise to those who had heard the rumour that she had died onboard the *Carpathia* just an hour or two before. Her stepson was there to meet her but said little. It may well have been out of respect and sensitivity as he said. But it might also have been because of resentment; Mrs Astor was thirty years her late husband's junior and he had divorced his first wife to marry her not long before. Her stepson was older than her.

Perhaps one of the saddest homecomings was that of the Ryerson family. Mrs Ryerson, aged forty-eight, was travelling with three of her children. She had said goodbye to her husband Arthur when they left the sinking *Titanic* in Boat 4, one of the later boats to leave. Arthur Ryerson had been lost.

What made their situation more poignant was their reason for making the crossing in the first place. Their eldest son had been killed in an automobile accident on Easter Monday, just a few days before *Titanic* bade her farewells to Southampton for the first and last time. They were going home already overwhelmed with grief and now this. There was just one moment of relief for the waiting Ryerson clan. The youngest son, Jack, had not been reported among the survivors to those ashore and now they saw the welcome sight of him looking down from the rails of the *Carpathia* to at least partly anaesthetize their grief.

All this was devastatingly sad, each loss representing an awful tragedy and a lost life that could not be replaced. However, less attention was paid to the fate of some of the immigrant families, of whom a number had been aboard. Few told the story for example of the Rice family who had boarded in Queenstown. Six of them had got aboard her and none of them had survived. Or the Goodwins; eight boarded in Southampton, none survived. Then there was the Panulas, immigrants who had also joined in Southampton; six sailed out, none got off. Or the Skoogs, more Southampton boarders; six got on, none survived. Four families (and there were others), all of them from different nations, each with different stories to tell. Yet they shared two things in common. They were all lost, each and every one of them. And all of them travelled in third-class.

Their tale sat uncomfortably with the heroic stories of women and children first that were already becoming legend within days of the catastrophe. Helen Allison, the tragic little first-class girl lost on the ship, became a heart-wrenching symbol of the extent of the tragedy. The image of her tugging her mother's coat-tails became a poignant and tear-jerking *memento mori* for the wider world. Few however mentioned poor Sidney Goodwin, aged one, his brother Harold, aged nine and his sister Jessie, ten who were all lost, along with their mother Augusta and their elder sister, Lillian, aged sixteen. They were all women or children but they were all lost too.

This is not to diminish the terror that tiny Helen or her mother felt as they faced the end together in unbelievably harrowing circumstances but it serves to make a wider point. People were interested in what happened to the first-class millionaires, the star-studded cast who played the main roles in the *Titanic* drama. They were far less interested in the third-class, the 'extras', who faced an equally terrifying fate with odds far more weighted against their survival.

No one seemed to care much about the third-class passengers. Logan Marshall, who chronicled the disaster in 1912, meticulously listed both first and second-class survivors and those lost when the great ship went down but noted that 'a list of third-class passengers and crew is omitted owing to the impossibility of obtaining the correct names of many'.

This is arrant nonsense. There were both crew and passenger manifests and although there were questions about some specific names, it is revealing that a fairly comprehensive list of names is now available a century later, albeit with one or two question marks, but it was not available in 1912. The truth was that no one much bothered about third-class nor, for that matter, the crew, who apart from officers and a few select other categories, such as the radio operators, the band (neither category actually really crew in the strictest sense of the word) or the engineers (who died to a man), attracted little public attention.

There were over 200 third-class survivors, and when they left the *Carpathia* they looked bedraggled, their clothing makeshift and their general appearance derelict. There was a Syrian woman among them, headed for Youngstown, Ohio, accompanied by a six-year-old girl. She had, the press reported, lost her husband and three brothers in the disaster, and was now largely on her own in a strange land. She was representative of many others of her class among the survivors. Many of the third-class had been travelling in families and few survived intact. For these, the journey to America had typically been the fulfilment of a dream, a voyage to a land of promise and potential in which their lives would take a dramatic turn for the better. But the dream had turned into a nightmare.

Among the survivors were two mysterious little boys. They were French and had been onboard the *Titanic* with their father, who had been lost. However, no one could find out much about them and they had been informally adopted by nineteen-year-old Margaret Hayes, a fellow survivor, who spoke French too. However, as the boys were only two and three years old, there was little that they could tell anyone about who they belonged to. Although there was a warmth between the newly-formed family, communication was still difficult, so much so that Margaret did not even know their names.

Miss Hayes had got off in Boat 7, accompanied by her Pomeranian dog. The two little French boys had been dropped into the last boat to be lowered from the *Titanic's* sloping boat deck, a collapsible put into the water just after 2.00 a.m., only a quarter of an hour before the ship's final plunge. Only later did the truth emerge and a happy ending of sorts emerged from this darkest of tragedies. Their real surname was Navratil, their first names Edmund and Michel. Their father, also Michel, had abducted them from his estranged wife, and they had boarded the *Titanic* under assumed names in Southampton. In the publicity that attended them after their extraordinary survival, they were recognized by their mother and eventually reunited with her.

Among those onboard the *Carpathia* was a stewardess, Violet Jessop, whose career would be to say the least extraordinary. She had noticed that, long before the *Carpathia* had docked, there were anxious shouts from the shore enquiring whether such-and-such a person was aboard. It was only then that the full extent of the *Titanic* disaster became apparent. Not only were those on the quayside frantic with worry, a concern exacerbated by the paucity of solid news that they had received. So too were those on the *Carpathia* who had survived the sinking of the *Titanic.* Until this moment they had hoped that other rescue ships might have picked up loved ones. Now it was clear that such hopes were in vain.

The surviving crew of the *Titanic* were not disembarked with the rest. They were instead taken by a tender, the *George Starr*, to Pier 61. From here, it was planned that they would be transhipped back to England onboard the *Lapland*. However, an American senator, William Alden Smith, had plans to keep some of them on American soil for rather longer than some of them wished.

And so at last some at least of the passengers of *RMS Titanic* had arrived in New York. Now they made their way towards an uncertain future. Some of them were of course much more fortunate than others. The first-class survivors had suffered losses, and the death of husbands and sons was a personal tragedy, but at least they had financial security to hold onto for the future. For the steerage passengers, all too often no such security pertained. Many had lost literally everything on the *Titanic* and were destitute in a strange country, normally with the main breadwinner of the family lost.

The following morning, kind souls ashore met the survivors with clothes they had collected to help people who had, in many cases, lost everything. They were laid out on tables, like a jumble sale thought Violet Jessop. The women in particular looked like wet hens, dressed now in old clothes many seasons out of date. But they, at least, had their lives. That night and the following morning, New York was the centre of the world with everyone looking on in a way which they might not perhaps do again until another disaster struck the city in 2001.

The same day that the *Carpathia* came in, 19 April 1912, a short distance to the north in Boston another, very unglamorous, steamer made her way into port. There were few journalists there to meet her, though there were some. They had heard, erroneously as it happened, that she was carrying some bodies from the wreck onboard. The *Californian* had arrived at the scene of the disaster just as the *Carpathia* had picked up the last lifeboat load of survivors. The journalists went away disappointed. There was no story to be had here.

The *Californian's* crew disembarked for a short spell of shore leave. One of them, the ship's carpenter McGregor, had a cousin living in Clinton, close to Boston, whom he went to visit. Chatting as relatives who only see each other occasionally do, carpenter McGregor related a strange tale of rockets in the night, of a ship in distress, of another ship that did not go to her aid. The journalists would certainly have a story to tell with this material if they ever got hold of it.

But for the moment, the world was looking elsewhere. As the *Titanic* survivors made their way ashore along with the passengers and crew of the *Carpathia,* among the latter was the young wireless operator, Harold Cottam. Cottam was a man on a mission, the nature of which would be the cause of much critical comment in some quarters. He was on his way to meet Frederick Sammis, a senior official of the Marconi Company in the nearby Strand Hotel. Sammis had arranged to meet him there and put him in touch with a *New York Times* reporter to whom he would sell an 'exclusive'. A four-figure sum was believed to be involved, which Cottam was to share with the *Titanic's* surviving operator, Harold Bride.

In the event, Cottam and Sammis missed each other. The latter had made his way through the thronged streets along with Signor Guglielmo Marconi. The impact of the disaster was to be double-edged for the great inventor who had been the first man to successfully send a 'wireless' message and had since proved himself a very astute businessman as well as an outstanding scientist. On the one hand, Marconi would be lionized as his invention had perhaps been responsible for saving the lives of those who did survive the sinking. On the other hand, certain aspects of his company's operations were to appear decidedly unethical.

Sammis and Marconi made their way up the gangplank and into the *Carpathia's* wireless shack. There they found an operator still hard at work, no less a man than Harold Bride from the *Titanic.* Despite being injured in the wreck, Bride – who could not walk properly as a result of his injuries and frostbite from immersion in ice-cold water – had helped Cottam deal with the huge volume of messages that were sent in the aftermath of the catastrophe and even now was getting off a few last communications.

It was time for him to leave his post; he had performed heroically. Now, unable to walk, he had to be carried ashore. He had suffered cruelly, both from the effects of frostbite and from having his legs crushed when he was perilously perched on an upturned collapsible boat. His survival was crucial in terms of the evidence that would later be unearthed at the enquiries that would soon follow, both in America and Britain, for he could tell an incredulous world of the half-dozen or so ice warnings that the *Titanic* had received before she hit the berg.

An extraordinary tale was about to emerge, one that would stun the world, then and now. It was a tale with the whole gamut of emotions and behaviours. That there was heroism was undeniable but that there was less heroic behaviour was equally apparent. There had been complacency too, on a staggering scale, a complacency exacerbated by fatal incompetence. The whole tragedy was, most poignantly of all, completely avoidable.

There would be debates aplenty about why the ship sank. Conspiracy theories would make their inevitable appearance as they always do with disasters of such magnitude that the human mind cannot comprehend them (witness for example the assassination of President Kennedy or the death of Diana, Princess of Wales). Others suggest that her construction was faulty. A rogue fire was fingered for the loss of the ship. There seemed to be a thousand theories as to what had gone wrong.

There was, and is, though, one fact amid the many disputed ones that is broadly incontrovertible (though people still argue over the odd one or two statistics, as if the debate was one of pure accountancy rather than human tragedy). Over 2,200 passengers and crew left Queenstown, Ireland for New York. Over 700 arrived at their final destination alive (most estimates are in the range of 705-712 survivors). This is their story, both the saved and the lost.

2

Three Ships:
Titanic, Carpathia & Californian

This is a story more than anything about people, especially the several thousand souls aboard the *Titanic*. But to ignore the ships involved in these momentous events would be like trying to appreciate a great drama without considering the set. In fact, there are three sets. The major scenes were played out of course on the *Titanic* itself but important acts were set on two other ships, the *Carpathia* and the *Californian*. Various other ships were also involved, though more peripherally; these included the *Mount Temple*, the *Frankfurt* and the *Olympic* and indeed others that were on the spot, some of them never securely identified.

But of them all, it is of course the *Titanic* that takes pride of place. It is time to consider her, for she is a core part of the myth. In modern times, Hollywood has billed her as 'the ship of dreams', unsurpassed both in opulence and size. That is not so far from the truth but, in the best traditions of Hollywood, it is not really the whole truth. It is worth looking at her credentials in more detail for in so doing a few myths may be reinforced but others merely dissolve.

She was indeed, as people liked to say at the time, the largest moving object ever made by man. At over 46,000 tons by volume, she was bigger than her closest rival for the title of the world's largest ship (which was indeed her older sister, the *Olympic*). At 882½ feet long, illustrations of the time showed her exceeding in length the height of the world's tallest buildings. In fact her size was a major problem for there were no ports in the world that could cope with her without being adapted. So far, so reinforcing.

But the *Titanic* was only one of a class of three super-ships, the second in a triumvirate which was meant to secure White Star's position as a world-leader in the shipping business. It was the first of the three, *Olympic* – after which the class was named – that really changed the rules of the game. For the class as a whole moved the goalposts. Each ship in it would be massively bigger than her rivals from other shipping lines.

To understand the impact of these super-ships perhaps a sense of relativity is useful. White Star's main rival on the North Atlantic route, certainly as far as ships sailing from Britain were concerned, was Cunard. The flagships of Cunard's fleet were the *Mauretania* and *Lusitania*. These ships were renowned for their speed, and were considered greyhounds of the seas. As a result of their powerful engines and sleek lines, the ships sliced through the choppy waters of the North Atlantic far faster than their rivals and the *Mauretania* had seized the coveted Blue Riband, the prestigious award that belonged to the ship that crossed the Atlantic in record time, in 1909; she would hold it for another twenty years.

White Star decided not to compete with Cunard for speed, which incidentally means that rumours that the *Titanic* was after a speed record on her maiden voyage are nonsensical; such a record was a physical impossibility. Instead, the *Olympic* class ships would compete on their size and on the grandness of their fittings. They would be 50 per cent larger than their Cunard rivals in terms of gross tonnage; the *Mauretania* and *Lusitania*, both launched in 1906, weighed 31,938 gross tons and 31,550 gross tons respectively. The new White Star ships were manifestations of brute strength and power, driven on with a staggering force of 55,000 horsepower. Coal stocks of 650 tons per day would be required to drive these monsters.

However, the *Olympic*-class ships would not have the field to themselves. Appropriately enough given the contest for supremacy between the British and German naval fleets that was then underway and would lead, among other factors, to a World War in 1914, it was German shipping lines that were giving White Star and Cunard the toughest run for their money. Ironically, the *Titanic* if she had stayed afloat would only have been the largest ship in the world for about a month. In May 1912, the Hamburg Amerikan Line planned to launch the *Imperator*, even bigger than the *Titanic*. No one could fault her interior design either; the man responsible for it had previously done the same for the renowned Ritz Hotel in London. So if the *Titanic* was the largest and most luxurious ship in the world when she went down, she would only have stayed that way for a few weeks.

The *Titanic* and her sister ships were built in Belfast by Harland & Wolff in their yards at Queens Island. The relationship between the company and the White Star Line was a crucial one commercially for the Belfast shipbuilder. Although the yard did not build exclusively for White Star, co-operation between the two companies was long established and vital for Harland & Wolff's continued viability. White Star gave Harland & Wolff something not too far removed from a blank cheque for the ships they built. The cost of building each ship constructed for White Star would be reimbursed with a profit margin of 5 per cent added on. This might not be much by modern standards but by those of 1912 it was considered more than satisfactory by the shipyard.

Much *carte blanche* was given to Harland & Wolff to design the ship too. Generally, White Star would map out a general idea of what was required from a particular ship and leave the fine detail to the shipyard to come up with. Of course, there would be regular meetings as work progressed during which White Star would ask for specific modifications to be made. However, taken as a whole the relationship between the two companies was one of mutual trust and respect, one in which cost considerations did not play the same overriding role as they might do in a modern commercial environment.

This relationship went back a long way, indeed to the birth of the White Star Line itself. In 1867, Thomas Henry Ismay purchased Wilson and Chambers, a bankrupt company whose vessels sailed to Australia, for the princely sum of £1,000. He worked closely on the scheme with Gustav Schwabe, who was employed by the Harland & Wolff shipyards in Belfast; his uncle, Gustav Wolff, was in fact a partner in the company. With the deal to establish White Star duly completed, Ismay entered into a contract with the Belfast shipyard to build three new vessels, each just under 4,000 tons each.

The first ship resulting from this collaboration, the *Oceanic*, came off the stocks on 27 August 1870. The year before, White Star had begun sailing the North Atlantic route. On 2 March 1871, the *Oceanic* crossed the Atlantic to New York for the first time. It was the start of a long and lucrative working relationship between White Star and Harland & Wolff. Before long, White Star had become one of the major players on the North Atlantic run, a classic Victorian success story of entrepreneurial businessmen striking it rich. The company's pennant, a vivid red background with a prominent white star, was one of the most familiar of all maritime sights.

On 1 January 1891, Ismay's son Bruce was admitted to the business as a partner. When his father retired just a year later, Bruce Ismay and his brother James took over the reins. Further developments followed. A new *Oceanic* was launched in 1899, sailing from Liverpool to New York on 6 September of that year. The relationship between White Star and Harland Wolff showed no sign of abating with the arrival of a new Chairman.

However, the world in which White Star operated was about to change dramatically. Increased competition between shipping companies had an enormous effect on prices. By the beginning of the twentieth century, a third-class ticket could be bought for £8, bringing trans-Atlantic travel within the range of many more people. Competition brought with it a hunger for profit. In 1900, the American Line was at the centre of the formation of a huge shipping organization that intended to dominate the North Atlantic market. Led by a financier of enormous wealth, J. Pierpoint Morgan, it started to buy up all other American shipping companies.

This was a serious threat, from which even White Star with its prominent position was not immune. Harland & Wolff, who built all White Star's ships, found that some of their clients in America were swallowed up. In 1901, Morgan approached the White Star Line, now under the control of Bruce Ismay, to broker a deal to add Ismay's company to his growing empire. Ismay's initial reaction was dismissive; the whole scheme was to him 'a swindle and a humbug'. However, Lord Pirrie, Chairman of Harland & Wolff, desperately wanted the scheme to go ahead and secure the future of his shipyard.

Money eventually talked. A huge offer, £10 million, was agreed as the purchase price of the White Star Line. A massive new consortium was formed as a result, known as the International Mercantile Marine (IMM). However, even this huge juggernaut of a company was not the end of Morgan's aspirations. Approaches were made to Cunard, White Star's main British rival. Cunard made no secret of these in an attempt to frighten the British government, who were increasingly concerned at so much commercial maritime power in the hands of Americans, into protecting them.

As a business ploy, it worked. The British government agreed in effect to subsidize future construction projects, such as those involving the *Mauretania* and the *Lusitania*, provided that the ships were handed over to the government in times of war for use as auxiliary cruisers. This ensured that the proposed Cunard merger with the new IMM was a dead duck. The potential use of these vessels as auxiliary warships also meant that they were theoretically safer than White Star's ships given their more extensive watertight arrangements. However, this of course did the *Lusitania* little good in practice.

There was no doubt where power lay in this new organization. There were thirteen directors, eight of whom were Americans. However, both Ismay and Lord Pirrie, the Chairman of Harland & Wolff, were also to be directors, though other senior members of White Star, including James Ismay, Bruce's brother, lost their places as a result of the takeover. Bruce Ismay, an astute businessman whose skills were appreciated by Morgan, probably the foremost moneyman of his generation, soon found himself as President and Managing Director of IMM and its subsidiaries.

In 1907, a fateful discussion took place at Downshire House, London, the Belgrave Square mansion of Lord Pirrie of Harland & Wolff. He and Ismay discussed a new class of ships, bigger than any ever built, to face up to the challenge of North Atlantic rivals like Cunard (who had launched the *Mauretania* and *Lusitania* just the year before) and the increasingly assertive German lines such as Hamburg-Amerikan and the North German S. P. Lloyd. In keeping with White Star traditions, the new ships would compete on size, not speed (several White Star ships had already held the unofficial title of 'largest ship afloat'), and also on the luxuriant nature of their fittings. It was from these dinner-time discussions that the idea of the *Olympic*-class ships emerged.

The main characteristics of these ships would be their scale and their opulence. However, it would not be fair to suggest that no thought would be given to safety. The three *Olympic*-class ships would be built with watertight bulkheads and compartments, and the ships each had a double-bottom, though the double-plating did not extend up the sides of the ship as they did in the *Mauretania* and *Lusitania*. However, the double-bottom ran the full length of the ship varying from 5 feet 3 inches to 6 feet 3 inches in depth.

When White Star's marketing materials were assembled, the company made great play on the design of their ships. Describing the *Olympic* and *Titanic* in 1910, publicity brochures proudly proclaimed 'these two wonderful vessels are designed to be unsinkable'. White Star could say, of course, that they did not actually say they *were* unsinkable, merely that they were designed to be so. However, it might be argued that this is mere semantics and that it encouraged a mythology that the ships could not sink to develop.

It was a trend that would be reinforced by a review of the ships' watertight compartments by the professional magazine *Shipbuilder* in 1911, which said:

> each door is held in the open position by a suitable friction clutch, which can be instantly released by means of a powerful electro-magnet controlled from the captain's bridge, so that in the event of accident, or at any time when it may be considered advisable, the captain can, by simply moving an electric switch, instantly close the doors throughout and make the vessel practically unsinkable.

Again, the word 'practically' was not quite definitive but many people clearly did think the new ships were actually unsinkable.

In the light of what later happened, the extent of the ships' watertight arrangements, comprising sixteen compartments, further divided by fifteen transverse watertight bulkheads, was significant. The way the ships had been designed meant that the first four compartments could be flooded and the *Titanic* or her sisters would still stay afloat. Given the fact that the worst that anyone could envisage was a collision at the point where two compartments joined, merely flooding the two of them, this was deemed more than adequate.

The ships had their passenger accommodation and main rooms arranged from A Deck (at the top, though above this was a Boat Deck) down to G Deck, giving six main decks. Below G Deck were the engine rooms and the hold storage, giving eleven decks in total. The watertight compartments extended up to D Deck fore and aft, and amidships up to E Deck, one deck lower. Both decks were well above the waterline and again this was thought to be more than sufficient. This design was to play its part in the events that were about to unfold on the *Titanic*.

The *Titanic* would be held together by 3 million rivets, as at the time welding techniques were not sufficiently developed to do otherwise. Modern research has suggested that the construction of these rivets, tiny and seemingly insignificant compared to the vast scale of the ship, also played a part in the looming disaster. Everything was on a gargantuan scale, adding to the veneer of immortality. The rudder, operated electrically, weighed 100 tons and each anchor 17½ tons. Given the sheer size of the ship it was easy to overlook the significance of 3 million miniscule rivets.

Titanic would be propelled through the water by three propellers, the middle one of which was driven by a turbine. Twenty-nine boilers and 159 furnaces provided the energy to drive these. Three gigantic funnels, 24½ feet wide at their broadest point, took the steam away. There was also a fourth funnel, a dummy for ventilation purposes. Her lines were sleek and elegant and, romanticism aside, she was indeed a beautiful ship.

The beauty extended to some of the accommodation provided on the ship. Two first-class suites had private promenades. Each of these was about 50 feet long and consisted of several rooms. One of these suites went for $4,350 for a trip. Those without private promenades retailed at a bargain $2,300. To give this some perspective, Harold Bride, the wireless operator on the *Titanic*, was paid $20 per month.

Opulence was a key consideration, so much so that IMM took over the company who traditionally supplied furniture and fitments for White Star's ships, Aldam Heaton and Company. The style opted for in first-class had a late Victorian/Edwardian country house feel about it. Magnificently-carved wood panelling was liberally applied. It was even there in second-class though the designs there were simpler. Third-class was mostly plain or painted in white enamel. The end result of the new class would be three ships that would raise the bar of transatlantic travel. Each of them would cost £1.5 million to build ($7.5 million in 1912 money).

The heartbeat of the *Titanic* was however to be found down below in much less glamorous conditions. Here, there were two reciprocating engines, one working each side propeller, and a turbine engine driving the central propeller. The largest boilers were 16 feet 9 inches in diameter and 20 feet long with six fires under each of them. The smaller boilers were 11 feet 9 inches long with three fires underneath. Housing huge furnaces that produced a Hades-like heat, the engine rooms generated a suffocating, sweaty atmosphere in which the firemen worked in thin singlets regardless of how cold it might be up above in what was, for them, another world.

The ship had its own refrigeration and ice-making plant, crucial given the vast stocks of provisions that were needed for each trip. There were a number of separate areas for different foodstuffs on the lower decks, mutton, beef, poultry, game, fish, vegetables, fruit, butter, bacon, cheese, flowers, mineral water, wines, spirits and champagne. The passengers would certainly not be hungry or thirsty during their journey.

The White Star vessels were essentially trans-Atlantic ferries. They were not built to be the quickest but they were expected to be punctual. Safety was also important though. Their watertight doors were meant to be shut automatically from the bridge in an emergency, at least at the lower levels (higher up, above the waterline, they needed to be closed by hand). However, there were floats in each compartment so that, if the automatic closing did not work, the doors would shut themselves when the floor of each compartment came into contact with water.

There was though one area where safety considerations should have weighed much more heavily than they did in practice. Not a lot of thought was given to the lifeboats onboard the *Titanic*. Specially designed 'Welin' davits allowed four banks of boats to be deployed on the ship. With sixteen sets of davits, this allowed up to sixty-four lifeboats to be carried, although Harland & Wolff initially thought that forty-eight was sufficient. However, once discussions between Harland & Wolff and White Star got underway the number was reduced to thirty-two and then sixteen. Surviving documentary evidence even allows the approximate time that this decision was made to be ascertained; sometime between 9 and 16 March 1910.

With another four 'collapsible' boats carried on the ship, this gave capacity at a push for only 1,178 people to be carried in the boats; not everyone agreed on the exact numbers but the figure was universally accepted to be in the region of this number. The Board of Trade rule of thumb was that one person took up 10 cubic feet so using this as a proxy based on the cubic capacity of the boats onboard resulted in space for 1,133 people.

It seems that the issue of lifeboats was not a major concern for the White Star Line. Alexander Carlisle, who was Managing Director of Harland & Wolff when the *Titanic* was built though he had left by the time of the disaster, later recalled that 'we spent two hours discussing the carpets for the first-class cabins and fifteen minutes discussing lifeboats'. It was Carlisle's idea to have the specially-designed davits but he did not push the point about the number of boats that should be carried with his client, the White Star Line.

If the ship was ever filled to her full capacity of 3,547 (including crew), this meant that there were not places for over 2,000 people on her. However, no one seemed to think that the boats would ever be needed; the ship, it was said on a number of occasions, was her own lifeboat. Not that the *Olympic* or the *Titanic* were breaking any rules. They were required to comply with regulations set by the British Board of Trade as far as their lifeboat capacity was concerned. Unfortunately they were now twenty years of date.

The specific problem was that the registry on lifeboat capacity were related to the tonnage of the ship. Up to a figure of 10,000 tons, there was a relationship between the size of the ship and the lifeboat capacity. It was when the tonnage exceeded 10,000 tons that the relationship went askew. Above this figure, there was a minimum capacity that was prescribed which was fixed regardless of the ship's size. There was, beyond this 10,000 tons benchmark, no relationship between the size of the ship and the lifeboat capacity.

This perhaps mattered little when the regulations were set in 1892. It was hard to conceive at the time that ships could grow significantly beyond this 10,000 ton limit. However, almost unnoticed, ships like the *Titanic* had grown much bigger than this and yet there had been no amendment to the regulations whatsoever. During the navel-gazing that followed the sinking of the *Titanic* the White Star Line was to point out, with accuracy if not particular sensitivity, that they had actually provided space for more people than they were required to by the law. The fact that there was not enough capacity for half the people onboard, even though the ship was only two-thirds full, proved just how inadequate the regulations were. In fact, *Titanic* and *Olympic* were just the worst examples of the problem due to their size; in 1912 reality nearly every ship over 10,000 tons failed to provide enough lifeboats.

The *Titanic* historian Walter Lord showed in his book *The Night Lives On* that out of thirty-nine contemporary British liners of over 10,000 tons, thirty-three did not have boats for everyone aboard them. Neither was the problem limited to British ships. The *St Louis*, an American liner, carried boats for only 54 per cent of her full complement.

The regulations did not even mention numbers of passengers but worked on the rather more impersonal measurements of cubic feet of lifeboat capacity. The Board of Trade regulations stipulated that a ship of the *Titanic's* size – any ship over 10,000 tons in size – should provide 9,625 cubic feet of lifeboat capacity (which equated to 962 people) and White Star had provided 11,328 cubic feet of it (equating in practice to 1,178 people). So White Star was comfortably exceeding the regulations, in terms of lifeboat capacity. However, *Titanic* of course was nearly five times above the maximum tonnage envisaged when the regulations were drafted. There was very little correlation between the number of passengers aboard and the lifeboat space required as a result.

Complacency was the problem. Sir Alfred Chambers was an adviser to the Board of Trade from 1896 to 1911. When quizzed about why he did not believe a change to the legislation was needed he said:

I considered the matter [of lifeboats] very closely from time to time. I first of all considered the record of the trade – that is to say the record of casualties – and to see what
immunity from loss there was. I found it was the safest mode of travel in the world,
and thought it neither the right not the duty of a State Department to impose regulations upon that mode of travel as long as the record was a clean one.

Risk management policies were presumably not high up Sir Alfred's
agenda. In fact, Chambers was reassured by the increasing scale of the
ships. He said:

I found that as ships grew bigger there were such improvements made in their construction that they were stronger and better ships, both from the point of view of
watertight compartments and also absolute strength.

He also considered that 'the traffic was very safe on account of the routes'.
He further believed that wireless telegraphy had helped improve safety
and, astonishingly, that the regulations should not be changed because
companies were voluntarily supplying more lifeboat capacity than they
were required to by law. He concluded with the jaw-dropping statement
that 'it is not desirable to encumber the deck of a ship with unnecessary
things'. It was a staggering litany of incompetent unconcern.

Harold Sanderson, the Managing Director of the White Star Line, was
another example of the *blasé* attitude that was all too prevalent. He felt
that in most cases it would be impossible to lower all the boats safely
anyway. He persisted in this surreal argument even after the *Titanic* had
sunk. The magazine *Fairplay*, capably representing the incredulity of a
general public shocked to the core by the disaster and the attitude of some
of those running the shipping lines, sarcastically told its readers that those
onboard 'could avoid all these [problems] by drowning at once'.

But most thought until after the event that the lifeboats on the *Titanic*
were there as an optional extra that would never be needed. Captain
Rostron told the American Inquiry after the disaster:

the ships are built nowadays to be practically unsinkable, and each ship is supposed
to be a lifeboat in itself. The boats are merely supposed to be put on as a standby. The
ships are supposed to be built, and the naval architects say that they are, unsinkable
under certain conditions.

The giant scale of the ship added to the sense of invulnerability that
even a prudent master like Rostron betrayed in his comments. *Titanic*
was in many ways a mirror image of her elder sister, the *Olympic*. She
was indeed the largest ship afloat (for a short time at least) even if she
was only just so. White Star were always looking for improvements

and modifications for their ships and some changes to the *Olympic's* basic design made *Titanic* about 1,000 tons gross heavier than her. The major variation between the two was that the promenade deck on the *Titanic* was partly enclosed in glass, in contrast to the *Olympic* where it was open to the elements though there were other more detailed differences too.

Construction first started on the *Olympic* with the *Titanic* following on a few months behind her, so that the two ships later developed side by side with the *Olympic* always a few months further into her gestation period than her sister. They were so large that Harland & Wolff had to specially adapt the shipyards to deal with them. The lucrative nature of the contracts for these ships meant that they had no commercial difficulty in doing so.

These ships operated in a hugely competitive environment. White Star was a hard-nosed business, always trying to obtain a strategic advantage commercially over its many rivals. This made passenger convenience vitally important. The cross-Atlantic passenger trade in 1912 was one with carriers from many nations jostling each other to gain an advantage. The *Olympic*-class ships hoped to do this by offering a range of services that, at the time, others could not match. *Titanic*, as the second in the trilogy, had extra features compared to her older sister. She was the last word in modern marine construction. Inside her massive frame, she had such sybaritic facilities as a Turkish bath, a gymnasium and a swimming pool filled with seawater (although not the first, this was still something of a novelty).

In Belfast, the ships quickly took shape (though the third would not go into production until later with a provisional name of *Gigantic*, a name that would ultimately change when it suddenly appeared too hubristic). The *Olympic* was launched on 20 October 1910, earlier than expected and by June of the next year was in Southampton awaiting her maiden voyage. Being so much bigger than her rivals, she astounded those who saw her for the first time. Much has been made of the *Titanic's* impact on those who saw her but she was only marginally bigger than the *Olympic*. The quantum leap had come with the first ship and her impact was correspondingly greater.

Bruce Ismay sailed on *Olympic's* maiden voyage, as he did with all major White Star ships, and was much impressed. However, being something of a perfectionist he saw room for improvement. Later, extra first-class cabins were added to the *Titanic* at his suggestion, including the two with their own private promenade decks. This meant an extra 100 first-class passengers could be carried (commercially as well as aesthetically attractive to Ismay). A bijou *café* was to be constructed, the *Café Parisien*, to be kitted out with top quality Crown Derby china. Most significantly, the *Titanic's* promenade deck was to be partly glazed over, in contrast to the *Olympic* which was entirely open; passengers had complained that they had been splashed with spray.

It was ironic that these changes contributed indirectly to the disaster, for the modifications needed led in part to a delay in the *Titanic's* maiden voyage and, if she had sailed when originally planned, then that fateful rendezvous with a rogue iceberg might never have happened. Not that this was the only reason for the hold-up though; on 20 September 1911 the *Olympic* had been involved in an accident and was forced to limp back to Belfast for repairs. As a result, work on *Titanic* took second place for a short time.

Titanic had sailed down the slipway in Belfast just a few months before. The launching was attended by more than 100,000 people, some in the shipyards, others watching from vantage points close by. Twenty-two tons of soap and tallow was required to lubricate the slipway as the 46,000 ton behemoth slipped sluggishly down into the River Lagan. Earlier that morning special steamers had made the short crossing over from Lancashire, England carrying invited guests and journalists. Stands had been laid on for these in the dockyards so that they would have a grandstand view of the launch.

It was a bright, clear day, 31 May 1911. A breeze ruffled the flags that fluttered next to *Titanic* on the gantry. At just about midday, the stands filled with the leading luminaries of the White Star family, including Bruce Ismay, J. Pierpoint Morgan and Harold Sanderson. Lord Pirrie, whose company had built *Titanic*, was there too (it was his birthday, and his wife's too). His role on this special day was effectively that of master of ceremonies on what was a day of celebration and self-congratulation.

There was a last inspection by Pirrie, then a red flag was hoisted to be followed, more noticeably, by a red rocket. This was the signal that launching was imminent. Wedges which were holding back the giant ship were hammered out until only a set of hydraulic triggers held her in position. There was a cry of 'Stand Clear' and men hurried like so many worker ants to safety.

One worker, James Dobbins, was trapped when a piece of wood-shoring had collapsed on him. He was pulled clear before the huge hulk of the *Titanic* crushed him to a pulp. However, he was unconscious, though he was still included in the head-count of workers by the yard's supervisor on the day. He was taken to hospital and operated on but died the next day. It was not an auspicious start to the ship's career.

This was a detail lost in the celebratory noise to those who were there to cheer *Titanic* off. At 12.13 p.m., a second rocket was fired to confirm that the ship was about to touch water for the first time. The hydraulic triggers were released and slowly, almost perceptibly at first, she started to move. There was no naming ceremony, no smashing of a champagne bottle against her hull, but there were barely suppressed gasps as she started to move towards the River Lagan. *Titanic* was about to float.

It took her just sixty-two seconds to make that short journey into the river's muddy waters. The anchor chains that had been specially positioned to arrest her onward movement were called successfully into play and *Titanic* stood there, like a puppy experiencing a swim for the first time, bobbing up and down, unsure of what to make of her new home. The crowd, duly enthralled by this wonderful spectacle, made their way back home or, if they were lucky, to the dinner party laid on by Lord Pirrie to mark the occasion.

However, there was still a great deal left to do before the *Titanic* was ready to carry paying passengers. The ship, currently just a hulk, was to be fitted out to meticulous specifications supplied by White Star. A massive document, over 300 pages thick, marked out in detail every part of her specification. There would be a wide range of styles provided, from the 'Adams' style in white to 'Louis XV' in grey for example. Individual touches were liberally applied; in contrast to modern approaches to luxury hotel accommodation there was no attempt at conformity in first-class.

Nothing was left to chance, at least not as far as the furnishings were concerned. The two magnificent suites would each have two main bedrooms, wardrobe rooms, bathrooms (with bath and shower fittings) and a sitting room. There would also be a servant's bedroom included. Each suite would have its own veranda and an enclosed promenade deck; a first for ocean liners. Situated next to the first-class entrance to the ship, these were undoubtedly the showpieces of *Titanic*. For those who, in 1912, wished to sail in style she was at the time the ship of choice.

Aesthetic concerns seem to have been the considerations that in the main concentrated the minds of White Star officials. Safety appeared to be a secondary consideration. However, the accident to the *Olympic* in September was important as it highlighted that navigating these massive ships might be something of an art-form only acquired through practice. She was on her way out of Southampton down the narrow channel that led to the open sea when the accident happened. At the same time, a cruiser, *HMS Hawke*, was in the area. She came up on the starboard side of *Olympic* as the latter slowed down to negotiate a difficult shoal. But the cruiser did not stop, as if made of a ferrous metal being attracted by a magnet, and slammed into the side of *Olympic*. The White Star ship was holed with a massive gash in her side.

The *Hawke* appeared to be on the point of capsizing but managed to limp into Portsmouth, which was fortunately close at hand. *Olympic* was forced to anchor off the Isle of Wight as the tides were too low to get back into harbour at Southampton. Her passengers were taken off by tender, the trip to America now clearly off. When she did get back into Southampton, it was only for temporary repairs that would enable her to return to Belfast where the only dry dock big enough to deal with her was.

This delayed *Titanic's* sailing date as there was not room to work on both those giant vessels at the same time.

An Inquiry was later held into the causes of the collision; Her Majesty's Government did not take kindly to their ships being hit by new super-liners, even British ones. The inquiry blamed the *Olympic* for the collision, finding that the suction unleashed by the huge ship when she displaced the shallow water irresistibly pulled the cruiser towards her. It was technically not Captain E.J. Smith's fault as the ship was theoretically under the control of the pilot at the time. However, it did not augur well for the future, though in some perverse ways it emphasized the *Olympic's* presumed invulnerability for, despite a huge hole in her side, she did not sink nor remotely threaten to.

White Star did not appear to have changed anything as a result of the accident, though this striking demonstration of the suction created by these leviathans might have had a detrimental effect on some of those in charge of the lifeboats on the night that the *Titanic* went down and were afraid that their small craft would be sucked under when the great ship dipped below the water. Indeed, the line contested the findings, disputing the decision that the *Olympic* was to blame for the collision. When the time for the selection of the *Titanic's* captain on her maiden voyage arrived, there was no hesitation in awarding the honour to Captain Smith.

In the meantime, preparations for the start of *Titanic's* career moved on apace. In January 1912, the call-sign 'MUC' was given to *Titanic* for use by its wireless operators (it was changed shortly afterwards to 'MGY'). The ship had powerful wireless equipment though, being in its infancy, there were still significant technical constraints around it. Atmospheric conditions played a major part in its utility. A range of 250 miles was guaranteed in any conditions, while 400 was commonly achievable in the daytime. At night it could reach a spectacular 2,000 miles if conditions were favourable. It was powered by its own separate dynamo so that, even if mains power might fail, it could keep going.

However, the start to *Olympic's* career continued to be problematic. Apart from the collision with the *Hawke*, she also lost a propeller blade and again had to come back to Belfast for further repairs. The date originally planned for the *Titanic's* maiden voyage – which fortunately had not been extensively advertised though it had been made public – was moved from 20 March to 10 April 1912. On 6 March, *Olympic* and *Titanic* were together for the last time as the older sister sailed out towards Southampton.

Belfast now concentrated on her younger sibling. The *Titanic* was taken out for sea trials in Belfast Lough on 2 April, a day later than planned due to bad weather. There was a skeleton crew of seventy-nine men allotted to the engine room for this, though one did not turn up on the day. Thomas

Andrews from Harland & Wolff and Harold Sanderson from White Star were the main corporate representatives aboard. Bruce Ismay could not attend and Lord Pirrie was ill. The Board of Trade surveyor, Carruthers, was there too. He knew the ship like the back of his hand by now. Also onboard were the Marconi operators Jack Phillips and Harold Bride. Their recently-installed equipment was functional but not yet working at full capacity.

At 6.00 a.m. that morning the tugs towed her slowly out, a delicate manoeuvre with little margin of error given the size of the ship. She stood high in the water, lighter than she would be as few supplies had been taken on yet. Along the shoreline, hundreds of awestruck spectators watched on in admiration as she glided gracefully by. The new super-liners were the source of great civic pride in Belfast. *Titanic* proceeded down Belfast Lough, still under tow, until she was about 2 miles off the coastal town of Carrickfergus, beneath the watchful eye of its magnificent Norman castle. The castle was a ruin, a reminder of a history now long gone. In contrast *Titanic* was a symbol of the modern world, of man's ingenuity, and a sign of his immutable progress as he headed towards a glorious future.

Now, the tugs cast off and *Titanic* was on her own, in control of her own destiny for the very first time. Then, the orders were passed down below to start the engines. Slowly, the ship started to come to life as a gentle vibration caused her to shiver, surprised at her own power. She moved through the water, increasing speed until she reached 20 knots. Then, she was slowed down until she was stationary. She was restarted again and a number of manoeuvres were carried out to test out her flexibility.

After the first lunch to be served onboard had been consumed (a typical English offering, with the main course a choice of roast chicken, spring lamb or braised ham), a stopping test was carried out. The ship was put at full speed, then, after passing a buoy that had been placed in the water, she was put full astern to see how quickly she would stop. At about 20 knots, it was noted that it took about half a mile to come to a halt.

By about 7.00 p.m. that evening it was all over. The trials appeared to have gone well, though they had been cursory. *Titanic* steamed back into a now-darkened Belfast. Satisfied, Inspector Carruthers signed her off as being fit for service for a period of one year from that day. One more key piece of paper needed to be signed. It was monogrammed by Sanderson for White Star and Andrews for Harland & Wolff, the formal handover document. The *Titanic* was now officially White Star property.

Just after 8.00 p.m. she was ready to go once more, this time for real. She would now head for Southampton and from there out on her maiden voyage. She bade her farewells to Belfast, as it turned out for the last time. Work continued incessantly as she set her course for the south coast of England; there were still a great many last-minute details to be attended to and most of those onboard were too excited to sleep anyway.

It was a 570-mile trip to Southampton. On the way over, *Titanic* passed close to her elder sister, steaming out from the port *en route* to New York. Somewhere off Portland, the two ships passed each other. Friendly greetings were exchanged between them over the Marconi wirelesses they carried. Twelve days later they would use the same medium to conduct rather more serious conversations.

The wireless operators had sent a stream of messages concerning the ship's performance to Bruce Ismay in White Star's Liverpool offices and were among the busiest people onboard. As well as the *Olympic*, they also got in touch with other ocean-going ships. The atmospherics were good that night; messages were relayed to Tenerife, 2,000 miles away, and contact was even made with Port Said in Egypt, 3,000 miles distant. The sea was smooth and calm though for a couple of hours they had to contend with fog.

By the morning then, she was in the English Channel. The first breakfast had been served, a choice of robust rather than elegant food: Quaker Oats, kippers, liver and bacon, grilled ham, sausages, minced chicken, omelettes and cold meats. *Titanic* then made her way gracefully up towards what would become her home port, reaching the Isle of Wight just as it was getting dark. She needed to coincide her arrival with high tide, which meant that her timing had to be impeccable. There was only a few feet of draft to spare in the harbour at Southampton and any miscalculation could have serious consequences.

The *Titanic* arrived at the head of Southampton Water, where six tugs came out to bring her in. Although dwarfed by her, they gently pulled her upstream and into her berth. She arrived at Berth 44 just after midnight on the morning of 4 April. There was no fuss, no fanfare. Everything in fact was surprisingly low key. George Bowyer, who had acted as pilot for the *Olympic*, an event he wrote of with much excitement, probably did the same for *Titanic* but if he did, he did not even mention it in later conversations. Arriving in the middle of the night, with no crowd out to meet her, her introduction to Southampton could not have been more unremarkable.

Perhaps the port was starting to become a little *blasé*. A local resident interviewed later, John Wright, described the *Titanic* as 'just another ship'. The world had been recently introduced to other great ships, the equally giant *Olympic* and the sleek greyhounds *Mauretania* and *Lusitania*, and he later admitted when asked about the *Titanic* that 'we thought not a lot about her until the terrible happening'.

The arrival of the world's biggest ship in Southampton could not have come at a better moment though. Since February, coal miners had been striking for a minimum wage and, as supplies of coal dried up, the ships that it fired were laid up in port as shortages bit. As a result, 17,000 people were unemployed in Southampton while the ships that many of them would normally have crewed were tied up in twos because there were not enough berths for them all. The employment both *Olympic* and *Titanic* offered provided a real boost to the local economy at a time when it was much needed.

This was not just in obvious ways, such as providing jobs for crew members. Other local people benefited too, such as F.G. Bealing and Son who provided all the flowers (these were refrigerated and brought out daily during the voyage and made a great impression on many passengers) or the launderers who could be required to clean up 75,000 dirty items every time one of the monster-ships arrived in port (White Star had its own laundry in Southampton).

There would be enough coal for the *Titanic*, partly because she would travel below maximum speed to conserve fuel and partly because stockpiles had been kept at the expense of other ships that would otherwise have used them. In some cases, passengers who had been booked on other ships were transferred to the *Titanic*, which must at the time have seemed an incredibly lucky break for most of them.

The ship was loaded up with all the provisions that would be needed to cross the Atlantic. Some were exotic, such as a new Renault car belonging to first-class passenger W.E. Carter or a jewelled and rare copy of the *Rubaiyat of Omar Khayyam*. Others were mundane, though the staggering volumes involved give a hint of how major a logistical undertaking each crossing was; 36,000 apples, the same number of oranges, 6,000 lbs of butter, 15,000 bottles of beer and 850 bottles of spirits for example. It was like feeding a small army on the march.

If *Titanic* was the setting for the main act, there were two other floating participants in the drama to consider. As *Titanic* prepared for her maiden voyage, her ultimate rescuer was on the opposite side of the Atlantic Ocean. The *Carpathia* would leave New York on 11 April, the day after *Titanic* left Southampton. With a gross tonnage of 13,603 tons, *Carpathia* was only a quarter of the size of the White Star super-liner. About 540 feet long, she could carry over 2,500 passengers.

The *Carpathia* had been built for Cunard in Newcastle in 1902. She had always sailed the North Atlantic route and, if made somewhat second-rate by the emergence of the *Mauretania* and *Lusitania*, she still played an important role sailing backwards and forwards between America and Europe. Emigration from Eastern Europe was a particularly lucrative source of business for Cunard and *Carpathia* had spent most of her time since 1905 sailing between New York and Trieste. Her current mission was due to take her from New York via Gibraltar, Genoa, Naples and Trieste to Fiume (then in Italy, now Rijeka in Croatia).

There were about 300 crew onboard, captained by Arthur Henry Rostron. She would carry 743 passengers on her east-bound voyage (128 first, 50 second and 565 third-class; the latter class composed of Italians, Hungarians, Austrians, Greeks and Serbians). This would leave plenty of room on her, a fact that would as it happened prove very useful. Most of her traffic would be coming the other way, on the return leg from Europe to America. The *Carpathia's* normal pattern was to sail west with a large number of emigrants aboard. The United States was still for many a promised land where they escaped the drudgery of poverty and could carve out for themselves a better life and a wealthier future. She would typically have far fewer people aboard travelling east, as she was now carrying tourists and emigrants visiting relatives back in the old countries.

It was not uncommon for crew members to work a passage to America using a berth on board a westbound ship from Europe and then disappear when they arrived. In 1912, fifty-seven crew members of the *Carpathia* would use a position aboard ship as a way to illegally enter the USA. This caused far more difficulty for the immigration officials in America than it did for the captain of the *Carpathia*. Crew members were signed on for the duration of just one specific voyage so that there were always plenty of replacements readily available to fill in for these deserters.

There were other disturbing influences at work onboard too. On one trip over from the Mediterranean the ship had picked up passengers in Palermo, Sicily. Soon after she left the port, the sign of a Black Hand was seen scribbled onboard. It was an unmistakable symbol of the Mafia, a suggestion that their shadowy representatives were on the ship exercising their power over some form of illegal immigration racket. The boatswain had indignantly wiped the marks off as soon as he found them; it did little good, they appeared again soon afterwards.

Although lacking the majesty and grandeur of the *Titanic* or indeed her newer Cunard sisters, the *Carpathia* was still a significant ship. The same could not truly be said of the *Californian*. Launched on 26 November 1901 in Dundee, she carried only forty-seven passengers (a theoretical maximum, she normally carried only thirty-five). She weighed 6,223 tons gross and was just short of 450 feet long. Passenger accommodation was provided on the portside, with officers and crew quartered on the starboard side.

Californian's principal *raison d'être* was as a bulk carrier. She initially carried mainly cotton, a trade for which her owners, the Leyland Line, had become well known. The Leyland Line was owned by International Mercantile Marine, J. Pierpoint Morgan's vast conglomerate. This made *Californian* and *Titanic* members of the same extended family; apart from this, they had nothing in common.

Captain Lord, her master, had been in command for less than a year. His current trip had not been a happy one. The ship has left New Orleans on 20 February 1912 with a cargo of cotton. When she arrived in Le Havre,

France, on 20 March 1912, 622 bales had been damaged, an inauspicious start to the voyage. Lord would have much explaining to do at the end of the trip.

She was due to return across the Atlantic on a more northerly route. Setting out from London, she would be taking a general cargo across the ocean headed for Boston but no passengers on this occasion. She left on her voyage on 5 April 1912. The *Titanic* would leave from a position a little further south-west five days later but her vastly superior speed would mean that within another four days she would more or less catch her up.

And so the three ships started out, with different destinations, different reasons for their voyages and very different clienteles. As the new glamour ship of her day, Lord and Rostron would have known of *Titanic's* maiden voyage. Captain Smith would also be aware of the existence of the *Carpathia*, sailing out of New York and a significant if not major part of one of White Star's principal competitors' fleet. However, the *Californian* would have not have meant too much to him. As an experienced mariner, he might have known of her existence but she would have meant little else to him. They inhabited vastly different worlds.

Three ships, three voyages, three destinations, three very different captains. Each ship on its own course, on a routine voyage which on the surface appeared to be as mundane as every other trip would be (the status of *Titanic's* maiden voyage excepted). Yet each man, Smith, Rostron and Lord was headed into the unknown. At the end of this voyage one captain would be dead, one would be a hero and one would be on the verge of ruin. There would be nothing mundane about the story that was starting to unfold.

3

The Players:
Captains & Crews

On the eve of the maiden voyage from Southampton, the crew of the *Titanic* snatched a few hours sleep in preparation for the hectic day ahead. The ship had been a hive of activity since her arrival, with one exception. On Good Friday, the ship had been 'dressed' – decorated with flags – making a splendid and, as it would turn out, unique sight. It was a gesture towards the *Titanic's* new port as unfortunately none of the residents would be allowed aboard to inspect the ship as they normally would be as there was simply too much to do. Over the Easter period, work had slackened off. In a much more religious age than our own, the solemnities of this sacred period in the Christian year were duly honoured.

Many of the crew that had sailed from Belfast along with the officers had taken the chance to grab a last bit of shore leave before the voyage. A number of them, including Captain E.J. Smith, lived in or near the port so that they were able to make a last visit home prior to sailing. A large number of the crew, most of whom were signed up in Southampton, were not due to arrive until the last day or so before departure; there was no point in White Star paying them for any longer than was necessary.

The cast of players that were about to be involved in this drama were something of a hotchpotch. Centre-stage were three sea captains, very different in terms of their experience and personality. They would have moved in very different circles up until now and their careers would only have touched tangentially though E.J. Smith of the *Titanic* and Arthur Rostron of the *Carpathia* had both sailed the cross-Atlantic route to New York even if the latter had been doing so for a much shorter time than the former.

Captain Edward John Smith – 'EJ' as he was known to many of the crew – was White Star's foremost commander. When the *Titanic* had entered into service there was little hesitation in transferring him from the *Olympic*, which he had looked after from *her* maiden voyage, to take control of the new ship. It was a voyage that would have had special significance for Captain Smith even if it had not reached its cataclysmic conclusion, for this would in any event

have been his last trip in charge before retirement. He would be going out at
the top of his profession; as a blunt comparison of his value, a Cunard captain
was paid £600 per annum (around $3,000), while a P&O Commander was
paid about £900. Smith's annual salary was £1,250. As another example, one
of the main protagonists in the drama that was about to be unveiled, Stanley
Lord, earned £240 a year plus an annual bonus of £50.

Captain Smith was now sixty-two years old and hailed from Hanley,
Stoke-on-Trent, something of an irony as this was about as far away from
the sea as it was possible to get in England. His father was a potter – the
area around Stoke was famous for its pottery-making with names like
Wedgwood achieving worldwide renown. However, Smith's parents later
opened a shop. It was an unlikely beginning to a seafaring career in which
Smith would ultimately reach the top of the tree.

By the age of thirteen, Smith had begun an apprenticeship in Liverpool.
In 1880, he entered into service with White Star as Fourth Officer aboard
the *Celtic*. Involved principally in the runs to New York and Australia, he
clearly made a marked impression on his employers as by 1887 he had
command of his first ship. Just one year later, he was accepted into the
Royal Naval Reserve meaning that he could be 'requisitioned' into action
as part of the Royal Navy should any war break out.

It enabled Smith certain honorific privileges in terms of what colours
he could fly on his ships but there was also a chance that he would have
to return the compliment by serving in action should the need arise and
such was the case in 1899. Smith and his ship at the time, the *Majestic*,
were required to transport troops out to South Africa as part of the Boer
War campaign. Apart from the normal hazards attendant to any maritime
navigation, there were no real dangers involved; the enemy did not have a
navy to speak of and instead relied on land-based guerrilla tactics in their
attempt to defeat the British Empire. Despite the lack of any exceptional
risk, he was awarded a campaign medal for his part in the war.

Smith acquired a good reputation within White Star. There were no
untoward incidents at sea involving him in his early career and his
passengers generally liked him. By 1904, he was routinely appointed
skipper of all new White Star liners for their maiden voyages; his command
of the *Titanic* was therefore the latest in a series of such honours. When he
took command of the *Baltic* in 1904, she was also the biggest ship afloat
just as the *Olympic*-class ships would later be. In 1907, after three years
smooth sailing as skipper of the *Baltic*, he took command of the *Adriatic*.
Then, in 1911, he was given the *Olympic*.

It was a career of outstanding achievement. In 1904, he had achieved
the ultimate White Star accolade when he was appointed 'Commodore'
of the line, the merchant marine equivalent of 'Admiral of the Fleet'. This
position meant that he was considered the foremost of all White Star

captains, all of whom were junior to him. He had given the line a career of accident-free voyaging and they appreciated it. All White Star officers were paid bonuses if they spent a year free of any accident on their ships; marine disasters were bad news commercially.

Developments in technology had helped breed complacency. Smith had a reputation as a safe pair of hands based on his track record up to taking command of the *Olympic*. However, given the cavalier approach that the *Titanic* disaster evidenced about attitudes to safety generally, not just on the part of Smith but of all sea captains at the time, this owed something to luck. He certainly seemed to be confident that an accident at sea was becoming an increasingly remote possibility.

He said as much when arriving in New York at the end of the *Adriatic's* maiden voyage in 1907 in a newspaper interview. He told the interviewer how in forty years at sea his experiences could best be described as 'uneventful'. In all that time he:

> never saw a wreck and have never been wrecked, nor was I ever in any predicament that threatened to end in disaster of any sort. You see, I am not very good material for a story. [Perhaps most strikingly he also said] I cannot imagine any condition which would cause a ship to founder. I cannot conceive of any vital disaster happening to this vessel. Modern shipbuilding has gone beyond that.

Smith was a man who managed to strike a balance by being suitably deferential, paternal even, to his passengers. Many first-class passengers for whom trans-Atlantic travel was a fairly regular occurrence would look out for his ships so that they could travel specifically with him. His ability to make his more affluent passengers feel properly treated earned him the nickname of the 'millionaire's captain'. But although he was always polite, beneath his bushy beard he seemed a man who was always quietly in control of a situation. His passengers, and indeed his crew, not only liked him but also had confidence in him.

In retrospect perhaps there might have been a few more questions asked after the collision between the *Olympic* and the *Hawke*. Although the pilot George Bowyer was in charge when it happened and was officially culpable, it is hardly likely that Smith was standing idly by doing nothing while the pilot was notionally responsible for navigation. To be fair to Smith, these new super-liners were unknown quantities that were so big that anyone might have struggled to come to terms with them. Nevertheless, within the space of a year he was to have two major accidents (including one sinking) as well as several near-misses on his CV, a distinct tarnishing of a previously unblemished record. For a man who had in 1907 believed it inconceivable that a major accident could affect any of his ships, this must have come as something of a shock.

In fact, the *Hawke* incident had been preceded by another little-reported near-miss, at the end of the *Olympic's* maiden voyage. As she was docking in New York on 21 June, one of the tugs assisting her was caught up in the wash of her propellers. The tug was powerless, like a puppy caught in the jowls of a huge mastiff that shook it around from side to side. She spun out of control and collided with the *Olympic*. It was only a minor bump which had no impact on the super-liner though it damaged the tug. For a few horrible seconds, it looked as if the tug would get caught under the stern of the *Olympic* but fortunately it managed to get itself at last out of the slipstream and limp back safely to harbour.

It appeared a minor incident at the time but perhaps Captain Smith was looking forward to a long and healthy retirement, leaving the problems of navigating these leviathans to younger captains. *Titanic* would be the thirteenth White Star ship he had commanded and her maiden voyage would give him a suitable finale after which he could spend more time with his family. Certainly he appeared to have a happy home life with his wife Eleanor and daughter Helen. He lived in a very comfortable if not extravagant villa in Southampton where, his daughter later recalled, he loved to lock himself in a room and watch the shapes he could make when smoking his favourite cigars. He would get particularly annoyed if anyone entered the room while he was doing so and disturbed the shapes he had manufactured.

It is easy to see how Smith would come across as a delightful and charming gentleman, though *Titanic's* Second Officer Charles Lightoller would remark that he could bark out an order with the best of them, doing so with such magisterial authority that the recipient felt obliged to respond at once. It is equally easy to see how his ability to talk in a quiet, urbane and respectful way to his more prominent passengers would ingratiate him with them. However, other qualities would be needed when the chips were down and it is debatable whether or not, when that time came, they were present in sufficient quantity.

Captain Arthur Rostron of the *Carpathia* was forty-two years of age. Like Smith, he was also a member of the Royal Naval Reserve. A Lancastrian by birth, he had first gone to sea aboard a naval training ship when thirteen years old. Two years later, he joined the merchant marine and began to travel extensively, visiting America, India and Australia. He was in the southern seas aboard a barque named the *Red Gauntlet* when he had what he believed to be his nearest brush with death when the vessel was nearly overwhelmed in a violent squall off New Zealand.

Rostron then journeyed to the western coast of South America before obtaining his extra master's certificate in 1894. His decisive career move came at the beginning of 1895 when he joined Cunard as a Fourth Officer on the *Umbria*. He was in this position when he visited New York for the first time. He then held positions on various Cunard ships until in 1907 he was appointed First Officer of the newly-launched *Lusitania*.

However, he never sailed on her. The day before he was due to leave with the ship, he was transferred to the *Brescia*, a trading vessel, as captain. He stayed in similar roles until 1911, when he was appointed captain of the passenger steamer *Pannonia* sailing between the Mediterranean and New York. Then in January 1912, he took over command of the *Carpathia*. It was a steady career and he had already climbed a significant way up the rungs of the Cunard ladder. However, he would reach its summit because of the effect that the *Titanic* disaster and his actions in dealing with its results had on his prospects.

Captain Stanley Lord of the *Californian* was very much the junior one of the three commanders. However, there was no reason to think that this would necessarily have remained the case if his reputation had not been blackened by the sinking of the *Titanic*. He was thirty-five years of age in 1912. Coincidentally he had been born in Bolton, within a few miles of Arthur Rostron's birthplace. Blue-eyed and lean, he had enjoyed a very promising start to his career.

After going to sea at thirteen (another coincidence; the same age that Smith and Rostron started their time at sea) he obtained his extra master's certificate at the age of twenty-three. This was an exceptionally young age to obtain the qualification; though Rostron had achieved the same when only twenty-four, Smith had been thirty-eight before he had got it. It made Lord a sought-after young man. One of the companies to offer him a post was the White Star Line but it was only as a Third or Fourth officer. Lord thought he could do better than that and turned the offer down.

Later, a Board of Trade examiner would recall that Lord had passed his exams 'most brilliantly', that his ability at sea had 'invariably been of the highest order' and that 'I have ever heard him spoken of as a humane and clever officer and commander'. These testimonials and his excellent exam results suggest a man possessed of significant talent. So too does the fact that he achieved his first command before the age of twenty-nine, again extraordinarily young. Although perhaps not well placed in the Leyland Line to be noticed by the powers-that-be in the International Mercantile Marine, there was nevertheless plenty of time for him to ascend further up the ladder. Here was a man of much promise, whose potential would in the end be sadly unfulfilled.

A captain could not be present on the bridge all the time and, when he was absent, his duties were deputed to his officers. Onboard ships like the *Titanic* and *Olympic* (and indeed *Carpathia* and *Californian*) there were a group of senior officers who took executive command when he was off-duty who were assisted by a group of junior officers in supportive capacities. The senior officers on the *Titanic* were Chief Officer Henry Wilde, First

Officer William Murdoch and Second Officer Charles Lightoller. The juniors were Third Officer Herbert Pitman, Fourth Officer Joseph Boxhall, Fifth Officer Harold Lowe and Sixth Officer James Moody.

Although some had served with Captain Smith before, these officers did not come together as a complete package and were required to learn quickly both how to work with the ship and also how to work with each other. Some of them were to have a particularly key part in the events of 14/15 April 1912. Charles Lightoller for example would be one of the star witnesses at both the American and British Inquiries that would follow the disaster. He would also have an extraordinary story of survival against the odds to tell.

In terms of individual biographies of those aboard the *Titanic*, that of Lightoller would take some beating both before and after the disaster. Going to sea in 1888, his second voyage on a ship known as the *Holt Hill* ended when she was dismasted and forced to seek shelter in Rio de Janeiro. The sense of excitement was compounded when they arrived there during a revolution and a smallpox epidemic. This however was nothing compared to what happened in 1889 when the ship was completely wrecked on a desert island in the Indian Ocean. Lightoller and his fellow survivors spent eight days there before being rescued by a passing ship and taken to Australia.

He was not put off by these experiences and returned to sea soon after in his first ship, the *Primrose Hill*. He was onboard her when the ship was hit by a cyclone that they barely survived. Then, while on a ship called the *Knight of St Michael*, the coal caught fire. Lightoller had been prominent in the measures taken to counteract the effects of the fire, thereby saving the ship, an action which resulted in his promotion. For a while his career was then accident-free, though he nearly died of malaria at one stage.

By 1898, Lightoller decided that a change might be good for him. He first tried his hand as a gold-prospector in the Yukon, though without success. He then tried his luck as a cowboy but finally decided to return to England, working his passage onboard a cattle boat. So by the age of twenty-five, Lightoller had been shipwrecked on a desert island, been a hero in a fire onboard ship, survived a cyclone, been a cowboy and a gold prospector and also experienced being penniless. If a novelist had come up with such a script, their publisher would have rejected it as being too fantastical.

Perhaps searching for a quiet life, in 1900 Lightoller had signed up with White Star. Then his life took a romantic turn. Meeting a young lady passenger onboard a ship he was working *en route* to Australia, he returned with her as his bride. They remained devoted for the rest of his life and Sylvia Lightoller would take a keen interest in the *Titanic* disaster. Now enjoying a steady but slow rise up the White Star ranks, Lightoller worked for some time with Captain Smith on the *Majestic* before transferring as Third Officer to the *Oceanic*. However, he had not been with Smith on the *Olympic* but this did not appear to have done him much harm as he was now down to be the First Officer on the *Titanic*.

But all this changed at the last moment when Smith decided he wanted Henry Wilde, whom he had sailed with on the *Olympic*, to be his Chief Officer. This led to a last minute reshuffle in *Titanic's* chain of command. Everyone else was bumped down a notch, including Lightoller, who now became Second Officer. At the time the previous Second Officer, David Blair, appeared unluckiest of all as he was dropped from the trip altogether. When this happened, he cursed his luck. His views presumably changed later.

All this was done at the eleventh hour. Blair had sailed over from Belfast on the *Titanic*. Then he was a victim of career politics. Wilde was due for promotion but no suitable opening had come up and he was asked to become Chief on the *Titanic,* perhaps in an attempt to soothe his feelings. There was a domino effect on the crew; Murdoch went down from Chief to First Officer and Lightoller from First to Second. Blair was the man to lose out altogether. He wrote to a friend that 'this is a magnificent ship, I feel very disappointed not to make the first voyage'. He left in such a hurry that he took one of the keys to the telephone in the ship's crow's nest with him.

He might also have been an unwitting party to a rather more serious situation, for on the trip down from Belfast the crow's nest binoculars went astray. Lookout Hogg used them on the way across from Ireland but they were lost when the lookouts tried to find them in Southampton. There was a box in the crow's nest for them but when the lookouts opened it, it was empty. Although it was not necessarily Blair's fault (the keys would normally be in the hands of the ship's First Officer) the confusion caused by this last-minute reshuffle was most likely responsible for the fact that no one knew where the binoculars were once the ship arrived at Southampton. It meant that the lookouts would be deprived of this ocular aid when they most needed it out in the North Atlantic. On such small matters can the course of great events hinge.

Unfamiliarity with the ship would be a problem for some officers too. The thing that struck people like Lightoller about the *Titanic* was her sheer size. He was an experienced seaman but, not having been on the *Olympic*, he had never seen anything like her. It took him fourteen days to find his way around the passageways of the ship. The gangway door was so big that you could drive a coach and horses through it. It took three joining officers a whole day to find it. This unfamiliarity was to have unfortunate consequences on the night that the Titanic sank as Lightoller would forget that A Deck was enclosed with glass windows, introducing a delay and inefficiency into the boat lowering process at a time that it could be least afforded.

First Officer Murdoch would play a key part in the *Titanic* tragedy too. During the disaster he took charge of lowering the boats on the starboard side of the ship while Lightoller in the main did the same for the portside. They would have significant differences in their approaches to the boat lowering which meant that, statistically, passengers (or more accurately male passengers) would have a far greater chance of survival with Murdoch than they would with Lightoller. Murdoch did not survive and indeed a few gossips suggested that he committed suicide. There is barely a shred of evidence for this and rather a lot against it, so the likelihood is that he died heroically on the ship from which he had helped passengers to escape until it was far too late to save himself.

Given the grand name William McMaster Murdoch when born in 1873 in Dalbeattie, south-west Scotland, he cut his nautical teeth serving on various sailing ships. Since joining White Star, in recent years his career had closely followed that of Captain Smith. He had been on the *Olympic* with him along with Wilde, so the two senior officers supporting the captain had worked together as a team for a while. Having both a Chief and a First Officer onboard the *Titanic* along with a captain who had all been on the largely similar *Olympic* made a lot of sense from White Star's perspective. They had brought as much experience to bear on the maiden voyage as they possibly could have done.

Among the junior officers involved in the tragedy Fifth Officer Harold Lowe would probably make the greatest impression on both events and on the investigations that followed them. Lowe was a Welshman, a man with a strong character and one would not suffer fools gladly, regardless of their ranking in any social or professional hierarchy. He also, events would suggest, had rather a penchant for using a revolver. Lowe might have made some important mistakes at the time but in the main he took control of the situation that enfolded when the ship went down far better than anyone else did.

Lowe's character showed itself at an early age, when in 1896, at the age of fourteen, he ran away from home rather than be apprenticed; he was, he explained later, not going to work for anybody for nothing. Unlike many of the other officers onboard, Lowe was very much a new boy, having only joined White Star fifteen months before the *Titanic's* maiden voyage. He was a total stranger among the ship's officer caste, in stark contrast to everyone else who knew each other well. This was also his first trip across the North Atlantic. He would not forget it in a hurry.

It would be easy to assume that the officers and crew of the ship were one homogeneous whole; easy but totally wrong. There were three main categories of crew; victualling staff, seamen and firemen – the 'black gang' as the latter were known. The victualling element included the stewards and the catering staff, many being what would now be called 'front of house' employees who would see and interact with passengers regularly. The seamen were composed of staff who would help the captain and his officers in the exercise of the navigational aspects of the ship, including for example men like the lookouts. The firemen worked below decks, firing the boilers, loading up tons of coal into the hungry furnaces that, devouring them eagerly, drove the ship on.

Many of the crew also had little or no idea who the officers were, other than those which they came into regular contact with because of their work. The firemen for example spent most of their time onboard ship far below, either in the engine rooms or in their quarters. Even Captain Smith would have been little known on a personal level by many of the crew, though his high profile as an instantly recognizable figurehead of the White Star Line would have meant that most would have known him at least on sight. Such sub-divisions within the crew would have important repercussions when the *Titanic* found itself in trouble.

There was another important difference to note too. Although the captain and senior officers were waged employees of the White Star Line, the rest of the crew were all casual staff, taken on for each voyage. The parts of Southampton where most of them lived were rough areas, subject to frequent fights when men came home from their voyaging and spent a large chunk of their wages on an extended drinking session. As one local put it, they would 'come home like walking skeletons, the stokers, and they had one glorious booze-up, which led to fighting and off they went again'.

Many crew members sailed on the same ships frequently despite the casual nature of their employment, though this was not invariably the case. Others opted for a bit of variety; thirty-two-year-old Able Seaman George Moore who was on the *Titanic* often opted for routes to Bombay during the winter months. In practice, many of the men had been working with White Star for many years. However, in 1912 times were particular hard for them. There was a national coal strike on which meant that many of the normally bustling liners were lying idle in the docks in the absence of enough fuel to power them.

The existence of the coal strike hinted at something greater, for this was a time of some social unrest and fraught industrial relations. White Star had only recently agreed to recognize trade unions and there had been several serious disputes about the wage levels of crew members. One particular union, recently set up, had the majority of the *Titanic's* crew as members. This was the British Seafarers' Union, which was based in Southampton. The Union was asked by White Star to select crew, especially seamen, stokers, trimmers and greasers for the maiden voyage.

There were 898 crew on the maiden voyage, 699 of whom were registered as living in Southampton though only 40 per cent of the total crew were born locally. Many had moved down from the north-west of England when White Star had relocated from Liverpool a few years before. Twenty-three of the crew were female, eighteen of whom were stewardesses. The crew were an eclectic bunch. Take the cooks for example. They were divided into categories, Vienna bakers, soup cooks, pastry cooks, coffee men, carvers, wine butlers, fish cooks and 'Hebrew cooks' for example.

The same was true of the stewards, such as library stewards, bedroom stewards, bath stewards – most bathrooms were still communal apart from a few first-class cabins – pantry stewards, saloon stewards. There were a host of other staff, from those working in the restaurant to lift operators (the lifts on the new ships were a novelty), Turkish bath attendants, gym instructors, cashiers and interpreters. There were also Post Office staff onboard – the post was an important revenue-earner for White Star. These men were employees of the British and US Post Offices, relatively well-paid when measured against their peers.

However, all was not well with the postal staff. They were most unhappy at their sleeping quarters. They were for one thing very noisy, being located among third-class cabins which were, as one inspector reported when reviewing the quarters, occupied by 'mostly low-class continentals' (jarringly patronizing language with barely-concealed racist undertones comes across time and again in reports of the disaster). The quarters were right next to a door through a main thoroughfare which frequently banged open and shut throughout the night.

The ship also had an orchestra (rather a grand name for what were in fact ensembles), in fact it had two. Although officially second-class passengers they were accommodated in the bowels of the ship, portside on E Deck. There were eight of them in all, five in a piano quintet and three in a piano trio. The former played for first and second-class passengers while the latter played in the *A La Carte Grill*, the exclusive restaurant on B Deck. Bandmaster Wallace Hartley led both.

Many of the crew slept in dormitories, sometimes surprisingly close to first-class accommodation (though barriers made this proximity invisible). Most of the crew were located on E Deck, which was connected by a wide working alleyway known as 'Scotland Road', close to a first-class passageway known ironically to the crew, as 'Park Lane'. It led to several sections of third-class accommodation on the ship.

With so many categories of staff, the crew was far from being a generic whole. Each segment formed a sub-stratum of its own, with its specific internal dynamics and its own brand of professional pride. A number of the crew relied on tips from grateful passengers to augment their wages.

Some of them, such as Steward Jack Stagg, were sorry that the *Titanic* was not fuller for, he complained in a letter home to his sister sent from Queenstown *en route* to America, he would probably only have one first-class table to look after. Wages varied greatly. Captain Smith, as mentioned, was paid £1,250 per annum and would receive a bonus each year that his ship avoided an accident. Seamen received around £5 a month, stewards £3–£4 per month. Harold Bride, the wireless operator, received £48 per annum.

The relationship between passengers and crew was closest with the stewards, who were in very regular contact with them. Some of the passengers had their own favourite stewards who they had sailed with on various ships for years. This would prove particularly beneficial to some of the passengers, who would in some cases owe their survival from the wreck to the fact that a friendly steward looked after them when it came to the time to load the lifeboats.

Sidney Daniels was one such steward. He had done ten trips on the *Olympic* and clearly made a fine impression for he was chosen to make the maiden voyage of the *Titanic*. In an interview later he teasingly said: 'they were picking out the best of the crew... pat my back a minute... best of the crew to go to the Titanic', and he was one of them.

The firemen working below decks on the other hand were rarely seen. They lived in their steamy caverns, far out of sight of passengers. They were a tough lot; even many of the officers were nervous of them, though it was widely thought that those from Southampton were less problematic than many from other ports. Their life was hot and dirty, and they earned every penny of their salary with bucketfuls of sweat.

Some crew were in special categories. The restaurant was run by Luigi Gatti, who had recently managed the Ritz restaurant. He moved to Southampton when he was awarded the commission (for he or his crew were not employees of White Star) for the restaurant on the *Titanic*. He was married with a young son, Vittorio. Shortly before *Titanic* sailed the little boy gave his father his favourite teddy bear as a good-luck charm. It was pulled out of the water with Luigi's body a few days later and returned to the family.

The wireless operators were also not strictly speaking White Star employees. They worked for the Marconi company and their role was primarily to provide a means of communication for passengers to other passing ships and to shore. It was known that they could be valuable in a crisis for a wireless operator, Jack Binns, had summoned help to a stricken liner named the *Republic* in 1909 and saved many a life as a result. Despite this crucial demonstration of their value, little thought had been given subsequently to how they might be best used, a state of affairs that would have a critical effect on the disastrous events that were about to unfold.

The regulation of wireless operators onboard ship would be shown to be distinctly amateurish.

The problem was that they essentially inhabited a little world of their own on their ships. The recently-agreed Berlin Convention had introduced some regulation into what was a shambolically-regulated industry but it had scarcely scratched the surface of what needed to be done to maximize the potential of this incredible invention. Some important things had happened as a result of the Convention. It confirmed that safety messages took precedence over all others, a crucial point when all the money from wireless onboard ships came from the sending and receiving of passengers 'wish you were here' messages. Some standardization had been introduced too, which was also vital. In the tidying up of the Morse code to be used (for speaking by radio had not yet been invented, only the dispatching of Morse messages) the international distress call 'CQD' ('Come Quickly – Distress') would be replaced by a new call, 'SOS'.

All this was well and good but the Convention got nowhere near the heart of the problems. In practice, operators did pretty much as they liked when they were at sea. If there were an emergency, then the skipper of the ship would for sure insist on safety messages taking priority; indeed most wireless operators would not need to be reminded of the fact. However, the rest of the time most captains took little interest in what was going on in the wireless shack.

Therefore, operators among other things would set their own working hours. In practice, this would invariably mean working in the day, when the huge majority of passenger messages were generated, and knocking off at night when things were much quieter. It was not quite so bad for the *Titanic* which, as the largest ship in the world, had two operators. However, many ships either had only one operator or, in smaller ships, none at all. The problems of inadequately regulated wireless telegraphy were about to come home to roost with a vengeance.

Other than Jack Phillips and Harold Bride on the *Titanic*, there were two other operators who played a key role in the story. One was Harold Cottam, the operator aboard the *Carpathia*. His role would swing between hero and villain at various stages of the story. The other was Cyril Evans, the operator on the *Californian*. He would play a key role, strangely, by playing no role at all until it was too late. If luck played any part at all in the unfolding disaster, it did so more than anything else by who did and who didn't pick up the wireless messages that were flying across the North Atlantic at the time.

Harold Bride in particular would be a first-hand witness to the heavy wireless traffic that dashed back and forwards across the ether when his ship struck a berg and therefore is one of the key characters in the tale. He was in many ways a typical example of the bright, dynamic and sometimes hot-headed young men who were attracted to the profession back then. He was just twenty-two when the *Titanic* sailed, hailing from Nunhead in England and only out of wireless training school for a couple of years. Wireless was new then and in such an environment youth was no obstacle, for no one was experienced in the medium. Despite his tender years, he was already a seasoned operator, having served on both the *Haverford* and then the *Lusitania*. He joined the *Titanic* at Belfast and was working the powerful apparatus aboard as assistant to Jack Phillips.

In many ways the wireless operators on both the *Carpathia* and the *Californian* were very like their counterparts on the more glamorous *Titanic*. Harold Cottam on the *Carpathia* had studied the Marconi system in London. He was the youngest ever graduate of the British School of Telegraphy, achieving this distinction when he was just seventeen years of age. He had spent his subsequent career partially in a shore-based station and partly at sea. He joined the *Carpathia* in February 1912. At the time of the *Titanic* disaster he was just twenty-one years old, one year older than Cyril Evans on the *Californian*.

The wireless operators were to play a seminal role in the events surrounding the *Titanic* but other crew members did too. Chief among them was perhaps one of the humblest of all men on the *Titanic*, lookout Frederick Fleet who, along with his mate Reginald Lee, was up in the freezing cold crow's nest when an iceberg loomed suddenly, far too late, into view. Fleet's life had been a tragic one and his story is perhaps the saddest of all those on the ship, certainly of those who survived the tragedy. Pathos had not finished with him even when he got back ashore.

Fleet had been born in Liverpool in 1887. He never knew his father and his mother abandoned him when he was still very young so he was effectively left to be brought up as an orphan. He grew up in a succession of foster homes and orphanages, being looked after at one time by the much-respected charity Dr Barnardos. He first went to sea in 1903 and had, since then, lived the same uncertain, financially perilous life shared by most of the crew in the absence of a permanent job. He was now paid £5 a month, though he received another five shillings (25p or $1.25 in modern financial parlance) as a small bonus for his job as lookout. The bonus recognized the uncomfortable nature of the lookout's job, stuck aloft in a draughty crow's nest and exposed to the elements.

Captain Smith's villa in Southampton, if not exactly a stately home, was about as far away from the life that most of the crew lived as it was possible to get. With an annual salary level twenty times above that of many of them and a lifestyle that incorporated invitations to swanky receptions that rich passengers liked to hold aboard ship he inhabited a different world than most of his crew. They were indeed a cosmopolitan lot, the officers and crew of *RMS Titanic*.

Before considering the passengers, who were equally varied in terms of their backgrounds and ways of life, there was a small group of people who were neither crew nor really in reality like any other passengers. There were a number of representatives of both Harland & Wolff and the White Star Line sailing on this maiden voyage, several of whom were to play prominent roles in the looming catastrophe.

Harland & Wolff had sent a small proving party, about twenty strong, out on the voyage. Their job was basically to deal with any snagging issues that arose and needed to be sorted out to give the ship a smooth run. At their head was the new Managing Director of the yard, Thomas Andrews, who had designed the *Titanic* and knew her better than anyone. Andrews came from a Presbyterian Northern Irish background and brought with him the reputation for hard work that often went with that particular culture. He was also a perfectionist and nothing would be left to chance in any effort to improve the *Titanic* for future reference. For most of the trip, he was thinking about minor details such as whether or not the number of coat-hooks that had been provided was sufficient. By the end of it, this was going to appear somewhat academic.

In the course of his search for excellence, Andrews would poke his nose in every corner of the ship. Nothing was out of bounds for him, from the most plush of the first-class areas to the darkest, dirtiest recess of the engine room. He was a charming if quiet conversationalist too; everyone seemed to think that when Andrews spoke to them he was really, genuinely interested in them and their problems. It was no doubt his natural way and was not in any way an act, but it also proved a remarkably useful asset in finding out what was going on in the ship and what could be made better.

Andrews was a truly popular man. He took an interest in what was going on below decks and, unusually for a white collar worker of the day, was widely respected for his calm demeanour and concern for details, both mechanical and human. Sometimes in the literature of the *Titanic* disaster there is a tendency to over-eulogize, to exaggerate the virtues of this or that particular hero. Not so with Andrews, for whom most people seemed to have had a genuine fondness.

Bruce Ismay was on the trip too, as usual making a point of going on a maiden voyage to make sure that everything went to plan. He had a brash exterior which hid an essentially shy personality. Sometimes demonstrative to the point of being overwhelming, this was merely an attempt to hide his innate reserve. His position was somewhat ambiguous. He did not seem to interfere with the navigation of Captain Smith's ship, giving him his due place as the captain and therefore in absolute charge of the *Titanic* while she was at sea. Indeed, he was normally careful to see that no one might mistake a genuine interest in his company's later super-liner for interference.

However, it was not always so. His innate insecurity led to him occasionally bestowing the benefits of his own particularly informed insight on other passengers on the ship. He and Smith did not spend a great deal of time in each other's company but did exchange pleasantries on occasion. In these ad hoc chit-chats Smith would bestow some small piece of information on him.

Sometimes Ismay would then pass it on. In most circumstances this would have appeared little more than a piece of braggadocio, the actions of a show-off wanting to impress with his knowledge and, by implication, power. However, in the scenario that was about to be played out it looked something much more than that, the actions of a man who was taking far too big a part in the sailing of the ship. Ismay would unwittingly chart a course right into the middle of a huge controversy and would find himself portrayed as the pantomime villain of the piece.

Now, this great collection of stewards, firemen, cooks, seamen, officers, gymnasium staff, postal clerks, wireless operators, shipbuilders and company owners were about to become, in theory, one vast crew responsible for looking after a group of passengers the size of a small town to enjoy a journey that they would never forget. Comfort and size were the key words for the *Titanic*, a name which in its very self suggested gargantuan bulk. The crew and their officers had never before been together as a homogeneous whole and it would inevitably take a while for everything to bed in. But no doubt all would be well in the end and the ship could look forward to many years of incident-free sailing across the mighty Atlantic.

4

An Ominous Beginning:
10 April 1912, Southampton

In recent years, the fate of Southampton and the White Star Line had become ever more intertwined. As the nineteenth century progressed, Southampton had increasingly become a port that dealt with passengers and mail rather than cargo traffic. The double-tides she enjoyed gave her a strong commercial advantage over many rivals, as it meant that ships could sail into and out of the docks more regularly than they could elsewhere. Her position astride the English Channel also helped to give her an edge. The port was therefore in a position of some advantage and White Star had sensed an opportunity in that.

Other shipping organizations had too. In 1893, the American Line decided to move its ships from Liverpool to Southampton, which was also becoming increasingly accessible in other ways. Since the opening of the first railway to the city from London in 1840, the south-coast port had been within two hours of the capital. The railways linked up with ocean steamers to take passengers across to France and the Channel Islands, ferrying thousands of them down to the docks and dropping them off literally next to the vessels they were due to sail on.

The city had had to grow to accommodate the increased volume of traffic that ensued. The deep Empress Dock had been built in the city in 1890, being opened by Queen Victoria. Then, the Prince of Wales Graving Dock, the largest in the world, was opened in 1895. These measures helped Southampton deal with bigger ships and more of them. But it was the decision of the American Line to relocate there which was crucial to the city's confident entry into the new century. However, ships carried on growing all the time and the docks needed to grow with them. This led to the opening of an even larger dry dock, Trafalgar Dock, in 1905.

The city grew alongside the port. The South-Western Hotel was opened in 1867, the largest in Southampton. It was purchased by the London & South Western Railway as part of their package offering; rail travel, accommodation in port and then transportation across the ocean. It adjoined both the station and the dock gates, and was therefore perfectly positioned as a transition point from land to sea travel. Elegant and sophisticated and within five minutes stroll of the ships it proved a great commercial success. On the eve of *Titanic's* sailing, many prominent passengers, including Bruce Ismay and Thomas Andrews, spent the night there.

It was in 1906 that White Star decided to relocate its transatlantic base in Britain to Southampton, a bitter blow to Liverpool where the line had been based previously. That same year, White Star appointed George Bowyer as the pilot for their ships in port. It was he who, six years later, would negotiate the *Titanic* out of Southampton docks and out to sea not, as it turned out, without incident. The year after, 1907, the company opened officers in Canute Road; they too would play a significant part in the great disaster that struck the city when the *Titanic* went down. Despite all this however the corporate centre of the business remained in Liverpool and would do so for some years to come. When the *Titanic* sailed, she still carried the name of Liverpool as her port of registration. She was planned to make a visit to the port on her way over from Belfast but this idea had been abandoned late on.

In 1907 one of the first White Star ships to sail out of Southampton was the *Adriatic*, commanded by none other than E.J. Smith. Although not on the same scale as the *Titanic* would be, she appeared huge to the residents of the city. White Star's move to the city had a hugely beneficial effect on Southampton. At the start of the Century, unemployment had been high and poverty rife there. It was a common sight to see men queuing up for work and their forlorn wives pawning what few possessions they had to gain a small amount of cash. The move of White Star to the city boosted employment prospects.

The port still needed to get bigger alongside the ships she was expected to accommodate. Large dry docks had been built but larger wet docks were needed too. The firm of Topham Jones and Railton was instructed to build a new 16-acre dock to a depth of 40 feet at low tide. Cargo and passenger sheds were built alongside to deal with the large number of passengers transiting through. The new dock would become the home of all White Star vessels in Southampton for the next few years.

The ongoing quest for size among the latest ships being built was becoming increasingly problematic for the port authorities. It would create even more difficulties with the advent of the *Olympic* class. The channel into Southampton was barely deep enough to deal with these monsters and White Star had written to Southampton Harbour Board in December 1908, telling them of their expectation that all necessary measures would be taken to ensure that dredging was duly undertaken to deepen the harbour. The response of the Harbour Board was that of all great bureaucrats throughout the ages; prevarication. 1909 came and went, and apart from mealy-mouthed platitudes nothing came out of the port authorities.

The problem of course was money. The work required would cost £100,000. When a meeting was held between White Star and the Harbour Board in January 1910, the latter's opening gambit was to offer to loan the money to White Star for the work to be done. There on behalf of White Star was Harold Sanderson, their General Director, who expressed astonishment that his shipping line was seriously expected to stump up the money when Southampton would be such a clear beneficiary of the traffic that the new ships would bring to the port. Thinly-veiled threats to relocate to Plymouth did the trick; the White Star Line could have their work done free and gratis.

Now all that work had come to fruition. *Titanic*, the second of the three new giants, was due to sail on the morrow, only a week or so after the *Olympic* had done the same. It would be the start of a regular weekly shuttle between Southampton and New York with the ships passing each other normally somewhere in the mighty ocean. The future seemed bright for the port. Now the crew began to make their way for the ship and hundreds of passengers converged on the south coast of England.

Bruce Ismay arrived on the night before *Titanic* sailed. His valet, Richard Fry, was there to meet him having travelled down to make sure that everything was in order. His secretary, William Harrison, was there too. Both men would also join the *Titanic* with Ismay and both would be lost. Fortunately, the Chairman's wife and children only came down to see him off and did not go with him on the fateful voyage.

Many of the ship's passengers arrived in Southampton on the day but certainly not all. For the rich crowd, the South-Western Hotel was certainly the place to be. Here they would be greeted by banks of porters dressed in their red uniforms and enjoy every luxury in the hotel's grand surroundings. Thomas Andrews had stayed there all week. He had left for the ship every morning at 8.30 a.m. and came back ten hours later to sort out any correspondence that had come in during the day. In other words, he was living up to his reputation as a veritable workaholic.

The first people to arrive on 10 April were of course the crew. The first day of a maiden voyage, and the preparations for it, were a nightmare. As the *Titanic* got ready for her big day, below decks was a hive of activity. Perfectionist Thomas Andrews was as usual a blaze of energy, taking the owners round the ship, interviewing engineers and crew and making sure everything was as shipshape as it should be. Even now, at the eleventh hour and fifty-ninth minute, he still noted tiny details that could be improved at a later stage.

Not everyone on the ship was happy. Some crew members had their own particular gripes to concern them. Steward George Beedem had worked on

Good Friday onboard the ship but owing to an administrative error had not been paid for his labour. He sent some money home to his wife with the letters he despatched from Southampton, explaining why the amount was short of that expected.

He was not in a good mood and had not even been able to locate a duster to clean the place up. Some of his concluding comments, made in jest, have a chilling ring about them: 'what with no dusters or anything to work with I wish the bally ship at the bottom of the sea'. The old phrase about being careful what you wish for comes to mind for the ship did end up at the bottom of the sea and so did George Beedem. As a reminder of how great the human tragedy of the *Titanic* was, his last words to his wife in his letter home was to ask her to think whether they should go for their own house or not. Despite his griping, Beedem was in an ambitious frame of mind.

Captain E.J. Smith spent his last night before sailing at home in Winn Road, Southampton. As he left at seven in the morning, dressed in a bowler hat and a long coat, he bumped into his paperboy Ben Banham and took his copy of the newspaper with him to read later. He had a Board of Trade inspection to handle at 8.00 a.m. and a taxi arrived to pick him up and take him on the short journey down to the docks. It was a bright, sunny day – 'summer weather' as Officer Pitman later called it. Captain Smith arrived at 7.30 a.m., to be met by his officers who had spent the night onboard.

Most local crew members opted to follow Smith's example though and stay at home. Able Seaman Joseph Scarrott kissed his sister and uttered a 'goodbye' to her. It later seemed odd, for his usual farewell was a 'see you soon'. He seemed to be acting out of character, for he delayed changing into his uniform until the very last minute. He had always had a set routine and today, for some reason, he was not following it. For reasons he could not explain, he thought that there was something distinctly out of the ordinary going on.

Smith and Scarott and all the crew, from the greatest to the humblest, all those responsible for sailing the ship and pampering her passengers, made their way to the docks. By 8.00 a.m., the crew was mustered and ready to spring into action. One of the early tasks to be carried out was a lifeboat drill. Two boats were prepared for lowering. Nine men got into each of them and they were lowered down to the water. No one seemed to think it might be a good idea to lower them full and see how many could be safely put in each boat (most of them had a notional capacity of sixty-five). Equally, no one gave much thought to allocating crew members to specific boats so that, in an emergency, everyone would know where to go. It was as if no one thought that the boats would ever be used for real.

Officer Lowe was one of those involved in the boat drill along with Sixth Officer Moody. Two boats were lowered, rowed around the docks and hauled up again. There were about sixteen men involved in this drill, an insight into the prevailing attitude that they would never be needed except in the event of a 'man overboard'. Perceived wisdom was that there should be a minimum of two sailors per boat and, ignoring the extra collapsibles that had been put onboard, there were sixteen boats, which required thirty-two sailors, twice as many as were being drilled if all the boats were needed.

One of the stewards, Edward Wheelton, later explained that a full boat drill was not possible as it would interfere with getting lunch ready for the passengers who would soon arrive. Food was more important than safety apparently. Certainly, the whole process was cursory, merely a formality that needed to be observed. Officer Lowe at least had some good practice for what was to come. The boats were safely lowered to the water, the men rowed round in circles a couple of times and then were hoisted back onboard and had their breakfast.

Not everyone in the crew was quite so *blasé* about the lack of a drill as the ship's officers were. Steward Percy Keene had previously served on the *Oceanic* under another respected White Star commander, Captain Haddock. There he noted that everyday the watertight doors were tested and each Sunday a lifeboat drill would be carried out. All the crew were required to take part, except for the firemen whose union had negotiated an exemption. He later remarked that this was not the case on *Titanic*.

Some of the stokers onboard were allowed ashore for a last drink before they sailed. They left while Captain Smith formally received the Board of Trade clearance certificates that had just been produced after the final inspection. It was something of a relief, for the Inspector, Maurice Clarke, was a stickler for detail and everyone was glad to see the back of him. His job was to clear *Titanic* as an emigrant ship and every fine detail was poured over until he was satisfied. Second Officer Lightoller and the crew generally thought that the Inspector was 'a nuisance because he is so strict', 'because he makes us fork out every detail'.

Other last minute visitors were more welcome. Norman Wilkinson was an artist who had supplied paintings for both the *Olympic* and *Titanic*. The subject of the one onboard the latter was Plymouth Harbour. On his way to Devon, Wilkinson decided to drop in and admire his handiwork *in situ*. Smith greeted him but apologized that he was too busy to show him round, so handed him over to the Purser. Wilkinson received his guided tour and duly saw his painting from more or less the same spot in the Smoking Room where Thomas Andrews would be seen for the last time when the great ship later went down.

Captain Smith's wife and his twelve-year-old daughter Helen also came onboard to bid the captain *bon voyage*. The Ismay family also visited for the same purpose. Smith missed his family when he was away from home and felt that he was missing out in particular on seeing Helen grow up. A *Titanic* survivor later said that Smith had told him he wanted to retire to see more of her. The Smith and Ismay family members who were not sailing then returned to shore to wave their loved ones off from the quayside.

At 9.30 a.m., the boat train pulled in beside the ship with second and third-class passengers. They passed through the massive passenger sheds and the third-class members of the assemblage were given medical inspections. Then they started to board, being greeted by stewards who led them to their cabins. The first-class passengers would arrive last of all on a train at 11.30 a.m., having left London Waterloo just under two hours previously. The train pulled up right to the side of the ship. The passengers, some of the elite of contemporary society, then made the short walk up the gangplank and onto *Titanic*, where they were greeted by the stewards, some of whom probably were distraught at the sight of some familiar and not too welcome faces, at least if the memoirs of people like Violet Jessop are to be believed.

Many of the stewards and stewardesses were old hands, well known to regular travellers, hence Jessop's ability to recognize certain faces. Also onboard was Steward Albert Crawford who would find himself unexpectedly in charge of a boat. He said that he was forty-one years old and had been at sea for thirty-one of them, having made his first voyage in 1881.

Some lucky souls cancelled their trips late on for a variety of reasons. J.P. Morgan had expected to be on his new ship but had cancelled when a business trip overran. The millionaire George Vanderbilt telephoned in his cancellation on 9 April. However, his luggage stayed onboard. The American ambassador in France, Robert Bacon, was supposed to be travelling back to the States with his family but his successor was delayed so he had to postpone his departure.

Many of the richer passengers were touring the Continent and would board the ship at Cherbourg but not all. W.T. Stead was perhaps the most prominent British passenger on the ship, a famous magazine editor and social reformer. A man of great social conviction, he was not afraid to court controversy in a good cause. In 1885 he published a work called *The Maiden Tribute of Modern Babylon*. This was an outstanding example of investigative journalism into the evils of child prostitution.

Like the best examples of its type, it led to real change. As a direct result of his efforts, the *Criminal Law Amendment Act* was passed, raising the age of sexual consent in Britain to sixteen, where it still remains. However, he suffered for his efforts. Nasty and self-serving sections of the press portrayed him as a paedophile as a result of his research and he was imprisoned for three months for his efforts. But others, incensed at the injustice, rallied round him, including especially prominent social reformers and religious figures.

In 1886 he wrote an article in the *Pall Mall Gazette* entitled *How the Mail Steamer went down in Mid Atlantic – by a survivor.* In it a hypothetical steamer collided with a ship in mid ocean. There was a huge loss of life because there were not enough lifeboats onboard. He concluded the article with a statement that this was exactly the sort of disaster that would occur one day unless something was done about the shortage of boats on modern ocean liners.

He followed it up with an article in the *Review of Reviews* in 1892. In it he wrote about a couple who were journeying to the New World when a passenger had a vision about another ship that had struck an iceberg. This was so vivid that she managed to persuade the captain to change course, as a result of which he avoided an ice-field. Little can Stead have realized that he was about to find himself in the middle of a real-life drama that in many ways mirrored the fictional stories he had already included in his publications.

In later life, Stead had turned to spiritualism. He had also become increasingly disturbed at the effects of war on humanity and had developed strong pacifist tendencies as a result. Now, aged sixty-three, with a bushy, white 'Santa Claus' beard, he was the epitome of a warm, welcoming grandfather figure. However, his gentility should not disguise his influence. He was on his way to America to address a pacifist conference, having been personally invited to do so by President Taft of America.

There were some prominent Americans onboard too. The Wideners were a well-known Philadelphia family. George Widener's father, Peter Widener, was a director of International Mercantile Marine, owner of the *Titanic*. Mrs Eleanor Widener was said to be the owner of one of the world's most valuable jewel collections. The family had just spent two months in Europe. During their trip, Mrs Widener had presented a set of thirty silver plates once belonging to the famous seventeenth-century courtesan Nell Gwyn to the London Museum, which had been opened by King George V that March.

Also boarding at Southampton was Isidor Straus, a partner in the prominent New York department store Macys. He was a well known politician and charitable benefactor. He had been a member of Congress between 1893 and 1895. He was particularly active in providing charitable assistance to Jewish immigrants. He was also on committees at Harvard, though he himself had never received a college education. He took great pride in his extensive library and was an avid reader. It was true to say that he could afford to indulge his leisure activities as he had a personal fortune reputed to be $50 million, the same as George Widener.

Bearded as were many men of his age at the time, Straus, now sixty-seven years of age, was approaching the twilight years of an industrious and successful life. He had worked his way up through hard graft and perseverance. Through it all he had been accompanied by his wife, Ida, four years his junior. They had travelled to Europe with their daughter Beatrice who was not making the return trip with them. Isidor and Ida, devoted to each other, were the perfect picture of a couple who had lived a long and happy life together.

Another first-class American passenger on the ship was Colonel Archibald Gracie. He had had a tough life. Married with four daughters, two had died very young, one particularly tragically in an elevator accident, and a third had passed away shortly after her marriage. His father, also Archibald, seems to have been an inspirational figure for him. Archibald Senior was a civil war veteran who had fought in one of the toughest battles of the war at Chickamauga.

His father had died when young Archibald was just five years old. Now fifty-three, he had been so in awe of his father that he had spent seven years writing a book called *The Truth About Chickamauga*. It had tired him out and he had journeyed to Europe aboard the *Oceanic* for a holiday. Now, he was on his way back, ready to offer his services to any single ladies who needed his protection. The idea, now rather a quaint one to modern eyes, was that men would offer to look after ladies who were unescorted as one of the social conventions of the day. Gracie took to it like a fish to water and would soon be looking after his own coterie of such single ladies.

With a dapper moustache and a well-mannered bearing, Gracie was an elegant middle-aged man still somewhere close to the prime of an affluent life, having been born into a rich family. There is in truth something of the appearance of a fusspot and a nuisance about him, albeit a very well-intentioned one. However, when it came to the crunch there were a number of ladies who were grateful for his protection in a real hour of need. In an old-fashioned way perhaps, Gracie was about to become as big a hero as his father had once been.

Of course, these were the ones who stood out. The vast majority of those on the ship were not in this category. Lawrence Beesley for example was a second-class passenger, a schoolmaster from Dulwich College who had decided to go on a tour of the United States. He had several reasons for choosing the *Titanic* to travel on. One was just the fact that she was new, part of an exciting personal adventure, but that was not all. Friends had travelled over the Atlantic in the *Olympic* and had commented favourably on her stability when the sea was rough. This was a very attractive proposition to Beesley.

He stayed the night of 9 April in Southampton. When he went down to breakfast the following morning, the four huge funnels of the *Titanic* could be seen towering over the shipping offices opposite the hotel window. Processions of stokers and stewards were making their way towards their new ship. As he rose from breakfast, Beesley overheard a conversation between fellow residents who were also about to board the ship. They spoke of the dangers of an accident at sea. He recognized them later onboard but they would not survive the very dangers that they were presently discussing.

He boarded the *Titanic* at 10.00 a.m. Two friends had come up from Exeter to see him off and together they toured the new ship. There were so many corridors that it was easy to become totally lost. They wandered casually into the gymnasium and were using the exercise bikes when McCawley, the instructor came in, accompanied by what they assumed were friends. They were not; they were photographers from the London press. As they worked out in a lackadaisical manner, other passengers came in, using the other equipment there including the electric camels and horses. In 1912 it was all a wonderful novelty.

Other more local passengers drifted in throughout the morning. Charlotte Collyer and her family had had a fine send off from their village, Bishopstoke, near Southampton, the day before. They had been led to a seat in the old churchyard – Harvey was a parish clerk and a much respected member of the local community – and had sat there while the bell-ringers climbed into the belfry and rang an honorary peal for them. Although Charlotte appreciated the gesture, it also seemed to generate somewhat melancholy emotions in her.

Charlotte Collyer and husband Harvey had gone to the bank in Southampton where they drew out all their life savings. She had been suffering from tuberculosis and they were going to a fruit farm in Idaho in the hope that the better climate would help her. When the clerk asked if they wanted a bank draft Harvey replied that notes would be fine. He put the money in his inside breast pocket on his coat where it remained even when the *Titanic* went down. There were several thousand dollars there. They had sent all their other possessions ahead on to the ship. Everything they owned was on her.

The Collyers, including their little daughter Marjorie ('Madge'), entered the ship through its second-class entrance. So too did the ship's musicians who were strictly speaking passengers. They were provided under contract by an agency, C.W. and F.N. Black of Liverpool. This had only been the case for a short time. Until quite recently the musicians had been employed direct by White Star. However, the agents had sensed a business opportunity and had approached the company to offer to supply the musicians at a reduced rate if, in return, White Star would contract solely with them. The deal had been struck and the company had saved itself a few pounds in salaries as a result.

The second-class passengers had the option of taking the stairs or getting on the elevator, still a novelty at the time. Third-class passengers were given slightly less spoiled treatment. They were inspected closely when they got onboard, though the English emigrants tended to get less rigorous inspection than did those from the continent and beyond. These formalities had to be observed as otherwise the passengers would not be allowed out of the immigration centre at Ellis Island in New York if the necessary criteria had not been met.

Third-class were arrayed in a widely-dispersed set of cabins, ranging from D Deck, down through E and F and finally onto G Deck. There were 296 such cabins in all. There was strict segregation of single men and women with males at the forward end of the ship and females at the stern, along with families. There were barriers in place to stop third-class getting into second and first-class areas. However, if this sounds harsh, not long before on other ships third-class were grouped together in dormitories rather like barracks. Separate rooms were something of a luxury and the facilities onboard contrasted favourably with what had been available for second or even first-class on ships not many years previously.

There was no such thing as a typical story for any passenger on the *Titanic* and it is a particular shame that accounts of the ship's tragedy do not feature more on the third-class passengers. The problem is that so little interest was shown in them as individuals, or indeed even as a class, at the time that no one bothered to tell their story. However, there were some terrible tales to tell from some of the families onboard.

Particularly poignant was the story of William Skoog, his wife Anna and their four children, Karl, Harald, Mabel and Margit. The Skoogs were Swedish and had emigrated to Iron Mountain, Michigan, some time before. However, they had become very homesick and gone back to Sweden in 1911. It was a move that had not paid off and now they had decided to try their luck in the USA once more. The Skoogs had already had a long journey having travelled via Stockholm, Gothenburg and Hull to reach Southampton.

Frederick Goodwin was a forty-two-year-old electrical engineer who had been persuaded by his brother Thomas, who had emigrated some time before, to take up a job at a new power station at Niagara. He had sold his home in Fulham and was now on his way with his wife Augusta and six children, the youngest, Sidney, just a baby, to try his luck. Things had already seemed to take a turn for the better. They had booked to go on a small steamer across the Atlantic but the coal strike had led to this particular sailing being cancelled and they had instead been transferred to this magnificent new ship. They could hardly believe their good fortune.

Marie Panula was Finnish. Her husband, Juha, was already in the USA and now she was off to join him with their five children. She had sold her farm in Finland for $1,200 and was travelling to America along with this and $76 in cash. Now the family, accompanied by the daughter of a neighbour back home in Finland, were setting out in this great adventure. They and hundreds of other excited passengers now sought out their new temporary homes in the rabbit warren of corridors below decks. Marie's sons, Ernesti and Jaako, were single men and made their way towards the bows of the ship where their accommodation was situated. The rest of the family, including baby Eino, were in a cabin towards the stern.

Also boarding in Southampton as part of third-class was the family of young Millvina Dean, just two months old. She was there with her parents, Bertram (a farmer) and Ettie and her young brother, also Bertram, aged one. They had originally been booked on the *Philadelphia* but the coal strike had led to their transfer to the *Titanic*. Millvina's grandparents, George and Gladys Light, came down to see the family off. They got onboard to do so, almost missing the bell that rang telling all non-passengers to leave in the process.

One other visitor to the ship almost did not get off either. R.C. Lawrence had been sent to the ship to deliver some typewriters to the Purser's Office at the last minute. As an inquisitive sixteen-year-old, he was unable to resist the chance to look around, overwhelmed by the magnificence of this floating hotel. He went into the gymnasium and tried some of the equipment out.

So engrossed was he that he lost track of the time and did not realize that midday, the time for departure, was approaching. Suddenly, the warning whistles that alerted everyone that sailing time was approaching blew, shaking him from his reverie. He made his way through the milling passengers and eventually found the gangplank off. By the time he arrived there, the ship had already started to move and a small gap had appeared between her and the quayside which he had to jump across.

Others had what would be, with the benefit of hindsight, amazingly lucky escapes. Joe Mulholland, a sailor, had an argument with one of the Engineering Officers and walked off the ship in a strop. Some of the crew were drinking just around the corner in the *Grapes* pub, not leaving until 11.50 a.m. Six of them left together and made their way into the docks. However, arriving here their progress was stopped by a passing train. Some of the men took a chance and ran across in front of the train, making it to the ship on time. But the rest waited until it had passed and by the time they reached the ship the gangway had been removed and the ship was already setting out.

Lawrence Beesley watched on as other latecomers missed the ship. A gang of stokers rushed up at the last minute even as the gangplank was being pulled up. A jobsworth officer stood guard and refused to let any of them on, even though they could easily have boarded. However much they argued the toss, he would not budge and let them pass. Cursing him, and their luck, they stood disappointed as the *Titanic* started to move cumbersomely away.

Yet perhaps the officer, who was Sixth Officer Moody, was not a jobsworth after all. Standbys had been kept on the ship until the very last moment, men who desperately wanted a job and a wage, far more than did those who had spent too long in the pub. Far better to give them a chance, reasoned Moody. And so a lucky six men were asked to sign on in place of those who had, at the last minute, failed to make the ship. However, there was then a hitch. The other standbys, who should have got off the ship at the last minute, had been left until it was too late to get off and they were now therefore stuck onboard.

The moment of departure had now arrived. Although there was a band playing, there was not a particularly great sense of occasion; Beesley described the scene as being 'quiet and orderly'. From the shore, the Ismays, the Smiths and others waved their farewells and, under the effective control of Pilot George Bowyer, the ship gracefully slid away. Half a dozen tugs pulled her carefully out as the crowd ashore followed her down the dockside as far as they could go. The order came to start the engines and the *Titanic* began to spring into life. Just after midday on Wednesday 10 April 1912 and the great ship's short career had now begun for real. As the *Titanic* swung slowly out, there was no cheering or hooting of ship's whistles from the neighbouring vessels, just the sight of the ship bursting majestically into life.

However, unknown to most aboard, *Titanic* already had a problem. The coal strike had come to an end on 6 April but it would take a while for shipping activities to get back to normal. The ship now had nearly 6,000 tons of coal to make the crossing. However, in the bunkers of Boiler Room 6 some of it had caught fire. While stokers poured water on it to dampen it down, engineers examined the bulkheads to see if they had been damaged. Chief Engineer Bell assured Captain Smith that everything was under control. The captain took the matter under advisement and decided to carry on as normal. If Inspector Clarke was aware of the problem, he did not mention it in his report.

Fireman Dilley said he fought this fire constantly with eleven other men down in the bunkers but could make no headway against it. Coal was piled in heaps, the top of which were wet but the bottom dry. Some of the dry coal had caught alight. The fight to put it out went on almost until the iceberg was hit and there was talk among the crew that they would have to empty the bunkers when they reached New York and get help to dampen the flames. It was eventually extinguished on 13 April but it is an interesting insight into attitudes to safety that the ship sailed off with the fire allegedly still burning.

The *Titanic* moved slowly away, friends and families of those onboard waving last farewells from the quay and following the ship as far as they could down the dockside. A further problem was imminent. As the *Titanic* moved out, she passed two ships moored side-by-side. On the inside, next to the dock, was the *Oceanic* and, tied up to her and closer to the passing *Titanic*, was the American liner *New York*. Both were victims of the coal strike and were idle.

Suddenly, there was 'a series of reports like those of a revolver'. It was the sound of the ropes holding the *New York* in position snapping as if they were as weak as a thin piece of string. Then coils of rope shot high in the air, like angry snakes rearing up, and then fell into the crowd on the shore, forcing them to scurry out of their way. Now, to the horror of everyone watching, the smaller American ship, deprived of its restraining hawsers, started to move into the path of the *Titanic*.

A great commotion broke out as orders were shouted in an attempt to stop the looming collision. Some of the sailors put out ropes while others hung collision mats over the side. On the bridge, Captain Smith and Bowyer worked together to try and stop a crash. Smith ordered the propellers to be stopped while two of the tugs, *Vulcan* and *Hercules*, attempted to grab hold of the meandering *New York*. Captain Gale on the *Vulcan* had dropped astern to pick up some workmen. He noted that the *Titanic* was drawing about 35 feet of water and it was close to low tide so she was quite near the bottom. White Star's urging of the Harbour Board to make sure that the channel into the port was properly dredged suddenly seemed particularly relevant.

Gale heard someone shout to him to try and push the *New York* back but she was too big for that. He was rather worried that his tugboat might be crushed to a pulp between the two liners if he tried. Instead, he managed to get a wire rope around the *New York*. Although it broke, he was straightaway able to get another line aboard her. He managed to grab hold of her when she was just 4 feet away from the *Titanic*. She managed to hang on while the *Titanic* passed. A number of sightseers had made their way onto the *New York*, crossing over from the *Oceanic*. They found themselves stranded until a gangplank was found to enable them to cross back to the *Oceanic* and, via her, to the quayside.

The *New York* drifted loose for a short time. Although tugs got lines aboard her, it was a while before her movement was arrested. She was eventually moored well away from the path of *Titanic*. Further lines were put on the *Oceanic*, to ensure that she did not have the same problem as the *New York*. *Titanic* had in the meantime moved back towards her berth. Eventually, an hour late, *Titanic* tried again and this time got into open water. There was a cinematograph photographer onboard who shot it all on his equipment with relish. Unfortunately, the film, which would have made fascinating viewing, currently lies 12,500 feet down in the North Atlantic.

Onboard *Titanic*, everyone breathed a sigh of relief. Joseph Scarrott wished that she had got closer to the *New York*, so that he could have jumped across and got off. He was more nervous than ever now. Everyone agreed it was a close shave. Captain Smith had helped to save the day by ordering the engines to be put hard astern when the *New York* looked as if she would hit. The backwash created had pushed her away as if a giant hand were fending off a puppy. On the one hand, it suggested that he was well able to manoeuvre even a behemoth like this. On the other, coming so close after the accident with the *Olympic* and the *Hawke*, it did suggest that there was a lot to learn about these new super-ships.

As a result of the *New York* incident, there was later a good deal of correspondence between White Star and Southampton Harbour Board. The company suggested that the problem arose because the water was too shallow and prevailed upon the Board to provide further dredging, which was duly done. Certainly the low tide had created a major unforeseen hazard, as the huge suction created when the *Titanic* passed the *New York*, even at low speed, tore her from her moorings with no apparent effort.

Of course, the passengers and crew made the incident a talking point aboard for a while though people had different opinions on it. The *New York* incident, in the opinion of Charlotte Collyer, did not frighten anyone onboard *Titanic*. It merely reminded the passengers how powerful she was. Colonel Gracie was standing with the Strauses when they witnessed the *New York* incident. Mr Straus told Gracie that he had made the maiden voyage with the *New York* a few years ago and had thought it 'the last word in shipbuilding'. Now she looked insignificant alongside the *Titanic*.

After this initial excitement, passengers and crew started to settle down. As she sailed down Southampton Water, from close-by on the shore, a young boy watched her pass from his house, Eaglehurst, near Fawley. Degna Marconi looked across the perfectly manicured lawn, 'like a carpet between house and shoreline'. As he watched from the French windows, 'passing ships seemed to sail right across the grass'.

That afternoon, he and his mother watched as the great ship went past. His mother should have been onboard but had had to cancel due to the onset of a fever that had laid Degna's brother low. His father Guglielmo should have been on her too but instead had boarded the *Lusitania*. However, his part in the *Titanic* story was only just beginning. His son and wife waved as the *Titanic* sailed towards her destiny. Young Degna was sure that some onboard waved back.

Many of the passengers were delighted with their accommodation but not all. One second-class passenger, Mrs Iminita Shelley, was not happy; she had not got the room she had booked. Her cabin was too small and she felt cold and ill. She made several complaints to her steward who appeared reluctant to do anything until the ship reached Queenstown. After threatening to report the situation to Captain Smith, she was moved but found her new 'cell' little better. It appeared half-finished and, when she asked the steward to put the heating on, he said he could not as it was not working.

There were those onboard with other concerns. A number of people later said that they had bad vibes about the ship and, although this might be a case of collective hindsight asserting itself, frequent reports along these lines were made. Eva Hart had arrived on the boat train with her family that morning. She had never seen a ship before and this one looked huge. They had been taken down to their cabin, where Eva's mother, Esther, said that she had decided she would never go to bed as long as she was on the ship.

Others took the incident with the *New York* as a bad omen; the father of Edith Brown, a second-class passenger, certainly thought so. People ashore were concerned too. Two brothers, John and William Hawkesworth, were both stewards on the *Titanic*. The wife of one of them had gone down to wave them off, something she had not done before. As the ship moved off, her son heard her say 'that ship will never reach New York'. Members of the crowd round about her muttered that she was a 'silly woman' at the time.

Titanic moved gracefully out into the open spaces of the busy highway that was the English Channel. She moved out to the east of the Isle of Wight with the great naval port of Portsmouth off to port in the distance. Gradually, England drifted out of sight. The great ship had survived a narrow shave but now she was safely out to sea. France loomed, then Ireland and, following that, on into the huge expanse of the North Atlantic. One week's cruising lay ahead, a week in which the crew could find their way around the ship and the passengers could sit back and enjoy the ride.

5

Outward Bound:
10–13 April 1912, Cherbourg,
Queenstown & the North Atlantic

After the dramas of her departure from Southampton and her near-miss with the *New York*, the *Titanic* sailed without further incident into the English Channel, an hour behind schedule but apart from that none the worse for her experiences. Her first stop was to be just a few hours later at Cherbourg in France, some 80 miles away. As she approached the Isle of Wight, greetings were exchanged with a nearby Red Funnel tug waiting to escort a new arrival in. Several warships were also in the area, reminding those aboard that Britannia still claimed to rule the waves. The island looked beautiful in its draping of blooming foliage, a pretty spring backdrop as the ship sailed into open water.

It was a beautiful day. For the ship, this short crossing was just a warm-up, like an athlete preparing before a long-distance endurance race. The sea was calm and the crossing as routine as it could be. *Titanic* sailed confidently across the busy thoroughfare that was the English Channel, dwarfing all the other vessels that she passed. Cherbourg, the gateway to Europe, was reached just as dusk approached. It had been a lovely crossing for those onboard.

Twenty-two of the passengers were just making the short four-hour crossing before disembarking in France. One of them, eleven-year-old Eileen Lenox-Conyngham, recorded her experience in a letter to a friend. The *Titanic* impressed her as the 'bigest [sic] ship in the world' and the swimming bath and gymnasium were a great hit with her, as indeed they were to many passengers given their novelty value as much as anything else. Eileen reminisced in later years that she was absolutely staggered at the size of the ship, which dwarfed the cross-Channel ferries she was used to.

However, it was not just the massive scale of *Titanic* that awed her but also her elegance. The beauty of her lines made a lasting impression. There was also her newness: 'it was so lovely, all the fittings were so lovely... the glass and the china and the flowers, everything was brand new'. As her group were just crossing to Cherbourg, they did not have a cabin, so they walked around the deck and sat on the benches before lunch much as any cross-Channel passenger would. This was the highlight of the trip for, as she said, normally 'we didn't have our meals with our parents, we had them in the school or the nursery and it was generally very plain food, milk puddings and rather dull things like that'.

The elaborate food provided for them was an unprecedented treat, prepared by the top quality catering staff specially recruited to serve on the ship. Replete with this delicious lunch in *Titanic's* enormous dining room, Eileen watched the tenders as they sailed out from Cherbourg to load more passengers on and take a few, such as her, off. Then it was on to tour Normandy, including the famous tapestry at Bayeaux, before travelling down to Paris. It was here that she saw a poster that read 'Blesse au mort le Roi des vessaux', a message that sent a shiver down her spine when she realized that it referred to her beloved *Titanic*.

Others experienced the sense of awe at the presence of the super-ship that Eileen felt too. Edith Brown was a fifteen-year-old second-class passenger travelling with her family. It was her aunty, already in America, who encouraged them to travel west. Her father decided to set up a hotel in Seattle and, after buying a job-lot of sheets and blankets, he went straight away to book their passage. In the hold of the ship there were, among other items for the Brown's new enterprise, 1,000 rolls of bed-linen. Now Edith excitedly looked forward to a new life. To her, *Titanic* was 'a great big ship – it really was a floating palace'.

Although Cherbourg was a deep-water port, her docking facilities could not deal with ships of this size and tenders were therefore needed to ferry passengers out from the shore; an issue for most ports around the globe which were simply not big enough to cope with the monster ships that were increasingly appearing.

As soon as *Titanic* had been launched on 31 May 1911, the *Olympic* had left Belfast immediately and set out for a two-day visit to Liverpool, the official home of White Star. On the same day, two tenders, *Nomadic* and *Traffic*, made their way out of the docks there and crossed sedately down St George's Channel and over to Cherbourg. They were there when *Olympic* arrived on her maiden voyage on 14 June 1911.

Ferrying passengers out to White Star's ships from the shore was to be the ongoing role of *Nomadic* and *Traffic* and they now sprung into action. *Nomadic* would carry those travelling first and second-class out to *Titanic* when she arrived while those in third-class would be on the *Traffic*. Thomas Andrews looked on with paternal pride at two of the less glamorous creations of his yard as they went about their business with efficiency and the minimum of fuss.

Just as English-based passengers could take a boat-train to Southampton from London, so too could French-based passengers from Paris, travelling from Gare St Lazare in the city to Cherbourg, and many did so. In France,

274 passengers were due to board *Titanic*, while 22 would be getting off (as well as a fortunate canary, which was also disembarked here). However, everyone was forced to wait; *Titanic's* captain had made no effort to catch up with the time lost due to the delayed departure from Southampton, interesting in the light of allegations later made against the ship's officers and their desire to arrive on time.

The ship in fact sailed over at a speed of around 15 knots, way below her theoretical maximum. This was fully in keeping with White Star's normal policy, which was to run ships in before driving them at full speed. Speed would be increased very gradually and it would probably take several trips before they even approached their maximum rate of knots.

There were 102 new passengers from further afield boarding at Cherbourg; Syrians, Croatians, Armenians and others from the Middle East. Few of them spoke English. This was a contrast to the wealthy first-class passengers, mainly American, who came aboard. They included Margaret Brown, Benjamin Guggenheim and his valet Victor Giglio (plus Guggenheim's mistress, who appears to receive less of a write-up in most accounts of the wreck) and Mr and Mrs Arthur Ryerson and their three children.

Attention was automatically drawn to the *glitterazzi* of first-class who came aboard at Cherbourg, the celebrities onboard, though there were many other stories to be told too, much less interesting to a culture that had become increasingly absorbed by the trappings of wealth. Given the fact that the cumulative wealth of those on the *Titanic* came to something in the region of $500 million – a huge sum in 1912 terms – it was perhaps inevitable that attention should be magnetically drawn towards the well-heeled element of the *Titanic's* passenger list.

The richest of the rich was John Jacob Astor, one of the wealthiest men on the planet. A Harvard graduate, JJ was forty-eight years old when the *Titanic* sailed. He had been born into wealth, wealth he added to by his own entrepreneurial ventures. A good chunk of his money had come from property speculation; one of his legacies was the world-famous Waldorf-Astoria Hotel in New York, part of a complex which was about to play ironically enough a key part in the *Titanic* story.

He also had an interest in matters military. This had led to him taking a part in the Spanish-American war at the turn of the twentieth century as a volunteer colonel. It is debatable whether his fighting skills were as valuable in this conflict as his other contributions during it, be it the loan of his yacht to the US government or the money he gave for the equipping of a mountain battery. Suffice to say, from then on he took great pride in being known as Colonel J.J. Astor, a nomenclature which stuck.

However, Astor was a man with a skeleton in the family closet. Back in 1891, he had married Ava Willing from an old and distinguished

Philadelphia dynasty. They had a son and a daughter together. But in 1909 JJ had divorced Ava and two years later had scandalized contemporary society by marrying eighteen-year-old Madeleine Force who was one year younger than his son. The couple longed for acceptance but they had not found it. Even the wedding had been a hush-hush affair, and according to the *New York Times* it was only half an hour before it took place that it had been publicly announced.

They had wintered abroad in Egypt and Paris, taking a long second honeymoon to let the gossips talk themselves out. However, they had many people to win over, even Stewardess Violet Jessop who remarked when she saw Madeleine:

> instead of the radiant woman of my imagination, one who had succeeded in overcoming much opposition and marrying the man she wanted, I saw a quiet, pale, sad-faced, in fact dull young woman arrive listlessly on the arm of her husband, apparently indifferent to everything about her.

Now there was something else to worry about; Madeleine was pregnant. As they stepped aboard the *Titanic* to sail back to the States, they must both have been nervous of the reception they would find there. They came with an entourage, a maid, a manservant, a private nurse and a dog. They would between them occupy rooms C62–64.

Mrs Charlotte Cardeza was one of the lucky occupants of the huge suites that White Star had had installed on the ship (she was in Suite B51). She was accompanied by her son, Thomas, her valet and her maid. As an insight into how the upper classes travelled on these trans-Atlantic ferries she was accompanied by fourteen trunks, four suitcases and three crates of other baggage. Travelling light this was not. When Mrs Cardeza later filed an insurance claim, it came to nearly $180,000 in value.

Also boarding here were Sir Cosmo and Lady Duff Gordon, representatives of the British upper class. Lady Duff Gordon was a renowned clothes designer, using the fashion label 'Lucile'. She was also the sister of the well-known novelist, Elinor Glyn. For some reason they were travelling as Mr and Mrs Morgan, a completely pointless subterfuge given their high-profile in social circles for they would have been known to most of the first-class passengers aboard.

Lady Duff Gordon had a 'past'. She was married in 1888 and had a child but was then divorced, creating something of a stigma at the time. She was left penniless. As a result, she went into dress-making which led to the start of a meteoric rise. She met Cosmo and they were married in 1900. Sir Cosmo was an interesting character, who had represented Britain at fencing in the 1908 Olympic Games in London. He was also a keen pistol-shooter and had lost an eye as a result of an accident while engaged in the sport. He was happy to engage in these pursuits while his wife dealt increasingly with the rich and famous including the future British queen, Mary. Eventually she would open up branches of her brand in New York, Paris and Chicago.

The couple did not enjoy a close married relationship and it was perhaps no surprise that they were in separate rooms on the *Titanic*. Lady Duff Gordon was not good with money and in fact her relationship with her husband had at first been a business one to compensate for this deficiency. After their marriage they often lived apart. To be frank, she came across as something of a snob and it was suggested that her acceptance at court would be more likely given the aristocratic connections she had gained through her marriage. However, her status as a divorcee always counted against her to an extent. Her superior ways were not made any better either by her husband; their collective actions in the drama that was about to unfold would ask serious questions about the principles of both of them, partly arising from a sense of their own innate superiority.

In contrast, Mrs Margaret Brown, who also boarded at Cherbourg, would show herself to be anything but a snob. She had certainly not been born with a silver spoon in her mouth. Although American, she was born to a family of Irish immigrants. As a young girl, she had a job stripping tobacco leaves. Her life changed in 1886 when she married a young miner, James Brown. During the following seven years, two children arrived and Margaret made a name for herself as an early-day feminist and a worker on the soup-kitchens that were so necessary in the poverty-cloaked mining town in which they lived.

However, times were initially hard and a great recession hit the mining industry. It was then that her husband came up with an innovative new technique that would enable him to access previously inaccessible seams of gold. It worked a treat and the Browns all of a sudden found themselves to be rich. It was the beginnings of a fabulous rise in their fortunes and they soon found themselves owning two homes.

Margaret was the possessor of vast stores of energy. She even turned herself to politics, running for the US Senate at a time when women were not even allowed to vote. However, all was not well domestically. Her husband could be violent and there were stories of affairs with other women. The couple were now effectively estranged. Whereas James Brown liked the simple life, Margaret had taken to money and the trappings of wealth like a duck to water. She had been with the Astors in Cairo when she received word that a grandson was ill and had decided to return home.

Margaret had been travelling with her daughter Helen, who had decided to stay in Europe for the time being. Margaret was accompanied by a friend, a Mrs Emma Bucknell, who was afraid to embark as she had had a premonition that something terrible was about to happen. So last minute was Margaret's booking that many of her family and friends did not know she was aboard. Noisy and gregarious, she would be popular with many but perhaps rubbed up some of the longer-established wealthy passengers, who disapproved of this loud member of the '*nouveau riche*', the wrong way. She would later become legendary as 'the unsinkable Molly Brown'. However, 'Molly' was not a name that she would have recognized and neither would any of her associates in 1912.

Other rich passengers came aboard at Cherbourg too. Benjamin Guggenheim was one of them, another multi-millionaire sometimes known as 'The Silver Prince' as he had invested successfully in the precious metal. Guggenheim had originally booked on the *Lusitania* but her sailing had been cancelled as she needed repairs.

Here was another man involved in a very public scandal. Although he was married, he also had a mistress, a French singer, Madame Léontine Aubart. Also with him was his valet, Victor Giglio, and his chauffeur, René Pernot. Guggenheim was a stylish man but one who had recently been slightly less lucky with his money. However, he was not exactly living on skid row and would leave decent sums to his children in his will, one of whom, 'Peggy', would famously open her home posthumously as a magnificent art gallery on the banks of the Grand Canal in Venice.

By around 8.00 p.m. that evening, the ship was ready to move again. Her giant anchors were pulled up ten minutes later and she pulled away from Cherbourg and west towards Ireland. Loaded up with this new batch of passengers and more mail, *Titanic* left the port behind at around 8.30 p.m. She headed north-west towards the Emerald Isle.

Passengers and crew nestled down for their first night on the ship, the former excited at the prospect that lay ahead and delighted with the luxury in which they were accommodated, the latter settling down to work. It was far from a perfect day as far as *Titanic* management was concerned; a near-collision with another ship and a late arrival at her first port of call. However, at the end of it all, there had been no permanent damage done. Hopefully things would improve as the trip went on.

The next destination would be Queenstown in Ireland. Queenstown (now known as Cobh) is on an island about 15 miles from Cork, in a harbour where the River Lee meets the Atlantic Ocean. During the nineteenth century, it had become an important port for emigrants escaping from the hardships of life in Ireland. Queen Victoria had visited here in 1849, her first visit to Ireland, and the port was named 'Queenstown' in honour of her. In the century between 1848 and 1950, over six million people emigrated from Ireland, half of them from Queenstown. The port had become the exit door from the island.

The *Titanic* arrived off Queenstown on the morning of 11 April at around midday. The Channel crossing had again been calm but the wind had a biting edge to it and kept most of the passengers off deck. Lawrence Beesley noted the rolling green hills and ragged grey cliffs that marked the coastline around Queenstown, giving it a beautiful if rugged setting. The pilot was picked up at the Daunt Light Vessel and, under his guidance, the ship edged her way cautiously into the harbour. However, as at Cherbourg *Titanic* was too big to come portside and she dropped her huge anchors 2 miles offshore. Two tenders, *America* and *Ireland*, brought out 1,385 sacks of mail along with 123 passengers, all but 10 of them third-class. There were some of the 30,000 people that would emigrate from Ireland in 1912 alone.

As the tenders made their way out to *Titanic*, Edith Russell (also known as Edith Rosenbaum; another first-class passenger who had boarded at Cherbourg) saw from her position on deck that the gangplank to the ship was held by ten men on either side as it shook and swayed. Edith was a successful and noted fashion correspondent who was returning from France to her native USA.

Yet more provisions were to be brought aboard, particularly tinned vegetables for the journey ahead. A steward remarked to Edith that although they had 'a good crowd' going over to America it was nothing compared to the return trip for which she was fully booked. She did not like the ship, which she thought was like a large hotel, stiff and formal, and much preferred the intimacy of smaller vessels. Not everyone was convinced that the ship was a marvel after all.

As the ship was anchored, waiting for the tenders to arrive from the nearby port, the passengers who were on deck looked up and saw the blackened face of a stoker peeping out from the top of the dummy funnel which acted as a ventilation shaft. The stoker had evidently climbed up there for a joke but to some onboard of a superstitious disposition it appeared to be a bad omen for the trip ahead.

A few lucky people, seven in all, disembarked. Most notable of them was Francis Browne, a teacher who was training for the priesthood. His importance derives from the photographs he took of his short voyage to Ireland, the only images of the passenger-carrying *Titanic* at sea that survive. Also making his way ashore, surreptitiously in this case, was a stoker, John Coffey, who was originally a resident of Queenstown. He planned to hide himself under some mail bags and smuggle his way ashore. Given the fact this was his home town, it is probable that he always planned to hitch a free ride home.

He turned to an old mate, John Podesta, and told him as the tender came out that he was going to climb down and go and see his mother. Podesta performed lookout duty for him and Coffey disappeared over the side. He hid under the mailbags as planned and was undiscovered when the tender made its way back into port, a fortunate escapee indeed.

A number of those aboard would post what turned out to be their last letters home via the tenders that steamed back to Queenstown. Many of them were mundane but their very ordinariness makes them all the more poignant. Steward George Beedem seemed to write to his family because it was expected of him but he didn't know what to say though he did mention the *New York* incident. He closed in a clumsy but strangely touching way (presumably addressing his young son, rather than his wife) 'glad you liked the pictures and I suppose those chocolate eggs have all disappeared down that great big hole'.

Harvey Collyer wrote home that, despite the ship's size, there was hardly any vibration as she moved; he was thankful that none of the family had suffered from seasickness yet. Second-class passenger Samuel Hocking complained that he had been kept awake by the rattle of bottles. He was however enjoying the cigarettes ('fags') that he had brought with him.

Everyday-ness was the pattern with the majority of these messages but there were even now hints that some onboard were concerned at some strange vibes they were feeling. Captain Smith's steward Arthur Paintin wrote home to his parents that 'we have now commenced the quick voyages all summer (bar accidents)'. An innocent enough comment perhaps but Chief Officer Wilde was more specific about his concerns. 'I still don't like this ship,' he said. 'I have a queer feeling about it.' There were a lot of stories about the *Titanic* being a fated ship but most appeared only after she had sunk with the benefit of hindsight. Wilde's premonitory concerns are the more striking as they were committed to paper before any accident had happened.

At 1.30 p.m., the *Titanic*, after its short stop, was ready to depart again. The new arrivals, who to the relief of the crew spoke a language they could understand, were taken to their quarters. The new batch of emigrants that came aboard earned a grudging respect from some of the *Titanic's* deck-staff, one of whom was overheard to say 'at least this lot speak English'. Among them were young men like Daniel Buckley, out to make his fortune in the west, and sixteen-year-old Kathy Gilnagh from County Longford. Both were travelling in (separate) groups of young, single Irish men and women hoping to find fame and fortune on the far side of the Atlantic.

Even as they sailed west towards America, final preparations were being made in New York for the *Carpathia* to sail the other way. The ship left dock at noon that day New York time (a few hours after *Titanic* sailed out of Queenstown). It was a fine, clear day on the other side of the Atlantic and, with the pilot safely dropped off, Captain Rostron and his ship passed the Ambrose Channel Lightship at about 2.00 p.m. She was set on a course which would bring her unknowingly slap bang in the middle of the greatest shipping drama of all time.

The *Titanic* in the meantime made its way slowly out to the lightship off Queenstown where the pilot was dropped off. Then she made her way out into the wide ocean and the 3,000 mile journey to New York. As she did so, she passed the Old Head of Kinsale, off which her great Cunarder rival, the *Lusitania,* would meet her dreadful fate three years later when she was torpedoed by a German U-Boat in the First World War. As *Titanic* left Ireland behind, one of the third-class passengers, Eugene Daly from Athlone, picked up his pipes and played 'Erin's Lament', a mournful farewell to the Old World as the ship headed towards the promise of the New.

The huge propellers sparked into life once more, churning up the sand off the sea-bottom just a few feet beneath the ship. A loud, noisy procession followed the ship out of the harbour and for a while into the open sea, hungry, screeching gulls after a meal. Young Jack Thayer, in first-class, noted that 'the weather was fair and clear, the ship palatial, the food delicious'. This voyage promised to be an absolute delight.

Nostalgic passengers watched from the rails as Europe slipped behind. As darkness fell that second night out of Southampton, the Irish mountains were the last thing that could be seen, dim and faint in the dropping darkness. When the curtain of the darkness was lowered, the gulls were still there but when the suns rays peeped over the eastern horizon in the morning they had gone. Ahead lay thousands of miles of the North Atlantic. As dawn broke, all that could be seen was the sea and the white horses of the waves that broke against the ship as she carved her way through the water like a knife.

For some, the views that unfolded during the next few days had a wonderful beauty of their own. The sea was unusually calm, so much so that few missed a meal through seasickness. The wind blew mainly from the west or the south-west, and had a decidedly sharp feel to it. Lawrence Beesley, who had never crossed the ocean before, was besotted by the light on the sea when the sun came up everyday, a dazzling array of pinks, oranges and reds that enchanted him.

Behind, the wake of the ship, churned up by those gigantic propellers, seemed to be like a road stretching out behind them to the very shores of Europe itself. Each night, the sun sank into the waves before them, a beacon it seemed lighting the road to America and the New World. Progress was steady, if not spectacular. The White Star Line had not built the ship for speed and anyway always treated their ships with kid gloves until they had been properly bedded in. Between noon on 11 April and the same time on the 12th, 386 miles was travelled. The next day, Friday–Saturday, 519 miles were eaten up and on Saturday–Sunday 546 miles.

For whatever reason, the second day's mileage had been less than expected and the purser told Beesley that they would now probably arrive in New York on Wednesday morning rather than Tuesday night as had apparently been expected at one stage. However, such information was later explicitly denied by Bruce Ismay at the American Inquiry where he said that they would aim not to arrive at the lightship off New York until 5.00 a.m. Wednesday morning. This, Ismay said, had always been the plan since before leaving Queenstown. As he said: 'There was nothing to be gained by arriving at New York any earlier than that.'

The more sedate pace of the *Titanic* compared to some of her rivals was commented on favourably by some of the more experienced passengers aboard. She had noticeably less vibration that most of them, making for a much more comfortable existence than many seasoned passengers were used to. She was a comfortable ship, easy on her passengers who, in the main, were enjoying an excellent and relaxing voyage.

From time to time, Beesley would look down (literally rather than metaphorically in this case) on the third-class passengers who were exercising in 'their' area at the stern of the ship. Some of them were playing a skipping game, of 'mixed-double type' as Beesley called it. One of the passengers (a Scot Beesley called him, though this was probably the Irishman, Eugene Daly) played the bagpipes, playing a tune that 'faintly resembled an air' as one of his dismissive companions put it.

He noticed in particular a man far better dressed then the others who looked aloofly on at a distance from his fellow third-class passengers. Beesley assumed that he was a previously well-off man who had fallen on hard times. There was another third-class passenger whose travel arrangements were somewhat odd for his wife was travelling in second-class. He would regularly climb the stairs up to the gate that separated second from third-class and converse with his wife.

It is not clear whether, in those more reserved times, Beesley merely assumed they were married because such intimate behaviour would, between an unmarried couple, have been unthinkable particularly given the social distinctions between second and third-class. A more cynical observer might have assumed that something more salacious was going on. Whatever the reality, Beesley would see the woman again after the *Titanic* sank but the husband, if husband he was, was lost.

Colonel Gracie enjoyed this crossing of the Atlantic. So far it had gone without a hitch across a placid, ripple-less ocean. He had spent most of his time reading and socializing and abandoned his usual regime of exercise; the Colonel liked to keep in trim and had boarded the ship full of good intentions that had not so far been fulfilled. He was enchanted with the experience; it was:

> as if I were in a summer palace on the seashore, surrounded with every comfort. [He too noticed that] the motion of the ship and the noise of its machinery were scarcely discernible on deck or in the saloons, either day or night.

Lady Duff Gordon was another who was having a thoroughly good time. She later reminisced:

> The first days of the crossing were uneventful. Like everyone else I was entranced by the beauty of the liner. I had never dreamed of sailing in such luxury... my pretty little cabin, with its electric heater and pink curtains, delighted me, so that it was a pleasure to go to bed. Everything about this lovely ship reassured me.

Second Office Lightoller, who as an experienced seaman should know about these things, also noted the lack of vibration. It was not that there was none but what there was appeared insignificant compared to the norm. It was as if the slight vibration was comforting, almost like rocking a baby to sleep, rather than the gut-churning tossing and turning that had been the usual state of affairs on many other ships.

As on all voyages, those aboard settled into a routine. Breakfast was served between 8.00 a.m. and 10.30 a.m., lunch between 1.00 p.m. and 2.30 p.m. and the evening meal between 6.00 p.m. and 7.30 p.m. (though in practice there was more flexibility over the times of this meal as opposed to the others). There was of course class segregation in everything, reflecting the mores of the time. For first-class, there was an *a la carte* restaurant that seated 137 diners at 49 tables in addition to the main first-class dining saloon. It was open between 8.00 a.m. in the morning and 11.00 p.m. in the evening daily for first-class passengers. Passengers received discounts if they decided to eat all their meals in here; $15 if their ticket cost under $175, $25 if it was more than this.

However, this reflected the fact that the Ritz Restaurant was about as exclusive as it was possible to be with prices to match. It was under the control of Luigi Gatti, previously of Oddenino's Restaurant, one of London's foremost establishments. Most of the staff were not British. There were twenty-six Italians, seventeen Frenchmen, six from Britain and Switzerland and one each from Belgium, the Netherlands and Spain. It was what would now be called a 'contracted out' venture with Gatti employing his own staff and responsible for his own accounts. Despite its exorbitant rates, it was nearly always fully booked.

Second and third-class passengers had their own dining saloons. There were 394 seats in the second-class and 473 in the third-class saloon. Bugler P.W. Fletcher was responsible for informing passengers when it was time for a meal, a rather incongruous clarion call summoning everyone to eat. For third-class passengers who wished to relax elsewhere, there were two bars; one forward on D Deck, the other near the C Deck smoking-room near the stern. These were furnished with individual chairs rather than the traditional benches that had in the past been used in ships for steerage passengers.

Beneath the (un-lettered) Boat Deck, there were six other public decks, lettered A to G with A the higher-most, and then beneath these the more open spaces of the holds and the engine rooms (though these could be quickly compartmentalized if the watertight door mechanism was activated. The Boat Deck was where (unsurprisingly) many of the lifeboats (eight lifeboats and all four collapsibles) were stowed but also where the gymnasium was situated. It was also where the first-class entrance was situated (adjacent to the gymnasium) and it had a first-class promenade area. In other words, many of the boats were located in a first-class area, a point that is not without significance. The remainder of the boats, another eight, were located in an area where there was a second-class promenade area.

Though there were nowhere near enough seats in the boats for everyone onboard, those provided gave space for more people than was required by the British Board of Trade regulations. There were fourteen large lifeboats, each with a capacity of sixty-five people (65.5 to be strictly accurate, with the half a person equating to a child). There were twelve oars provided for the oarsmen in each boat, along with six spares.

There were also two smaller 'emergency boats', each with a capacity of forty. These were kept permanently ready to be lowered, as they were to function as boats that could be launched quickly if, for example, there was a 'man overboard' situation. In addition, there were four 'collapsible' boats. These were not 'blow up' boats as their name might intimate but boats with a fixed bottom and sides that needed to be pulled up. Their capacity was deemed to be forty-seven. Unfortunately, two of them were almost inaccessible, as they were stored on the roof of the officer's quarters and as they each weighed several tons they were also impossible to lower down to the Boat Deck where they would have to be launched from. This gave an intimation of the state of mind reigning; no one could envisage that they might actually have to be used.

In summary, there was capacity for about 1,178 people in the boats. *Titanic* was now headed across the Atlantic with over 2,200 voyagers. If the boats should be needed, there would not be room for over 1,000 of those aboard. It was just as well that the *Titanic* had not been full up, otherwise there would have been over 1,000 more people left stranded in the event of a serious accident.

At Belfast, before setting out for Southampton, Fourth Officer Boxhall and his fellow officers had checked out the lifeboats to ensure they were properly provisioned with food and water. He believed they were and checks on the recovered lifeboats later seemed to confirm this. However, this was only half the story. In keeping with the shoddy attitude towards lifeboats prevalent on the *Titanic*, the officers do not appear to have told those who might be in charge of the boats if they were ever used where the provisions were stored. And they certainly did not have lights stowed on them, as Seaman Samuel Hemmings would have to dish them out to everybody when they were needed.

There were other issues concerning the lifeboats too. There was supposed to be a list which assigned members of the crew to different lifeboats. However, it had not been posted before the ship left Southampton and it was not until she was out at sea that lists went up. Even then, not all of the crew appeared to be aware of its existence and were as a result only vaguely aware of where they should go in the event of an incident.

Beneath the Boat Deck, on A Deck, there was a first-class smoking room, the first-class lounge, a covered first-class promenade area, a veranda and the palm court. Here also was the first-class library, open from 8.00 a.m. until 11.30 p.m. Then on B Deck was the highest-placed accommodation, consisting of a number of first-class cabins and the two enormous and very expensive suites. There was also a second-class promenade area located towards the stern.

Here too, adjacent to the first-class restaurant, first-class passengers could relax in opulent Gallic grandeur in the Café Parisien, an original touch that White Star hoped would prove irresistible to well-heeled travellers. With massive windows giving extensive sea views but the ambience of an exclusive French pavement café, this was all part of another passenger-pampering experience. Furthest forward on B Deck in the open came the forecastle and the poop deck.

On C Deck there were more first-class cabins (Colonel Gracie was in C51 on the starboard quarter just past amidships), and nearby the maids' and valets' quarters. Here too was Jack Thayer, seventeen years of age and a typical adventurous youth for his age. He was in a first-class cabin next to his parents who were also making the trip.

C Deck also housed a barbers' shop where passengers could have a cut or trim, and the telephone exchanges. Here too second-class passengers such as Lawrence Beesley could visit the free lending library or promenade. To the rear, segregated of course, was a third-class promenade area as well as a General Room and a Smoking Room for steerage. The General Room housed a piano, around which the passengers could enjoy a hearty sing-song. Another first-class dining room was on D Deck, along with a reception room. The second-class dining room was located towards the stern here, along with a number of second-class cabins forward and aft. The hospital was on D Deck too, along with a third-class open area forward.

It is noticeable that all three classes 'shared' the same decks. However, in practice the different areas were sectioned off so that third-class could not stray into first or second-class areas and so on. The trend was continued on E Deck (where all three classes had cabin space) and F Deck (where second and third-class accommodation was located). G Deck had a large number of steerage cabins and also the crew quarters forward. Some of the crew were also housed on the port side of E Deck, where there was a long corridor known as 'Scotland Road' stretching half the length of the ship.

Other public rooms were to be found on F and G Deck. The Turkish baths for example were on F deck as was the swimming pool, while the squash courts were on G Deck (though because of their height the open space above them stretched to F Deck too), next to the Post Office area. The Turkish baths were open between 10.00 a.m. and 1.00 p.m. for ladies and between 2.00 p.m. and 6.00 p.m. for gentlemen. Tickets could be purchased from the purser for $1. The swimming bath was 32 feet long, 13 feet wide and 6 feet deep. It could be used by gentlemen between 6.00 a.m. and 9.00 a.m. and thereafter by ladies and gents at the same time as the Turkish baths. It was free of charge and filled with sea-water. The squash court could be hired for a fee of 50 cents for a half-hour session. For those who wished for expert tuition, professional Fred Wright was available for hire to help improve their game.

First and second-class passengers could move up and down this honeycomb of rooms and decks via the ship's elevators; stairs had to be good enough for third-class. The first-class passengers were warmed the instant they entered the ship by the six electric heaters in the entrance. There were even revolving doors to keep the nippy sea-breezes out when the ship was underway.

The décor on the ship was stunning. First-class passengers had oak-panelled corridors leading to the smoking room and lounge. There was also oak-panelling in the second-class dining-room and smoking room. The oak-panelling even extended to the third-class smoking room with its teak tables and comfortable benches. The distinguishing factor between classes was the degree of ornamentation on the carving, with the most ornate naturally in first-class. However, there was no denying that as a whole she was a floating work of art.

While the passengers relaxed, the crew got on with their work. Down below, hidden from view, they toiled invisibly in their subterranean world. Stokers, trimmers, greasers did their work, four-hours on, four-hours off. The engineers' shifts were four-hours on, eight off (but they were still on call for four of those). There would be the occasional distraction to distract them from the monotony. Assistant Engineer George Ervine wrote to his mother in a letter posted from Queenstown that they had had an alarm drill and also practised closing the watertight doors.

For some, this was no pleasure cruise. Thomas Andrews had gone along on the maiden voyage to see if the ship operated as efficiently and smoothly as possible. A disciplined man, every morning his steward Henry Etches took him fruit and tea at 7.00 a.m. Etches would next see him again when he dressed for dinner at around 6.45 p.m. in the evening. In between times, Andrews did not stop working. He was also normally very late going to bed at night. He was generally pleased at the ship's performance so far but there was always some improvement, however minor, that could be made.

Perhaps some of the busiest crew members onboard the *Titanic* were the ship's Marconi operators, Jack Phillips and Harold Bride. The wireless shack was next to the first-class entrance on the starboard side. Messages cost 12s 6d (about 63p or $3.15) for the first ten words and 9d (about 4p or 20 cents) for each additional word. To give an idea of the relative cost of this, it is useful to recall that Harold Bride was paid £4 or $20 per month so he certainly could not have afforded to send many on his own account.

Wireless was still a novelty back then and first-class passengers in particular loved to show off to their friends by arranging for a message to be sent. The *Titanic* had one of the most powerful sets of wireless apparatus around, and it could transmit 400 miles in the day time. This meant that not only could passengers send messages to shore-based wireless stations when within 400 miles of land but could also contact friends and relatives on passing ships. After all, there was no trans-Atlantic flying in those days and the rich and famous were crossing the Atlantic with some regularity in many cases.

Between Southampton and the night of 14 April, the *Titanic's* wireless operators despatched some 250 messages. The operators tapped out their messages in Morse on their equipment though with communications travelling across the ether very quickly. Although such communication still had a long way to go before it could be regarded as perfected, it was still a vast improvement, particularly in terms of safety, than what had gone before.

Before the advent of wireless, it was not unheard of for ships to disappear without trace. One such was the White Star ship *Naronic*, a 470-foot long vessel that left Liverpool bound for New York in 1893. It carried seventy-four passengers and 3,600 tons of cargo. It never arrived in New York. A message originally given out by the company suggested that it had struck an iceberg though this statement was later retracted. However, the story was given added credence when four different bottle messages were washed up.

One came ashore in New York Bay and was dated 19 February 1893. It said simply 'Naronic sinking. All hands praying. Have mercy on us.' Another, picked up in Virginia on 30 March of that year said among other things 'we were struck by an iceberg in a blinding snowstorm' and ended laconically 'goodby [sic] all'. Although a few of her lifeboats were found empty no other trace of the *Naronic* was ever discovered. An Inquiry was subsequently held that dismissed the messages as hoaxes (though as they were found on both sides of the Atlantic this seems to have been fairly well organized). However, a British ship the *Hummel* arrived in New York on 5 March 1893 and did report sailing through extensive ice-fields.

The story mirrored that of another ship, the *Pacific*, which was lost in 1856 along with 286 souls. A bottle message later picked up stated 'ship going down. Confusion onboard. Icebergs on every side. I know I cannot escape'. Both disasters were intriguing, in particular that of the *Naronic* whose lifeboats were found within 100 miles of the position in which the *Titanic* would founder.

February appeared to be a particularly bad month for disasters at sea. In that month in 1896, the *State of Georgia* disappeared, in 1899 it was the turn of the *Allegheny* and in 1902 the *Huronian*. All of them were sailing on the North Atlantic route and their losses were a mystery. The advent of wireless in theory made it much less likely that ships would disappear without some kind of message being sent as to their fate, which was welcome. But among other things the lack of information in the past perhaps bred complacency as mariners underestimated the danger of ice in the region. In modern times, icebergs can appear in the area of the Grand Banks, into which the *Titanic* was sailing between February and October (though the period to August is particularly busy in this respect). Indeed, the US Coastguard, which set up ice patrols in response to the *Titanic* disaster, estimated that before its foundation 113 ships were lost as a result of collisions with icebergs.

All these sombre events however were a long way away from anyone's thoughts. Everything was now going swimmingly well and they would be in New York in just a few days time. The wireless operators carried on sending their 'wish you were here' messages by the dozen. However, just now and then a jarring note burst in on them, warnings that there was danger ahead. At the time they seemed routine courtesy calls, wishing the *Titanic* luck and adding, almost as a codicil, the fact that such-and-such a ship had encountered ice. It was only later that their true significance would be truly realized, and by the time that it was it was far too late to matter.

6

Into the Ice Zone:
14 April 1912, North Atlantic

A smooth sea and a calm crossing. The cruise across the Atlantic could not have been more idyllic. No squalls to speak of, no roller-coaster waves, no corrugation of the water, no riding the rollers like a bucking bronco. Experienced travellers who had seen the ocean at its worst gave inward thanks for a delightful voyage. Yet ahead, unseen, lay a sinister, menacing presence, a granite-hard barricade of frozen-solid ice, capable of tearing the heart out of any unsuspecting ship made of frail steel, a bank of ice perhaps 25 miles long and 5 miles wide. Ahead of it like ferocious guard-dogs lay rogue bergs dozens of feet high with piercing spurs jutting out below the waterline reaching down into the depths for hundreds of feet.

All across the Atlantic messages had been racing across the ether from ships warning passing neighbours of ice ahead. However, many vessels did not have wireless so they could not take such measures. They would either have to pass the news on via the use of Morse lights when they were close enough to do so, or log the position of the ice and report it when they arrived at their destination. This might not be for days, by which time their information might well be too old to be of any use.

Even those ships that did have wireless aboard usually had equipment that was of a limited range. This meant that information could only be transmitted to ships within a few hundred miles. However, this would often be forwarded via a relay system. Ships with decent wireless apparatus aboard therefore had a good chance of knowing about ice long before they reached the region where it was located. However, it was of course necessary for them to do something with that information if it was really to be of any use.

Captain Smith knew early on that there was ice somewhere ahead of him on the track. Indeed, in the American Inquiry, Fourth Officer Boxhall suggested that 'the Captain gave me some wireless messages from Southampton, I think, that we had before we sailed, which I put on the chart'. Captain Smith definitely received notification on the evening of 12 April from the French ship *La Touraine* that she had passed through ice.

She was headed east towards Europe so for her the danger had passed. However, Captain Smith was steaming towards it at a rate of knots.

The information did not worry him unduly. Ships sailed a prescribed route with those travelling west from Europe on a track many miles to the north of those going east, with a view of course to limiting the possibility of collision at sea. In recognition of the increased danger of ice, both tracks were moved south during the ice season, an arrangement that had been in place since 1899. Sharing these same routes had an added safety dimension; if a ship was involved in an accident then there was theoretically a good chance of another being in the vicinity to help. There was always a danger that sometimes ice would drift further south than normal of course. 1911/12 had seen an unseasonably mild winter and much more ice had broken off than normal. Captain Smith did not fully appreciate how extensive the ice ahead of him was.

He did not take many measures to pass the information on either. Boxhall marked some positions on a chart with the label 'ice' against it but Third Officer Pitman did not know if this meant a single iceberg or a large ice-field; two very different things. Details were posted on a blackboard but there did not seem to be much pressure to look at it. No doubt Smith would have said that the senior officers were the ones who needed to know and they were informed. However, the whole impression given was that ice was an irritant rather than a potentially fatal danger.

Perhaps the most fraught place to be that Sunday morning on 14 April was the wireless shack. The apparatus had been playing up earlier on in the trip. In those days, the wireless operators had to do everything for themselves including fix their kit when it malfunctioned. They were as much hobbyists as employees, required to get their hands dirty when the occasion demanded. In these early days of telegraphy, there were few manuals to follow and identifying a problem and finding a solution to it was often a matter of trial and error.

The apparatus had malfunctioned on Friday night and Phillips, the senior operator, had spent most of the night fixing it. By Saturday morning the kit was operational again. However, there was a huge backlog of unsent telegrams to despatch, business worth a lot of money to the Marconi Company. Having had no sleep and with a mountain of messages to get through, Phillips was tired and irritable. It was just as well that Bride was there to help him out but they would be lucky to get rid of the backlog by the time they reached New York. So much for Sunday being a 'day of rest'.

Then at 9.00 a.m. that morning another message arrived. It same from the *Caronia* and reported ice in the region of 42 degrees North, 49 to 51 degrees West. This was a wide area and suggested that whatever ice lay ahead was extensive. The *Caronia's* operator was politely thanked for his information and the message was passed on to *Titanic's* bridge.

Few people onboard the ship knew anything about the ice ahead. For most of the passengers the day would be even more leisurely than usual. There would be Divine Service at 10.30 a.m. This was as much a social as a religious event, when passengers would dress in their 'Sunday best' in an effort to impress their fellow seafarers as much as possible. It was also the only time that class segregation was broken down as the service was open to all passengers.

For most of the passengers, Sunday 14 April was a day that began as the most unremarkable of days. Lawrence Beesley was one of those who went to the service in the Saloon. However, when he went out on deck after it was over, he was struck by the plummeting temperature. He reckoned that it was not the wind off the sea that was blowing but the motion of the ship through the water that created a breeze. Whatever the cause, the briskness of the temperature kept most passengers off deck.

Colonel Gracie awoke determined to get out of the bad habits he had got into. He had been so busy looking after his coterie of unescorted ladies that he had abandoned his normal healthy routine. It was time to put that right. The Colonel was not a man to do things by halves. He would have a work out on the squash court first of all before breakfast. After a half-hour squash game he would then have a dip in the heated swimming pool. He planned to do the same the next morning and arranged another early morning session with the squash professional accordingly. He would also go to bed earlier than he had been doing so far in the trip. It would be back to normal for the Colonel.

He has also attended the morning service. He was there with an old friend, 'Clinch' Smith. Gracie noted that one of the hymns was 'Oh God, Our Help in Ages Past', his friend's favourite. The next time the Colonel would sing the hymn was in rather more sombre circumstances. The service finished at 11.15 a.m., and Gracie went out to enjoy the rest of a rather leisurely day. Fifteen minutes later, a lifeboat drill would normally be held on a Sunday. For reasons unknown to anyone except Captain Smith, it would not take place today.

After the service, Lawrence Beesley went into the library, where he met an old acquaintance, the Reverend Ernest Carter, a Church of England clergyman. They exchanged conversation comparing their two universities – Carter was an Oxford man, Beesley from Cambridge – in a friendly sparring manner. The Reverend was disappointed that there was no evening service scheduled so he had asked the Purser if he could hold a congregational 'sing-song' later on. Permission was duly given and such a service was to take place at 8.30 p.m. that evening, once more in the Saloon.

The library was crowded that day; many people having been driven in by the cold. Through the windows Beesley could see two children playing in a covered area; he would later learn that they were the Navratil children, Edmund and Michel, aged two and three respectively, two little non-English speaking mites who would become unwitting celebrities in the days ahead.

For Beesley, there were mundane matters to attend to, baggage labels to be filled out and handed back to the Purser before they arrived in New York. There were also baggage forms to be completed for the Customs authorities. Beesley had some money that he now handed over to the Purser for what he thought would be safe-keeping. He put in a self-labelled envelope, took his receipt and put it carefully in his pocket.

Being a young man with warmer blood, Jack Thayer did not mind the cold so much. He enjoyed this bright, clear day. He spent most of it walking around the decks with his mother and father. A confident young man, he spoke to a number of the passengers including Bruce Ismay, Thomas Andrews and Charles Hays, President of the Grand Trunk Railway in Canada.

As the day wore on, it got colder. However, there was a promise of something exciting ahead. Bruce Ismay pulled an ice warning out of his pocket to show it to the Thayers but assured them they would not reach the region where it was situated until 9.00 p.m. that evening. At the time, it looked like a harmless bit of showing-off. It would later assume more sinister overtones.

Ismay had lunched with Captain Smith, and one passenger later claimed he overheard them talking about the ship's speed. At midday, the ship's position had been calculated from the sun as was always the case. This was the object of some interest; some of the passengers had been betting on how fast she would be travelling. The resultant position showed that she had travelled 546 miles in the past twenty-four hours. But several more ice warnings had come in since that of the *Caronia* had been received. The Dutch liner *Noordam* had unambiguously reported 'much ice' in a similar position to that given by the *Caronia*. This arrived about fifteen minutes before midday.

After dealing with this message, the wireless shack then returned to its normal routine of sending and receiving passenger communications. About midday the Strauses had sent a radio message to their son and daughter-in-law *en route* to Europe onboard a passing ship. They received a message back in reply. But then more ice warnings were received, with two more arriving in quick succession. Second Officer Lightoller, who came on watch as a relief for lunch, heard of an ice warning at about 1.00 p.m. though he was not sure which ship it had come from.

The *Baltic* had sent a message at 1.42 p.m. It reported ice in the region of 41 degrees, 51 minutes North, 49 degrees, 9 minutes West. Captain

Smith gave this message to Ismay who put it in his pocket (though he later handed it back to the captain). It was this message that Ismay later showed to Emily Ryerson and the Thayers.

Mrs Ryerson allegedly told her friend, Mrs Mahala Douglas, that she asked Ismay if they would slow down as a result of this information, to which he supposedly replied: 'Oh no, we will put on more boilers and get out of it.' Just three minutes after this came in, another message was received from the German liner *Amerika* reporting ice in the region of 41 degrees, 27 minutes North, 50 degrees, 8 minutes West. The latter was never acknowledged by Captain Smith so it possibly never reached the bridge.

The ship steamed on towards America and also, despite the warnings, largely unconcernedly towards the ice ahead. Just after 5.00 p.m. that evening, the temperature gauge started to plummet. Within the space of just two hours, it would drop by 10 degrees Fahrenheit. At about 5.50 p.m., the ship changed direction, officers would later suggest as a precaution against the ice ahead though the adjustment was in fact minor and made little difference. Ten minutes later, Second Officer Lightoller came on the bridge to begin his four-hour shift in charge, taking over from Chief Officer Wilde.

As was the norm, the temperature of the water was taken at two hour intervals. It showed that the water temperature was dropping. Surviving *Titanic* officers said that this was no indication of nearby ice but not everyone agreed. Interviewed at the American Inquiry, Captain Moore of the *Mount Temple* agreed that it was not a reliable indicator of being near bergs but could indicate that a more substantial ice-field was nearby. To give this some context, unlike many of the *Titanic's* officers, Captain Moore had a great deal of experience in dealing with ice in the North Atlantic.

While Lightoller was making sure that the water temperature was being taken, all over the ship passengers were getting themselves ready for the second main formal event of the day, dinner. The Wideners would hold a small dinner-party with a select group in attendance, including Captain Smith. The captain mixed easily in such company, his avuncular presence and reassuring, quiet manner endearing him to all (though Mrs Widener later signed an affidavit confirming that he had drunk absolutely no wine or intoxicating liquor during the meal). For most passengers, meals would be taken in their dining rooms, dependent on what class they were in. Bruce Ismay ate with Dr O'Loughlin shortly after returning the ice warning he had in his pocket to Captain Smith; the captain had asked for it as he wished to post it on the bridge for his officers to see.

It was about 6.30 p.m. when the Thayers went down to their rooms to dress. Jack's parents had been invited to join friends for dinner so he decided to dine alone at his regular table. After enjoying his meal, Jack ordered a coffee. A man about thirty years of age came over to talk to him. He was Milton Long, son of a judge, who was travelling alone. They had a long chat – Jack found Long an invigorating conversationalist. After about an hour, Jack decided to turn in after taking a brisk walk around the decks.

It was really cold now, and the night was as black as pitch, with only the stars providing any natural light as there was no moon. There was a slight haze on the horizon. Jack walked up to the Boat Deck, which was quiet and deserted. The wind was whistling through the ship's wires as she sped through the water and smoke billowed out of her three working funnels. To Jack, it felt like one of those nights when it was good to be alive. About 11.00 p.m. Jack decided it was time to retire for the night. He had a brief chat with his parents and, after opening his window to get some fresh air in the room, donned his pyjamas and got ready to climb into bed.

Miss Elizabeth Shute had turned in too but was so cold that she could not sleep. The air was damp and clammy, so much so that it reminded her of the time she had visited an ice cave on the Eiger in the Alps. Eventually she became so cold that she got out of bed and turned the electric fire on. Although the glow took the edge off the frigid air, she was nervous and unable to sleep.

Charlotte Collyer had enjoyed the quality of the meal at dinner time, though she thought it a trifle too rich and heavy. She listened to the orchestra for a while and then retired to bed. Her husband joined her later and chatted to her for a while. It had been another pleasant day and their new life in America was getting ever closer. She looked forward to the prospect with a mixture of excitement and apprehension. Her young daughter, little 'Madge', was taking things in her stride as children of her age tended to.

Colonel Gracie was determined to make the most of the social opportunities aboard the ship but equally determined now to get a good night's sleep. After his meal, he had adjourned to the Palm Room for coffee while listening to the *Titanic's* band. His good friends 'Clinch' Smith and Edward Kent were there too. The men were resplendent in their formal dinner suits and the women stunning in their elegant dresses. The Colonel was a happily married man but it did not stop him from noticing that there many beautiful women aboard.

Then, playing out the traditional routines of the era to perfection, it was on to the Smoking Room, an all-male preserve. It was an excellent environment for a cigarette and a good chat with some of the many personalities aboard. These included Major Archie Butt, President Taft's military aide, with whom Gracie enthusiastically talked politics, and also Clarence Moore, with whom he discussed adventure (Moore had once helped a journalist obtain an interview with a famous backwoodsman outlaw).

Frank Millet, the famous artist, was also in the Smoking Room, along with the rich businessman, Arthur Ryerson. Gracie also chatted with John B. Thayer (Senior, Jack's father), who was a Second Vice-President of the Pennsylvania Railway and George Widener, son of a Philadelphia streetcar magnate. It was a wealthy, not to say spectacular, collection of luminaries.

However, all good things must come to an end and Gracie was determined not to stay up late. Having had a crammed evening, at around 10.00 p.m. he bade his goodnights and turned in. He climbed in to bed and drifted off to sleep, determined to wake ready for the workout he planned early next morning. The extra rest would come in useful but not in the way that he expected it to.

After dinner, Lawrence Beesley had gone to the Saloon for the congregational hymn-singing. There were about 100 other passengers present. Those there were to choose their favourite hymns, and there was no set structure to the service. The Reverend Carter was in his element as a sudden celebrity aboard ship. Before each hymn was sung he would, from his encyclopaedic memory, relate the story that had led to its writing.

Inevitably, the hymn 'For Those in Peril on the Sea' was one of those sung in what Beesley later remembered as a hushed silence. Later he would also, in a quote to the historian Leslie Reade, admit that the Reverend had said: 'We're not in peril but others may be. Let us sing the hymn for them.' Beesley omitted the reference from his subsequent book, saying that 'it might have seemed like a criticism of God'.

About 10.00 p.m., the service wound up. Stewards brought coffee and biscuits around to the passengers. Beesley and the Carters (the Reverend's much-loved wife Lillian was aboard too) indulged in social chit-chat until 10.45 p.m. and Beesley then retired to his cabin. Unknown to him, just over 20 miles to the west, a gigantic block of ice lay directly in the path of the ship, waiting to rip the heart out of her. A shadow of death loomed ahead.

Across the ship, things were wound up for the night. The routine was similar for most of those aboard, regardless of class. Major Arthur Peuchen, a chemist from Montreal, had been through a routine very similar to Gracie; a nice meal – he thought it was particularly fine, even by the *Titanic's* high standards – followed by a smoke and a chat. Although no one bothered to ask them later what they were doing at the time, down below single third-class passengers like Daniel Buckley would probably have enjoyed their humble meals too (though humble was a relative term, it was still good chow) and may well have gone to the bar for a few beers or to the General Room for a sing-along.

Families like the Panulas, the Skoogs and the Goodwins presumably turned in early given the fact there were quite a few young children around. However, perhaps the head of each household also enjoyed an ale or two before turning in. At the other end of the wealth scale, a few gambling types played cards. There were one or two professional 'sharks' aboard who were adept at extracting money from other people's wallets. Some more conservative observers would later suggest that the playing of cards on the Sabbath would bring bad luck.

Rich food, hymn-singing and card-playing were a world away for many of the crew, who might as well be living in a parallel universe. Down below, the firemen continued to shovel coal into the furnaces that kept the ship moving, choking on the dust and sweltering in the heat. The stewards and stewardesses rushed around like worker ants, looking after their passengers every need. This was no day of rest for them. Some however were luckier. The seamen aboard would normally be expected to help scrub the decks at the end of the day. However, in token recognition of the fact that this was a Sunday they had been given the night off, which was much appreciated given the frigid air outside.

When Second Officer Charles Herbert Lightoller took over on the bridge at 6.00 p.m. that night, he was aware that there was ice ahead but he did not realize how extensive it was. No one had yet joined up the dots of the ice warnings that had come in and the size of the ice barrier that they cumulatively intimated.

It was also uncertain how much the *Titanic's* officers regarded it as a real threat. There had been no recorded case of a major ship definitively being sunk by a berg, with the stories from the old days when ships had disappeared seeming to be both ancient history and unproven cases anyway. The last significant incident involving ice was when a German ship, the *Kron Prinz Wilhelm*, had had her bows crushed in 1907 but had limped safely into port. Anyway, the fact that she had been hit but had survived seemed to suggest that ice could damage a modern ship but was unlikely to sink it.

A number of ice warnings had been received. Fourth Officer Boxhall had dutifully marked the positions of the ice on the chart when they came in but no one seemed to take a lot of notice of them. Third Officer Pitman later recalled looking at the markings on the chart but believed they intimated that the ice was to the north of the track where the *Titanic* was travelling.

At around 7.30 p.m., the wireless operators on *Titanic* picked up a communication between the *Californian* and the *Antillian*. It stated:

Six-thirty pm, apparent ship's time; latitude 42 degrees 3 minutes North, longitude 40 degrees, 9 minutes West. Three large bergs 5 miles to the southward of us. Regards. Lord.

Harold Bride took the message up to the bridge, though Captain Smith did not receive it directly as he was at dinner. Given Bride's confusing evidence at the London Inquiry, it is not clear that anyone ever received it.

There was in fact an interesting story behind this message. The *Californian* had originally tried to send it direct to the *Titanic*. However, Harold Bride – who was on duty at the time – was too busy preparing his accounts to answer it. He therefore got it second hand from the *Antillian* (Bride recalled it as being from the *Baltic* but given the timings he appears to have confused himself).

There was a delay of half an hour in getting the information as a result. As it happened, the delay was not important – but as Bride did not know what the message was it might have been. It does not speak much for the priority placed on safety by *Titanic's* wireless operators. It would also have been completely understandable if Cyril Evans, *Californian's* operator who would later be given a rude brush-off by Jack Phillips on the *Titanic*, got a bit fed up with it all.

Wireless had become highly regarded since the emergence of Jack Binns, who was probably the most famous wireless man in the world in 1912. His fame dated back to 1909 when his ship, the White Star Line's *Republic*, was hit by another vessel, the *Florida*, off the coast of Nantucket and began to sink. Wireless was then a fairly new gimmick but Binns had proved its worth magnificently. The distress calls he sent out from the *Republic* were picked up by another vessel, the White Star liner *Baltic*, which came to the rescue. As a result of Binns' messages, nearly all the passengers onboard the stricken liner were saved.

Binns became a celebrity which also led to him being called as a witness to the subsequent American Inquiry into the loss of the *Titanic*. He was asked if information about hazards to navigation such as icebergs were always sent as a priority. Specifically, he was questioned whether 'this is regarded as the most important information that can be communication from one ship to another'. His response was in the affirmative. It is doubtful if it was a point of view shared by the *Titanic's* wireless operators based on the attitudes in evidence during the day.

Onboard the *Titanic*, Sunday 14 April ended with the promise of a quiet night and Lightoller thought the sea was as flat as a sheet of glass. He had already taken some precautions by instructing lamp trimmer Samuel Hemming to secure the hatch and skylight over the crew's galley so that the light from it would not get in the way of the lookouts vision in the crow's nest. At about 7.40 p.m. he had also taken some stellar observations to confirm the ship's position with Third Officer Pitman; they showed the ship to be exactly on track.

Lightoller had passed on his reading from the stars to Fourth Officer Boxhall so that he could work out the ship's position. Just over an hour later, he ordered carpenter John Maxwell to go and look at the water supply on the ship which was about to freeze. As the evening wore on, the captain excused himself from his dinner party with the Wideners and came up on the bridge to see how things were. At 8.55 p.m., a conversation took place between Lightoller and Captain Smith. In most circumstances it would have been the most mundane of dialogues, yet retrospect would present it as a discussion dripping with significance.

The conversation lasted for twenty-five minutes, mostly small talk between two vastly experienced seafarers. The subject of ice was raised, as both men knew that it would not be far ahead. They noted how clear the night was, giving both men comfort that they would spot the ice long before they were on it. They thought that there might be reflected starlight off any bergs. Captain Smith was concerned enough to instruct Lightoller 'if in the least degree doubtful, let me know', However, he was not concerned enough to either stay on watch for longer or get the ship to slow down as a precaution, nor did he put on any extra lookouts. Lightoller took a mental note and worked out that they would be in the region of ice at around 9.30 p.m.

The thought of slowing down did not cross anyone's mind. This was reflective of the generally cavalier attitude prevalent among most sailors at the time. Lightoller, who had been sailing in ice regions for many years, said later: 'I have never known speed to be reduced on any ship I have ever been on in the North Atlantic in clear weather on account of ice.'

Sir Ernest Shackleton knew more about ice than most people. He would later be marooned in it for months in Antarctica after it had caught his ship in a vice-like grip and crushed it slowly to pulp. Along with all his men, he had survived the experience in one of the most amazing stories of survival ever written. He was called as an expert witness to the Inquiry that would be held into the *Titanic's* loss in London. After being asked how easy it was to spot bergs at night, he was asked whether there should be extra lookouts posted if you were travelling at 22 knots in an ice zone (*Titanic's* approximate speed on the night of 14 April). His reply was blunt and to the point: 'You have no right to go at that speed in an ice zone.'

Lightoller's watch drew to an end. It had been quiet; 'nothing to see and nothing to hear' as he recalled it with the striking of the bell at half an hour intervals the only sound to break the monotony of the gentle noise of the sea as the ship's prow carved through it. At 10.00 p.m., it was time to knock off. First Officer Murdoch came to relieve him. As usual, there a few minutes of chit-chat when the changeover took place. Important information would be passed on during this conversation which also gave the new man on the watch time to get his eyes adjusted to making out things in the darkness. Perhaps the most important this particular night was that it was expected that the ship would be up around the ice at around 11.00 p.m. at the latest (Lightoller thought it would be earlier than this but for some reason said nothing).

Lightoller and Murdoch were old acquaintances. Among other things, they spoke of old times for a while. They both commented on how well the ship was performing, of her lack of vibration and of the general comfortableness of the voyage so far. All in all it was a very mundane conversation. There was little comment about the ice. Both men commented on the weather and particularly on the crystal-clear visibility that night.

Lightoller had already instructed Sixth Officer Moody to phone up to the crow's nest to tell the lookouts to watch out for small ice and 'growlers', low-lying chunks of ice that were hard to spot and potentially very dangerous. What he did not know was that, at around 9.40 p.m., another ice warning was received. It was from the *Mesaba* and told the *Titanic*:

> Ice Report: In latitude 42 degrees North to 41 degrees 25 minutes North; longitude 49 degrees West to longitude 50 degrees 30 minutes West, saw much heavy pack ice and great number of large icebergs, also field ice, weather, good, clear.

Phillips was alone on duty, a tired Harold Bride having turned in for a brief nap. He was busy with commercial messages and could not leave his post to take the ice warning up to the bridge. He shoved it under a paperweight and left it there.

Lightoller knew of several of the ice warnings that had been received though he dismissed them by saying that they were in positions that did not affect the Titanic on the track that she was on. He later felt that the message from the *Mesaba* was especially important. It gave a position that was right ahead of the *Titanic*, directly on her track. Phillips read the message, as did Bride. However, they did not know its importance. While Phillips sent trivial messages from passengers to the shore station at Cape Race and received equally trivial messages in return, this vital message lay under a paperweight with the intention of passing it on when things were quieter. Lightoller never knew of its existence until it was far too late to matter.

Tragically, three missing letters at the start of this clear message of danger directly in the path of the *Titanic* may have sealed the ship's fate. The wireless officer on the *Mesaba* failed to prefix the warning message with the letters MSG – Master's Service Gram – that required Phillips to return a personal acknowledgement receipt from the captain. The space in the report used for the MSG prefix was instead filled with the words 'Ice Report'.

Lookouts Fleet and Lee made their way into the crows nest at 10.00 p.m., taking over from Symons and Jewell. Jewell gave them very specific instructions; 'keep a sharp lookout for small ice'. They knew therefore that there might be ice ahead. It would not be easy to spot though. It was a dark night without a cloud in the sky. The stars shone in the heavens like a million diamonds spangling a black velvet dress. But there was no moon to illuminate the sea ahead.

The flatness of the sea was a problem too. It meant that they would not see any waves breaking on the ice, a tell-tale sign that would have been invaluable. It was not helpful that they did not have any binoculars either, though opinions were divided as to how useful they were. Some felt that they were important for identifying an object once you had spotted it in outline but no good for picking it up in the first place. Anyway, they would need to keep their wits about them. Still, the cold night air would blow on them in their lofty, exposed perch and make sure they stayed wide awake.

They were due to finish at 12.23 a.m. the next morning. The reason for the odd time was that the ship was due to change her clock by forty-seven minutes next day. As ships moved west across the ocean they would need to reflect their movement in the time aboard ship. The convention was to set the time based on where they expected to be at noon next day. However, the adjustment was done pragmatically. Therefore, when Fleet and Lee finished at 12.23 a.m., the time would be put back to midnight. Then when it reached 4.24 a.m., it would be put back again, this time to 4.00 a.m. By doing it this way the changes would take place when the passengers were fast asleep.

Having handed over to Murdoch, Lightoller did a final round about the ship before turning in. With a mile of corridors to cover, this was not an easy task. He had wandered between fore and aft along the passageway called Park Lane that ran the length of the ship. He finally reached the aft-deck where he checked that the Quartermaster was alert before finally reaching his room and preparing for bed. He climbed beneath the covers which he pulled around him in an attempt to warm up quickly and enjoyed the pleasant sensation of slowly thawing out.

While this was happening, there was another ship not too far away from the *Titanic* that was also aware that an ice-field was nearby. However, just how close the *Californian* was would later become a matter of intense debate, a debate which to this day has never satisfactorily been resolved and probably never will be.

Captain Stanley Lord, Master of the *Californian*, had never been in ice before and had been concerned at what he might find when he got near it. He had known it was ahead of him for some time. As far back as 9 April he had received a warning from the *Nieuw Amsterdam*, which had been followed by further updates from the *Caronia* the day before and the

Parisian on 14 April. When his ship got close to the ice region he had put an extra lookout on the bow. He also stayed on the bridge with another officer when he was not due to be on watch. Both actions contrasted rather positively with what was happening on the *Titanic* at the time.

The ship was well on her way towards Boston on her journey from London. Her home port was normally Liverpool but the change in the point of departure for this trip had led to one or two hiccups in organization. Cyril Evans, the wireless operator, had been so disorganized that in his hurry to get a wireless chart for the journey he had picked up the one for the South rather than the North Atlantic. The *Californian* had set out from the Royal Albert Docks at 1.30 a.m. on Good Friday 5 April, the very day that *Titanic* had been enthusiastically dressed in flags in Southampton.

At 7.30 p.m., Chief Officer Stewart had calculated *Californian's* position from a sighting from the Pole Star. The ship sailed on for another two and a half hours with Lord watching intently from the bridge. Chief Officer Stewart was replaced at the end of his watch on the bridge at 8.00 p.m. by Third Officer Groves. Stewart stayed with him for a few minutes while his eyes adjusted to the darkness and then went down below, not to appear centre stage until 4.00 a.m. the next morning.

Groves later wrote of this famous night in an unpublished manuscript, *The Middle Watch*, and it is worth bearing in mind that what he saw generally in terms of conditions was what the *Titanic* saw too. He recalled:

> the night was dark, brilliantly clear without a breath of wind and the sea showed no signs of movement with the horizon only discernible by the fact that the stars could be seen disappearing below it.

At 10.15 p.m., Lord saw a brightening on the western horizon. He screwed up his eyes and tried to focus on it. A couple of minutes of close attention and now he was sure – ice! He rang the engine-room telegraph to full speed astern and ordered the helm hard aport (which would turn the ship to starboard). She slowed down, turned sharply and then stopped, under half a mile away from a huge ice-field.

At about 10.30 p.m. (*Californian* time) Lord saw a light coming along (his memory was confused on this point; at the British Inquiry later, he thought it was closer to 11.00 p.m.). He saw the green light on her starboard side and could also pick out one masthead light. It was a strange night. Lord later recalled:

> We had been making mistakes all along with the stars, thinking they were signals. We could not distinguish where the sky ended and the water commenced.

He then spoke to the Chief Engineer and told him that he planned to stop for the night. He pointed out the steamer, which was getting closer, but was to the south and east of the *Californian*. Then he went down to see Cyril Evans, the wireless operator. Evans, like all wireless operators at the time, was not a paid-up member of the crew, though he received one shilling a month as a notional wage from the Leyland Line in addition to his salary from the Marconi Company. A bespectacled young man, with the looks of an egg-headed school-boy, Evans had little to do with the Captain but he was meticulous in passing any information that might be important on. On his way down, Lord met Evans coming up. Lord asked him if he had any ships. Evans replied that he had picked up the *Titanic*. Lord told the operator that the ship he had seen was definitely not her. He was sure that the ship he could see was a cargo steamer.

At any event, he told Evans to wireless the *Titanic* to tell her that they were stopped because of the ice. Captain Lord could also have ordered a Master Service Gram to be sent to the *Titanic*, which would have required an answer from the Captain of the other ship. However, he did not do so.

Evans returned to the wireless shack and started to tap out his message. He was underway and got as far as 'We are stopped and surrounded by ice' when he was interrupted mid-sentence by an irate Jack Phillips. Phillips had been struggling manfully to catch up with his commercial messages when the message from Evans came crashing in, deafening him because he was so close.

'Keep out! Shut up! You're jamming my signal. I'm working Cape Race,' he angrily responded. Although Evans would later say that he did not take umbrage at the response, he could not have been criticised if he had done. Suffice to say that if Jack Phillips, who would later act heroically in the looming crisis, had taken the time to take the message down and deliver it to his captain then the crisis might not have happened at all.

Caronia, Baltic, Amerika, Californian, Mesaba, Californian again. Six messages in all, six chances to avoid a calamity. The first two were taken to Captain Smith, the third was not. The fourth was allegedly delivered to the bridge but later no one was sure that the Captain (or anyone else) had seen it. The fifth was left lying under a paperweight while the sixth was not even completed because Jack Phillips was too busy to take it. It does not speak highly of the way that the wireless operators worked or the way that their information was processed on the bridge. It was slapdash and amateur. The looming catastrophe was an accident waiting to happen.

Evans, duly chastised, carried on working until around 11.25 p.m. *Californian* time and then turned in. His ship was going nowhere, her engines had stopped and she was just drifting slowly with the current. He could be confident that it was going to be a quiet night. Just about five minutes later, *California's* officers on the bridge signalled the nearby stationary ship with a Morse lamp. There was no reply to this. The Morse messaging continued but with no response whatsoever.

Lord went down below to his quarters. Third Officer Charles Groves was on watch until midnight, He had not seen any ship until 11.10 p.m. Given the unusual light that night, he did not even think, when he saw a single light in the distance, that it was a ship he was looking at, thinking it might be a star rising. However, within fifteen minutes he could clearly see two masthead lights and it was obvious that what he was looking at here was a vessel of some description. He went down below and told Captain Lord that there was a ship to the south of them.

The ship was now about four miles away at most from the *Californian*, Lord thought. Whatever she was, Lord did not believe that the ship he could see was the *Titanic*. He later insisted that the ship in view was 'something like ourselves – a medium sized steamer'. However, Third Officer Groves did not agree with him. Lord came back to the bridge and they watched the ship together. Groves later related that he had spent no more than three minutes on the bridge in this brief visit. However, Groves' later evidence was confusing. He said that the ship was to the south of them and moving west but showing her red light. This does not make sense; if the red light was on the port side, if it were to the south then the ship must have been travelling east, not west. It was not the only item of confusing evidence to emerge from the ship that night.

When Groves had a conversation with Lord before knocking off that night, he told Lord that 'she has been stopped since 11.40... she is a passenger steamer. At the moment she stopped she put her lights out'. This would be the subject of much debate later, partly because Lord did not remember the conversation. The coincidence of times was suggestive. Although there were those who suggested that the ships were operating with different times in operation, others said this was not the case. The appearance of the lights going out might be, they argued, the effect that would be seen when a ship made a sharp turn to avoid something such as an iceberg.

All this only became significant with hindsight. Lord was getting tired and would turn in soon. He would return down to his chart room and get some rest. The captain's cabin was something on an inner sanctum, a holy of holies that people entered with a feeling of discomfort not too far off dread. Lord would later be quoted in the *Boston Journal* – and admittedly newspapers have not been above embellishing a story for effect over the years – when asked about his cabin that 'no member of the crew has ever been in this room, and none of them come near the place except to clean up'. If accurately accredited, this suggests a man who did not seem to inspire men by his accessibility.

The *Californian* was now quiet, Third Officer Groves thought it especially so. He tried to call up the nearby ship with his Morse lamp but she did not respond. The stillness was only disturbed by the plaintive sounds of someone singing the melody 'Annie Laurie' down below. Lord was exhausted and he needed to recoup his strength to find his way through the ice in the morning. He would wait until Second Officer Stone came on watch at midnight and then get some shuteye. Nothing much should be happening now that his ship had stopped for the night.

7

Collision:
23.40, 14 April 1912, North Atlantic 49 Degrees 57 Minutes West, 41 Degrees 44 Minutes North

Titanic steamed through the darkness of the night, her sharp prow cutting through the chill water like a knife through butter. Despite the warnings of ice ahead, the ship was going at nearly 22 knots, as fast as she had ever been and indeed as fast as she would ever go. The decks were quieter now, a somniferous hand had descended over the ship and most people had turned in for the night. Few were abroad on this cold night, with the temperatures plummeting and the air icy.

But a small number of those onboard were still wide awake. High up in the crow's nest, Fleet and Lee peered intently into the inky blackness. The stars were bright but were of little help in picking anything out. Ahead of them, everything bore an ebony hue, with no disruption at all to the monotone darkness apart from the diamond-like stars high above. At sea level, there was nothing. No sign of any ice, no sign of a wave, no sign even of another ship's light. Lee remembered seeing a haze on the horizon. He was insistent that Fleet said to him that 'if we can see through that, we will be lucky'. However Fleet denied ever saying any such thing and Lord Mersey, Chairman of the subsequent British Inquiry, thought this was a too convenient explanation to justify not spotting any ice until it was too late.

Able Seaman Joseph Scarrott was on watch, which as a sailor meant that he was basically on call awaiting whatever instructions might emanate from the bridge. He heard the bells struck for 11.30 p.m., and a few minutes passed without any interruption to the dull monotony of life onboard a great liner at night. No parties or *haute cuisine* for these men, just a series of unexciting chores. It was approaching 11.40 p.m., just another three-quarters of an hour before knocking-off time and the promise of a warm bunk down below, especially appreciated by the lookouts in their lofty eyrie. It would not be a moment too soon. It was a perishing cold night, and steamy vapour trails came out like the breath of a dragon every time they exhaled.

Suddenly, Fleet was shaken to the core. There ahead, looming out of the darkness, some 500 yards ahead, something lay directly in their path.

Given the coldness of the air, given the warnings they had received earlier, it could only be one thing – ice. At first it was not that big, just the size of two tables as Fleet later recalled (it would become clear during subsequent investigations that he was not a good judge of distance or scale). However, as they came closer, it grew in stature until it was something very large indeed.

As the berg loomed into view, Fleet frantically rang three bells – the signal for an object dead ahead – and rushed to the telephone that connected the crow's nest to the bridge. The answer came quickly, said Fleet, a simple 'What do you see?' from Sixth Officer Moody. Fleet gasped out: 'Iceberg, right ahead!' (though first-class passenger Major Peuchen, in evidence at the American Inquiry, would say that Fleet had told *him* that he did not get an immediate reply when he rang the phone). Almost simultaneously, Murdoch had spotted the berg from the bridge and was already starting to take evasive action.

Many years later, Fleet would tell of how he had watched in horror as the berg loomed in the distance, getting inexorably closer, its pointed top giving it a sinister and menacing appearance. He told his mate Reginald Lee to climb down out of the crow's nest; there was no point in both of them being there. Lee actually started to do so but then changed his mind and returned to the viewing platform.

The forty seconds that followed were the longest of Fleet's life. Each second seemed to last an hour and yet the leviathan still did not move (some later suggested that the rudder was too small for the size of the ship). She seemed to dart straight as an arrow for the berg. Then at the last moment she slowly started to turn away. She began to swing with agonizing lethargy to port but it was too late, far too late, and she struck just before the foremast. There was just the faintest grinding noise that Fleet could hear but no noticeable jar. To him, it was nothing more than 'a narrow shave'. However, Lee distinctly heard a 'rending of metal' as the berg scraped along the ship's side.

In reality it was anything but a close shave. It was in retrospect a pity that she moved off line at all, though of course it was completely natural that the ship's navigators should try and escape a collision. A head-on crash would have stoved in the bows and undoubtedly led to loss of life but most of the watertight compartments would have been unaffected. She would certainly have listed but would probably have floated. However, the apparent glancing blow had torn holes in her side which compromised the integrity of a number of the watertight compartments. In truth, whatever anyone did now, the ship was doomed. It had taken years to plan and build her. It had taken just seconds to condemn her to oblivion.

When Murdoch had seen the berg, instructions were sent down at once to the engine rooms. Far down below in Boiler Room 6 as in all others a series of lights gave automated instructions to those working in the bowels of the ship as to what was expected of them; white meant full speed ahead, blue slow and red stop. A red light flashed on. Leading stoker Fred Barrett was in charge and immediately shouted to his men to 'shut all dampers'. His men rushed to comply but before they could fully do so there was a crash.

On the bridge, the man with his hand on the helm was Quartermaster Hichens. As the berg loomed inexorably closer, closing in on him as if he were about to run headfirst into a wall, Murdoch frantically shouted to him to try and steer around it. Hichens responded: 'Hard astarboard. The helm is hard over.' Then came the blow.

Slight though it may have been, Captain Smith was already rushing out of his cabin to find out what the problem was. 'What is it?' he asked. 'An iceberg,' responded Murdoch. 'I put her hard astarboard and ran the engines full astern, but it was too close; she hit it.' He explained that he planned to port round the iceberg and then put the helm hard over the other way so that the stern of the ship would swing clear but that she had been too close to avoid the berg. Captain Smith told his First Officer to shut the watertight doors but Murdoch responded that he had already done so. Smith looked at the commutator, which measured if the ship had any list; within a few minutes it told him that she was already listing 5 degrees to starboard.

Questions would later be asked about the *Titanic's* lookout arrangements. For example, the lack of binoculars in the crow's nest later became a bone of contention. Lookouts Hogg and Evans had asked for them in Southampton but were told there were none though they had had them on the way over from Belfast. Hogg was later interviewed and was surprised that they were not issued to them, thinking that they would have made a difference. Fleet would later be asked if he could have spotted the ice earlier with binoculars. He would insist that 'we could have seen it a bit sooner'. When asked how much sooner, he responded pointedly: 'Well, enough to get out of the way.'

It was a point of view not shared by Second Officer Lightoller. He actually considered that binoculars were detrimental to the lookouts. However, there is an element of self-defence in this assertion perhaps. It was the Second Officer's job to know where the binoculars were and, with Lightoller taking over the role from Davy Blair at the last moment, this piece of knowledge had been lost. But others also thought 'glasses' were of limited value, such as Seaman Thomas Jones, who had served as a lookout on other ships though not on the *Titanic*. Lookout Archie Jewell on the other hand thought that they were 'very useful'.

There was also the lookout's positioning to take into account. Sir Ernest Shackleton had described how he always posted lookouts in the bows of the ship when looking for ice (a strategy that Captain Rostron, master of the rescue ship *Carpathia*, would employ later that night). Captain Lord had done the same. Yet Captain Smith did not think this was necessary, He had gambled on a normal lookout service spotting the ice before he reached it and he had lost. The price of the forfeit would be enormous.

Across the ship, the collision registered in many different ways to many different people. The majority of those aboard felt little, though it depended to a great extent on where you were; those lower down and on the starboard side where the collision happened felt a much greater force than those elsewhere.

For example, Lawrence Beesley had been lying in his bed reading and had suddenly been conscious that the vibrations of the ship seemed to increase. The mattress was his usual indicator of such things and now it seemed to be a stronger sensation of rocking in it than he had ever felt before. It made him think that the ship was moving more quickly than ever. Outside his room, he had heard the muffled voices of stewards talking in the corridors as he started to get drowsy. And then he felt something, a disturbance to the regular running of the engines and an increase to the vibrations.

Jack Thayer was winding his watch and about to retire when he felt the ship sway. She had veered to port, as if she had been gently pushed. The shock was very slight, so much so that if he had have been holding a glass of water he was confident he would not have spilt a drop.

Little Eva Hart was in her cabin with her family, in a comfortable four-berth with a table her nervous mother used for her sewing. Her mother had been worried about being on the ship from the start and had refused to sleep in a bed at night. She later described how she felt a little 'bump'. It did not register very strongly because the cabin was on the portside, far away from the point of collision. She straight away woke Eva's father up. He went away at once to find out what had happened and came back, reporting the accident to his family. He would later tell them that they were going to launch the boats but they should not worry too much, for he was sure they would all be back onboard for breakfast.

Asleep in his cabin adjacent to the wireless shack, Harold Bride did not realize that there had been a collision at all. He got up as planned just before midnight to relieve Phillips who had been very busy. Phillips told him that he thought the ship had been damaged and would probably have to return to Belfast for repairs (perhaps he was aware of a practical problem; there was no dry dock in the USA big enough to deal with the *Titanic*).

Bride had planned to be up earlier than usual, as it had been a particularly trying day. The problem with the apparatus had taken them seven hours to fix. At last, after trial and error, they found that one of the components had burnt out and replaced it. The timely discovery and fixing of the problem was one of the few strokes of luck that the *Titanic* experienced that night. The thought of the *Titanic* being without her wireless at this crucial moment does not bear thinking about.

There were three rooms in the wireless shack: a sleeping room, a dynamo room and an operating room. Bride, tired, had soon fallen asleep when he went to bed but had later woken, to hear Phillips sending passenger chit-chat to the shore station at Cape Race. When the iceberg was struck, he felt no shock or jolt at all. He was barely aware that anything had happened.

Fifth Officer Harold Lowe was also not woken by the impact and slept on until he heard the sounds of voices outside of his door. He was amazed when he went out on deck and saw people milling around with lifebelts on. He got up and noticed something strange about the ship. When someone later suggested at the Inquiries that she was listing he corrected the statement; she was, he said, 'tipping', not listing, that is angling forward rather than sideways. Lowe was a cautious man and at some stage went into his cabin and picked up his revolver just in case it might be needed.

Quartermaster George Rowe was on watch towards the stern of *Titanic* when the collision came. He saw a massive berg float past, at first thinking it was a close shave with a sailing ship. However, the seriousness of the situation did not dawn on him at all. He went back on watch and while throughout the rest of the ship the drama unfolded, he was oblivious to what was happening. He would later see a lifeboat go past at around half past midnight and telephoned the bridge to report it. Incredulous, they asked him to report to the bridge. Rowe, the last person to find out perhaps that they were in trouble, would later play a part in firing off distress rockets.

Lightoller was about to fall asleep when he was shaken awake by a vibration passing the whole length of the ship. It was not a violent sensation. However, there had been such a distinct lack of vibration during the trip so far that the break to the mundane smoothness was enough to disturb him. He was up in a second. Not bothering to throw on anything over his pyjamas he ran first to the port side of the ship, then the starboard. He could see nothing in the icy darkness and with the frigid air biting into him gratefully made his way back to his warm bunk.

Others tried to see the berg too but few were able to. One exception was Steward Crawford who went out and saw the iceberg, 'a large black object, much higher than B Deck, passing along the starboard side'. In contrast, Pierre Maréchal, son of a vice-admiral of the French navy, Lucien Smith, Paul Chevré, a French sculptor and A.F. Omont, a cotton broker, were playing bridge in the Café Parisien when the ship struck. They went outside, looked over the edge to see if they could spot the cause of the collision, and then returned to their card game having failed to do so. One returned to the café to pick up his cigar, which he had left burning there, saying that he couldn't waste it. None of them thought that the collision was serious. Maréchal was among the survivors, as was Chevré and Omont. They all had winning hands that night, unlike Smith who perished.

Major Peuchen was just on the way back from the Smoking Room making his way to bed. Just before he reached his room, it felt as if the ship were hit by a heavy wave. He was not at all perturbed and continued to make his way to his cabin. It was not until about half an hour later that he noticed that the ship seemed to be listing. James McGough, a buyer for Gimbel Brothers, was asleep in his cabin when he felt a wrenching sensation, not severe or terrifying. He thought perhaps the ship had hit a heavy swell though he was perturbed enough to go up to the deck to see what was wrong.

Third Officer Pitman was in bed when the collision came; it woke him up. It seemed to him as if the ship was coming to anchor. He dressed and went outside but he saw or heard nothing. So unperturbed was he that he went back to his quarters and lit himself a pipe. Steward Edward Wheelton, perhaps remembering what had happened to the *Olympic* not too long before (just back in February), thought that the ship had dropped a propeller. He thought it would mean a trip back to Belfast for repairs.

Many people were unperturbed by the accident, barely noticing it at all. However, some were more concerned by it. Governess Elizabeth Shute noticed that 'suddenly a queer shivering ran under me, apparently the whole length of the ship'. The strangeness of the sensation disturbed her and she jumped out of bed. However, excessively reassured by the sheer magnitude of the ship she was on, she went back to bed but it was just a very short space of time before a friend from a nearby cabin knocked on her door and told her to get up. She told her that they had struck an iceberg; if she was quick she might still be able to catch sight of it out of the window.

The collision also made a strong impression on Edith Brown. She was asleep but felt a great vibration cause the ship to shiver as if in fear. Colonel Gracie was 'enjoying a good night's rest when I was aroused by a sudden shock and noise forward on the starboard side, which I at once concluded was caused by a collision, with some other ship perhaps'. He jumped from his bed and turned on the light. He glanced at his clock, which he had not yet reset; it said it was midnight (Gracie thought this made it about 11.45 p.m. ship's time). He went out into the corridor but could see no one. However, there was 'a great noise of escaping steam'. Most noticeably, the ship had stopped.

At the time of the collision, Harvey Collyer was getting ready for bed. It felt to Charlotte as if the ship had been picked up by a giant hand and shaken a couple of times before she came to a halt. Charlotte felt a long backward jerk, followed by a shorter one. Despite the sensation, she was not thrown out of her bed and her husband stood steady on his feet. There were no strange sounds, no noises of steel being ripped, but the main thing they noticed was a negative sensation, the lack of motion as the ship stopped.

Margaret Brown had retired to bed and was reading. Mrs Bucknell had repeated her premonition that very night; her Cassandra-like warnings were starting to get annoying. When the ship struck the berg, Mrs Brown was thrown to the floor. The engines stopped immediately but, being unable to see anything obviously wrong, she returned to her reading.

It was the crew and third-class passengers, furthest down in the ship's bowels, who experienced the greatest shock. When the ship struck, Seaman W. Brice heard a rumbling that lasted 'about ten seconds'. George Beauchamp, a fireman who was on duty at the time, heard a noise that was 'like thunder, the roar of thunder'.

The boiler rooms were the most obviously affected. In Boiler Room 6 there was a tremendous bang and the starboard side of the ship was pierced. Water started to rush in from a hole about 2 feet above floor level (it was later estimated that this was about 24 feet below sea level). Men had to jump under the rapidly closing watertight doors to escape. They planned to return but when Fireman Barrett climbed back towards Boiler Room 6 he could not get back in it for it was already under about 8 feet of water – this in the space of just about ten minutes.

He had no doubts at all about the seriousness of the crash. If the water rose by 14 feet in total, just another 6 feet, it would come up through the plates of the floor above and then slop over into the next watertight compartment. It would inevitably pull the *Titanic* down by the head. He had already looked in the coal bunker on the other side of the watertight compartment, a vast, cavernous space, capable of holding 500 tons of coal. It was empty and he could see that water was coming in – he likened it to the flow of water one might see coming out of a fire hose. At any event, the *Titanic's* hull had been breached even beyond Boiler Room 6 and there was no doubt that she was in serious trouble.

The nature of the damage caused by the collision has been made clearer by the discovery of the wreck. Dives on the ship have located some of the iceberg damage. The *Titanic* was held together by wrought iron rivets rather than welded as a modern ship would be, with the plates of the ship overlapping each other. When the ship collided with the berg, the effect of the collision was to 'pop' the rivets, causing the plates of steel that they had held together to part. Through the gap created as a result, water started to stream in.

The rivets were made of wrought iron, a mix of iron and slag. If there was too high a proportion of slag, that would compromise the strength of the rivets. A small sample of rivets has been rescued from the ocean bed where the wreck lies and these show a higher than expected proportion of slag in the rivets, suggesting that some of them at least are not of top quality which would make them less resistant to the impact of a collision.

The damage caused was not a long, continuous slash, which would probably have sunk the ship much quicker. It had long been assumed that this was the case, as if only a catastrophic hull failure could sink such a vessel. But in reality it was only a series of small holes in the side of the ship, totalling little more than 12 feet square in total, that did for her. The sea did not come pouring through in a rush but in several places was more like water coming out of a series of fire hoses. But most importantly it affected a number of the watertight compartments and this was enough to doom the *Titanic*.

Intriguingly Barrett later testified to the British Inquiry that here was the bunker where coal had caught alight before the ship started her voyage. As a result of this, it had been emptied though not until it had burned for days. Barrett could see that it had dented the watertight compartment that was adjacent to it though it was not obvious to him whether or not this was contributing to the rate at which water was coming into the next compartment. Leading Fireman Hendrickson had been one of those responsible for getting all the coal out of the bunker. He could see when he was finished that the bulkhead next to it was dented and some of the paint on it had been scorched off.

Further back Fireman George Cavell was in another bunker shovelling coal. When the shock came, the coal in the bunker came tumbling down on top of him and he only escaped with difficulty. He heard the warning bell ringing, telling him that the watertight doors were about to clamp shut. Then the lights in his stokehold went out. It must have been terrifying but Cavell managed to fumble his way up onto deck where one of his mates told him that they had struck a berg. He later went back to draw the fires in the boiler room. When he got there, there was no water in it and he started to dampen the fires. However, they had to abandon this with the task uncompleted as the water started to come in over the floor plates. By the time they left, the water was up to their knees.

Daniel Buckley was in a cabin deep down in the ship forward, along with all the other third-class single men. He was quartered with three others in his cosy cabin. Like many in his situation, he had decided to go to America to 'make some money'. Unlike those higher up in the ship, he heard a 'terrible noise' when the ship struck the berg. However, he did not get up at once. When he did a short time later, he had a shock; his feet were wet as a trickle of water was running into the room. He tried to rouse his room-mates but they were having none of it; 'get back into bed. You are not in Ireland now', was the response.

Lookout Archie Jewell was in his quarters and was awakened by a crash. He ran up on deck and saw a lot of ice. Perhaps thinking that this might indeed be very serious, he went below to dress properly. He also noted that the ship was stopped. Able Seaman Ernest Archer felt what appeared to be 'a grating sensation... like an anchor'. He went forward to see if he could ascertain the problem. There were pieces of ice on the forward deck when he arrived there. They were just small lumps, rather than big chunks.

The crew had easy access to an open area forward and they took advantage of it to see what had happened. Going out into the freezing air, they saw the small globules of ice on the deck. Some of them took them back inside to show their shipmates the evidence that they had sailed close to a berg. This was how Seaman Frank Evans first knew of the accident when one of his shipmates came in with a lump of ice from the forecastle.

Joseph Scarrott was having a cigarette when the ship struck. He was standing around the forecastle and therefore had a grandstand view of events. The collision shook the liner from stem to stern but was not as violent as might have been expected, reflecting the fact that she had struck a glancing blow. The ship shook as if the engines had been put full astern, which indeed they had been. Scarrott ran down the ladder to tell his mates what he had seen, an iceberg about the height of the Boat Deck which reminded him in shape of the Rock of Gibraltar. The crew turned out to see what was happening, getting out of their bunks and going up on deck.

But even down below there were many who were initially unaware of the serious nature of the situation. Boatswain's mate Albert Haines had good reason to celebrate the religious conventions of the time. Normally at night he would have been scrubbing the decks along with Seaman Brice but because it was a Sunday they were excused duty. Soon after the collision, Haynes heard air coming out of and water going into the forepeak. He reported to Chief Officer Wilde that the water was coming in and was told in reply to go and get all the men from his area up from down below.

Although he was disturbed by the collision, Steward Charles Andrews went back to bed but got up again when he heard the sounds of water. Mistaken impressions that the accident was not serious were quickly being put right. On the bridge, Captain Smith ordered the carpenter to go and sound the ship to find out how badly she was damaged. Chief Steward John Hardy was sent around to shut some of the upper watertight doors; only those lower down were automatically closed from the bridge.

Down the dim corridors a few hand-picked men made their way towards the bottom of the ship, to ascertain how bad the damage was and whether the watertight doors and the pumps combined would keep the ship afloat. It was time now to gather the evidence and reach a rapid conclusion about what would happen next. When the evidence was put together, no one could quite believe how dreadful the conclusion emerging from it would be.

8

A Troubled Silence:
23.41–24.00, 14 April 1912

It was easy to believe at first that there was nothing to worry about. This was no instantaneous catastrophe. When the *Empress of Ireland* went down in 1914 with the loss of over 1,000, it sank fourteen minutes after being hit by another ship. The year after, the *Lusitania* went down eighteen minutes after being struck by a torpedo. In both instances, it was almost immediately obvious that the vessel would sink. Not so with *Titanic*, where the awful realization of the extent of the disaster dawned slowly, almost imperceptibly. This was would be no instant death but a long, lingering demise, almost as if it were happening in slow motion.

Major Peuchen had gone out on deck to have a look around. He saw a thin layer of light ice in the forecastle area. However, there was no sign of any imminent catastrophe. He went to tell his friend Hugo Ross that 'it was not serious; we have only struck an iceberg'. Shortly afterwards he was bringing other acquaintances forward so that they could have a look at the ice too. But then Peuchen noticed that the ship had started to list and that started to worry him. His friend Mr Hays reassured him that, as a minimum, the ship was good for another eight to ten hours.

Lawrence Beesley had been reading in his bed. All he heard was the continuing murmuring of stewards. Then the ship slowed and stopped and the vibration that was somehow a comfort disappeared. This was the first sign to him that something might be wrong. He equated it to being in a room with a loud clock; while it was ticking, one was unaware of its presence but the minute it stopped, the noise was missed. So too with *Titanic's* reassuring vibration.

He too theorized that perhaps a propeller blade had been dropped, an accursed nuisance as it might well mean a trip back to Belfast for repairs. He jumped out of bed and donned a dressing-gown over his pyjamas. Then he put on his shoes and made his way to the hallway near the saloon. There was a steward there and Beesley asked him why the ship had stopped. The reply was a reassuring one: 'I don't know sir but I don't suppose it is anything much.'

He then climbed three flights of stairs and walked out onto the deck. The freezing night air cut him to the bone. He looked over the side into the black night but there was no sign of anything there to alarm him, certainly no iceberg looming threateningly out of the darkness. There were just two or three other people idling around there, none of whom knew of anything to worry about.

He looked through the windows of the smoking room and saw a small card school continuing to play as if nothing had happened. One of them said that he had seen an iceberg looming above the ship through the window and they had certainly felt more of a sensation than Beesley had. They guessed that the berg was about 90 feet high. But it made so little impression on the card-players that they returned to their game virtually without a break. One of them laughingly suggested that it had probably caused some damage by scraping off the new paint. This group of passengers was certainly not at all bothered. One even suggested that someone should go out and fetch a cube of ice for his whisky. This was enough for Beesley. Joining in the laughter, he then made his way back below decks and returned to his cabin to read.

The engines had stopped almost at once. To Jack Thayer, the quietness and stillness of the ship was extremely disconcerting after four and a half days of her hypnotizing vibrations. All he could hear was the breeze blowing in through his open window. Then he heard the sound of running feet and muffled voices as people hurried past in the corridor trying to find out what had occurred. He did not bother to get dressed but just put on his slippers and threw on an overcoat before venturing out.

His father decided he would join him. They made their way up to the deck. The intense darkness meant that they could see next to nothing when they looked over the rail. However, when young Jack looked forward he saw ice scattered across the forecastle in small chunks. There were just two or three others around when Thayer Senior and Junior arrived there (young Jack was first, hurrying up while his father was dressing) but they were soon joined by a number of others. They eventually found a member of the crew, who told them that they had hit an iceberg. He tried to point it out to the Thayers but they could not see it in the darkness.

After a few minutes the ship started up again but then chugged to a halt once more, this time for good. Greaser Frederick Scott was down below in the engine rooms so was better placed than most to know what happened. He thought that the ship went slow ahead for ten minutes and then slow astern for five. Quartermaster Alfred Olliver also noticed that the ship went half-speed ahead for a short time and then stopped. Situated where they were, the Collyers could hear the coughing and spluttering of the engines clearly. They were not alarmed. Harvey reassured Charlotte that there had been a slight accident in the engine room and he did not even propose to go and investigate further.

However, he then decided that he should after all try and find out more information. Charlotte and little Madge nearly fell asleep again. But, just as she was about to drop off, Harvey came back into the room and woke Charlotte up once more. 'What do you think?' he asked excitedly. 'We have struck an iceberg, a big one, but there is no danger, an officer just told me so.'

Harvey told her that the collision did not appear to have disturbed many people and there were only a few inquisitive souls up on deck. He said that he too had passed a card game in full swing. Their cards had been thrown off the table when the ship struck but they had been so little disturbed by this that they had quickly resumed their game again.

After the collision, Colonel Gracie had dressed hurriedly and then went up to the Boat Deck. He found only one other person there, a young lad. It was a beautiful night, cloudless, with the stars shining brightly. However there was no sign of any ice or icebergs. At this stage he had no idea that it was an iceberg that had been hit. He vaulted over the gate into a second-class area. He expected to be challenged by the ship's officers but saw none. This was a situation that would change later on, especially when third-class passengers were trying to get up to the Boat Deck.

Gracie crossed over onto the port side onto A Deck but could still see nothing wrong. Here he saw Bruce Ismay, effectively White Star's senior official, who wore a day suit and was hatless, as he normally was. 'He seemed too much preoccupied to notice anyone,' Gracie recalled. At the foot of the stairs he met a number of other people gathering including his great friend 'Clinch' Smith. Smith showed him a small sliver of ice, which he suggested Gracie should keep as a souvenir.

It was here that Gracie heard for the first time what had happened. The story came from someone who had been in the Smoking Room when the ship struck. He had rushed out to see what it was and came back to tell of an iceberg '50 feet' higher than the ship. Gracie also heard that the mailroom was already filling with water and the clerks were working stoically in 2 feet of it. They were transferring the mail to higher decks where they hoped it would be safe.

Elizabeth Shute was not aware of any confusion or noise of any kind at this stage. The stewardess came and told them she had learned nothing from the investigations she had carried out as to what had happened to the ship. Along the corridor, heads were peeping out of open stateroom doors, trying to find out what was going on. The atmosphere was, as Miss Shute significantly described it, 'sepulchrally still'.

Now the Graham family, whom she was accompanying, and Miss Shute were all dressed. Margaret Graham, nineteen years of age, was nibbling at a chicken sandwich but was clearly unnerved by what had happened; the meat kept falling from the sandwich as her hands were shaking so much. Her tension infected Miss Shute too. For the first time she was frightened at the situation, more perhaps because of the uncertainty than any specific dread.

Going out into the corridor Miss Shute saw an officer passing. She asked him if there were anything wrong but he reassured her that he knew of nothing. However, his calm demeanour did not put her at ease for she heard him enter a cabin further down the corridor and tell someone inside, *sotto voce,* that 'we can keep the water out for a while'. Realizing that the situation might indeed be grave, Miss Shute hurried back in to put on some more clothes: a coat and skirt, slippers (quicker to put on than shoes) and a lifebelt which the stewardess helped to fit.

Eavesdropping was a good way of finding out what was going on. Dr Washington Dodge, a first-class passenger, went out and heard someone say that the ship had stopped as she had struck some ice. When someone questioned this, the man who had made the statement boldly suggested that he should go and look at the forecastle and see for himself, as it was covered in fragments of ice. Dodge went out, strolled along the promenade and looked down on to the deck below. There he saw a large amount of ice debris, amounting in total to several cartloads worth he guessed.

It was while he was standing here that Dodge overheard a conversation that for the first time alerted him to the seriousness of the situation. Two stokers were engaged in a discussion. One asked the other (addressing him as 'sir', it was presumably a more senior member of the crew that he was talking to) if the collision had been serious. The reply put the onus back on the questioner; it was suggested that he should know better than anyone if the ship was badly damaged as he had just come up from below decks and would have better information than most onboard as to whether she had sprung any leaks or not.

The stoker, he who had asked the question in the first place, remarked that 'the water was pouring into the stoke 'old when we came up, sir'. It was not a reassuring exchange to overhear. Dodge looked out over the rails and could see no ice or bergs. However, some of the steerage passengers were amusing themselves engaging in a surreal game of football played with chunks of ice. Dodge pondered on what he had heard and realized that this could be a rather tight corner to be in.

In the meantime, on the *Californian* Third Officer Charles Groves continued to ponder on the ship he could see nearby. Groves was sure that she was 'a passenger steamer' with 'a lot of light'. Lord disagreed but Groves was insistent. He said: 'It is, sir. When she stopped her lights seemed to go out, and I suppose that they have been put out for the night.' He thought that the ship had stopped at 11.40 p.m. The British Inquiry would seize on this as the time that the *Titanic* hit the berg. They intimated that what appeared to be the lights being put out for the night might instead be the *Titanic* making a sharp turn to avoid something.

There were just two problems with this apparently incriminatory evidence. Firstly, there was the issue of the ships' times. There is much debate about what the time difference between the two ships was. Time at sea is a complex subject but the basic premise is that ships sailing west set their clocks based on the next day's noon position. There are different views of what the time difference between *Titanic* and *Californian* was. Some suggest that the *Californian* was twelve minutes behind the *Titanic*, others that she was seventeen minutes ahead. Therefore, it is impossible to state with confidence that the time at which Stone saw the lights go out was the same time that the *Titanic* swerved to miss an iceberg.

The second issue is a much more basic one. Groves said that he had a conversation with Captain Lord debating whether or not they were looking at a passenger steamer. Lord had no recollection of such a conversation ever taking place. It would be something of a habit; Groves was one of just three officers on the *Californian* who would later claim that they had had a conversation with their captain at some stage that night which he could not recall, the other two being Second Officer Stone and Apprentice Gibson.

Back on the *Titanic*, after returning to his room following his initial foray out to see what had happened, Second Office Lightoller now lay snugly in his bed. He felt he should so something but reasoned that, if he were needed, someone would surely come and get him. It was about ten minutes after the collision when there was a knock on his door. It was Boxhall, who told him quietly that there was something wrong. Lightoller responded that he already knew there was. Then Boxhall told him of the collision with the ice. The ship had been pierced and water was now in the mail room on F Deck. Then he left. Lightoller got dressed and went out on deck to try and make himself useful.

The impact had awoken Bruce Ismay but he had stayed in bed for a short time. He then went out into the corridor to see what was going on. He asked a steward but he had little information so Ismay put a coat on and went up on deck. He went to see the Captain, who told him that they had struck ice. He then sought out the Chief Engineer who felt that the blow had been a serious one but that the pumps would be able to keep the water out. Such confidence would soon start to evaporate.

It can only have been a few minutes after the berg was struck that Smith came into the wireless shack, as he still had not received the results of the inspection into the damage that he had ordered. He told Phillips and Bride that the ship had struck a berg and that they should make themselves ready to send a call for assistance. However, they should hang on until he knew more.

Thomas Andrews then came on the bridge to see Captain Smith. He and the carpenter then took a backstairs tour of the Titanic to inspect the damage. It soon became clear that it was terminal. She was designed so that any two of her compartments might be flooded and she would stay afloat. Even the first four watertight compartments could be breached but she would still not sink. She would be at a pretty uncomfortable angle it was true but she would at least have remained on the surface. But the way in which she had hit the ice had allowed water into six compartments; too many for the ship to live. Andrews made his way back to the bridge with his awful and unbelievable news.

A terrifying picture started to emerge, though at this stage only a few people were aware of it. On the bridge, Captain Smith had quickly taken steps to ascertain the full extent of the damage. As well as Andrews, Fourth Officer Boxhall had been sent below to try and find out how serious the damage done to the ship was. Initially, he could find none – he must have been looking in the wrong place. When he reported back to Captain Smith, he was asked to go and find the ship's carpenter. However, it was the carpenter who found Boxhall and told him that *Titanic* had been holed and was taking on water fast. While the carpenter made his way to the Captain to make his report, Boxhall continued to journey down into the bowels of the ship.

He arrived at the Post Room, where the mail clerks were working frantically – they had about 400,000 items of mail to worry about. The lowest deck, where the post was stored, was already virtually flooded with water within 2 feet of the deck on which Boxhall was now standing. He could clearly see mailbags floating. There was no doubt that there had been serious damage and Boxhall hurried back to Captain Smith to tell him the bad news as soon as possible.

First-class passenger Norman Chambers had also gone down to investigate. He saw some mailmen who had come up from the Post Room who were wet through. Looking down he could see that the water level was up to within 18 inches of the next deck. He could see letters floating on the surface. He was not though especially alarmed and made a joke of it. He was confident that *Titanic's* watertight compartmentalization would more than cope with any problems.

First-class stewardess Annie Robinson was on E Deck in her cabin. When she was disturbed by the collision, she got up and dressed. She went down below and saw that the Post Room was already flooding. She saw a man's Gladstone Bag floating on the surface of the water. She also saw the carpenter, lead-line in hand with which he had sounded the ship. He looked 'absolutely bewildered, distracted'. He said nothing but the look on his face told a million words. Stewardess Robinson knew well enough how dangerous icebergs were; she had already been in collision with one onboard another ship, the *Lake Champlain*.

Third Officer Pitman had also been down below in an attempt to ascertain the extent of the damage. He saw none but bumped into a group of firemen coming up from down below carrying their 'bundles', their personal possessions. They told him that water was coming into their quarters. He made his way down to a hatch where he could look down into the bottom of the ship and see for himself the water coming in.

It was the crew and third-class passengers far below who realized that there were serious problems first, probably even before those in command on the bridge. Those of the crew who were up on deck noticed a large amount of ice and snow on the starboard deck. However, it did not seem to have been a serious collision so most of them trooped down again, cursing the situation more for the fact that it had disturbed their sleep than for any sense of danger they felt. They had not been back in their cabins long though before the boatswain came in and told them all to get up and help in uncovering the boats.

Fireman Jack Podesta had gone to find out what had happened. As he looked down a spiral ladder that gave him sight of what was happening down below he saw several men running along. He could hear the sound of water rushing into the forward hold. He returned to his room where he tried to rouse his shipmates. One of them, Gus Stanbrook, laughed at him, thinking it a huge joke.

Some down below heard evidence of problems before they actually saw it. Able Seaman Edward Buley was quartered with some of his colleagues in the front of the ship. They noticed the sound of water coming in although they could not yet see anything. There was a hatchway in the forecastle with a tarpaulin across it. Water could be heard rushing in below it.

Seaman Samuel Hemming also heard the 'hissing noise' of the air escaping from the forepeak. He had not been too disturbed at the time of the collision and had gone back to his bunk after getting up to investigate. He was soon shaken from his lethargy, when the boatswain came in and said:

> Turn out, you fellows, you haven't half an hour to live. That is from Mr Andrews. Keep it to yourself and let no one know.

It was about midnight now and even at this early stage it seems that those in authority already knew that the ship was doomed. However, they seemed surprisingly lax in appraising some others of the fact, especially those responsible for loading the lifeboats soon afterwards.

Steward Joseph Wheat was quartered on F Deck next to the Turkish baths. He was awoken by the collision. He woke his room-mate and then went out to find out what had happened. He found out that the ship had been holed and that water was coming in forward. He then went down to the Post Room on G Deck where he too saw the staff moving the post bags up from the rising water. He also saw water already starting to creep up the stairs. He then saw it to start to slowly cover G Deck where he was standing.

He then went up to manually close the watertight doors by the Turkish baths (only the watertight doors down in the lowest areas of the ship were closed automatically from the bridge). There were in fact two there. One he managed to close himself, the other had to be closed from above (E Deck) and he had help to shut that one. It helped delay the spread of the water but nothing more. The way that the bulkheads had been constructed meant that they did not go up high enough and water would inevitably tip over from one compartment to the next as the forward sections of the ship dipped down into the water. It was perhaps significant that it was not Wheat's job to close these watertight doors and he did so on his own initiative. In order for the *Titanic* to stay afloat for as long as possible there had to be a system in place for closing the doors manually and it is not clear that there was any such thing in operation.

Now aware that his ship was in real trouble, Captain Smith re-entered the wireless shack about ten minutes after his first visit and asked Phillips to send out a message for assistance. The recently-held Berlin Convention had decided on a new code, 'SOS', as the standard international distress code. It was about to make its debut. In the meantime, Boxhall worked out the position of the ship for transmission to other ships. As it was night he could not take a position and had to rely on 'dead reckoning'. This was a process by which the ship's last known position was taken as a starting point and a new position calculated by taking her speed and bearing since then.

Unfortunately, for whatever reason Boxhall calculated a position that was significantly wrong. This was not known at the time but was confirmed when the wreck was discovered in 1985. There was however plenty of evidence for those who cared to look at it with an open mind that the position was obviously wrong even in 1912. It did not make much difference to those aboard the *Titanic* that night, though it might have done. However, it may have been a significant factor in explaining what became known as 'The *Californian* Incident'.

It was now time to start getting the passengers up on deck. There must be no panic. Perhaps the wireless operators might pick up a ship close at hand. The chances of passenger survival would be made better if those aboard could be encouraged to stay calm. However, it was time to start taking precautionary measures just in case. This would be the job of the stewards.

The approach taken was contingent on what class a passenger happened to be in. In first-class, Steward Henry Etches went to look after his charges, a small, select group including Benjamin Guggenheim. He helped Guggenheim and his secretary dress in their lifebelts, taking them out of the wardrobe where they were stored and putting them on. Guggenheim did not think much of them.

Steward Cunningham also looked after first-class. There was no emergency alarm system onboard so it was up to the stewards to muster all the passengers. The polite and deferential system adopted by the first-class stewards was not replicated by others. The stewards responsible for third-class had large numbers of people to look after and just flung open doors and told those in the cabins to get up. Cunningham on the other hand was a first-class steward with only nine rooms as his responsibility. After making sure all his passengers were organized, in a surreal touch he went round each empty room and turned off the lights. It was a bizarre gesture of normality.

The approach was less deferential in second-class. Steward John Hardy and others went around waking passengers up by throwing doors open and telling them to get up and put lifebelts on. Hardy would later recall that the order to do so was given within five minutes, though this sounds inherently unlikely given the time it would take to assess damage to the ship adequately.

There was much less control in third-class areas. Steerage passenger Olaus Abelseth was on G Deck forward, not far away from Daniel Buckley. He had gone to bed at around 10.00 p.m. When he heard something, he was not quite sure what, he got up to investigate. There was quite a lot of ice on the starboard side of the deck he noticed. The officers around wanted Abelseth and those with him to go back down again but he was not satisfied.

Abelseth was travelling with his brother-in-law and his cousin. They were also accompanying two female passengers across the Atlantic who were quartered towards the stern with the other single women. One of them was a sixteen-year-old girl whose father had asked Abelseth to watch out for until they reached Minneapolis. They eventually all went up on deck together, though some time elapsed before they got there.

The initial response then was for first-class stewards to rouse their passengers but those travelling in second and third-class had far less assistance. Passengers like Abelseth had to show initiative rather than rely on the stewards to tell them what to do. It was natural that in first-class, with stewards looking after a small number of passengers, then there would be more one-to-one attention. However, as the night went on, the disparity in treatment between first-class and the rest would get ever more marked.

But still at this stage for most people there was no sense of panic or urgency. Paul Maugé, who worked in the *a la carte* restaurant, poked his head out of the door but was told by a steward 'there is no danger, it is better that you go to sleep'. There was little sign of imminent disaster and most people aboard still assumed that there was nothing to worry about. The immediate emotion of most people was curiosity rather than fear. Hardly anyone on the *Titanic* had any idea that the ship had just over two hours to live. And those who did know were generally not letting on.

9

Uncovering the Boats:
00.01–00.30, 15 April 1912

Armed with the still fairly private knowledge that the maiden voyage of the world's largest ship was transforming itself into a nightmare of Dante-esque proportions, Captain Smith now had to face the unthinkable. There were twenty boats located on the Boat Deck and they needed to be prepared for use. With over 2,200 souls onboard they also needed to be prepared mentally to use them. They somehow had to be persuaded to leave the largest ship in the world and be lowered 70 feet onto the vast North Atlantic in comparatively tiny lifeboats. This would be no easy task. Everything must be done quietly, in an orderly fashion. Nevertheless, it was now time to uncover the boats.

However, there were some practical issues making the situation even worse than it already was. Four of the boats were collapsibles with sides that had to be pulled up before they were lowered. Two of these were readily accessible on the deck area, the idea being that when the ordinary lifeboats next to them had been lowered away, they could be fitted in the davits and filled too. However, the two stowed on top of the Officer's Cabin would be very difficult to get down onto the Boat Deck, weighing several tons each as they did.

In addition, the lack of a meaningful boat drill was also about to show itself as a critical problem. There had been no instructions issued to the passengers as to which lifeboat they would use in a time of emergency; how could there be when there were not enough lifeboats to go around? It was little better with the crew either. On the Friday before, lists had gone up detailing members of the crew to various lifeboat stations but not everyone seems to have read them or even known of their existence. Even those who did sometimes chose to ignore it on this particular night. And by definition, as only sixteen men had taken part in the cursory lifeboat drill at Southampton, some of them would not even have had a practice at rowing a boat. Indeed, it would later emerge that some of them had never rowed a boat before, full stop.

There was a further problem, one that was effectively a death sentence for nearly 500 people aboard who might otherwise have been saved. It revolved around the so-called 'lowering capacity' of lifeboats, that is how many people could safely be lowered in the boats as opposed to be on them when they were afloat on the water. Second Officer Lightoller epitomized the issue. He had been onboard both when the lifeboats had been tested in the trials in Belfast and also when the boat drill had been held in Southampton but he had never seen a lifeboat filled to anything like its full capacity. He therefore believed there was a risk that, if too many people were put on the boats before they were lowered, then the ropes lowering them would break or the boats might buckle with disastrous results. Such was not the case but Lightoller believed it was, and he would be responsible for supervising the lowering of the boats on the port side.

There was therefore no such thing as a formal drill for loading the boats in place. Lightoller contrasted the Merchant Navy with the more disciplined approach of the Royal Navy. He explained it away by saying that in the Merchant Navy men were expected to show initiative. In his later justification of the lack of formal organization, he was to reveal much about the amateurish nature of the way in which the ship was run. It seemed as if the maxim was for every man to make his own decisions.

Rather than formal organization, it was a case of the officers aboard making it up as they went along. But, to use another cliché, everything would not be alright on this particular night. Instinct, which the Second Officer claimed was the best thing to follow in such situations, would not be sufficient. Lightoller would later claim that the loading of the boats that night went off without a hitch. On an occasion where myths soon began to overlay reality, this would turn out to be one of the more unjustified interpretations of events.

Organization was made more difficult by the noise of steam blowing off through the exhausts now that the engines had been stopped. The sound of this was deafening and officers could barely make themselves heard above the din. The seamen came pouring out on deck. It was too noisy to tell them what to do so hand signals had to suffice for directing them. The boats were uncovered, an act with an ominous symbolism with the *Titanic* alone in the cold, dark sea.

Charles Joughin was Chief Baker on the ship. Each boat was provided with some hard-tack biscuits (in the event many occupants would not be able to find these though few if any really looked) but Joughin now delegated his thirteen men to pick up any loose bread they could find for the lifeboats. They each eventually came up to the Boat Deck carrying four loaves of bread each with them.

Large numbers of passengers were also appearing, their faces understandably etched with fear. Lightoller tried to reassure them with a smile but, even as the covers were taken off the boats, he was aware that the ship was starting to settle. Soon the Bosun's Mate, whom Lightoller had delegated with the task of uncovering the boats, came over to report to him that the job was done. The Second Officer nodded in recognition and intimated that it was time for the boats to be swung out.

As Lightoller prepared the boats, he noticed Bruce Ismay round about. After those fateful discussions with Captain Smith and Andrews on the bridge which confirmed the imminent fate of the *Titanic*, Ismay had gone back to his room, presumably to get some warmer clothes on, and then back up onto the bridge. Here he heard the Captain giving an order to the crew about the loading of boats. He went to the Boat Deck and spoke to one of the officers there (perhaps Pitman) about loading them up. He admitted freely that he started to give orders to the officers: 'I met one of the officers. I told him to get the boat out... ' though he did not recall which officer it was. Then, in his words, he rendered all the assistance he could in putting the women and children in. Throughout it all, he noticed no signs of panic on deck.

In the meantime, some of the passengers had noticed a strangeness about the ship and the way she was sitting in the water. 'Clinch' Smith and Colonel Gracie had by now noticed a list. They did not mention it to any others as they did not wish to alarm them. Smith and Gracie resolved to stay together if a crisis ensued. Gracie pictured the two of them on a raft with no food or water. The two of them went back to their staterooms to prepare themselves for the ordeal ahead. Gracie packed his three large travelling bags so that they could be transferred to another ship should the need arrive. The raft still appeared a very distant possibility.

As he moved through the ship he saw stewards assisting men and women into their lifejackets. Steward Charles Cullen came up to Gracie and helped him to put his on. Returning to A Deck on the port side towards the stern Gracie found the unprotected ladies he had formed an acquaintance with during the trip. These were Mrs Charlotte Appleton, wife of an old school-friend, Mrs Malvina Cornell, wife of a New York judge, and Mrs Caroline Brown, wife of a Boston publisher. They were all sisters, returning home from the funeral of their sibling, Lady Victor Drummond. Also there was Miss Edith Evans, their friend; Gracie had not been introduced to her before and did not yet know her by name.

The Strauses were present too, along with Mr and Mrs Astor, as well as Hugh Woolner, son of a famous English sculptor and H. Björnström Steffanson, a young Swedish army lieutenant; he knew Gracie's wife's relatives back in Sweden. Soon the band began to play. The songs they played were cheerful and not hymns. Gracie was certain that they never played 'Nearer My God to Thee' and later said he would have made a point of noting if they had done so as a particularly inappropriate, even morbid, selection in light of the possible fate that was beginning to loom, hardly calculated to calm the nerves of those aboard.

Jack Thayer had quite early on noticed a list to port (the original list had been to starboard, and presumably changed as successive 'watertight' compartments were filled) and also felt that the ship was distinctly down by the head. After going outside to investigate, the bitter night air forced the Thayers, father and son, back inside into the warmth of one of the lounges. There was a fair crowd gathered now, dazed and unsure what was happening. Just then, Bruce Ismay and Thomas Andrews passed. Knowing Andrews on a social basis, the Thayers asked him what the problem was. He replied quietly that he did not believe that the ship had much more than an hour to live.

It was around 12.15 a.m., that the stewards passed the word around that everyone was to put on their lifebelts. By the time that the Thayers returned to their staterooms, both Mrs Thayer and her maid were fully dressed. Young Jack put on some clothes; a green tweed suit and several jumpers along with his coat. He put on his cork lifejacket and then his overcoat on top. He had after all been outside for the past half an hour and he knew better than most exactly how freezing the night air was.

He then returned to A Deck which was now getting very busy. He bumped into his new-found acquaintance Milton Long and they decided to stick together. There was a great deal of noise by now. The band was doing their best to give a surreal semblance of normality by playing lively numbers but nobody was listening to them. Jack and Long went out on deck and found the boats ready to launch. This was clearly a serious situation but there was as yet no sense of panic or crisis.

Amazingly, onboard the stricken ship the routine of ship life still went on. Lookout George Hogg and his mate still took over from Fleet and Lee at 12.23 a.m. ('old' *Titanic* time which was due to change to midnight to keep the clocks aligned with their longitude). Of course, they might have been invaluable now as the eyes of the ship picking up signs of other ships in the area. It is interesting, perhaps one might think crucial in terms of later allegations against the *Californian*, that they saw no other ship from their lofty eyrie. However, the lookouts, in common with most other crew members, did not seem aware of how serious the situation was. A while later, when Hogg saw people milling around on the decks with lifebelts on, he phoned the bridge to ask if they were still needed in the crowsnest but got no reply.

Down below, Lawrence Beesley was aware of the volume of voices outside his cabin increasing and thought that he should go out and find out what was happening. He decided to dress this time, putting on a thick Norfolk jacket and trousers and then making his way up to the deck. More people were up there now, asking each other what had happened, unaware of any specific problems. The night was so cold that he walked up and down merely to keep warm.

He decided to go down again but as he did so, he passed an officer. He watched as he moved across to Boat 16 and took the cover off. No one seemed to bother too much about this and neither was there any sign of any concern, let alone panic, among the passengers milling around. Yet as he looked down the deck Beesley was sure he saw a tilting downwards towards the bows, as if the ship were listing. It was a sensation that was exaggerated when he walked down the stairs, which seemed to him to be throwing him forwards.

Back on D Deck, where his cabin was situated, he met three ladies engaged in conversation. They asked him why they had stopped, to which Beesley replied that they were now moving again. However, when they insisted that the throb of the engines was absent, he took them to a bathroom and, when they placed their hands on the bath, they could still feel that reassuring vibration (an interesting story this, confirming indeed that the ship's engines did restart for a short time though perhaps slightly later than some suggested). He then went back to his cabin again, passing unconcerned stewards in the corridors as he went.

In his corridor, he met another man, getting dressed and putting a tie on. The stranger laughingly told him to peep in and look at his neighbour. In the top bunk of the room was a man, wrapped up in bed, telling the unwelcome intruders that if they thought he was going out on a freezing deck on a night like this, then they had another thing coming. Beesley returned once more to his room and put on some underclothes. After a gap of about ten minutes, he heard a steward pacing the corridor, shouting: 'All passengers on deck with lifebelts on!'

Beesley put on his lifebelt and started to walk up towards the upper decks but was stopped by a lady who said that she had no lifebelt. He took her back down to F Deck where her cabin was and a steward found it for her. Once more climbing towards the deck, he passed the Purser's office and heard the clanging of a door inside; the Purser, he felt sure, was emptying the safe of some of its more valuable items.

Returning to the top deck, there were a considerable number of people there now. Some were fully dressed, prepared for a cold night, but others seemed to have just thrown on whatever was at hand at the time that might be warm. The ship had stopped again and there was virtually no motion. Looking over the side into the darkness, the water seemed even further below than it actually was. To Beesley, the ship felt like a rock. Onboard, on the top decks at least, all was calm and quiet. Passengers kept out of the way and said little, though the noise of steam escaping from the exhausts was so deafening that they could not have heard each other anyway.

Passengers were still pouring up now (Beesley estimated the time as being about 12.20 a.m.). The crew were working on the lifeboats and, as the crowd watched, the crank-handles on the davits were turned and the boats started to lift and then move towards the side of the Boat Deck. Women and children were then ordered down to the deck below and men to stay where they were. Several women refused to leave their husbands but were persuaded to do so. The separation of women and men started to impress upon some of those present that the situation was perhaps more concerning than they had thought.

Major Peuchen, sensing trouble, had gone to his room to get some heavy clothes on. When he came up towards the Boat Deck, he saw a number of people congregated around the top of the Grand Staircase. Several of the ladies, he noticed, were crying. Mrs Anna Warren, a first-class passenger, had gone back to her room and put on some warm clothes. She and some friends went to the foot of the Grand Staircase on D Deck. As they were there, Mr Andrews rushed by, going up the stairs. When asked if there was any danger, he made no reply. However, another passenger noticed a look of terror in his face. Not long after word arrived that the squash courts were underwater, as was the baggage hold. The forward part of the ship was starting to fill.

The Collyers had been about to turn in again when the sound of quite a few people passing the cabin disturbed Charlotte. The noise they made reminded her of rats running through an empty room. She looked at herself in the mirror and was shocked at how white her face was. She put a dressing gown on over her nightdress and tied her hair up with a ribbon. She noticed that the ship appeared to be tilting slightly as she wrapped Madge up in a blanket. No valuables were picked up for everyone thought they would be back in the room soon, but they now made their way up to the open deck.

Being disturbed, Margaret Brown looked out into the corridor. She saw a man, pale with fright, who told her to get her lifebelt on. He was a buyer from Gimbel Brothers, a company based in Paris and New York. She put her lifebelt on and dressed in her furs. She then made her way up to the A deck where she saw Mrs Bucknell again who reminded her of their premonitory conversation earlier that evening. Some still made light of the situation. Mrs Vera Dick, from Calgary, Canada, was told to put on her lifebelt by a man who told her that 'they are the latest thing this season'.

Others however were shaken from any complacency in the most alarming way. Mrs J.B. Mennell (her married name in Gracie's book; at the time of the disaster she was unmarried Elizabeth Allen) was told by the maid of her aunt that the baggage room was full of water. She replied that she should not worry, as the watertight doors would have been closed and she should go back to her cabin. When she got there (it was on E Deck) it was already filling with water.

Elizabeth Shute passed by the palm room, where just two hours before she had been thrilled by a concert given by the ship's orchestra. She was struck by the surreal nature of the situation. Most of all, that great ship, which for five days had powered across the Atlantic, now lay still, unmoving, the vibrations which had been so marked while she was on the go now worryingly absent. Even the passengers were quiet, standing meekly on the staircase, waiting for instructions. To her, the most unnerving thing was the sight of all those white lifebelts, an unmistakable but quite unnecessary reminder that something was wrong.

Far down below, on *Titanic's* lower decks, the stewards were getting their passengers up and dressed. Steward George Crowe was quartered amidships on the lower deck. When he got up, he saw lots of stewards and steerage passengers moving from forward (where the single male steerage quarters were) to aft. Daniel Buckley heard the stewards going along the corridor, shouting: 'All up on deck! Unless you want to get drowned.'

Buckley made his way to the upper decks with no problem but when he got there he noticed that he did not have a lifebelt when most others did. He went down below to get it but when he returned to the lower decks the water had already risen up four steps. When he arrived back on the lower deck, there were still a number of his fellow passengers down there. The girls, he noted, were excitable and in tears, with the men trying to console them.

Buckley was one of the few third-class survivors to testify at the US Inquiry (better at least than the British equivalent, which did not bother calling any). He was an uncomfortable and sometimes contradictory witness who did not seem to want to metaphorically rock the boat. For example, he said that he was not aware of any attempts to prevent steerage from going up to the boats, but then immediately contradicted himself by saying: 'they tried to keep us down at first on the steerage deck. They did not want us to go up to the first-class place at all'.

However, there is perhaps an explanation for this apparent contradiction. The most likely scenario is that steerage were not kept, like rats waiting to drown, below decks but they were required on the whole to stay in their own above-deck areas and not permitted to trespass into first-class areas. In ordinary circumstances, this would just have reflected the social apartheid of the time. However, in the current case it was a matter of life and death because the Boat Deck was mainly in a first-class area. Therefore, there was discrimination against third-class in favour of both first and second-class, just because of where the boats were.

Buckley corroborates this interpretation when he witnessed such a case of segregation going on. He saw one of the *Titanic's* sailors throw a steerage passenger back over 'a little gate'. This was the barrier between the top of some stairs from down below and the first-class deck. The sailor then locked it but the steerage passenger was furious. He broke the lock and chased after the seaman. The irate passenger did not seem as bothered by escaping as by his desire to catch the errant sailor, saying that if he caught him he 'would throw him in the water'. This was the opening that many steerage passengers were waiting for. After that Buckley noted 'they could not keep them down'.

However, below decks was a rabbit-warren and passengers who did not know their way around might find themselves trapped in a *cul de sac*, literally a dead end. Only one man seems to have done much about this problem, which affected third-class passengers almost exclusively given their location on the ship. His name was Steward John Hart. About three quarters of an hour after the collision, Hart took third-class women and children from third-class to the first-class companionway. He had been given orders to take them to the Boat Deck. It would however take him a long time to get there.

Certainly water was by now pouring into the forward parts of the ship. Able Seaman John Poingdestre had gone back to his quarters to pick up his boots – he reckoned that this was about three quarters of an hour after the collision. He was coming out again when a wooden bulkhead (not a watertight compartment) separating his quarters from third-class suddenly collapsed and water came cascading in. As he made his way back he noticed a large number of third-class passengers from forward along with their luggage. They had escaped from the corridor below but were only in the open area behind the forecastle, still a long way from the Boat Deck.

At some stage some of the firemen and engineers had returned to the engine rooms in an attempt to man the pumps. One of them was trimmer Thomas Dillon. In order to allow the men down below to move around more easily some of the watertight doors were re-opened by hand. Dillon did not remember them ever being shut again.

Titanic's main hope now lay in any ships that might be close at hand that could come to the rescue. This put a huge onus on the ship's wireless operators. The call for help had gone out – 'CQD', the old call, first of all. Bride had laughingly suggested that they should send out the new call, 'SOS', as it might be the last chance they ever had to use it. Captain Smith told him that the berg had struck amidships. The wireless operators (or specifically Phillips, as there was only one set of apparatus) had immediately sent out the message.

Bride, however, does not always come across as a reliable witness and his evidence, certainly for a *New York Times* interview that he gave later, should be treated with a liberal pinch of salt. For example, he stated in this that Phillips had seen the iceberg ten minutes before they struck it. It is not clear how he had done this when Fleet had only seen it from the crows-nest about forty seconds before the ship hit it.

Responses to the messages soon came in. The first was from the *Frankfurt*. Their wireless operator went off to tell his captain the unbelievable news that the new super-liner had struck a berg and was in urgent need of help. By the time he came back across the ether, Bride could already feel the ship starting to sink by the head. Bride, whose job during the time that followed appeared to be the important one of 'go-between' for Phillips whereby he would keep the Captain informed of developments as they emerged, took it to the bridge.

Other messages went out across the waves urging help. On the *Virginian*, the operator was simply not believed at first by the Officer on watch. He was being dismissed from the bridge with a flea in his ear for his warped sense of humour when he kicked the captain's door (he had turned in for the night) and woke him. Only when his report was delivered to the captain in person was he believed and the ship headed in the direction of the position given in the distress call.

The boats were provisioned with food and water but not everyone seemed to know where the provisions were kept as later a number of shortages were later reported. However, they certainly did not have pre-stored lights in them. The lamps were kept in a special room and now it was the job of Samuel Hemming to fetch them and dish them out to each boat. However, he would not manage to do this for all of them.

Far down below attempts were still being made to draw the fires. Leading Fireman Charles Hendrickson had been asked by engineer John Hesketh to fetch some lamps to help light the engine rooms to do this. As he made his way down through the lower decks, he passed through crowds of third-class passengers carrying their trunks and possessions with them away from their flooding quarters. He did not take much notice of them at the time but when he later returned from down below he saw that there were still there, sitting around as if awaiting instructions.

In the meantime, some few miles away (how many was soon to become a matter of heated debate) the *Californian* still lay virtually stationary, just drifting almost imperceptibly in the current. An intriguing tale was to emerge from one of her crew members at a later stage. It came from 'donkeyman' Ernest Gill. He said that he had come up on deck at 11.56 p.m., *Californian* time. The stars were bright, it was very clear and he could see for a long distance. The ship's engines had been stopped at 10.30 p.m. and she was drifting in ice floes. Looking to starboard, he could see a 'large steamer' about 10 miles away moving at full speed. He would later tell the British Inquiry:

It could not have been anything but a passenger boat – she was too large. I could see two rows of lights which I took to be porthole lights and several groups of lights which I took to be saloon and deck lights. I knew it was a passenger boat. That is all I

saw of the ship... She was a good distance off I should say no more than 10 miles and
probably less.

Captain Herbert Stone, Second Officer of the *Californian*, had come on
the bridge at 12.08 a.m., *Californian* time. He also saw a steamer to the
south-south-east, stopped. He saw:

> one masthead light, her red sidelight [displayed on a ship's port side] and some small
> indistinct lights around the deck which looked like portholes or open doors. I judged
> her to be a small tramp steamer and about 5 miles distant.

In fact, it was Lord who briefed him about the other ship when Stone
began his watch. The Captain had told him that they were stopped in the
ice and he did not plan to move again before the morning. He pointed
out the nearby steamer to him, noted that she was stopped and instructed
Stone to tell him if the two ships should drift any closer to each other. Lord
then went below to the Chart Room leaving Stone in charge of the bridge.
He later recalled that it was about 12.10 a.m.

Stone replaced Groves who now also went off watch. Groves went down
to the wireless shack before turning in. He fancied himself as something
of an amateur wireless operator and often tried his hand with Cyril Evans
guiding him. However, Evans was tired and perhaps a trifle miffed after
Titanic's rude rebuff just over an hour before. Groves put the headphones
on but could hear nothing. He did not realize that the dynamo that drove
the power supply had wound down and that there was no charge left in
the apparatus. At about the same time, *Titanic's* wireless operator Jack
Phillips had started to transmit his distress signals.

Apprentice James Gibson came up on the bridge of the *Californian* at
about 12.15 a.m. He shared a coffee with Stone, and Stone pointed out
to him the ship on *Californian's* starboard beam. To both of them (and to
Captain Lord) it appeared to be a ship with one masthead light (though
Third Officer Groves who had seen her earlier thought that she had two).
As Gibson looked over, he saw a flash come from the other vessel. At first
he thought it was a Morse lamp signalling and he started to Morse her
back. However, when he looked through the binoculars he could see that
it was not a Morse lamp messaging them at all but a flickering light.

He could also see a port side light and the faint glare of other lights on
her after deck. He remarked to Stone that she looked like a tramp steamer,
an assessment that the Second Officer agreed with. To Gibson, the ship he
was looking at 'had no appearance at all of a passenger steamer'. At about
12.25 a.m., Gibson went below to pick up a new log. He returned soon
after as he could not find it and then went off the bridge once more, this
time for nearly half an hour.

So the Second Officer and the Apprentice of the *Californian* both felt that they were looking at a tramp steamer, as had Captain Lord. However, Ernest Gill believed that he had seen a passenger steamer; so too did Third Officer Groves. These were two very different sets of views. It would not be the last difference of opinion to emerge about what was seen and done onboard the *Californian* that night. The conflicting, confusing and downright contradictory story of the *Californian* incident was already being written. And, even as it was, the fate of the *Titanic* was becoming more and more certain.

10

Lower Away:
00.31–01.00, 15 April 1912

Some 50 miles south of the *Titanic*, on the more southerly east-bound track and therefore well out of danger, the *Carpathia* was proceeding towards Europe unconcerned by anything other than the normal anxieties of the ship's passengers and crew. Harold Cottam was the only wireless operator onboard the *Carpathia*. Like all such technicians on such 'one-man ships' he did not work regular hours but largely decided them for himself.

The job was not very well paid (about £4 10s a month) but there was a certain glamour about it that attracted a significant number of young men to join up, take the training course and become an operator. His apparatus was not the best available with a normal effective range of about 250 miles, much less than that of the *Titanic* or even the *Californian* for example.

It was pure luck that Cottam was still up, as he normally turned in about midnight. Cottam was waiting for a reply from the *Parisian* to a message he had sent earlier and would otherwise have been in bed with the wireless off. There had as yet been no reply so he then switched over to the Cape Race land station to see if there was anything of interest from there, after which he planned to turn in – the reply he was waiting for was routine and not urgent. He heard a batch of mundane commercial messages from Cape Cod for the *Titanic* and decided to contact her to see if she was aware of them.

He must have been stunned when he got the reply from Phillips on the *Titanic*: 'Come at once. We have struck an iceberg. It's CQD Old Man.'

Betraying his incredulity, Cottam asked: 'Shall I tell my captain? Do you require assistance?

The answer ended any lingering doubts: 'Yes. Come quick.'

Cottam ran to the bridge, where First Officer Dean was on watch. Together they went to see Captain Rostron. The two men barged in without knocking, which irritated the very correct master, a stickler for discipline. However, he reacted in a flash when they passed on the news, though he too was shocked, asking Cottam if he was certain that his information was correct.

On receipt of this almost incredible information, Captain Rostron sparked into life. *Titanic's* distress call was received at 12.35 a.m. *Carpathia* time (Rostron recalled this was 10.45 p.m. New York time). Rostron ordered the ship to be turned around and *then* asked if the radio message was correct. Then came his orders, a meticulous list made all the more impressive as it was improvised under enormous pressure. They are worth mentioning in detail as they give a fascinating insight into the mental prowess of a sea captain of outstanding quality. They included the following provisions:

– The Chief Engineer to summon another watch of stokers and make all possible speed.

– The First Officer (who was currently on watch) to prepare all the lifeboats.

– The English, Italian and Hungarian doctors to deal with First, Second and Third Class survivors respectively. Each doctor to have supplies of stimulants and restoratives on hand.

– Rooms to be freed up to accommodate survivors. These included not only cabins but also dining rooms, smoking rooms and the library.

– Pursers to be ready to receive survivors onboard and prepare a list to be sent by wireless as soon as possible.

– Stewards designated to keep *Carpathia's* own passengers out of the way.

– Coffee, soup, tea etc. to be made available in the saloons along with blankets.

– All boats to be swung out and all gangway doors to be opened.

– A chair slung at each gangway to hoist injured or infirm survivors up onto the ship.

– Ladders to be made ready to hang over the side and canvas and ash bags to be made available to pull small children up.

– Rockets to be prepared to be fired when they got closer to *Titanic's* reported position to reassure those aboard her that help was on the way.

It should be borne in mind that this was not a list that Rostron had hours to think about, it is what he came up with more or less on the spur of the moment. He required that each officer delegated a task report back to him personally to confirm that it had been satisfactorily carried out. This meticulous attention to detail provides a marked and very unflattering comparison to Captain Smith's actions on the *Titanic* that night.

Rostron also differed in another important respect. He of course would have been only too well aware of the dangers of ice from the parlous position that the ship he was trying to aid was in. However, it seems clear enough from his general approach that he would have been cautious with ice around anyway. Aware of the risk he was taking, he put on extra lookouts; he had two men placed forward on the deck and one in the crow's nest. It was, he later said, always his policy to post a man forward in times of risk as they would often spot objects in front of them before the lookout in the crow's nest would.

After passing on the shock news to Rostron, Cottam returned to his post, wide awake now. A few minutes later he picked up a conversation with the *Frankfurt*. Then another message came in for the *Titanic* from her older sister, *Olympic*. The *Titanic* did not pick it up; Cottam asked the *Titanic* if she had received it and she said no, so Phillips then made contact with his opposite number on the *Olympic*.

As the reply from the *Carpathia* came in, Bride took it to Captain Smith on the bridge. It cannot have been entirely good news; Rostron's predicted arrival time of four hours later would leave *Titanic* at the bottom of the North Atlantic for a good couple of hours at least and probably more. However, it was better than nothing and maybe other ships might be raised via wireless. Clearly, Smith was concerned as he came back to the wireless shack with Bride. *Olympic* was now in communication too though she was much further away, far too far to be of any practical use.

When Bride went to tell Captain Smith of the *Carpathia's* response, he had to push through a crush of people to do so. Then he returned to the shack, where Phillips told him to get dressed. In the excitement, Bride had forgotten that he had not done so. He went to his cabin, put on his clothes and returned with an overcoat for Phillips, as the night was icy cold. From then on, he went to the Captain's cabin every few minutes with updates.

In the meantime, the *Frankfurt* did not reply to the initial message from the *Titanic* for another twenty minutes and when she did come back her message was vague; she clearly had not understood how serious things were. However, the seriousness of the situation did not seem to have dawned yet on Jack Phillips either. Rather than exercise some patience, Phillips – by now in communication with the *Carpathia* whose operator clearly *had* grasped the full extent of the *Titanic's* plight – told the *Frankfurt's* operator that he was a 'fool' and to stay out of future conversations.

This was extraordinary, especially as the *Frankfurt's* signal was so strong that the *Titanic's* operators thought she was quite close, though as it happened she was too far away to provide practical assistance in time anyway. Another ship, the *Mount Temple*, had later been in communication with the *Frankfurt* which helped confirm her position, which was too far to the west to be of use.

At the American Inquiry that was held after the loss of the *Titanic*, Senator Smith, the Chairman, was quite rightly much disturbed at this flippant attitude on the part of the *Titanic's* operator and suggested strongly that the sinking liner should have tried to explain her situation more patiently even if the *Frankfurt's* operator was indeed a 'fool'; this was no time for *prima donnas*. Other ships were picked up too, such as the *Baltic*, too far off to be of assistance (about 350 miles) but informed by the *Caronia* of the *Titanic's* precarious position anyway.

At 12.30 a.m. (ship's time) Captain James Moore, skipper of the *Mount Temple*, had been awakened with a message from the Marconi operator. It had come in from the *Titanic*; it ended 'come at once. Iceberg'. Moore went to the Chart Room, worked out the ships' relative positions and steered east. They were about 49 miles away, he calculated (though this was understated by at least 8 miles because Boxhall had worked out *Titanic's* position incorrectly). Before setting off, he gave instructions that the 'fireman' should be woken up; if necessary, he was to be given a tot of rum to encourage him; an interesting management technique that one is unlikely to see copied in the modern world.

As the night went on, the *Mount Temple* would be a distant observer of other wireless messages sent to the *Titanic*. She picked up several from the *Olympic*, (500 miles away from the *Titanic*) asking first of all 'are you steering south to meet us', which clearly intimated that the seriousness of the situation was not at all clear to *Titanic's* sister.

Others picked up the distress call too but were too far distant to get there in time to make a difference. Gilbert Balfour was a travelling inspector for the Marconi Company and was onboard the *Baltic* when he picked up *Titanic's* CQD. The ship immediately turned around but was in no position to help though it did not stop her doing her best.

By the time that *Titanic's* boats were swung out and ready to lower, the water was already nearly level with the deck at her bows. Yet revealingly Lightoller still did not think that the ship would sink. In his evidence in New York, where he generally said as little as possible, this was one question that seemed to put him on the defensive. When asked why he did not take more risks when lowering these first boats, he said emphatically: 'I did not know it was urgent then. I had no idea it was urgent.'

Here was a strange chain of events. The man tasked with lowering the lifeboats had not yet been told by his captain that his ship was going to founder. It is a shame; maybe Lightoller might have thought about putting on a few more people if he had known the grave extent of the damage that had been caused to the ship.

Lightoller had been to see the Captain to suggest that the lifeboats should be lowered with women and children loaded. Again, this is suggestive. The Second Officer suggests to the Captain what should be done, not the other way round. It seems as if Captain Smith, overwhelmed by the magnitude of the disaster which now not only loomed but was unavoidable, had retreated into a shell and left the decision-making to others. Nothing could have been more undesirable at such a time. A firm hand was needed but no one was there to provide it.

Lightoller saw Captain Smith several times during the rest of the ship's life but the Captain seems to have been surprisingly peripheral. The Second Officer would later have a vague recollection of seeing his Captain on the bridge towards the end. His last direct orders to Lightoller, given now, were to lower away women and children. However, this is not a decisive instruction but a response to Lightoller's own suggestion that he should start to lower the boats.

It was a similar story for Third Officer Pitman. When he first got up to the Boat Deck, he saw Bruce Ismay. Pitman did not immediately recognize Ismay, though it slowly dawned on him who he was. Uncertain what to do, Pitman was soon chivvied up by Ismay who said quietly that 'there is no time to waste', a clear sign that the White Star Chairman was well aware how serious the problem was. Unsure what he should do, Pitman made his way to Captain Smith and told him that Ismay wished him to lower the boats. Smith replied: 'Go ahead, carry on.' Again, the Captain was responding to a question from his officer rather than taking proactive control of the situation.

Lawrence Beesley believed that Ismay transmitted the seriousness of the accident to many of the officers on deck. This begs a serious question, namely why Captain Smith did not proactively issue orders for the boats to be filled rather than rely on a company official to take the initiative in doing so. Smith also does not seem to have informed Lightoller of the parlous situation they were in which exacerbated an already dangerous state of affairs when the boats started to lower away soon after.

That lack of pro-activity was to have disastrous repercussions. Without clear instructions to follow, Lightoller decided to lower boats, with the exception of a few crew members to row, almost exclusively with women and children. While this might appear initially to be a gallant and chivalric gesture, it was one founded perhaps more on romanticism than common sense for many of the first boats to leave from the port side, where Lightoller was loading, were to go away half full.

At a later enquiry into the disaster, Lightoller would be directly asked why he had adopted this policy, which contributed significantly towards the loss of 500 lives that might have been saved. The Second Officer insisted that he had not filled the boats up more because he did not consider it safe to do so as the weight of a full boat might cause the ropes lowering her to break (evidently not correct as later on some would be lowered when nearly full). He repeatedly insisted later on emphasizing the difference between the lowering capacity and the floating capacity of a lifeboat. When pushed on the point as to why these first boats in particular were so empty, Lightoller came back with the damning reply 'because I did not know it was urgent then'.

This requires just a moment's reflection to see just how complete an indictment of the lack of leadership on the *Titanic* that night this comment is. Captain Smith and Thomas Andrews had been in early discussions when it appeared that the survival of the ship was highly unlikely. However, the Captain had not seen fit to let his Second Officer, who was taking a leading role in loading the boats, in on the secret. It appears that the enormity of the crisis was overwhelming the great ship's captain.

Perhaps because of this lack of information, there was no panic in the loading of the boats until much later. The men, who were debarred from access on the port side, made no attempt to rush the boats; 'they could not have stood quieter if they had been in a church', Lightoller recalled. Seamen were deputed both to row the boats when they were afloat but also to help lower them, though there were too few of them and Lightoller would have trouble in manning them properly.

Boats with odd numbers were on the starboard side and were loaded mainly under the supervision of First Officer William Murdoch. The rule here was women and children first but men could go if there was room left for them. Those boats with even numbers were on the port side and were loaded under the watch of Lightoller. The rule here was women and children only. This was a policy followed with virtually no flexibility, an approach that sentenced dozens of men to death.

As Jack Thayer went out on deck, the noise of the steam escaping from the Titanic's funnels was still deafening. Jack and Milton Long tried to converse for a time but it was pointless so they went back inside into the crowded entrance hall where it was also much warmer. While they were there, they heard the stewards pass the word around that there were boats for them on the port side. Jack said goodbye to his mother and her maid at the top of the stairs on A Deck. The women then made their way out to the Boat Deck. Unknown to him, they were making for Boat Number 4, the launching of which would be a total fiasco.

Thayer father and son then made their way to the starboard side, probably thinking that this was where their boats would be lowered from. They could not understand what was happening; everybody was waiting for orders and no one was giving them. Few knew where their boat was as there had been no lifeboat drill. It was noisy but the deck was still well lit. People generally kept out of the way, letting the crew get on with their jobs, whatever they might be. Some second and third-class passengers soon started to arrive, making the crowd even larger.

The Collyers stood together waiting for a boat. Charlotte did not recognize anyone else around her and could not see anyone from first-class. Suddenly she saw a stoker come up from down below, his fingers badly cut, so much so that she thought they had been amputated. The sight suddenly sent a sensation of fear coursing through her. She noticed that

First Officer Murdoch put guards by the gangways to stop anyone else coming up from down below.

Boat 4 was supposed to be the first boat lowered away, armed with orders to go around to the gangway. The Bosun's Mate was sent with a party of men to go and open the lower deck gangway door but they were never seen again, probably trapped in the maze of corridors as the invading sea rushed in. However, thanks to an aberration on Lightoller's part, this boat would not reach the water for over an hour.

The problem was that Lightoller ordered it lowered to A Deck. There were hawsers there that he thought he could tie the boat up against the side of the ship with. However, he forgot that this area was enclosed. He sent a steward down to open the windows but then decided that he might as well lower them from the Boat Deck after all. He had though in the meantime sent passengers like Mrs Emily Ryerson down to A Deck along with other women and children. Here they waited for further instructions, unaware for the moment that Lightoller had changed his mind. This was not a good time to be making things up as you went along.

The first steps had been taken to lower the boats. Another harrowing suggestion of the serious situation the ship was in was about to appear. Captain Smith now decided that the ship should start to launch distress rockets. The task was delegated initially to Fourth Officer Boxhall. He pulled the rockets out of their storage cupboard and prepared one to fire. It shot up into the air, bursting at several hundred feet, exploding in a shower of white stars. There was a thud like a mortar shell. From the decks of the *Titanic*, necks craned upwards, those watching all of a sudden terribly aware of the danger they were in.

Fifth Officer Harold Lowe had been standing by Boat 3 when the first distress rocket flared up. It lit up the whole deck and there was a loud explosion which he found 'deafening'. It illuminated the nearby figure of Bruce Ismay, whose face must have been a picture of disbelief and shock. Lowe noticed that the Boat Deck was not crowded; just a 'little knot of people' gathered around the door of the gymnasium. There was still no sign of panic, yet the firing of the first rocket ratcheted up the tension by another notch.

The man-made stars bursting in the sky above the still ship woke people up to the emerging crisis. Everyone on the deck looked up in alarmed fascination as the rocket shot up into the ebony night and then erupted above them. As others started to follow, those aboard the *Titanic* now knew without a doubt that their ship, the 'practically unsinkable' vessel that was the biggest moving object ever built by man, was in distress.

As Beesley stood on the deck, two ladies approached a nearby officer and asked him if they could go onto the Boat Deck. He told them that they could not but should instead go to their own boats, pointing them elsewhere. They were second-class passengers and Beesley took the officer's actions as a sign that a form of class discrimination was being applied to filling the boats, though of course there is some logic in what the officer was saying as there were boats in the second-class part of the Boat Deck. However, when the policy was examined more closely it did not make sense at all; there were boats in first and second-class areas but none in third so where were third-class passengers supposed to go?

At this very moment, a rumour went around the starboard deck where Beesley was standing. It was to the effect that all male passengers were being lowered from the port side. Nothing, it transpired, could be further from the truth as Lightoller, who was in charge on that side, was lowering women and children only. But most of the men did make their way to the port side, leaving the starboard Boat Deck area virtually deserted. It was a sequence of events that, as Beesley later realized, led to his own personal salvation.

As he stood there (Beesley reckoned that the time was about 12.40 a.m.), a cellist from the ship's orchestra came round the corner, rushing down the deck and banging his cello on the planking as he did so. Beesley then looked over the side and saw that several boats were in the water. Officer Murdoch also leaned over and shouted to the boats to go around to the gangway door and wait to take off more passengers there. Murdoch then turned and walked back to the port side.

Boxhall started to fire these rockets off at roughly five minute intervals. It is debatable if this was in line with international distress regulations, which prescribed that rockets were to be fired off at short intervals – was five minutes a 'short interval' or not? But there was now a ray of hope for those on the ship. A light had been spotted just off the *Titanic's* sagging bow. She was close enough for Captain Smith to tell Boxhall to try and contact her with a Morse lamp (a device that flashed out messages in Morse Code by sending light signals to match the 'dots' and 'dashes' of the code). This in itself suggested that she appeared to be quite close for it was unlikely that a Morse Lamp would be seen more than 10 miles away.

Boxhall was not sure of the colour of this other ship's lights at first but looked at her more closely through his binoculars. He first saw her two masthead lights, then her red side light. The distance that a red light was required to be visible for was 2 miles, again an indicator of how close the other ship was; Boxhall, who recalled that she had 'beautiful lights', estimated she was about 5 miles off, making allowances for the clearness of the night. He was also convinced that the ship he could see was moving. He had seen her green (starboard) sidelight at one stage but for most of the time could see her red (port) light. Captain Lord later told how his ship, somewhere to the north, slowly swung round after midnight because of the current 'and showed him [the ship nearby] our red light'. This too might be regarded as significant.

Boxhall's evidence about the ship he was watching moving towards them was one of Captain Lord's strongest arguments against the mystery ship being the *Californian*. Just about the only thing all witnesses from the *Californian* agree on is that the ship was motionless all night, apart from a very slow drift. If a ship was seen to be moving therefore, the argument ran, it could not be the *Californian* that the *Titanic's* people could see.

The only problem with this apparently flawless argument is that Boxhall's evidence was contradicted by a number of other witnesses. Others who saw the light give very different accounts. Second Office Lightoller thought she was 'perfectly stationary', Pitman said that the light he saw had 'no motion in it, no movement'. Lowe saw the lights at two intervals an hour apart and they seemed to be in the same place while Fleet said: 'It never moved.' Steward Alfred Crawford also thought that they did not move. However, Quartermaster Hichens took the opposite view, telling the British Inquiry that 'the light was moving, gradually disappearing'. William Lucas saw the light and thought that it got further away every time they looked at it.

The eye-witness evidence of a stationary ship accords exactly with the situation aboard the *Californian* that night. Crawford in particular noted that the ship he could see was not at anchor – how could she be in the middle of the ocean – but was one that was moving irregularly because of the wind and current. That too was exactly what was happening to the *Californian*. But against that, the evidence of Boxhall, Lucas and Hichens suggests that the opposite was the case. The enigma of the so-called '*Californian* incident' that would later unfold is dogged by such contradictory evidence meaning that analysts can make pretty much what they want of it, ignoring some evidence and using other items to support their case as they wish.

Another contradictory witness now makes a re-appearance. At around 12.30 a.m., *Californian* time, Ernest Gill of that ship said he went out on deck for a cigarette. By this time, he could not see the ship he had spotted earlier. About ten minutes later he saw a rocket, which he thought was a shooting star. However when he saw another flash in the sky he realized what it was and was certain that it was a signal from a ship in distress. But he did nothing and, assuming the officers on the bridge would see it, he went back to bed. He was awoken at 6.30 a.m. next morning by the Chief Engineer of the *Californian* who told everyone to get up and prepare to render assistance as the *Titanic* had gone down.

Back on the *Titanic*, news had by now started to reach the passengers that a ship was on its way according to the wireless operators. This buoyed their spirits. Gracie pointed out to some of his fellow voyagers a white light on a ship 'which I took to be about 5 miles off and which I felt sure was coming to our rescue'. J.J. Astor asked Gracie to point it out, which he did. However, the light would prove to be a devastating disappointment; 'instead of growing brighter the light grew dim and less and less distinct and passed away altogether'.

When the order to lower away had been given, Gracie had escorted his charges up to the Boat Deck from A Deck. He saw Sixth Officer

J.P. Moody barring the progress of all men passengers to the boats. He also saw a baker bringing out bread onto the deck to be loaded into the lifeboats, one of Joughin's entourage. One of Gracie's *coterie*, Miss Evans, told the Colonel that a fortune teller had told her to 'Beware of water' and that 'she now knew she would be drowned'.

Gracie then went to look for two acquaintances, Mrs Helen Candee and Mr Edward Kent. On the way he met Frank Wright, the squash professional onboard and remarked that they might have to postpone their game arranged for the morning after. Wright smiled hiding the truth; he knew that the squash court was already underwater.

Gracie returned to his stateroom to find it locked (he was looking for blankets). Steward Cullen told him that this was to prevent looting. They then went to get blankets together from the stewards' quarters. Gracie then went forward along A Deck still looking for his friends. In the smoking room, he found Archie Butt, military aide to President Taft, Clarence Moore and Francis Millet, the well-known artist (plus one unidentified individual) playing cards. No one else was there but they were playing as if they did not have a care in the world. Gracie never saw any of them again although a lady would tell him that she had seen Butt on the bridge just minutes before the last lifeboat rowed away (Gracie thinks it more likely that he stayed where he was; most of the card players bodies were never found though Millet's was).

Gracie then returned to the port side, hovering between the Boat Deck and A Deck. He rejoined 'Clinch' Smith who told him that Mrs Candee was already off in a boat. He was on the Boat Deck when he heard the first rocket and then witnessed the *Titanic* Morsing for help. He saw no response from the ship in the distance and now feared for the first time that the *Titanic* might sink before all the lifeboats could be launched.

Boat 7 on the starboard side was probably the first one to be launched. Lookout Archie Jewell was in the boat (an odd statistic; there were six lookouts aboard *Titanic* and all of them survived). First Officer Murdoch had ordered women and children to the boats and then ordered Number 7 lowered away. The boat was to stand by the gangway. She remained the nearest to the *Titanic* for a time, even after other boats were lowered.

Mrs Helen Bishop, a first-class passenger, was also on the boat. She had been on deck and had seen the Captain tell Astor something in an undertone. Astor came over to Mrs Bishop, in a group of six women, and told them they should put their lifebelts on (they had left these down below). They all went to put them on and when they returned found very few people on deck. Mrs Bishop was pushed into the boat with her husband, Dickinson Bishop, and it was lowered with twenty-eight people aboard. Five people were transferred on to the boat from another one at a later stage but then she was rowed away to avoid the suction expected when the great ship went down.

French aviator Pierre Maréchal also got in. There was no rush at the boats, everything was calm and orderly. He heard no order of 'women and children first' or 'women and children only'. James McGough, another first-class passenger, also got in. He had also gone down to get his lifejacket and when he returned he saw the boats were being loaded. He said he *did* recall an order of 'women and children first'. There was some hesitation before anyone got into the boats. McGough insisted he was pushed in the boat by one of the officers (though of course such claims might be treated with cynicism; it was not 'heroic' for a first-class man to survive this disaster).

There was a significant sense of 'survivor guilt' among the men who survived the wreck. This was compounded by the veneer of heroism that contemporary society attached to those who went down on the ship. Men, especially first-class men, were supposed to go down with the *Titanic* after giving up their places for women and children aboard. It was therefore difficult to explain how over fifty first-class men survived.

McGough was a perfect example of the dichotomy. He said that he was forced into Boat 7 so that he could row, implying there were not enough men in it. This does not make sense. There were fifteen men in this boat out of a total of twenty-eight people (he says there were forty). McGough's account hints at several pieces of what would now be called 'spin'. As well as his unconvincing reasons for his presence in the boat, his over-estimation of the number of people aboard in total was typical of virtually every account that appeared that discussed the subject of how many people were on each boat.

Quartermaster Alfred Olliver fumbled for the plug between the feet of the people in Boat 7 as it was lowered. When it hit the water, the sea started to rush in and Olliver had to scramble around to put the plug in properly. But at last she was safely down. Onboard her, those who had been lowered away looked up the huge sides of the ship, like a cliff towering above them in the darkness, not quite believing the situation that they were in.

As Lightoller passed along to Number 6 boat, he was conscious of the band playing '*jazz*' in the background. He was not a fan of such music but it gave a reassuring veneer of normality at a time like this. It would be lowered away just before 1.00 a.m. Capable of carrying sixty-five people, there were about twenty-eight aboard, a fitting precedent for what was to follow under Lightoller's watch. It would under the command of Quartermaster Hichens, the same man who had been at the helm when the berg had struck and had tried desperately to avoid it.

First-class passenger 'Madame de Villiers' appeared, dressed in a nightgown and slippers; Margaret Brown noticed she had no stockings on but that she had a long woollen motoring overcoat over her. Realizing the seriousness of the situation where presumably she had not done so before, she was going to go back to her cabin to pick up her valuables when Mrs

Brown talked her out of it. After some hesitation, 'Madame de Villiers' got into the lifeboat.

'Madame de Villiers' however did not exist. She was in fact Berthe Antonine Mayné, a Belgian cabaret singer. Her life story might come as a surprise to those who think this was a puritanical, prudish era. She was described in one contemporary publication as 'being well known in Brussels in circles of pleasure, and was often seen in the company of people who like to wine and dine and enjoy life' – the last phrase in particular might be a hint at all kinds of vices. During the winter of 1911, she had met a young Canadian hockey player, Quigg Baxter, while performing. The two soon became lovers. 'Madame de Villiers' had been installed in first-class cabin C90. Now she bade farewell to Baxter on the deck of the *Titanic*. A tragic *denouement* to this passionate affair was fast approaching.

Mrs Brown in the meantime started to walk away to see what was happening elsewhere. However, she had barely moved when someone caught her by the arm insisting that she too got in a boat. She was dropped 4 feet into the lifeboat. As the boat was lowered it was nearly swamped by a stream of water coming through a porthole from D Deck. Margaret Brown grabbed an oar and pushed the boat away from the side of the deck. When they reached the water, as flat as a millpond, she looked up and saw Captain Smith looking down at them. He told them to pull for the light in the distance.

Mrs Helen Candee, also in Boat 6 (the lady that Gracie had been looking in vain for), handed an ivory miniature of her mother to Mr Edward Kent (it was later recovered from his body). He was reluctant to take it, perhaps seeing it as a bad omen or having a premonition that he would not survive. When the boat was half lowered, it was noticed that there was only one man in it. Lightoller looked for a volunteer and Major Peuchen climbed out along a spar and down a rope into it, drawing on skills he had gained as an experienced yachtsman. As the boat began to be lowered, Peuchen was conscious of rockets being fired off and exploding over the ship.

The shortage of men in Boat 6 had arisen because of some confusion in loading it. Seaman Samuel Hemming had been in the boat helping to load it and Lightoller had assumed he would go with it. However, Hemming had stepped out of the boat at the last minute, thinking that he was more useful on deck. Unaware of the fact, Lightoller had lowered the boat with only one man aboard, hence the need for Peuchen's acrobatic performance. Peuchen anyway later wondered why boats were not being lowered with more people in them. However, he later had to live down the fact that he was a man who had survived the *Titanic* – a quite nonsensical attitude given the fact that he had been ordered into a half-empty lifeboat with hardly any men in it to row it.

Peuchen commented later on the perfect discipline on the ship. He also noticed 'about 100' stokers on deck before the boat was launched; an officer came along and drove them all off the boat deck as if they had no right to be there. However, Mrs Candee also noticed this but saw it rather differently, praising the men for the way in which they obeyed the order when they could have overrun the boat if they had wished. She also noted the brave behaviour of her steward; when she advised him to save himself too, he replied that there was 'plenty of time for that' – he would not survive.

When Mrs Candee entered the boat, she slipped on the oars and broke her ankle. The lowering of the boat proved difficult and jerky; and she was in agony but also terrified that the boat at one stage would be swamped. On getting onto the boat, Peuchen had fumbled in the dark for the plug. He could not find it. Hichens shouted: 'Hurry up, this boat is going to founder!' Peuchen thought he meant the lifeboat but he did not; he meant the *Titanic*. Lookout Frederick Fleet and Peuchen were then responsible for the rowing.

They later discovered an 'Italian' 'stowaway' in the boat; he had a broken wrist and was no help in the rowing. However, this disdainful slur with its racist connotations that Peuchen directed implicitly at him was unwarranted on two counts. It seems likely that he was an injured boy ordered in by the Captain, and Mrs Candee also did not think that he was an Italian.

Frederick Fleet could see a white light. The boat's untrained crew headed for it, shining brightly over on their port bow. But it seemed to be pulling away from them all the time. It is interesting that Fleet, who had not been able to see a light from the crow's nest where he had been until 12.23 a.m. could now see one when he was almost at sea level half an hour later.

Major Peuchen could also see something but believed it to be a reflection, 'an imaginary light' as he called it rather than a genuine sign of hope. Mrs Lucian Smith, also in Boat 6, believed it to be a star. Peuchen thought that it was to the north of *Titanic*, a compass bearing he worked out from the direction of the Northern Lights (though not everyone agreed; Third Officer Pitman thought it was to the west). Lightoller, when lowering the boat, had told Hichens, who was in charge of it, to 'pull toward that light'. Hichens, who thought he was looking at a trawler, proceeded to do so.

Peuchen's comments on the light are interesting, as they suggest just how many different versions of it many witnesses saw that night. Peuchen did not think that:

> from my knowledge of yachting that it was a boat light. The northern lights were very strong that night. It might have been some reflection on ice. I was not satisfied it was the light of a steamer by any means.

Contrast this view of a yachtsman and a man who was on his fortieth trans-Atlantic crossing, with that of an experienced sailor like Fourth Officer Boxhall who believed that he *was* looking at a steamer with green and red lights showing and you have a neat example of the dichotomy of evidence concerning any so-called 'mystery ship'.

There were though a large number of witnesses who saw the light, though they did not agree on what kind of ship it was or indeed if it was a ship at all. Quartermaster Alfred Olliver, in Boat 5, could not be sure whether the light he could see belonged to a ship or a star. But Able Seaman George Moore's boat, Number 3, which would be launched soon after, rowed for a bright light just 2–3 miles away on the starboard bow. He thought it was a trawler.

With the loading of the boats underway, Lightoller would get into a rhythm. Each boat was lowered until its gunwales were level with the Boat Deck. He would then stand with one foot on the gunwales, the other on the deck, take women and children by the arm and virtually lift them over the gap. Two crew men were deputed to accompany each boat but it was not long before he was short of them. With the ship now starting to dip lower, it was important that he developed an efficient loading process.

Third Officer Pitman was loading up Boat 5. There was a big crowd around the boat. He asked for more women but there were none to be seen so he let a 'few' men in – this does not ring true, as statistics prepared later suggest that there were as many men as women in the boat. The embarrassment felt by male survivors who did not live up to the heroic idealistic picture that was later developed was evidenced by Pitman's subsequent statements to the US Inquiry. Here he stated that there were half a dozen men in the boat – other evidence suggests that there were in fact at least ten. Murdoch told Pitman he was in charge and to row around to the gangway and take more passengers off. By the time the boat was lowered away, Trimmer Hemming had not managed to provide her with a light.

Steward Etches also perpetuated the myth of men giving up their places for women. He later said that Boat 5 took in thirty-six ladies. However, there were only forty people in the boat, of whom fifteen or more were men. Bruce Ismay was on the scene. He called out asking if there were any more women to be loaded. One appeared, a stewardess, who was loaded onto the boat. She would not initially get in because 'I am only a stewardess'. Bruce Ismay said: 'No matter, you are a woman, take your place.'

As the boat was being lowered, a German-American physician, Doctor Frauenthal and his brother, jumped in. This created some controversy. Mrs Annie Stengel, a first-class passenger, was on the boat. She stated that her husband, Charles, drew back from the boat but that four men proceeded to jump in as it was being lowered; these presumably included Frauenthal and his brother, who was also there. Frauenthal she thought weighed about 250 pounds and was wearing two life preservers. He wanted to be with his wife, who was also in the boat. This was perhaps understandable as they had only been married for two weeks. However, on the way in he struck Mrs Stengel forcefully, breaking several of her ribs.

First-class passenger Norman Chambers also got in, he said because his wife would have got out if he did not. But all this nonsense about men getting into the boats was rather fatuous. There was still room for twenty-five passengers in the boat when it was lowered and there were no women around. Mrs Stengel also protested too much (though perhaps her cracked ribs provided some justification); her husband later got off in another boat. Another first-class passenger, George Harder, said that the lowering of the boat was jerky but they got down safely enough. There was trouble with getting the plug in and also cutting the boat free from the *Titanic*. He suggests there were hardly any men on the boat, which is simply not true.

While on the Boat Deck, Chambers could hardly hear himself think, the terrific noise of steam escaping making it virtually impossible to hear anybody in the vicinity. As his boat was being filled, he did hear an officer say 'that is enough before lowering. We can get more in after she is in the water'. His boat was then lowered. Damning the sailors responsible for looking after the boats with faint praise, Chambers later remarked harshly but truthfully:

> We were then lowered away in a manner which I would consider very satisfactory, taking into account the apparent absolute lack of training of the rank and file of the crew.

Mrs Anna Warren said that by the time she reached the Boat Deck there were not many people there. She also heard a deafening roar of escaping steam. Mr and Mrs Astor were close by but did not try and get in this boat but went back inside (perhaps J.J. Astor's best chance to survive had been missed). When it came to the time to lower the boat, both men and women moved towards it. Mr Warren was assisting women on the deck elsewhere and she did not see him again. The boat was only lowered she thought with great difficulty and Mrs Warren was worried that the boat would be swamped when it hit the sea.

Also onboard Number 5 was Paul Maugé, clerk in the Ritz kitchen. He had been billeted in third-class quarters. He awoke after the collision and went up to see what was going on. He went to wake up the chef and then returned through the second-class saloon. Here, he saw that the kitchen assistants were not allowed up onto the boat deck. When Maugé saw the boat being lowered, he jumped into it. He advised the chef to copy his example but he was too portly to do so. Once Maugé was in the boat he told the chef to jump once more but again he was unwilling to do so. As the boat was lowered, members of the crew still onboard the *Titanic* tried to pull Maugé out but were unable to do so. He saw no passengers being prevented from entering the Boat Deck but thought he was let past because he was not dressed like a member of the crew.

There was some debate about how many these boats would hold. First-class passenger George Harder, who had come aboard at Cherbourg, counted thirty-six people in the boat. He was aware that it was said that the boats would hold sixty people but he did not believe they could; even with this number in, she seemed full. It is not immediately obvious how then some boats were filled by the end of the night with twice as many people as this.

Fifth Officer Lowe had helped to load the boat and had almost come to blows with Bruce Ismay in the process. Ismay was desperate to get the boats off as quickly as possible. According to the officer, he was 'overanxious and he was getting a trifle excited'. Urged to move more quickly, the hot-headed Welshman turned on him and told him:

> If you will get the hell out of it I shall be able to do something. Do you want me to lower away quickly? You will have me drown the lot of them.

Ismay, publicly berated, sloped off to Boat 5. Seasoned older hands looked on in horror, sure that there would be a reckoning at a later stage.

Third Officer Pitman ordered the boat to pull far enough away to avoid suction when the *Titanic* went down. As they moved away, they realized that the ship was going down slowly by the head. The full horror of what was slowly happening to the great ship was more apparent from the sea than it was onboard. However, even then there were still those who thought that the ship would not sink. Pitman was convinced she would stay afloat. It would be another hour before he believed the ship was doomed.

This might be why these first boats were lowered with spaces for many others on them. It was a policy that inspired perhaps one of the most memorable quotes of that memorable night. Stoker Walter Hurst watched on disbelievingly and commented: 'If they are sending the boats away, they might as well put some people in them.'

It was a problem that Dr Washington Dodge noticed too. He watched on as the boats began to be lowered. He was not impressed by what he saw. Not a boat would pull away he noted that would not have taken between ten and twenty-five more people. He saw no women or children on decks and observed that, as soon as everyone in the immediate vicinity had been got aboard, the boats were lowered away. This made sense provided that all passengers had been brought to the Boat Deck so that they could take their places in the boats. This of course was not the case. If there was no one else to load and the boats were being lowered only half full, yet there were not enough places available for half those aboard, then huge numbers of passengers were being kept in some place other than the Boat Deck. Major Peuchen was insistent:

> Every woman on the port side was given an opportunity. In fact, we had not enough women to put into the boats. We were looking for them. I cannot understand why we did not take some men. The boats would have held more.

Here were several valid observations. Firstly, there were no more women or children to load but a number of them would be lost. Therefore, there were not proper arrangements in place for making sure that all the women and children were being brought up to the Boat Deck.

Also, Lightoller and Wilde on the port side should have been allowing more men into the boats. For men to give up their lives to let women off in the boats might be regarded as chivalrous. For them to give up their lives when boats were being lowered half empty might be regarded as pointless.

But even the officers seemed unsure how many a boat could safely hold. Lowe reckoned that the maximum lowering capacity of a sixty-five-person boat was fifty. This was twice as many as Lightoller, who reckoned that the lowering capacity was an incredible twenty-five people only. There were also problems emerging concerning the number of seamen available to row. A number had been sent to open gangway doors so that more people could get off when the boats were in the water. They never returned and were presumably lost. Now some boats were being lowered with hardly any seamen in them. A proper boat drill might have helped.

Stewardess Violet Jessop was now up on deck after staying down in her cabin in the 'glory hole', as the steward's quarters were known, for a while after the collision. She and her room-mate remained there for a time until a steward came to fetch them, hurrying them up as, he explained, the boat was sinking and they needed to get off. There was a bizarre exchange while they argued about what to wear including which hat was the most appropriate attire to wear in a lifeboat.

When she went outside, the coldness of the night air had caught Violet by surprise so she went below to pick up more clothes. Passing an open cabin, she saw an eiderdown, which she went in to get. She threw it around her shoulders. She noticed the empty rooms, still well lit, with jewels left lying on dressing-room tables and in one a pair of silver slippers thrown off carelessly by someone in their haste to get dressed and away.

On her way back to the Boat Deck, she had passed a group of four officers casually standing and chatting. They smiled and waved in recognition as she passed. She later said that the four men were Captain Smith, Ismay, Purser McElroy and Doctor O'Loughlin though as she supplied these names four decades after the event we cannot be sure that her memory was not mistaken.

On her way up, she also passed a young woman remonstrating with an officer who was refusing to allow her father to accompany her into a boat. He had explained that the decks must be cleared of women and children before any men would be allowed through. She had then met Jock Hume, the violinist of the band, who were getting ready to play at the time. He was a great friend of Violet and he explained to her that they were going to provide music to keep the passengers' spirits up.

Two pantry boys appeared carrying bread to load onto the lifeboats. Despite the signs of serious events unfolding, there was no panic on deck. It helped that people could see the ship's lights on the horizon; these were frequently being pointed out. In fact, she noted that those on the ship cheered up as the light appeared to be coming closer. Nevertheless, someone suggested to the officer in charge of loading that the boats were being lowered with too few people on them and, when he decided to put more in, there was a surge as people pushed forward trying to get aboard one.

Amid all the signs of impending doom, one small loss of crew discipline struck home to Violet, the sight of a steward standing with cigarette in hand. It was unthinkable in normal circumstances that a member of the crew would do so amid all the passengers and it was a sign of the erosion of the supposedly unbreachable barriers between crew and passengers that forcibly brought home the nature of the situation they were all in. It is interesting that several of the passengers would later complain of crew smoking in their presence.

Passengers kept on coming up to Lightoller and asking them if the situation was serious. He kept on smiling back at them, saying that the loading of the boats was just a precaution. Yet the frequent trails from distress rockets being fired high into the night sky gave the lie to his reassurances. The cascade of stars that spangled forth when they exploded added a distinctly ominous tint to the atmosphere.

Lightoller too could see the light of a ship. He estimated that it was just a few miles away. He reasoned that the boats would soon be picked up. He carried on with his plan to open the gangway doors, ask the boats to stand off by them and pick up more passengers from his sinking ship. Although it suggests a plan of sorts, it was unnecessarily complex. The boats could be lowered with a full complement without buckling. Lightoller's plan added unnecessary time and complexity when time was short and simplicity highly desirable. It was a mistake, as his captain should have told him. But Captain Smith remained peripheral.

Steward Hart had arrived with his batch of third-class passengers from down below. He had about thirty women and children in tow. He took them to the side of Boat 8 and left them there. However, it was not immediately obvious that he had not been wasting his time for none of them got off in it. This was incredible; the boat had a capacity of sixty-five but only had about thirty people in it when it was lowered. Hart in the meantime had gone down below to pick up more third-class passengers and bring them back up to the Boat Deck.

The single male passengers billeted forward in the ship had been flooded out and forced towards the rear of the ship. They made their way along the corridor known as Scotland Road carrying their baggage with them. Many of them were foreigners without a word of English. Interpreter Müller had his work cut out helping them out. Despite that, there seemed to be no chaos or panic among them at this stage.

Boat 3 on the starboard side would be lowered at about 1.00 a.m. Able Seaman George Moore helped load the boat. Once more, there were not enough women on the Boat Deck to fill it with female passengers, so when there were no women left, the men were loaded. 'There were a few men passengers', Moore later said, not wishing to puncture any myths; however, this was a very misleading statement. There were about ten male passengers out of the thirty in the boat and, when members of the crew were taken into account (there were a large number of stokers in it) the men aboard comfortably outnumbered the women. Strangely, try as he might Lowe could not find any more passengers to put in the boat.

Elizabeth Shute was one of those who did get in. She felt that the boat had been lowered amid the greatest confusion. Orders were shouted by rough seamen, left, right and centre. As the boat was lowered the 70 feet or so to the icy Atlantic, the falls stuck and one side started to dip down faster than the other, threatening to throw all its occupants into the sea. With difficulty, the problem was addressed and at last Boat 3 reached the sea in safety, though to Miss Shute the open sea did not seem a very safe place to be.

Way down in the bowels of the ship, matters had taken a significant turn for the worse unknown to those on deck. At around 12.45 a.m. Boiler Room 5 was almost empty. However firemen Fred Barrett had stayed below with a few mates to operate the pumps in an effort to buy some more time. One of them, Second Engineer Jonathan Shepherd had fallen down a manhole and broken his leg. He had been taken to a pump room to try and make him comfortable.

While Barrett and Second Engineer Herbert Harvey valiantly continued their efforts, all of a sudden things took a dramatic twist. Without any warning, the bulkhead between Boiler Rooms 5 and 6 suddenly disintegrated. A torrent of water, cold and chilling, burst through. Barrett climbed as quickly as he could up the escape ladder. As he turned, he saw

Harvey heroically rush towards Shepherd to try and get him out. He was too late. Shepherd was completely engulfed by the onrushing wave.

This was a terrible personal disaster but it was also another fatal blow for the ship. *Titanic* had taken another hit, another cavernous boiler room was flooded and the ship lurched further down at the head. The terrible mathematical certainty that the ship must sink as each successive compartment was filled and the vessel tipped lower in the water was starting to dawn on most of those onboard.

In contrast, it was hard to imagine a quieter night than the one being experienced by the *Californian*. Stopped in the ice, the ship had effectively closed down. Captain Lord had been down in the chart room, reading and enjoying a smoke. At about 12.35 a.m. *Californian* time, Lord had called up to the bridge through the speak tube in the chart room. He wanted to know if the ship he had seen earlier had moved any closer. Stone replied that there had been no change at all in her position.

It is important to note that, at this time at least, there was nothing to alert the suspicions of anyone aboard the *Californian*. The nearby ship had stopped and had not attempted to contact them, either by Morse lamp (not all ships had them) or rocket. She appeared to be doing exactly what Lord was doing, namely stopping for the ice until daybreak enabled her to find a way through. Lord decided to turn in for a few hours sleep. It had been a long and draining day. He told Stone to contact him if he needed anything and, still fully dressed, stretched out on the sofa in the chart room and began to doze off. He was soon in a deep sleep.

Second Officer Herbert Stone was now on his own. The apprentice, James Gibson, had gone off on an errand and Stone had the bridge to himself. He kept an eye on the ship to the south, staring at her with his binoculars from time to time. He paced slowly backwards and forwards across the bridge. It was about 12.45 a.m., ship's time, when he thought he saw a flash in the sky. He thought that it was a shooting star, of which he had seen a number that night. Now though his attention was firmly fixed on the nearby ship.

As he watched, there was another flash followed by several more at intervals. He could not though make out what they were. He was unsure whether they were signals of some sort, recognition devices used by ships at sea, or something of more sinister import. However, he was puzzled by them, more than anything else by their low altitude and the fact that they did not appear to be coming from the nearby ship. He was uncertain what to do so for the time being he took the most unsatisfactory option possible; he did nothing.

The rockets were undoubtedly unusual but he could not believe there was anything to worry about. And so as, somewhere not too far off, the boats of the doomed leviathan were lowered into the water, those on watch on the *Californian* went about their business as if this was just another quiet night in the North Atlantic.

11

The Looming Crisis:
01.01–01.30, 15 April 1912

On the *Titanic*, the atmosphere was still fairly calm, though there was an increasing sense of anxiety developing. Boats had started to be lowered and rockets had been fired, both signs that those in command of the ship were concerned that the ship was in danger. However, *Titanic* was so big, so substantial, so solid. It was still inconceivable to many that she might sink.

To the south, the *Carpathia* was now hurrying with all the speed she could muster to the rescue. It was clear to those commanding her that the situation onboard the *Titanic* was parlous. They received a message from the *Titanic* at around 1.00 a.m. *Carpathia* time, stating laconically 'engine room nearly full' – presumably this was not long after Leading Stoker Fred Barrett had been flooded out when the bulkhead collapsed down below. There was no time to lose and Captain Rostron anxiously watched as the minutes ticked past in this race against time.

The passengers gathered around the lifeboats on *Titanic's* Boat Deck. There was an emphasis on women and children being lowered away first but some women refused to go, wives who would not be parted from husbands or children from parents. Charlotte Collyer was one of them. She saw Harold Lowe loading the boats; despite his youth, he had a presence about him which imposed itself on others who felt compelled to obey his instructions. One passenger in particular seemed to her to be interfering too readily in the boat-loading. She had seen Lowe ordering him away peremptorily. Only later did she think that the busybody passenger was J. Bruce Ismay. However, at some stage he moved off to load other boats and Charlotte Collyer lost sight of him.

Colonel Gracie had initially been kept back from the boats but the policy had now changed and he was not prevented from approaching them. Wanting to be helpful, he started to play a role in loading them, there being in his opinion no time to lose. He was now on A Deck, where boats were being loaded having been lowered from the Boat Deck. Lightoller was standing, one foot in the lifeboat, the other on the rail of the deck, his stentorian voice, with its lilting accent, giving firm instructions to those getting on the boats. Women, children and babies were passed through the open window to him.

A staircase led from the Boat Deck directly down to C Deck and Lightoller went down it every so often to gauge the water's progress. He watched with horrified fascination as step by step the water started to climb the stairs, the electric lights that it devoured burning on for a few eerie seconds before they at last went out forever; Lightoller recalled that this weird sight created a 'ghastly transparency'. The deck lights were still on though which meant that the dynamos were still doing their work. One woman waved a cane with an electric light in it, almost blinding Lightoller as he worked. This was Mrs J. Stuart White and, however inconvenient her cane might have been at the time, it would do good service later on (or so she claimed).

Mrs White gives the impression of being someone who would now be euphemistically described as 'high maintenance'. She was in many ways the epitome of the first-class passenger, spoilt and pampered. She comes across as being something of a metaphorical bulldog and, without wishing to be disrespectful, her photographs suggest an uncanny physical resemblance to one too. She was convinced that none of the men were particularly heroic that night for the simple reason that none of them thought the ship would sink so they were quite safe staying where they were. As she prepared to leave the ship, she heard comments from them suggesting that they would all need passes to get back onboard in the near future.

She was not impressed at the quality of the crew onboard the lifeboat either. She was shocked to hear them asked, before they got in, whether or not they could row. She had a point, as it transpired that very few of them could and some of the women had to help out. It was a shame, Mrs White grumbled, that the crew were in the boat at the expense of some of the men passengers, 'athletes and men of sense', as she called them; she was presumably referring to the first-class element.

As the seriousness of the ship's position was now becoming more obvious, Lightoller now ordered the boats filled to the maximum capacity he dared. It is certainly true that later boats would have more people on them than those loaded at the beginning but it is equally true that they still had space in them. Lightoller was struck by the calmness of those entrapped in the looming crisis. There was a young honeymoon couple on deck, walking calmly up and down. The new husband asked Lightoller if there were anything he could do to help.

While he was loading the boats, Chief Officer Wilde asked Lightoller if he knew where the firearms were. They were not needed yet and were merely being sought as a precaution. Murdoch did not know where they were so Lightoller went, accompanied by him, the Chief Officer and Captain Smith to the place where the firearms were stored. As they left, the

Chief Officer handed a pistol to Lightoller. Not thinking he would need it, he put it carelessly in his pocket along with a few cartridges.

As he returned to his post, Lightoller saw Mr and Mrs Straus standing by the deck house. He asked Mrs Straus if he could take her along to the boats but she replied in the negative. Mr Straus tried to persuade her but she was not having any of it. Neither was another unnamed young woman who was sitting on deck with her husband. Lightoller asked her to if she wished to be escorted to a boat. Her reply was immediate: 'Not on your life, we started together, and if need be, we will finish together.'

Lightoller continued to look at the nearby ship as his own sank lower. He could not understand why she did not respond to the *Titanic's* frequent requests for help. He had been reassuring passengers all the time he had been lowering the boats with her presence but it was increasingly obvious that she was not going to come to the rescue. The frustration and desperation that must have been felt is unimaginable.

Jack Thayer and his father now decided that they ought to make sure that Mrs Thayer had safely got into a boat. Down on B Deck, the lounge was full of people and they had to push their way out onto the open deck through a crowd. The crush was so great that Jack and Milton Long were separated from Thayer Senior. Jack would never see his father again. At the time, he assumed that both his mother and father would make their way safely onto a lifeboat and he made his way to the starboard side with Milton Long to see whether there was any chance of getting off there.

By now, Jack noticed that the bows of the great ship were underwater. He said later that he could still see the boats 500 or 600 feet away though as only one of them had a light and it was such a dark night this was doubtful unless he could see them in the reflected glare of the rockets that were still shooting up every five minutes or so. But he insisted that they were 'plainly visible' so perhaps the starlight was indeed bright enough to illuminate the scene.

The lights were still burning on the great ship and the exhaust steam was still roaring. The band continued to play, though they had life preservers on by now. Thayer noticed a man come through the door carrying a bottle of Gordon's Gin which he had been liberally helping himself to. He told himself that the man would, for certain, not be one of those lucky enough to survive the night but he was wrong.

The irony was that Jack Thayer and his father did not know that his mother, waiting to get in Boat 4, was still on the *Titanic*. Lightoller kept changing his mind about where the boat should be lowered from. He had first of all decided that it should be filled from A Deck and then changed his mind to the Boat Deck after being reminded that A Deck was enclosed. He now changed his mind again; she would be filled from A Deck after all from the opened windows.

Steward George Dodd told the passengers waiting to go back to A Deck. Mrs Thayer was getting annoyed at this to-ing and fro-ing, with every justification. This was not just inconvenient, it was also clear that there was real danger on the ship and time was of the essence. Another person waiting to get on Boat 4, Mrs Martha Stephenson said that when they came up the stairs onto the Boat Deck they saw Captain Smith, looking very worried. The ship was listing heavily to port. She saw the rockets going up, which alarmed her. It suggested that any wireless messages that had been sent were not having any effect and that the situation was growing serious.

However, the sense of urgency had not yet fully transmitted itself to the people responsible for filling the boats. Boat 8 was about to be filled. It had a capacity of sixty-five people; survivors' accounts suggest that between twenty-eight and thirty-five would actually get in it, including Mrs J. Stuart White. Able Seaman Thomas Jones was one of those aboard. As he got in the boat, Captain Smith was on hand, asking him if the plug was in the boat; he replied in the affirmative. He then asked for any more ladies but there were none. The Captain and a steward then helped drop the boat gently down the side of the ship. Captain Smith had also instructed Steward Alfred Crawford to get in, pull for the light and land the boat there and then come back for more passengers.

The Captain of the *Titanic* clearly thought that the mystery ship was very close if this was his expectation. Crawford believed he could see two lights, one on the foremast, one on the main of this mysterious vessel. 'Everybody saw them' was his assessment but they could make no headway towards reaching them. Crawford reckoned it was at most 10 miles away and was sure that it was a steamer as a sailing ship would not have two lights. As he pulled away from the *Titanic*, he saw that she was making water fast at the bows.

Mrs Straus had at one stage started to get into Boat 8, along with her maid. However, when she had one foot on the gunwale she stepped out again and stood by her husband. She said defiantly: 'We have been living together for many years, and where you go, I go.' The Strauses then sat themselves down in deck chairs on the enclosed A Deck, waiting for their fate. Someone suggested to Mr Straus that no one would object if an old man got in a boat but he was not having any of it. He would not seek to gain an advantage over other men. The irony of course is that if he had gone to the other side of the ship, he would have had no problem in getting in a lifeboat with a clear conscience.

Fourth Officer Boxhall had been frantically trying to contact the nearby ship with a Morse lamp and frustratingly was getting nowhere. Worse than this, as the night wore on she turned around and presented her stern light as if she was preparing to move away. He could not make out what she was but was convinced that she was not a fishing boat. Rockets still shot up at regular intervals. By now, Boxhall had been joined by Quartermaster Rowe. However, the other ship seemed to be taking not a blind bit of notice of them.

In the meantime, Second Officer Stone on the *Californian* was increasingly confused. By 1.15 a.m. *Californian* time he had seen five rockets shoot up into the air. It is now that we enter the murkiest, muddiest, most indecipherable part of the story of the so-called *Californian* incident.

Stone had seen five rockets, all white. He said in a signed statement later that he informed Lord of the fact: 'I, at once, whistled down the speaking tube and you came from your chartroom into your own room and answered.' The phrasing would imply that he immediately told Lord of the rockets (Gibson said that Stone had told him that he had reported to Lord after he had seen the second rocket) but exactly how many he had seen when he reported to Lord is somewhat ambiguous in Stone's statement.

Lord seemed to confirm that some time had elapsed before the rockets were reported to him. In his own later affidavit, he confirmed that he was informed of the situation by Stone 'at about 1.15 a.m.'. However, this is directly contradicted by the evidence given by Apprentice James Gibson in a statement given immediately after the disaster and before any formal Inquiries had begun on 18 April.

Gibson's recollection was that he had been below decks and had returned to the bridge at about 12.55 a.m. Stone had told him that the other ship had fired five rockets and he had already reported the fact to Lord after he had spotted the second one. This would have put the time closer to 12.45 a.m. than 1.15 a.m. *Californian* time. Stone however also thought it was about 1.15 a.m. Two to one evidence; that is about the best odds one could get on anything reported from the *Californian* that night.

Informed of the rockets, Gibson had first of all tried to contact the ship with the Morse light but got no response. He then picked up his binoculars and trained them on the ship. He was actually looking through these when:

> I observed a white flash apparently on her deck, followed by a faint streak towards the sky which then burst into white stars. Nothing then happened until the other ship was about two points on the starboard bow when she fired another rocket.

Stone thought that the rockets were appearing very low down, and may well have come from a point beyond and behind the ship he was watching. Gibson however clearly thought that the rockets were coming from the ship he could see. The fact that Gibson was actually watching through binoculars when the rockets were fired makes his account the more difficult to refute.

No one on the *Titanic* saw any rockets fired from any other ship that night, at least not until several hours later when the *Carpathia* was steaming towards the lifeboats. Therefore, it is almost certain that the only ship firing rockets in the area that night was the *Titanic*. If Gibson was right and the ship he was watching was also the ship firing rockets (and the ones he saw were white as were those fired by Fourth Officer Boxhall), then the ship he could see must have been the *Titanic*.

Lord's recollection of the conversation he had with Stone earlier (which of course Gibson did not hear as he was not on the bridge at the time) contradicted Stone in several crucial details. Stone reported 'seeing lights in the sky in the direction of the other steamer which appeared to me to be white rockets'. Lord however recollected that Stone had reported to him that the other steamer 'had fired a white rocket' in the singular. Stone's recollection was that he reported to Lord after seeing the fifth rocket. Gibson's account of what happened is more ambiguous and suggests that Stone may have reported the rockets after seeing the second one (Gibson was not there at the time so was quoting second-hand).

There are two important differences to emphasize here. Firstly Stone said that the rockets came from the direction of the other ship. Lord recollected that Stone had told him that the signals came from the other ship itself, not just from her general direction, a point of view that corroborates Gibson's opinion that the rockets came from the nearby ship (though of course Lord had not seen any rockets himself and might merely have misheard Stone or drawn the wrong conclusion). Secondly, Stone said he reported rockets in the plural, Lord only remembered hearing of one in the singular.

Reading Stone's version it is easy to interpret the situation as being that the ship he could see and the rockets were not directly connected; that is indeed consistent with his other evidence when he thought that the rockets came 'from a good distance beyond her'. However, Lord believed that the rockets were coming from the ship itself as did Gibson.

Secondly, it is perhaps easy enough to dismiss one isolated rocket as nothing too much to worry about. Company recognition signals were sometimes used back then. However, Stone had seen more than one when he reported to Lord. To anyone attuned to imminent danger (which Lord, as his earlier precautions attested, was) then being aware of this many rockets might have suggested that a serious situation was unfolding not far away from him. But amazingly, if Stone did report the rockets after seeing just two of them, he then saw three more rockets before Gibson came back and did not report further to Lord until much, much later.

There was also another man who claimed to have seen the rockets. This was 'donkeyman' Ernest Gill (a donkeyman was the quaint name for an engineer from the engine room). He was back on deck he said, having another cigarette, at about 12.30 a.m. He was standing there for about ten minutes when he saw a white rocket, though he too thought at first that it was a shooting star. Just short of ten minutes later, he saw another flash and thought to himself that 'that must be a vessel in distress'.

This appears to be fairly decisive evidence but there are several flaws with it. It has been suggested by some that Gill is an unreliable witness, partly on the grounds that he confessed to some of his shipmates that he expected to make money from his story (though this in itself does not mean that it is false). However, it was a freezing cold night and he must have been finding it very difficult to sleep if he chose to spend this length of time in the open.

Most difficult to explain away is what he did *not* see. He said that now there was no ship in sight, he could just see the rockets about 10 miles away. But both Stone and Gibson quite clearly saw both a ship and the rockets at around the same time.

There was also the problem of what Gill did *not* do. He did not report the rockets to anyone else at the time. He said:

> It was not my business to notify the bridge or the lookout but they could not have helped but see them. I turned in immediately after, supposing the ship would pay attention to the rockets.

At best this shows a seriously cavalier attitude and an astonishing lack of any sense of responsibility. It is easy to see why those who felt that Captain Lord was unfairly singled out as the villain of the piece did their best to discredit Gill as a witness, suggesting that he merely developed the story after the event in an attempt to make some money out of the disaster.

Neither did it help Gill's case when he was inconsistent in the accounts he gave at different times in his later evidence. In his original affidavit Gill described how he had seen 'a big vessel going along at full speed' at around midnight. By the time that he got to London he was much less confident, merely saying that 'I did not stand to look at the ship but I supposed she would be moving'.

He would also say to the British Inquiry that he could not be sure that what he had seen was a company recognition signal or a rocket. However, when asked if he regarded the rocket as being of any significance he said: 'No, not any importance. It was a signal... ' This is very different from being convinced that he was watching a ship in distress. He could not even be sure what direction the ship he was watching was travelling.

Captain Lord would later be publicly castigated for his inaction and would vigorously deny that he had been close enough to the *Titanic* to make any difference to the situation. He would argue that the ship that could be seen close to his was emphatically not the *Titanic*. A brutal war of accusation and counter-accusation would break out. People would take sides in a battle between the so-called 'pro-Lordites' and the 'anti-Lordites'. The debate continues to this day, fought out with huge passion and partisanship by supporters and opponents of Captain Lord alike.

The weapons used by the participants include bewildering (and ultimately currently unprovable) arguments about what time it was on each ship, the relative positions they were both in and hugely complex discussions about what coloured lights could be seen from each ship at a given time. In the latter, geometrical diagrams that are more suited to a mathematics degree than a history book appear prominently.

They are academically fascinating no doubt and they underscore a commendable search for truth which is the foundation of all historical study. However, boiled down to their basic principles it is virtually impossible to arrive at a conclusion one way or the other with any confidence. The root of the problem is that there were just a handful of eye-witness accounts surviving from those aboard the *Californian* to act as evidence. They are shot through with contradiction of which the above is just one example.

To be charitable some at least of the key witnesses were mistaken on several key points. To be more cynical, some of them are simply not telling the truth. The nub of the debate is which one, or several, of the witnesses you choose to believe or disbelieve. In the absence of any other evidence, this is – in the tradition of all great courtroom dramas – down to the observers' assessment of the credibility of each witness. Unfortunately, there are some serious questions to be asked of some of the witnesses on both sides of the case, including Captain Lord himself.

A further problem was one that relates directly to the conduct of the investigations that followed the disaster. Both were deeply flawed in terms of their conduct. This does not necessarily mean that they arrived at the wrong conclusion with regards to Captain Lord's inaction. However, it means that in the superficial attitude they took to arrive at that conclusion they did not test the evidence thoroughly. Limited cross-examination of contradictory witnesses was not pursued with appropriate diligence, leaving a number of question marks unresolved.

For the historian this in itself is a tragedy. In the American Inquiry key witnesses were not called. In the British Inquiry contradictions in the accounts of key witnesses were not questioned and probed. In total, because of this amateurish (supporters of Lord would say 'biased') approach much of the evidence that might have helped clear up the debate was not collected. With the passing of time and the death of all the key witnesses there that night, it is now gone forever.

Lord's reaction, when informed of the rocket, or rockets, by Stone was to inform the Second Officer to carry on keeping an eye on the nearby ship and continue his previously unsuccessful attempts to contact her by Morse lamp. Gibson was to be sent down to him with any further information.

Lord then went to lay down again, where he soon began to fall into a deep sleep, soothed by the hypnotic sound of the keyboard he could hear being clicked as the Morse lamp sprang into action once again.

Lord said that he had been reassured by his conversation with Stone. He had asked the Second Officer if what he had seen had been company signals, to which Stone had replied that he did not know. However, he took reassurance from the fact that Stone also reported that she had changed her bearing to the south-west which Lord took to mean that the ship was under way and moving further away from the *Californian* (as indeed Stone later confirmed *was* what he meant). This is consistent with what Stone said to Gibson soon after. He took a compass bearing of the ship and told the apprentice: 'She was slowly steering away towards the south-west.'

The arguments around what Lord could and should have done have several dimensions. The first is a pragmatic one; if he had tried to make his way to the *Titanic* could he have arrived in time to make a difference? In the absence of concrete information, his first step would have been to wake up Wireless Operator Evans and ask him to try and find out what was wrong. In a few minutes he would, if he was fortunate, find out of the unfolding disaster on the *Titanic*. He would then have ordered the engines to be started up and made his way towards the ship. Assuming they were not slowed down by any ice (and as he was on the same side of the ice-field as the *Titanic* then that would possibly have been the case though several *Californian* witnesses describe ice to the south of them) he would then have set off towards the *Titanic*.

Let us assume that Lord was indeed first informed of the problem at around 12.45 a.m. *Californian* time (which may as noted have been different from *Titanic* time). Let us assume then that he had found out about the problem via wireless and started the engines at around 1.00 a.m. How far away he actually was from the *Titanic* is of course a matter of great debate. However, taking as yet another assumption that it was 10 miles then that was an hour's steaming away from the ship; it is unlikely to have been any less than that as neither ship could see each other's attempts at Morsing each other and the *Titanic*, the largest ship ever built, would surely have been unmistakable if she had been closer than this distance.

Taking all these best case assumptions, then it would not have been much before 2.00 a.m. before the *Californian* arrived. By then all *Titanic's* lifeboats had been launched (though some of the collapsibles were still left). Lord could have lowered his own and certainly saved some of those in the water. However, the vast majority of those still on the *Titanic* would have still perished.

The greatest tragedy of all this though is that Lord did not wake up Cyril Evans in an attempt to find out whether there was a ship in distress or not. Lord would later admit to being dissatisfied with Stone's replies about the nature of the rockets but he still chose not to wake up the operator. Supporters of Captain Lord argue that this was because the true power of wireless had yet to be understood. It is not a convincing argument; Lord had already seen fit to send several warning messages that evening using it.

In the meantime, Gibson tried to call the other ship up without any joy. Stone at one stage turned to him and said: 'Look at her now; she looks very queer out of the water; her lights look queer.' Gibson looked at her through his glasses. To him the ship he was looking at seemed to be listing to starboard. Stone then remarked to Gibson that 'a ship was not going to fire rockets at sea for nothing'. The rockets were white and exploded in starbursts. However, there were no explosions to be heard. It was a quiet night. The absence of any explosive sound meant one of two things; either that what they were watching were not distress rockets or that they were being fired from a spot quite a long way off. But they looked just like distress rockets were supposed to look, so that left only the latter explanation.

Gibson carried on watching the ship; her red port side light seemed to be higher out of the water than it had been previously. Stone in the meantime postulated about the ship he could see and what the rockets meant. He concluded that 'there was something the matter with her'. But for whatever reason he was not concerned enough to go and wake his captain up again. He would come across as a very confused witness. He did not believe that the rockets he saw were company signals, yet he did not think they were distress rockets either, so it is not clear just what he thought they might be. As he watched the ship he was sure that she was steaming slowly away and he could not understand why a ship doing that would send up distress rockets. But he also thought that the direction of the rockets was changing in line with the change in direction of the ship he was watching.

Most damning of all this is the vocabulary of the witnesses. Quotes of lights looking 'queer', of ships that appear to be listing, of vessels that look as if there is something the matter with them, suggest something very out of the ordinary. Bear in mind too that the *Californian* was stopped because of the danger posed by an immense ice-field and it is quite incredible that nobody's suspicions were alerted by a series of out-of-the-ordinary indicators in an area of known danger. It is hard to understand how observers from the *Californian* looked on impassively and did nothing.

There was also, to reiterate, no doubt that those on the *Titanic* could see something they thought was a ship from where they were. Pitman in Boat 5 saw a white light on the horizon, which he thought lay on *Titanic's* track to the west. However, he was not sure what it was and thought that it could have been one of their own lifeboats. He could see no other lights, such as a red side light, and believed that the craft to which the light was attached was stationary. In his view, it was about 3 miles away. He did not think it was a sailing vessel or a steamer; certainly he did not believe that anything was coming to the rescue.

Once they were safely lowered, Jones and the oarsmen in Boat 8 'pulled for the light, but I found that I could not get to it; so I stood by for a while'. Jones was certain that he could not see any children and very few women when he left the ship. He did however notice the Strauses in the vicinity of the boats on deck though he could not hear them speak as steam was blowing from the funnels and the noise was deafening.

There was also a first-class passenger in Boat 8, a woman of rare poise and beauty. This was Noelle, the Countess of Rothes. Born into money with a wealthy landowning father, she had married into it too when she was wed to Norman Leslie, the 19th Earl of Rothes in 1900. The event made the society pages of the best London newspapers and the couple entered easily into the high society of late Victorian and early Edwardian England. As well as socializing, they enjoyed the other facets of contemporary English aristocracy; hunting, boating and riding.

Her husband was no stay at home aristocrat though. Noelle was active in charitable circles but her husband also looked for business opportunities; being a Lord was no guarantee of permanent wealth in these changing times. He travelled widely and in 1912 had gone to Florida to look at the possibilities of making money from a citrus farm. The Countess was now on her way to join him.

A photograph of the Countess taken in 1907 shows a woman of exquisite beauty, a woman of elegance and style rather than sensuousness. In an understated way, Jones – who was in charge of the boat – was also most impressed by her. He noted that 'she was a countess or something' and that 'she had a lot to say so I put her to steering the boat'. This might not sound like much of a compliment but in fact Jones was very taken with the Countess. He would later present her with the brass plate from the boat and they would keep up a correspondence after the disaster.

Also in Boat 8 was the discontented Mrs J. Stuart White. She was disgusted to look up and see stewards smoking cigarettes; what she wondered could be less appropriate at a time like this? But she confirmed the story that an officer (though she didn't name him as Captain Smith) told the boat to row for the lights. In her view, the light was 10 miles away.

She had her cane with an electric light on it which was just as well as the light that had been put in the boat was next to useless. No one seemed panicked or frightened but there was, as she put it, 'a lot of pathos when husbands and wives kissed each other goodbye'. She later claimed that her cane was stolen; Lightoller said that he was so infuriated by 'the damn thing' when she had been waving it around on deck that he had ordered it thrown over the side. It seemed a suitable end to it; in riposte to her questioning as to how appropriate it was to smoke at a time like this, it is difficult not to wonder how appropriate it was to worry about such things at a time like this. Lightoller must have been tempted to throw her in too along with her cane.

It was about 1.10 a.m. when the most controversial boat on the *Titanic* started to lower away. This was Boat Number 1. It was one of the two emergency boats, always swung out ready to be lowered, with a capacity of forty.

Colonel Gracie, a heroic man no doubt but one who saw many aspects of the disaster through rose-tinted spectacles, says that there was no disorder in loading or lowering this boat. This is hardly surprising as there were so few people on it, twelve in all. In addition, the fact that this was the fourth boat from the starboard side and yet it was only just over a quarter full shows how desperately poorly organized the whole loading sequence was. Fifth Officer Lowe later suggested there were twenty-two people in the boat which shows he either had a very poor memory for figures or he was something of a story-teller. With Sir Cosmo Duff Gordon also onboard, a man whose actions would later come under very public scrutiny, this was without doubt the most controversial lifeboat launched that night.

Lookout George Symons had already helped launch Boats 5 and 3 and was then asked to help with Emergency Boat 1. First Officer Murdoch was in charge of loading it. Two women ran out on deck and asked if they could board. Permission was duly granted. There were no more women in sight so the boat was lowered. Just before leaving the Boat Deck, Symons – who had been put in charge – noticed a white light on the port bow about 5 miles away. As they started to pull away from the ship, Symons noticed that the water was now up to C Deck at the bow, coming up to a spot right underneath the ship's name. Symons had been told to lie 100 yards off the *Titanic* and await further orders. He did so for a short time (perhaps quarter of an hour) then pulled further back as he was afraid of the suction when the ship eventually went down.

First-class passenger Charles Stengel, whose wife was already away in a boat, had also climbed in. When he reached the Boat Deck there were no other passengers around and permission was freely given him to get aboard. It was a fair jump from the Titanic to the boat and Stengel tumbled, effectively falling into the boat. Murdoch laughed, saying that this was the funniest sight he had seen all night. Less amusing however was the way that the boat was lowered. The lowering was uneven, the unpractised seaman struggling to co-ordinate their efforts, and the boat almost tipped its occupants into the water far below. Stengel confirmed that Boat 1 later followed a light that could be seen in front of the bows.

He personally felt that this was not the light of a ship but merely the Northern Lights reflecting off bergs. However, this was rather a minority assessment. Most people, including a large number of experienced seamen (which Stengel was not) were sure that what they could see was the lights of a ship.

Stengel also seemed to be somewhat embarrassed at his own personal position. He explained that Boat 1 was nearly full: 'I do not think it had a capacity for any more than were in it.' This was one of the more ludicrous statements of the night, as (to recapitulate) Boat 1 had a capacity of forty and had just twelve people in it. It was perhaps also a feeble attempt by Stengel to explain why this boat, not even half full, did not go back to pick up any more survivors from the water when the boat sank.

He also said that people seemed slow to come up onto the Boat Deck. Whether this was another attempt at self-justification or a more accurate statement which might reflect the fact that people were not being allowed up into a first-class area is not immediately clear. However, most accounts from those in Boat 1 suggest that there were no other passengers waiting to get in when she was lowered which begs the question, where were they?

Sir Cosmo Duff Gordon and his wife Lucy were in it too. They had already tried to get into Boat 7 but that was full by the time they arrived – it was in fact less than half full, but given the cavalier attitude to loading the boats that was prevalent on the Boat Deck that was close enough. They next tried Number 3, where there was enough room for Lady Duff Gordon but not for Sir Cosmo and she would not go without him (though again, this boat was less than two-thirds full).

They asked an officer, presumably Murdoch, if they could get in and he replied that he wished that they would. Lady Duff Gordon later said that she thought she was destined to drown. She had turned down the chance to go in several boats because she would not go without her husband. However, she could see no other passengers waiting to get in the boat. She was now lifted gently into the boat. Safely lowered, the boat began to move slowly away from the wallowing ship. However, Lady Duff Gordon's brush with controversy had only just begun.

Boat 9 was away soon after, also from the starboard side. There were a significant number of second-class passengers on board, all but one of them women, and three single third-class men, who must have shown their initiative to get on the boat deck, possibly by climbing up cranes to get out of their third-class areas.

Boatswain's mate Albert Haines was in her too. He believed that the boat was more or less full when two or three men, presumably the third-class 'interlopers', jumped into the bow (it is true that the boat was fuller than some, with about fifty people aboard). To him, 'the boat was chock-a-block'. Murdoch told him to stand off, well clear of the ship. They pulled about 100 yards off to a point from where they clearly saw that the *Titanic* was going down by the head.

Quartermaster Walter Wynne was one of seven crew members in the boat. He gave a clear description of the light that could be seen nearby. He could see the lights of a steamer, red at first, then white, about 7–8 miles away. Steward William Ward noticed that Officer Murdoch, Ismay and Purser McElroy were nearby when the boat was being loaded. A sailor got in with a bag and said that he had been instructed to take control of the boat. Haines, who was actually in charge, told him to get out which he duly did. One old lady made a great fuss and refused point-blank to get in. A French lady fell and suffered a minor injury.

In the darkness, the women struggled to gauge the drop from the deck to the boat. Ward was told to get in and help load it. As there were no women left on deck, a few men were allowed to climb aboard. There was some difficulty in laying hold of the oars, as they were tied together and no one had a knife.

James Widgery, a Bath Steward, had seen that a number of passengers were already on deck by the time that he arrived at the boats. He went to Number 7 first but that was already being readied for lowering. He was then sent to Number 9. He confirmed the story about the old lady who would not enter; she was frightened and refused to board.

In the meantime, the illusory hope of that light flickered in the distance, frustratingly not moving any closer to the ship. One of the most detailed accounts of the light came from Able Seaman Edward Buley in Boat 10. He said:

> There was a ship of some description there when she struck, and she passed right by us. We thought she was coming to us; and if she had come to us, everyone could have boarded her. You could see she was a steamer. She had her steamer lights burning. She was off our port bow when we struck, and we started for the same light, and that is what kept the lifeboats together.

He told the American Inquiry that 'I am very positive' that she then stayed stationary for about three hours and then she made tracks. She was only three miles away, he reckoned, and he saw two masthead lights but not her bow light. At one stage they thought she was coming to pick up the lifeboats – 'we saw it going right by us when we were in the lifeboats'.

Unfortunately his statement is rather confusing. He implies that the ship was there when the berg was struck, but if she was then no one else on *Titanic*, including her lookouts, saw her. He says that she was stationary for three hours (which could, loosely applied, implicate the *Californian* though she was actually still for much longer than that) but then makes much of the fact that she seemed to be moving quite significantly, which would definitively rule out *Californian*. Perhaps his choice of words was merely clumsy but if so it is a pity because his statement almost generates more questions than answers.

Seaman Buley had been put in charge of the boat by Chief Officer Wilde. Seaman Frank Evans had also been told to get in by Wilde. William Burke, first-class dining room steward, was also ordered in though he did not say by whom. He had initially gone to Boat 1, which was the boat he had been assigned to. Baker Charles Joughin was putting women and children in the boat. Murdoch was also at hand. There was a 2½ foot gap between the ship and the lifeboat and 'he was catching children by the dresses and chucking them in'.

Joughin recalled Wilde telling the stewards to keep men back, though the order was superfluous as they were doing it anyway. The stewards, firemen and sailors formed orderly lines and passed the women along. They had difficulty finding more women to put in, though Joughin did notice some who would not be parted from their bags. He thought that the gap to the boat was about 4–5 feet and women had to be dropped into it. He did not himself get into the boat, thinking that that would give a bad example, and instead went back to his room down below to reinforce himself with a drop of liquor.

A woman in a black dress did not jump far enough and was caught between the side of the ship and the lifeboat. She was pulled in by the men on the deck below, returned to the Boat Deck and jumped again, this time successfully. One man (a foreigner) jumped into the lifeboat as it was being lowered. Evans seemed disgusted at his action. The foreigner, possibly Neshan Krekorian, perhaps thought it slightly pointless to stand around waiting to die while half-empty lifeboats rowed away from the doomed leviathan.

Evans however suggested at the American inquiry that the boat was pretty full, which comparatively speaking it was with perhaps fifty-five people in total aboard her. Also in the boat were the Dean family, Ettie, young Bertram and Millvina Dean. However, Bertram senior was left on the ship and was lost. The fate of Millvina was rather different. She would be the last of the survivors to die, passing away on 31 May 2009, exactly ninety-eight years after the *Titanic* was launched.

They rowed away for several hundred yards where they eventually tied up to Boat 12. This had been loaded by Seaman Frederick Clench and Second Officer Lightoller with Chief Officer Wilde passing women and children on to them. There was only one seaman, John Poingdestre, in her when she started to lower away so Wilde told Clench to jump in. They were told to keep an eye on Boat 14 and keep together. Only one male passenger got in, a Frenchman (unnamed) who jumped in as she was being lowered. This might not be heroic but it was certainly rational;

there were twenty spare places in the boat. Poingdestre heard Lightoller order the boat to stay close to the ship. They would eventually tie up with collapsible D and three other lifeboats.

Two of the second-class passengers in Boat 12 were Mrs Imanita Shelley and her mother, Mrs Lutie Parrish. One of the sailors had run up to Mrs Shelley, who had been standing on deck, and told her to get into the boat. There was she recalled a 4–5 foot gap to jump. 'The boat was filled with women and children, as many as could get in with overcrowding.' A 'crazed Italian' jumped in, landing on Mrs Parrish and badly bruising her leg. They had been told to head for the boat launched ahead of them. She noticed the men aboard acting in exemplary fashion, putting their clothes around half-dressed women and children.

Poingdestre also noticed a significant change in mood as Boats 12 and 14 were being loaded. Whereas all had been calm before, now passengers were starting to panic. A group of men – he thought that they were second and third-class passengers – began to crowd the boats and Poingdestre and Lightoller only kept them back with difficulty.

Boat 11 was lowered from the starboard side just before half past one. Seaman Walter Brice recalled that the boat was lowered from A Deck. Steward Charles Mackay said that the boat collected the women from the Boat Deck first and then gathered a few more on A Deck. As the boat was then lowered away, the women complained that the boat was so packed they had to stand. They were also unhappy that the men in the boat were smoking. However, the account of Assistant 2nd Steward Joseph Wheat differed slightly. He also said that Murdoch ordered the boat to be lowered to A Deck but that this was because there no one on the Boat Deck and that was why the boat was lowered down to the deck below.

One of the women in the boat was Edith Russell, who had never felt comfortable on the ship. When a male acquaintance suggested she should get in, she was reluctant as her clothes were so tight she could not climb onto the boat. As she explained, she was 'a prisoner in my own skirts'. However, she was helped on, along with a toy pig covered in white fur that played a tune known as the *Maxixe*.

When an officer asked if there was a sailor onboard, there was no reply so Seaman Brice had climbed out along the falls and lowered himself into the boat. He took over the tiller, by which time the boat had been filled with women and children. There were several problems when the boat was lowered. Firstly, she was nearly swamped by an outflow of water pouring out from the side of the ship. This was the discharge from the pumps that were being worked onboard the Titanic. Then, the ropes snagged.

Quartermaster Sidney Humphreys was in charge. He looked for a light onboard but could find none so he made some improvised torches from lengths of rope. The boat was not very well equipped; Steward McKay was unable to find any compass in the boat when he looked for one.

Steward Ernest Wheelton had previously seen Thomas Andrews looking into rooms to see if there was anyone there. When he arrived on deck, Boats 7, 5 and 9 had gone and Number 11 was already in the davits. Murdoch ordered him in. When the boat was almost full, Murdoch asked if there were any sailors in the boat. When the answer was in the negative, two climbed in (including the aforementioned Brice). Wheelton also confirmed that the boat was lowered from A Deck.

The stories so far are of passengers standing by the boats, patiently waiting their turn or resigning themselves to their fate. However, there are other stories to tell that cannot be fully told for the simple reason that most of the people who need to tell them did not survive. Hundreds of people were still nowhere near the Boat Deck and their tale can only be told by frustratingly but inevitably incomplete titbits of information.

Gathered some way away from the Boat Deck with his small group, Olaus Abelseth and his companions were among those who heard an officer say that they should be quick, for there was a boat coming. Abelseth still did not have his lifejacket and went back down below to pick it up. When he returned, he saw a lot of steerage passengers using cranes as makeshift ladders from the steerage open area up onto the Boat Deck. There was no other way, for the gates allowing access via more conventional means were locked. Yet both Inquiries would later insist that there was no discrimination by class; one of the more unsustainable conclusions of two unsatisfactory Inquiries.

To these poor souls, any hope of survival was receding rapidly. Steward Hart, an unsung hero, had been doing his job as well as he was able and escorting groups of steerage women and children up to the boats but he was on his own in his efforts. Most other third-class passengers seemed to have been left to their own devices. Any hope of survival rested either on their own initiative or on plain old-fashioned luck. The men would not heroically give up their places to the women and children here. Most of them would have no say in the matter. By now, the majority of those in third-class had already been condemned to a watery grave. And the moment at which they would look with terror into the dark abyss of their destiny was now less than an hour away.

12

Nowhere to Go:
01.31–02.00, 15 April 1912

The real horror of the *Titanic* disaster was the sheer drawn-out nature of the ship's death. It was only by degrees that the true magnitude of the pending disaster revealed itself to those on deck or down below. The gradual tipping of the ship as the bows sank lower beneath the waves and the angle of the stern rose correspondingly higher, and the listing of the ship to port or starboard (both seem to have happened at some stage during the two hours and forty minutes it took for the ship to go down) began to tell its own tale. Now a new terror was about to emerge; the lifeboats were about to run out.

The fact that there were not enough places for all onboard would soon become apparent but it was certainly clearer now to the officers loading the boats who started to fill them with many more passengers than were on the earlier boats. It was an awful situation, the horror of which was now fully dawning on those on the ship. Before long, over 1,500 of them would have nowhere to go.

Boat 14 was one of the next to be lowered, with about sixty people in her. Seaman Joseph Scarrott was initially put in charge of the boat, his bad vibes about the ship that he had felt back in Southampton now fully justified. Some men tried to rush the boat, 'foreigners' as he described them. Discipline was beginning to break down now that the urgency of the situation was more apparent. One man had to be thrown out three times. Fifth Officer Lowe came along and Scarrott briefed him on the problems he was experiencing. Lowe took hold of his revolver and decided to take charge of what was a deteriorating situation.

Seaman Scarrott told how 'half a dozen foreigners' tried to jump in when there were still women and children to be loaded but he beat them off with the tiller. When Scarrott told Lowe what had happened, he took out his pistol, a Browning automatic. The tension was now palpable and a sense of panic was becoming increasingly evident. Lowe fired shots down into the water as a warning against any attempt that others might make to enter the boats when they were not allowed to. Greaser Frederick Scott was watching on and thought he heard him say: 'If any man jumps into the boat I will shoot him like a dog.'

Lowe believed that the boat was crowded to capacity and might buckle under the weight. He saw a lot of 'Latin people', like 'wild beasts' waiting to jump in as the boat as she was lowered down the side of the stricken ship. Lowe fired several shots (Scarrott remembered two, Lowe reckoned three) from his pistol to keep the crowd back, taking care to fire into the gap between the boat and the side of the ship so that no one was hit.

Lowe had been looking after the lowering of Numbers 12, 14 and 16, which were all put down at more or less the same time. Sixth Officer Moody suggested that Lowe should get in Boat 14 and take charge of the small flotilla. Lowe agreed and climbed in. Two men tried to jump in and Lowe chased them out. Lowe filled Boat 14 and Moody Boat 16 with women and children; Lightoller was also in the vicinity part of the time. One man, an 'Italian' it was suggested, dressed as a woman in a shawl and crept in the boat. Another man, Charles Williams (a second-class passenger), was asked by Lowe to get in to row (this contradicts Colonel Gracie who said that only one male passenger got off on this side).

Charlotte Collyer and her young daughter were here too. Boat 14 was about half full when someone grabbed young Madge from Charlotte Collyer's arms and threw her in a boat. So sudden was the move that she did not even have time to say goodbye to her father. Charlotte clung desperately to her husband even as the deck slanted more steeply beneath her feet. She did not want to leave Harvey but she did not wish to abandon Madge either, leaving her with an agonizing decision to make. Two men virtually ripped her from her husband's arms and dragged her away. Harvey urged her to be brave and told her that he would get off in another boat. Whilst not everybody on board the *Titanic* acted heroically, some certainly did.

Charlotte was hurled bodily into the boat, landing on her shoulder and bruising it badly. As other women were waiting to get on behind her, she looked over their heads, seeking a last view of her beloved Harvey. All she saw was his back, as he walked away from the boat towards the other men. At the last, Officer Lowe jumped in and ordered the boat lowered away. Then a young lad climbed into it, barely more than a schoolboy. He fell among the women and crawled under a seat.

The women wanted to save him but Lowe would not have it. The Officer drew his pistol and threatened to blow his brains out. This only made the lad beg for his life, so Lowe tried a different tack. 'For God's sake, be a man, we have got women and children,' he simply said. Madge took Lowe's hand and begged him not to shoot the youth. The Officer smiled and the youth regained his composure and climbed back aboard the ship. There was barely a dry eye in the boat. Quite what it proved though is not clear. There was not a lot of room left but room there was and one more person aboard would not have sunk her. There were no more women and children on the spot to enter the boat anyway.

Eva Hart and her mother were put into Boat 14 without too much trouble. Eva bade farewell to her father, though she did not understand what was happening. He told her to hold her mummy's hand and be a good girl. Then the boat was lowered away. Eva was understandably terrified. She would never see her father again and the events of that night were to give her nightmares for years. Hers was one of many poignant farewells to be said on that cold and terrifying night.

Also off in Boat 14 was Edith Brown. She, like many others, had seen the lights of another ship from the Boat Deck, however the lights seemed at some stage to go out. She recalled being able to see the ice for miles around. She said that a number of her fellow passengers felt that the ship was unsinkable so had gone back to bed after the berg was struck even though there were ice fragments on the ship.

Edith's father had been the picture of calmness on the ship, saying nothing of the seriousness of the disaster and smoking on a cigar. After he put his wife and daughter in the boat, he simply walked away. It was not until Edith was on the water that she could see how the ship was sinking as the lights slowly slipped under the waves.

Charlotte Collyer told how, as the boat was on its way down, a steerage passenger, almost inevitably an 'Italian' according to Charlotte, leapt in. He fell upon a young child, injuring her. Lowe caught hold of him and flung him back on deck. As the boat continued its downward motion, Charlotte looked up and saw the 'Italian' being beaten to a pulp. Eventually the boat hit the water with a thud and prepared to move off.

Charlotte's evidence, like that of many others, is suspect in places. She says that when the boat reached the water those aboard could see the berg that had hit them for the first time, yet most survivors suggest that the sight of the ice was a shock when the sun first came up so she was certainly capable of embellishing a story. It is difficult to separate fact from fiction and the best that can be done is to seek corroborating details from other sources.

Some of the accounts come across as being dramatized and stereotyped, such as Charlotte's 'Italian'. Charlotte would also lose a beloved husband and the conduct of a coward made Harvey Collyer's undoubted heroism even more heroic in comparison. It does not mean that such things did not happen, just that much of what has been written, often in all probability in good faith, needs to be interpreted with caution.

About 5 feet from the surface of the water, the tackle got tangled and the boat had to be cut free. Steward George Crowe who was in the boat had also feared that she would be rushed by a crowd, 'probably Italians, or some foreign nationality other than English or American' as he jarringly described them (all these accusations against Italians would later prompt a complaint from the Italian Ambassador and an apology from Fifth Officer Lowe).

Crowe also heard the pistol shots fired by Lowe but was sure that no one was hurt. They did however succeed in stopping the rush. Apart from a woman crying, there was little disturbance. Not long after reaching the water, the boat seemed to have sprung a leak and several onboard had to start bailing her out. Some of the men used their hats to do this, a rather nice symbolic summation of some of the organization onboard the *Titanic* that night.

Miss Sarah Compton, a first-class passenger, could not even see the boat when it was her turn to board. She was virtually thrown into it. This was the general experience of the women who found it difficult to climb into the boats. She noticed that it proved difficult and jerky to lower the boats. Boat 14 eventually struck the water very hard. Once they were safely on the sea, they rowed about 150 yards away, holding their position close to the *Titanic*. The boat later tied up with Boats 4, 10, 12 and Collapsible D.

Boat 16 went away on the port side soon after. Able Seaman Ernest Archer said that everything was still quiet when the boats were being loaded. Young Steward Charles Andrews, just nineteen years of age, witnessed the fact that no steerage men were allowed in, having being told by the 'officer' loading the boat not to allow it. She went away with fifty-six people in her, pretty full but still with nine spare places. One of those on the boat was Karen Abelseth, sister of Olaus.

Olaus Abelseth and his group had been clustered towards the stern of the ship. Eventually, an officer came and shouted for the women to make their way forward. The gates were opened and Abelseth's two female companions were allowed through. However, the men were to stay where they were for the time being.

Archer still did not think the ship was doomed: 'To tell you the truth, I did not think the ship would go down. I thought we might go back to her again afterwards.' Steward Andrews was so convinced that he could see a light behind the sinking ship that he thought it was a vessel coming to the rescue.

Also in Number 16 was Stewardess Violet Jessop who noted that the crowd parted to let through a large crowd of third-class passengers, mainly foreigners, in. They rushed to the boat and for a moment it seemed as if there would be a breakdown in order. However, the officer in charge of loading regained control and the boat was lowered. But it was lowered in a jerky fashion, tipping first one way and then the other, threatening to deposit its passengers in the water far below.

As Violet got in, a baby was put in her arms. As the boat made her way down the side of the ship, it passed decks where lights still burned brightly through the portholes, illuminating the boat in searing rays of light before it disappeared again into the darkness. As she looked up, she saw people looking over the decks at them. Then, the boat hit the water with a crunching thud, which alarmed the baby and set if off crying. Someone shouted out an order for the men in the boat to row and the few there set to it. Violet noticed one of them, a stoker, dressed only in a thin singlet to keep him warm. He was still blackened with coal dust and his eyes were red from working with the furnaces. He took a cigarette from his pocket and started smoking it after offering Violet half of it.

Violet recalled that she had always wanted to see *Titanic* from a distance to appreciate fully her size and splendour. Now, in these other-worldly circumstances, the chance had unexpectedly arrived. It was, as she later described it, an incredible sight:

> My *Titanic*, magnificent queen of the ocean, a perfection of man's handiwork, her splendid lines outlined against the night, every light twinkling.

And yet as she continued to gaze fascinated at the ship, something incredible was happening. She counted the lines of light that blazed from her deck by deck. She counted to six. Looking a few minutes later, she saw only five, then four. There was no doubt about it, despite her shocked incredulity. The *Titanic* was sinking.

The women in the boat started to weep, quietly in the main, overwrought by the immensity of the horror unfolding before them of which they were front-row observers. Now more in hope than expectation, Violet scanned the horizon once more for the lights of the ship they had seen. She should be getting nearer now but she was sure that they were in fact further away. It was now clear that there would be no last minute reprieve from this direction.

Leading Stoker Fred Barrett had now arrived on A Deck, where only boats 13 and 15 were left. The two were lowered more or less together (this evidence contradicts the British Inquiry times noted by Gracie which suggests they were lowered ten minutes apart). The fall in Boat 13, the first to be lowered, had to be cut by Barrett, only just in time as Boat 15 was almost on top of her by this time. Barrett took charge but was overcome by the cold. Someone covered him with a blanket to help him warm up.

Dr Washington Dodge confirmed that Boats 13 and 15 were put in the davits at about the same time. He overheard an officer say that they would lower them from A Deck. He saw a group of around sixty people gathered around Boat 15 and decided to make his way down to A Deck. There were only about eight women there he later recalled. In fact he was mistaken; over twenty women got aboard. Dr Dodge, along with many other male survivors it seems, wished to justify his ongoing existence by suggesting that it would have been a futile waste of a life to stay aboard when there was plenty of room to go (a perfectly natural thing to do when there was space in the boats to do so). He was lucky; Steward Frederick Ray, who looked after him onboard the *Titanic*, was one of those in the vicinity and told him to get in.

Steward Ray recalled there was a fat lady who did not want to get into the boat. The size of the tiny craft when set against the magnitude of the vast sea was terrifying. However, she was given little option and was put onboard. A baby, wrapped in a blanket, was handed to someone in the boat, to be followed in by the woman carrying it. As they were lowered, they left three or four men by the deck rail. Ray saw them moving towards Boat Number 15.

More third-class passengers were reaching the Boat Deck, only now there were hardly any boats remaining. Daniel Buckley was one of those crowded around, with things now clearly desperate and likely to become more so. When Boat 13 was being lowered, a large number of men rushed her, including Buckley. The officers forced them out, firing shots in the air to drive them off according to him, replacing them with a mixed group of steerage passengers. Buckley, crying through fear, however managed to remain in it. A woman had thrown her shawl over him and disguised him. He thought it was Mrs Astor but this was wishful thinking; she would be in Boat 4.

Even now, some passengers were more terrified at being adrift in an open boat than they were of remaining on the *Titanic*. A woman in Buckley's boat, Bridget Bradley, got in, thought better of it, and tried to get out again. Fortunately for her, one of the sailors pulled her back in and the boat was then lowered away with her still in it.

As Boat 13 was being lowered, Lawrence Beesley looked over the side and saw that it was now level with the rail of B Deck. It appeared fairly full to him. There was a shout for more ladies to make their way to the boat but no reply. One of the crew looked up to Beesley, on the deck above, and asked if there were any more ladies on his deck. When the reply was in the negative, the friendly voice then suggested that Beesley should jump in. He sat on the edge of the deck and dangled his legs over the side. Throwing his dressing gown, which he had draped over his arm, into the boat first of all Beesley then jumped.

Almost as he landed, there was a shout that there were more women on B Deck. Two ladies were then passed over into the dangling lifeboat. Their story was revealing. They told Beesley that they had been on a lower deck and had climbed up to B Deck not by the normal stairway but up an iron ladder used by the crew. Other ladies had been in front of them but one of them was a large woman and her progress had been slow. Quite why women, presumably third-class (there were eighteen of them in this boat), had to climb iron ladders to reach the boats is something of a mystery and poses some intriguing and uncomfortable questions for those who believed there was no class discrimination in play.

Then, just as the boat was being lowered away, a family appeared on deck, husband, wife and baby. The baby was handed to a lady at the stern and the mother got into the middle of the boat. The father jumped in as the boat was being lowered. The only family fitting this description in Boat 13 were the Caldwell's, second-class passengers from Illinois. Boat 13 was lowered slowly and jerkily down the side of the *Titanic*. Its occupants looked bewilderedly through cabin windows whose lights still burned brightly.

As they neared the water, someone noticed the pump discharge. There was a hole 2 feet wide and a foot deep with a large volume of water pouring out. They shouted up to those lowering the boat to stop at once, fearing they would be swamped. Fortunately, their shouts were heard and the lowering was halted. Now they used the oars to push themselves away from the side of the ship and the discharge that threatened to deluge them. However, no one onboard knew how to release them from the tackle that had been used to lower them so they had to cut themselves free.

Now in the water, they had started to drift along the side of the ship. A serious situation was quickly developing for Boat 15 was being lowered on top of them. When it was only two feet above them, they shouted up for those lowering the latter to stop. In the nick of time, they did so. Boat 15 dangled there while Barrett cut the rope.

Dr Dodge found it was difficult to get hold of the oars. They had been tied together with heavily tarred twine. In addition, they had been placed in a spot where they were difficult to access, beneath the seats in the boat. He wondered at the attitude of those sitting on them, who did not seem inclined to move themselves so that the oars could be reached. With difficulty, the oars were at last put in position and used to push the boat away from the side of the ship.

The boat was once more poorly prepared. There were no lights onboard and those tasked with rowing were ill-equipped for the task. They headed for a lifeboat that was carrying a light but, although it only appeared to be a quarter of a mile away, they never managed to reach it.

When the boat started to pull away from the ship, it was realized that there was no one in it who was an obvious candidate to command her. Eventually a stoker was nominated for the dubious honour. It was decided that they should stay close to other boats. Those in the boat appeared to know that help was on its way but believed that it was from the *Olympic*. They too saw a light and rowed towards it, two lights, one above the other but as hard as they rowed they were unable to make any progress towards it. The lights in the end drew away and then disappeared altogether.

However, that was as yet in the future, for at the moment what grabbed their attention was the unbelievable sight of the *Titanic*. The scene was a dramatic one. The sky was without a cloud and the stars shone with rare brilliance. So thickly were they clustered that there seemed to be more stars than black sky that night. Then there was the intense, bitter cold.

There was hardly a breath of wind, just a cold, motionless chill that froze those in the boat to the bone. The sea was the third element of this trinity. It was calmer than any of the seamen aboard ever remembered it. One said that it reminded him of a picnic, so flat and waveless was it.

But these were just the backdrop. The great ship itself dominated the view from Boat 13, still close at hand. She stood quietly, almost as if she had accepted her fate. She sank ever so slowly deeper into the sea. Beesley thought her like a wounded animal. Her massive bulk dominated the view. Her black outline stood silhouetted against the sky and the stars. She looked beautiful save for one thing. She was still brightly lit but the lines of lights were slanting at increasingly crazy angles.

Boat 15 was also initially loaded on the Boat Deck and then taken down to A Deck to pick up a few more passengers. It is symptomatic of the confused evacuation techniques in use that there did not even seem to be a clear idea of where the boats should be loaded from. The boat was then taken down to B Deck, where there were far more people waiting to board. Fireman George Cavell believed that about sixty people were put in from this lower deck and that there were about seventy in total aboard her when she was lowered. He thought most of the female passengers who boarded were 'Irish girls'.

Fireman William Taylor insisted later that he had been assigned to Boat 15 all along and that is where he made his way. Although he and the crew got in on the Boat Deck, the lifeboat was then lowered down to A and then B Deck to fill her up. Most of the passengers loaded here he thought were steerage including a number of women and children. He looked around and could see no others left, though there was a large crowd of men. Boat 15, in common with many others, then started to head for the light of a ship.

Steward Rule said that about six men were put in on the Boat Deck and she was then lowered to A and B Deck. By now, there was a slight list to port. Scouts were sent along the deck to look for more women and children; there were none. There was then a rush when men were asked to step aboard. There were not enough places to go around and a number were left standing where they were.

Steward John Stewart was in this boat too. He may have been the last person to see Thomas Andrews alive. He saw him in the otherwise empty Smoking Room as the end approached, staring blankly at the picture of Plymouth Harbour. His lifejacket was lying on the table. When Stewart asked him if he was going to make a try for it, Andrews did not even bother to reply. Boat 15 got away about three quarters of an hour before the ship went down so stories that have Andrews still in the Smoking Room at the very end may or may not be true.

By this time, Hart had arrived with another party of third-class passengers. Boat 15 was the only one left on the starboard side; a large number of third-class passengers had got off in Boat 13, presumably the party he had escorted up before. Boat 15 was filled with Hart's passengers. However, there is some confusion in his account. He suggests that most of the loading took place on the Boat Deck which contradicts Cavell's evidence previously quoted. He says that only ten further people, including a man with a baby in his arms, entered from A Deck. Hart was then ordered into the boat by First Officer Murdoch. He perhaps deserved his place in the boats more than most given his efforts in saving some at least of the third-class passengers.

Hart also saw some women and children left but intimated that they remained on the ship by choice as frequent requests for more women and children were made and none responded. Hart stated that no women were stopped from entering the boats. He could still see a masthead light from the Boat Deck as Boat 15 was lowered. He confirmed that the stewards as a group did their best in helping third-class to the boats; however, the evidence suggests that he alone took the initiative in doing this.

Apart from the collapsibles there were only two boats now left on the *Titanic*, Numbers 2 and 4. Number 2 was an emergency boat, capable of carrying forty people in her. Despite the situation, incredibly there would still be room for fifteen more in her by the time that she was lowered. One of those who got off in Number 2 was Miss Elizabeth Allen. She said that while she was on the deck waiting to get on a boat she did not hear the band once. A line of men, about eighteen long, 'officers' as she described them, got in and were ordered back out again by an officer who called them all cowards. However, apart from a couple of pathos-ridden goodbyes, there was no panic.

Even as Boats 2 and 4 were prepared, Collapsible D was also being got ready to be slotted into the davits once they were free. Some of those in Boat 2 did not speak English; these presumably included the Kink family from Switzerland. The loading was directed by First Officer Murdoch. As the boat was being filled, Able Seaman Frank Osman saw several steerage passengers come up to the Boat Deck. The men, steerage as well as others, stood back while the women and children got in and there was still no panic. However, there were other accounts stating that Lightoller had to order several men out of the boat with the aid of a pistol (which was not loaded).

The boat was lowered away. It only had to travel some 15 feet to the water rather than the 70 feet that would normally be the case. Someone shouted to the lifeboats from the ship through a megaphone, telling them to row around to the starboard side; this may well have been Captain Smith as he was seen with a megaphone elsewhere that night. Boxhall rowed around, thinking he could take off maybe another three people. However, when he got about 22 yards off the ship he felt a little suction and feared that the boat might be pulled under if the Titanic sank. He was also disturbed by the number of people still on the ship looking to get on a lifeboat and he was afraid that his small craft would be overwhelmed.

Boxhall did manage to find a box of rockets which they had loaded thinking mistakenly that they were biscuits. They would prove useful later when the *Carpathia* was heading towards them. He did not steer for the light as, according to Osman, he was not sure if it was there or not. Osman however believed that it was and that it was sailing away from them. Perhaps Boxhall, who had for an hour and more being trying to Morse the ship and attract her attention with his rockets, had given her up as a lost cause. But Steward James Johnston was in the boat too and was convinced that he saw the white and red lights of a ship away in the distance.

By now, Boat 4 was the only lifeboat, other than the collapsibles, left to lower. Mrs Martha Stephenson noticed that on returning to A Deck again the lights were still on. The boats were lowered parallel to the window and deck-chairs formed a precarious bridge across the gap. With the list now worsening, some men felt that the women would not be able to make it across. A ladder was called for but before it arrived the women were in. Mrs Stephenson found it quite easy to jump across. She saw Colonel Astor saying goodbye to Madeleine and asking what boat they were in. There were some blankets thrown into the boat, which later proved invaluable. Every woman on the deck at that time was taken off.

Colonel Gracie personally carried Mrs Astor over the 4-foot rail. He then heard J.J. Astor ask Lightoller for permission to enter – he explained that she was 'in a delicate position' because of her pregnancy – but the officer refused while there were still any women and children left onboard. Lightoller recalled the conversation in which Astor asked for the boat number; he thought that he might be the subject of a complaint at a later stage.

Mrs Ryerson also got on the boat. Her boy Jack was with her. When an officer tried to stop him getting into the boat, her husband argued the point (young Jack was only thirteen) and won. Mrs Ryerson then turned and kissed her husband who was standing with Mr Thayer and others very quietly. Mrs Ryerson fell in the boat and scrambled across others onboard to the bows of the boat. An officer checked how many women were aboard; the reply twenty-four was shouted back. Mrs Ryerson watched:

> the ropes seemed to stick at one end. Someone called for a knife, but it was not needed until we got in the water as it was but a short distance; and then I realised for the first time how far the ship had sunk.

The deck was only about 20 feet from the sea. She could see 'all the portholes open' (which would not have helped the ship stay afloat for any longer) and the sea pouring in through them. The decks were still lit.

There was only one seaman in the boat so the cry for more went up and several men ('not sailors' according to Mrs Ryerson) climbed down into the boat. Someone shouted to the boat to go to the gangway, where presumably more people might be taken off. By this stage, barrels and chairs were being thrown overboard for use as impromptu rafts. Few were in doubt now that the great ship, pride of the White Star fleet, was soon to plummet to the ocean depths.

Quartermaster Walter Perkis lowered the boat and walked aft. However, then someone called out for another man in the boat so he slid down the lifeline from the davits into it and then took command.

Greaser Frederick Scott had gone to the starboard side but could see no boats there. Going to the port side, he heard a shot and an officer, presumably Lowe, shouting that if any man approached a boat without his permission he would 'shoot him like a dog'. Boat 4 laid off close to the ship. Scott tried to climb down a rope into her but fell in the water, where he was picked up. He recalls the time as being nearly 2.00 a.m. Greaser Thomas Granger would also be picked up in much the same way.

With no lifeboats left, now was the time to start launching the collapsibles. The first of them to be lowered was Collapsible C. It was obvious as the ship lurched lower and the boats were now nearly all gone that the situation was becoming parlous. By now a circle had been formed around the boats and only women were being let through. Quartermaster George Rowe was in charge of her. Chief Officer Wilde wanted a sailor and Captain Smith ordered Rowe to get in. A pantryman, Albert Pearce, entered the boat carrying two babies under his arms.

The collapsible had a nominal capacity of forty-seven and would be lowered with about forty people in her. However, another controversial incident was about to occur. Bruce Ismay had been around the lifeboats from the very beginning and had played an active part in the loading of them. Now, the boat was about to be lowered, one of the last left, and there was a space in it. He looked around for other people to go but could see none (which again begs the question where were they then?). Just as the boat was about to be lowered, Ismay stepped in. Perhaps he was unnerved; he had certainly felt the sensation of the ship sinking under him and could see that she was going down by the head.

The story of Ismay's entry into the boat is one of the great controversies of the disaster and Rowe was an up-close witness to it. Chief Officer Wilde asked if there were any more women or children to be loaded but no one replied or stepped forward. Rowe could not see any, nor for that matter could he see any men on the Boat Deck. He was fairly certain that Wilde did not suggest to either Ismay or fellow first-class passenger William

Carter that they enter the boat though, and intimated that they took the decision for themselves. Ismay explained his decision by saying merely that there was a place in the boat and there was no one else around to fill it.

However, he took no measures to enquire whether any steps had been taken to find anyone else on the ship who could get in, though as the boat was already being lowered it was presumably too late for this anyway. Yet Ismay also admitted to Sir Robert Finlay, appearing at the British Inquiry on behalf of the White Star Line, that he knew there must have been others left aboard who had not yet got in a boat, and would not do so. At the last moment, he opted to become a passenger rather than the Managing Director of the White Star Line. Whatever the rights or wrongs of his decision, it was one that would haunt him for the rest of his days.

Rowe could see a bright light about 5 miles away, two points off the port bow; he thought it was a sailing ship. He only noticed it after he got into the boat. As it was lowered, the *Titanic* was listing 6 degrees to port. The collapsible kept bumping the ship's prominent rivets as it was lowered, and Rowe had trouble keeping it away from the side. Because of the rubbing, it took a good five minutes to reach the sea. They then rowed towards the bright light – Ismay recalled this too in his later evidence – but made no progress towards it (Rowe believed that it was a white stern light), so in the end they turned around and headed for the green light of another lifeboat.

There were still over 1,500 people left on the ship, a number of them from third-class. The fate of third-class passengers was often a grim one and for them more than any other class (except for second-class men, who statistically suffered more deaths than any other category of passenger in percentage terms) the odds of survival were stacked against them. For once, absolute statistics do not tell the whole story. Of the third-class passengers 177 did survive but nearly 70 of these were on the collapsibles, the last boats to leave (two of which were not launched properly).

Twenty-eight also got off in Boat 13 and 38 in Boat 15, both of which owed much to the dutiful attentions of Steward Hart who led groups of third-class passengers through the rabbit-warren of passageways up to the Boat Deck. This left just thirty-seven in the other fourteen boats, many of which survived purely down to their own resourcefulness and a wise inability to do as they were told.

Edward Ryan from County Tipperary was one example of a man who survived because he used his wits. He wrote to his parents in May 1912 that he had a towel around his neck as he stood on the deck. He threw this over his head and let it hang at the back. His waterproof raincoat also helped disguise him. He walked stiffly past the officers who simply did not bother to look at him thinking that he was a woman. He got off in Boat 14. Although his actions may not seem very heroic, he perhaps thought that as there was room for more people in the boat, it seemed a bit pointless just to hang around to die.

There was also evidence, though few bothered to look for it very hard at the time, that third-class passengers had been forcibly restrained below decks until it was too late for them to escape. A young seventeen-year-old, Kathy Gilnagh, reported that she was held back with her friends by a barrier manned by a seaman. It was only when James Farrell, another third-class passenger, yelled at him that he meekly relented.

Another third-class colleen, Annie Kelly, stated later that the staircases up from third-class were blocked for fear that the passengers would overwhelm the boats. They were stopped from coming up until the last moment, though Annie survived because a friendly steward made a point of leading her up to the Boat Deck.

Margaret Murphy, also in steerage, was quoted in the *Irish Independent* of 9 May as saying that the doors were locked leading up from third-class. Male passengers in particular were shouting and swearing at the sailors and scuffles broke out. Women and children were praying and crying, terrified at the dreadful fate that loomed. Some of the sailors then battened down the hatches, saying that by trapping air below decks the ship would stay afloat for longer. All this contrasts markedly with the mythology that soon developed which suggested that passengers meekly hung around waiting to die with an air of calm resignation.

Seaman John Poingdestre saw an estimated 100 men waiting with baggage beside a ladder to second-class which was blocked by stewards. Charlotte Collyer saw guards being posted to stop more passengers from coming up on deck. All in all, there is not only evidence that third-class passengers were disadvantaged, the evidence that exists is compelling and conclusive.

Olaus Abelseth was still trapped towards the stern as the ship dipped lower. The women had been gone for some time before there was a shout for 'everybody'. However, by the time Abelseth, his brother-in-law and his cousin eventually got onto the Boat Deck it lacked many boats. On the port side, the last boat was being lowered so they moved over to starboard. Here, an officer was looking for sailors to man a boat. Abelseth had been a fisherman for six years but said nothing because his companions did not want him to go. He stayed where he was, his position increasingly precarious.

Some tragic stories were later reported concerning the steerage passengers. Catherine Buckley had been persuaded by her sister Margaret to join her in America where she had already settled. Her parents did not want her to go. She was lost and when Margaret later turned up at her parents' home, the door was slammed in her face amid accusations that she was a murderess.

Denis Lennon and Mary Mullin, also from Ireland, had fallen in love and eloped together. Realizing where they were headed, Mary's brother,

Joe, set off after them and only just missed them as the tender carried them out to the *Titanic* in Queenstown Harbour. He hammered the barrier keeping him back from the departing *Titanic* as she left Queenstown in frustration, an emotion that turned to something rather stronger when news came that both had been lost in the disaster.

Jack Thayer, still aboard, noticed that there was now an increasing sense of panic. A number of men were competing for the few places left but he could see no women waiting to get on. He watched as Bruce Ismay stepped into the last boat to be lowered. He was still a very young man and felt understandable pangs of regret that he was going to be deprived of so much of his life.

Jack Thayer and Milton Long now debated whether or not to try and get into one of the last boats. The ship was clearly sinking by the head, though her rate of submersion was still quite slow. However, the sense of panic was now strong and they felt that the boats would certainly be overturned in the chaos they felt was imminent. They watched in horror as one boat that was being lowered stuck on one side and almost tipped its occupants out. They shouted out for the lowering to be stopped and it was. The boat at last reached the water safely.

Thayer and Long now believed that the last boat had gone, being unaware of the collapsibles still left onboard. They discussed how best to survive. Thayer wanted to climb out on one of the lifeboat falls, scramble down the ropes and swim out to one of the boats. They were still about 60 feet above the water, too far to jump without a serious risk of knocking themselves out or killing themselves. They walked up some stairs on the starboard side, quietly sending messages to their families in their prayers.

Second Officer Lightoller was also left aboard. He kept going to look at the emergency stairs to gauge how quickly the *Titanic* was sinking. It was now obvious that not only was she going but she was going very soon. It would be unforgivable if she should sink with any boats left aboard; time was of the essence in loading them.

On his way back to the boats, he met a party of the officers, one of whom, a Junior Surgeon, smiled at him and asked 'Hello Lights, are you warm?' Despite the coldness of the night Lightoller had taken off his coat and was working so hard that the sweat was pouring off him. He bade the officers goodbye and then returned to the boats, determined to offload them as quickly as possible.

With just collapsibles left to worry about, Lightoller now met the engineers coming up from below. They had been released from duty a while back but had stuck to their posts even when they could no longer do much good in anything save a moral sense. In theory, they all had an allotted place in the boats. In practice, as Lightoller himself admitted, this was a farce with insufficient space for less than half the people onboard.

There were many alleged heroes onboard ship that night, some deserving of the attribute, others less so. Every single engineer onboard the *Titanic* that night was lost. The roll call of the lost is a fitting indicator of the heroism of the engineers aboard, a sacrifice that was commemorated with a magnificent memorial in Southampton after the event.

Those already safely off in the boats now stood off to the side, unsure what to do. In Boat 3, with Elizabeth Shute aboard, the tendency of those aboard was at first to stay close to the *Titanic*. Her great bulk provided a misleading reassurance. However, the mirage of security was increasingly appearing misplaced. The bows of the ship were dipping ever lower in the water, her profile becoming portentously darker as lights disappeared under the water. They looked in vain for a light to assist them in the boat but found nothing. Neither were there any biscuits for sustenance nor any water. The boat was completely unprepared for the crisis, and if a rescue ship did not appear quickly then the prospects for those who survived the initial disaster did not look good.

Messages for help had gone out and been answered. The *Mount Temple* had picked up a message from the *Titanic* to the *Olympic* saying that her engine rooms had flooded. Captain Haddock had replied 'am lighting up all possible boilers as fast as I can'. Sadly for all aboard the *Titanic*, he was too far away to make any difference. To the south, perhaps still 30 miles away, the *Carpathia* was going as fast as she could. It would be several hours before she arrived.

The desperateness of the situation was felt equally by most of those in the lifeboats. Most of them could not find any provisions even if they were in fact there. They had seen no sign of a rescue ship other than the illusory light of a distant vessel that did not seem to be doing anything to help them. It was a terrible situation to be in. However, it was preferable even then to that of those left on the ship, sagging every lower in the water, her lights still burning but now burrowing down deeper into the ocean. Time was evidently running out.

13

Waiting for Oblivion:
02.01–02.17, 15 April 1912

It was 2.05 a.m. There were now about 1,600 people left aboard the *Titanic*. There were three collapsible boats yet to be launched with a capacity of slightly less than 150. The odds against survival were now stacked against those who had not got off the ship which was dipping lower and lower into the ocean.

That was not all. The *Titanic's* builders had thought of most things; Turkish baths, swimming pools, gymnasiums, elevators. Thomas Andrews had earlier, in a very different world, made a mental note to attend to some of the smallest details that were wrong when he returned to Belfast, including the design of the ship's coat-hooks. Given all this attention to detail, it was unfortunate that nobody had bothered to put two of the three remaining collapsibles in a place from where they could easily be launched.

Dotted around the *Titanic*, those in the lifeboats looked back towards the stricken ship, the centre of their universe. Boat 14, with Charlotte Collyer aboard, moved away from the *Titanic* and stopped perhaps half a mile away. Charlotte looked back and saw the ship looking 'like an enormous glow worm'. The lights were still burning brightly, illuminating both the decks and the cabins. The only sound that reached her was that of the band playing a lively ragtime number. Although she could not make out any details, she could see clumps of passengers huddling together on deck. The whole scene was one of terrible beauty, made worse by the fact that her beloved Harvey was still somewhere onboard.

The band had had a busy night. Purser McElroy had ordered all the musicians to assemble around midnight. They had started to play in the A Deck lounge where there was a piano; obviously, only one of the pianists could have played. They were later asked to move to the Boat Deck lobby by the main stairs. An upright piano was located there, so one of the pianists could have carried on playing there too.

The makeshift band was then dismissed and made their way back to E Deck to pick up warm clothes and lifebelts. They reassembled outside on the Boat Deck, near the first-class entrance vestibule. No piano was available here, so they must have been down to a maximum of six players now. These would have been Roger Bricoux and Jack Woodward, cellists, and Fred Clark on bass. Wallace Hartley and Jock Hume played violin while George Krins played viola. Although there is much uncertainty about what they played, that they were playing for quite a while as the ship started to founder is attested to by a number of sources.

With most of the boats gone, those left on the *Titanic* could now only wait for the end, for a watery, bottomless oblivion to overwhelm them. Lightoller was in charge of loading Collapsible D, the only easily accessible collapsible left. Despite the situation, he had the greatest difficulty in finding women. When he asked if there were any around, someone replied: 'There are no women.' The boat, which was the last one to actually be lowered, was almost full. There were lots of Americans nearby, all of whom gave assistance. Some men got in, seeing the space, but then more women appeared so they got out again.

Colonel Gracie had been on the Boat Deck with Lightoller. A frantic search for more women passengers found none. There was now a marked list to port and Gracie feared that the ship was about to capsize. Lightoller, repeating the instructions of Chief Officer Wilde, ordered all onboard to move to starboard to try and even the weight up. (Another witness, Samuel Hemming, also saw Captain Smith telling those left aboard to move to starboard. It is not clear if these are two separate events or the same event confused). Gracie reflected pensively back over his life, feeling that his end was now a certainty.

As they moved to the starboard side a large crowd has assembled by the rails. They included John Thayer and George Widener. Gracie also saw to his horror Mrs Caroline Brown and Miss Edith Evans suddenly appear. Miss Evans told how she had got separated from her friends in the crowd (she now gave Gracie, previous to that night a stranger, her name for the first time). Gracie in the meantime noticed the crew trying to lower a collapsible from the roof of the officers' quarters.

Other passengers prepared themselves for the end. Benjamin Guggenheim, dressed in his best, passed on a message to Steward Johnston:

> Tell my wife if it should happen that my secretary and I go down and you are saved, tell her I played the game out straight and to the end. No woman should be left aboard this ship because Ben Guggenheim was a coward.

He asked Johnson to tell his wife that his last thoughts were of his wife and his daughters, conveniently ignoring the presence of his mistress in a nearby lifeboat.

Perhaps though this was a time to ask for forgiveness, a formal kind of confession now that the end of life was near. One of those aboard the ship as she neared her end was a man called J.H. Rogers, though he was not registered under that name. He was a card sharp but at the end he was helping women into the boats. To one of these he handed a note, saying laconically 'if saved, inform my sister, Mrs F.J. Adams of Findlay Ohio, lost'. His mother broke down when informed of his fate. She had not heard from him for two years, his last known location being London.

As Lightoller was trying to lower Collapsible D, he was 'rushed' by third-class passengers and drew his pistol to make them leave the boats they had entered. There was still some room as a crew member now approached asking Mrs Brown and Miss Evans to enter the boat. Gracie led them back towards the port side. As he did so, a line of crew barred his progress.

As the two ladies approached the boat, Miss Evans insisted that Mrs Brown got in first. However, Miss Evans was then unable to enter the boat. There was a 4-foot-high gunwale to climb and Miss Evans could not do it. It appears that she lost her nerve. She said 'never mind, I will go on a later boat' and then ran away and was not seen again. Lightoller later insisted that when he lowered the last boat, there were no women on deck. Gracie confirmed this saying:

> Neither the second officer not I saw any women on the deck during the interval there-after of fifteen or twenty minutes before the great ship sank.

But there were 106 women left somewhere who went down with the ship.

Lightoller believed that a couple of 'Chinese' stowed away in the boat; 'foreigners' unscrupulously trying to save their lives being a constant feature of this very Anglo-Saxon drama. By now, he could see water coming up the stairway that led to the Boat Deck. There seemed little more he could now do, having conscientiously if not always efficiently overseen the loading of the boats. Chief Officer Wilde suggested that Lightoller take command of the collapsible when it was lowered. 'Not damn likely' came the reply.

Among those who got off in the boat were Quartermaster Arthur Bright who had been firing the rockets along with Quartermaster Rowe and Fourth Officer Boxhall. Bright had later gone up to the Boat Deck, where the collapsibles were stowed on the deck until they could be put in the davits after the lifeboats had been launched. He had helped launch C on the starboard side and then returned to D on the port side where he was fortunate enough to find a place.

Seaman William Lucas was also in the boat. He could see that there was not long left now. However, he could also spot some way off a faint red light, the sidelight of a distant ship that was obviously now not going to come to help. He could see the hint of a masthead light, perhaps 9 miles away. The water was up to the bridge by the time the boat was launched. John Hardy, a second-class steward, saw that by the time the boat reached the water there was a heavy list to port. He recalled speaking to Murdoch a good half an hour before he left; Murdoch already thought that the ship was a goner back then.

When they left there were no women or children to be seen on the deck. There were not even any male passengers left according to Hardy, which does rather conflict with Gracie's account of many passengers gathered by the rails. It also contradicts Lightoller's recollection that there was a significant crowd on the deck now. He had ordered a cordon to be formed of crew and 'reliable' passengers to stop the boat being rushed.

When Hardy was asked where the missing 1,500 people were by Senator Fletcher at the American Inquiry that later followed, he said: 'They must have been between decks or on the deck below or on the other side of the ship. I cannot conceive where they were.' The boat, including a number of Middle Eastern women, was now lowered about 40 feet into the water.

One passenger, Frederick Hoyt, was picked up from the sea by the collapsible. His wife was already in the same boat. Hoyt had just seen Captain Smith who had suggested that he go down to A Deck to see if there was a boat nearby. Hoyt did as the Captain suggested, saw D about to be lowered and decided to swim out to her. It therefore appears to have been a complete fluke that his wife was onboard.

Hugh Woolner also made his way to a deserted A Deck along with Mauritz Björnström Steffanson. By now the lights were glowing red. He said: 'This is getting to be rather a tight corner. I do not like being inside these closed windows. Let us go out through the door at the end.' They walked out on deck, and as they did so the water rolled over their feet. They both hopped onto the gunwale, preparing to jump; otherwise they would have been trapped against the ceiling and would have undoubtedly died. The list was quite great by now as there was a 9-foot gap between the ship and the boat.

Collapsible D was just then being lowered. Woolner saw there was a gap in the bows and suggested to Steffanson that they should jump into it. Steffanson jumped in first, somersaulting into the boat. Woolner landed half in the water. Steffanson was standing up and pulled him in. After his rescue, Woolner would proudly tell how he had pulled men, 'foreign' steerage passengers, out of another boat that had previously been lowered. He did not explain what moral difference if any there was between getting into a boat when it was on deck and jumping into one when it was being lowered.

The wireless operators had continued to do everything they could to get help as quickly as possible. When Bride had been running his errands to Captain Smith, he had noticed the lifeboats being loaded. As the ship's situation worsened, the wireless had weakened. Then the Captain had put his head in the cabin to tell them that the engine rooms were starting to fill with water and that it could only be a matter of time before the dynamos no longer worked. Word was passed on to the *Carpathia*.

At one stage a woman had entered the shack and fainted. The wireless operators revived her with a glass of water and sat her in a chair. Her husband then came in and took her away. Bride then went outside where the water was now almost up to the boat deck. Even now, Phillips continued to keep the wireless going. Bride went back to his cabin to get his lifebelt and also extra clothes to keep him warm. He then went back to the operating room and put a lifebelt on Phillips while he continued to work. Phillips asked him to go outside and see if there were any boats left. He himself had been out not long before and came back seeing that things looked 'very queer'. Bride took this to mean that 'the sooner we were out of it, the better'.

Bride did so and saw about twelve men trying to get a collapsible from a position near one of the funnels. It was the last boat left. Bride went to help them and then went back to the wireless cabin to tell Phillips that all the boats were now gone. Then Captain Smith came in for one last time. He told them both:

Men, you have fully done your duty. You can do no more. Abandon your cabin. Now it's every man for himself. You look out for yourselves. I release you. That's the way of it at this kind of time. Every man for himself.

Only when the water started coming into the wireless shack did Phillips and Bride abandon it. Bride related how, at this last moment, a stoker crept into the cabin and took the lifebelt off Phillip's back. There was a scuffle and the stoker ended it lying on the floor unconscious, or possibly even dead. It has the feel of a story made up for the benefit of a media hungry for sensational tales, with Bride's assertion in the *New York Times* that he hoped the stoker was killed and that he would rather the assailant had walked the plank or stretched a rope with his neck having a particularly grating note to it.

Bride and Phillips made their way out on deck, where the junior operator noted that there were still some passengers without lifejackets on. It was presumably now, or shortly after, that Bride saw Captain Smith for the last time, as he claimed later that he saw the Captain dive off the bridge and into the sea (Lightoller recalled seeing him for the last time, presumably shortly before this, walking across the bridge). The band was still playing, ragtime as Bride remembered it later. Phillips ran towards the stern and that was the last that Bride ever saw of him.

Others had already taken matters into their own hands. Charles Joughin, the baker, could see that there was not going to be enough room for everyone – including him – in the boats and threw about fifty deckchairs over the side, reckoning that they at least would float and give him something to hang onto. He was in the pantry on A Deck, underneath the Boat Deck, taking a drink of water when he heard a crash and the sound of running feet over his head. He made his way out and saw a crush of people moving panic stricken towards the stern as the ship ploughed yet lower into the freezing ocean. He managed to keep himself clear when all of a sudden the ship took a large list to port. Most people were thrown over in a bunch but Joughin managed to keep himself away from the chaos.

Sidney Daniels had been helping load the boats pretty much from the start. He had been vaguely aware of the band playing lively tunes in the background. Now all the boats were away save the last collapsible. Someone shouted out for a knife as they tried to cut the ropes which lashed it to the top of the officers' quarters. Daniels took his out of his pocket and passed it up.

Lightoller had climbed back on top of the officers' quarters with a view to cutting down one of the collapsibles from there. There was another seaman, Samuel Hemming, there helping him. Together they cut the ropes holding the boat down and jumped round to the inside, intending to take hold of the gunwales and throw the boat down on the deck. However, the deck was no longer there, as it was rapidly disappearing underwater. There was no chance of lowering the boat now, they just dropped it into the water and hoped that anyone struggling in the ocean would be able to climb into it.

Steward Edward Brown jumped into the boat and called for the falls to be cut. However, as the water rolled up the deck, he was swept out of the boat and into the water, though he soon bobbed up to the surface because of his lifebelt. He was surrounded by people struggling for their lives whose fight to live was so determined that they tore some of the clothes from him. However, Brown – who could not swim – managed to climb into the collapsible that had by now floated off the ship.

As the end approached, Colonel Gracie was with J.J. Astor, John Thayer Senior, George Widener and 'Clinch' Smith. Once they realized the lifeboats had gone, the situation 'was not a pleasant one'. He recalled the old Trojan hero of school days; '*vox faucibus haesit*' ('his voice stuck in his throat') he reminisced, in a way that spoke eloquently of his classical education. Inwardly, Gracie muttered a valedictory 'goodbye to all at home'. He then learned that there was one collapsible boat left on the roof and decided to try for that.

A crewman asked if anyone had a knife and Gracie handed his over. Some oars were propped up against the officer's quarters so that the collapsible could be lowered down them as if it were a ramp. However, the boat crashed onto the deck, breaking several oars in the process. Then an officer from on top of the quarters asked if there were any seamen left – Gracie believed he was cutting loose the other collapsible boat. Amazingly a couple of the crew were still debating whether or not the ship's watertight compartments would keep her afloat.

Young Jack Thayer was still in the company of Milton Long. They went to the Boat Deck where there was just this one boat left but such a crowd around it that they did not think it was worth the bother of trying to get into it. They then stood by the rail just back from the bridge. There was a big list to port and Thayer feared that the ship might turn turtle at any moment.

As Lightoller moved to the starboard side to see what was happening there, the ship took a sharp plunge forward. Lightoller theorized that probably one of the internal bulkheads had just collapsed and the water was now pouring through the gaping hole that this would have left in the ship's structure. The water submerged the bridge and came rushing up the decks. As it did so, it overwhelmed huddled groups of people.

Sidney Daniels had left them to it and wandered around the deck. He could see that the sea was now almost up to the bridge and it could only be a matter of time before *Titanic* was immersed in a watery grave. 'Time to leave,' he thought. With the water already up to his knees he climbed up onto the deck-rail and launched himself into the sea. He swam out a short distance and came across another man hanging tight to a round lifebuoy. Swimming past this – he thought it was too close to the ship and would be badly affected by the suction when the ship went down – he saw something in the distance. Moving closer to it, he saw that it was an upturned boat, Collapsible B.

The wave had swept over Harold Bride too. He was surprised to see that Collapsible B was still on deck. They simply could not launch it. He recalled:

> Twelve men were trying to boost it down to the Boat Deck. They were having an awful time. It was the last boat left. I looked at longingly a few minutes; then I gave a hand and over she went.

In fact, as Bride approached to help, there was a sudden wave rising up the deck. It carried the boat off as Bride grabbed hold of an oarlock. It was soon afloat in the sea with Bride firmly attached to it. The trouble was that when it landed in the water, Bride was trapped underneath it. He had to swim out from under her and up to the surface. Here, he would soon find himself surrounded by hundreds of men fighting for their lives.

Seventeen-year-old John Collins, a cook, was on his first voyage and it was turning out to be one he would never forget. He had run across to the port side of the Boat Deck along with a steward, a woman and two children. The woman was in tears. The steward had one of the children in his arms, the mother the other. Collins took the child from the woman and made for one of the boats. Then a message arrived. There was a collapsible being loaded on the starboard side and all women and children were to make for there. Collins was just turning around when the water came coursing on up the deck and washed the child out of his arms. He was then pulled underwater where he remained 'for two or three minutes'.

He came up close to the upturned collapsible. He was only 4–5 feet off and there were people on it already. They did not help him on however; their eyes were fixed on the sight of the ship as its death throes started to convulse her. The bow was underwater and only the stern was now visible. There could only be minutes left before the final denouement.

Gracie saw the wave too. All of a sudden the water swept up the deck and struck the bridge. Thinking that the last collapsible would be overwhelmed by the vast number of people trying to board her, Gracie and his friend 'Clinch' Smith decided to try another escape route. They moved towards the stern and then:

> There arose before us from the decks below a mass of humanity several lines deep, covering the Boat Deck, facing us, and completely blocking our passage towards the stern.

The sudden arrival of all these previously unseen people horrified him. Able Seaman Frank Osman believed he saw something similar. He was on one of the later boats to leave (Number 2, lowered about 1.45 a.m.) and could therefore still pick out details on the sinking ship as he was not far off her. He saw that 'the steerage passengers were all down below and after she got a certain distance it seemed to me that all the passengers climbed up her'. He saw 'a big crowd of people' go up to the top deck.

This then was the truth. Hundreds of people had not made it to the Boat Deck, in particular steerage passengers including women and children. They all moved towards the stern where they found their way blocked by the fence and railing dividing first and second-class. Shocked to the core by the nightmare that was unfolding before him, Gracie saw the water rise further up the decks. It started to roll over him. However, like a surfer he managed to ride the wave and climbed on top of the officers' quarters. Tragically, 'Clinch' Smith disappeared beneath the waters, never to be seen again.

With the end now approaching, some of those left onboard had now decided to gamble all with one last desperate throw of the dice. Jack Thayer stood quietly by the rail, feeling very sorry for himself as well he might. He thought of the pleasures in life he might have enjoyed that he would now be deprived of. He reckoned it was now about 2.15 a.m. and the rate at which the ship was sinking had now noticeably increased. The water was up to the bridge and he reckoned that the bow was now about 60 feet underwater. The crowd surged up the decks towards the stern in an attempt to earn another few minutes of precious life.

The lights now went dull, though they still continued to burn. The roaring of the exhausts stopped, to be replaced by the noise of a mass of terrified humanity believing that the end was nigh. Muffled explosions could be heard inside the ship. All of a sudden, the ship dipped forward. There was a rumbling roar far below, perhaps some of the boilers breaking loose as the *Titanic* was now at an impossible angle. The noise reminded Thayer of standing under a railway bridge when a locomotive passed overhead. Mingled with it were the noises of thousands of pieces of crockery being smashed to bits.

Martha Stephenson saw that the *Titanic* was now well down in the water. There were no lights in her boat (Number 4) and the seaman aboard her did not know how to cast off which alarmed her as she feared they might be pulled down with the *Titanic*. They had been asked to go to a gangway to take people off but it was not open. She was now alarmed as people were throwing things into the water and there was a distinct sound of china crashing. She implored the others to pull away from the ship.

They would later pick up three people from the water. One of them had a flask of brandy in his pocket and was drunk. The brandy was immediately thrown in the water and he was chucked into the bottom of the boat with a blanket over him. The three rescued men told the others how fast the ship was sinking and again Mrs Stephenson implored the others to row out of the danger zone.

Quite what to do now the end was near was an issue that exercised many people in the boats dotted around on the open sea. This was a classic clash between moral values and the instinct to maximize one's own chances of survival. Major Peuchen heard the sounds of a whistle and the boat stopped. Those aboard Boat 6 all felt that they should row back towards the ship to try and pick up survivors. However, Quartermaster Hichens who was in charge would not assent; 'it is our lives now, not theirs'. He had been all for rowing back to the ship when the lifeboat had been first lowered and the passengers had had to remind him that Captain Smith had ordered the boats, when launched, to stay together and row away from the ship. Now he had evidently had a change of heart.

He now ordered the passengers to row as hard as they could so that they would not be sucked under when the *Titanic* sank. In fact, Margaret Brown said that he admonished them all that it was pointless to row away as the suction would be so great when the ship went down; he had apparently lost his nerve. He further told them that the explosion of the boilers would tear the icebergs apart and overwhelm the boat. He reminded them of the *New York* incident when the *Titanic* had left Southampton.

Eva Hart sat in Boat 14, struggling to make sense of what was happening. For a girl of seven, the feeling of terror was overwhelming. There were several moments that would haunt her to her dying day. One of them was the panic from those left onboard after all the boats had gone. Perhaps she could not see what was happening but she could certainly hear it. She felt terrified, not least because her beloved father was somewhere in that mass of humanity.

On the now doomed ship, Thayer and Long were now standing by the starboard rail next to the second funnel. They had decided to jump for it and avoid the struggling scrum of swimmers that would soon be in the water. Now was the time. They shook hands and Thayer took off his coat, thinking it would encumber him when he was in the sea. He sat on the rail and pushed off with both his hands and legs so that he did not hit the side of the ship. It was about 15 feet to the water. As he hit it, a freezing cold got hold of him as if he was in a vice.

Then he was seized by something else, the tremendous suction of the ship as it sank lower. It dragged him down. He managed to hold his breath however and push hard enough to break free of the dying ship's grip. He surfaced about 40 yards away from the ship. He later noticed that his watch had stopped at 2.22 a.m. Sadly, Milton Long – who had jumped just a few seconds later than Thayer – did not make it.

Seaman Samuel Hemming looked over the side with all the boats now gone. He reasoned that he should get off the ship before the panic that would inevitably ensue when the *Titanic* dipped under. Hemming looked over the starboard rail first but could see nothing. However, looking over the port side, he could see a boat not too far off. He climbed down a rope into the water and swam out a distance of about 200 yards to it. This was his lucky night. One of his mates was onboard and held out his hand to help him aboard (this was Boat 4).

Steward Andrew Cunningham had waited until all the boats had gone and then thrown himself into the water. He thought that he was in the sea for half an hour and swam about three quarters of a mile until he was also picked up by Boat 4 which had stayed relatively close at hand (note the difference in perception; Hemming thought that it was 200 yards to Boat 4, Cunningham believed it was three quarters of a mile).

Richard Norris Williams Junior was one of those scrambling to stay alive. He was not helped by a thick and heavy fur coat that threatened to drag him down even though he had a lifebelt on and he threw it off. He also kicked off his shoes and then swam across to Collapsible A some 20 yards away. He climbed aboard, up to his waist he said in water.

All around, the 700-odd souls sitting in the lifeboats looked in disbelief at the sight before them. There, before their eyes, the greatest ship in the world now loomed at a crazy angle. The lights had burned right until these very last moments but they were about to go out for ever.

If for them it was a nightmare, what must it then have been for those still on the terrifically slanted decks who waited in terror for the end? The slope of the deck had got increasingly steeper, making it harder for the hundreds still on the ship to stand. Now oblivion beckoned, hidden beneath 2 miles of freezing, black water. Now the terror was about to reach an awful conclusion.

One of the few people to survive from the mass of humanity that now remained on the ship, steerage passenger Carl Jansson, later told how:

> we were suddenly plunged into darkness... I could not accustom myself to the change for several minutes. I think I was in a sort of daze and have no clear recollection of what happened afterward or how long a time had elapsed. Suddenly I heard shrieks and cries amidships... People began to run past me toward the stern of the ship, and as I started to run I realised that the boat was beginning to go down very rapidly... Her nose was being buried.

The end of the world was nigh.

14

Descent into Hell:
02.18–02.20, 15 April 1912

The awful climactic moment was imminent. Those left aboard the ship prepared themselves for their end. For most, death would come and claim them, embracing them in an icy, suffocating grip. However, there were just a few lucky souls who were about to enjoy a miraculous reprieve but they were in a tiny minority. Beneath the starlit sky, the *Titanic* started to point upwards, a giant finger pointing up to the heavens while her now submerged bows reached down towards the ocean depths far, far below.

The *Titanic's* death throes had been long and extended so far. However, most witnesses thought that once the water passed the bridge, everything happened much more quickly. In fact, Joseph Scarrott was more specific. He thought that the decisive moment came when the port light, forward of the bridge, went under and after that the rate at which the ship began to sink accelerated dramatically.

Charlotte Collyer thought she could see from her boat a crowd huddling together on the deck around a man who had climbed upon an object, perhaps a chain or a large coil of rope. She thought it might have been a priest, Father Byles, whom she had seen earlier, leading a terrified congregation in prayer, offering what consolation he could as his flock approached the valley of the shadow of death. For him, the moment was especially poignant; he was on his way to America to conduct his brother's wedding. As he ministered to them as well as he could, she thought that she heard the band playing 'Nearer My God to Thee'.

Closer to the doomed liner, Jack Thayer had a grandstand view of what was about to happen. Already, the cold was starting to suck the life out of him but he could not take his eyes off the sight of the mighty *Titanic*. She was surrounded by a glare; it almost looked to him as she was on fire. She was continuing to sink lower into the water, which now lapped at the base of the first funnel. Onboard, the mass of those remaining were running back towards the stern which was at an ever-increasing angle.

As the ship sank lower Lightoller dived with it, while Colonel Gracie hung onto to the railings on the officers' quarters roof and was pulled under. 'I was in a whirlpool of water, swirling round and round,' he later recalled. He swam away from the starboard side of the submerged hulk. It was not cold, presumably because the boilers, the fires of which had been extinguished, were still warm.

What happened in the last few moments aboard ship was told graphically by Second Officer Lightoller. Still on top of the officers' quarters, he looked down on the people that still struggled to get away from the deathly grip of the water. As the bow sank down, the stern started to rise up and groups of people started to make their way up the increasingly-slanted deck. As he watched, he started to realize with horror the futility of their actions. By becoming part of a crowd they were lessening their chances of survival. Although it was natural to try to hang on to a few seconds of extra life, he reasoned that he needed to stay cool and think calmly if he were to live.

As he rationalized the situation he believed that now was the right time to get off the ship. He dived headlong into the water. As he hit it, it was like being stabbed by a thousand knives. His rationality left him for a second; he saw that the crow's-nest was still above the water and swam for it but quickly realized that this was a foolish thing to do. Instead, he swam to starboard, trying to get away from the ship. He was working hard to make any progress when he felt a heavy weight in his pocket. It was his revolver, now more useless than ever, and he flung it into the water.

Water was now pouring into the stokeholds through a grating. The suction this created threatened to hold Lightoller down. At any moment, he expected the wire cover to break. If this were to happen, he would be sucked down into the innards of the ship and his end would be a foregone conclusion. Just then, a rush of air from inside the ship forced him up, away from the stokeholds. He was briefly pulled under again, but once more broke through, this time for good.

As he reached the surface, Lightoller was aware of many others in the water around him, some swimming, others drowning. He thought it an utter nightmare of both sight and sound. He had come up next to an upturned boat but he made no attempt to get on for the time being and was content merely to hold onto a rope that was dangling over its side. As he watched the black silhouette of the ship rise ever higher he saw more and more people sliding down its steepened decks or plummeting over the side into the water.

Even as he watched, Lightoller saw with horror the forward funnel start to break away from the ship. It had been held by two substantial stays but the immense strain on the *Titanic* now broke the port one loose. The starboard stay lasted for a short time longer but this too then snapped. The effect was to send the funnel crashing over the starboard side of the ship. It fell into the water with immense force, missing Lightoller by inches. Others were far less fortunate and were crushed.

There was however a luckier side-effect for some. The wake created by the funnel falling forced the upturned boat some 50 yards away from the *Titanic*. Lightoller had held onto the rope and now felt it was time to get on top of the collapsible which he duly did. Even at the acute angle she was at, Lightoller noticed that the lights still burned aboard the *Titanic*. At this moment, there was a massive crash, possibly as the boilers left their beds and went crashing down through the doomed ship (though a number of boilers have been found on the wreck still *in situ* in the engine rooms).

A crew member, John Hagan, on the upturned collapsible B along with among others Lightoller, described how the ship starting shaking noticeably when it was part submerged. He looked up and saw the forward funnel falling. It missed him by about a yard. Although the wave pushed them further away from the doomed ship, several of those onboard the boat were washed off as a result. Hagan hung on for grim life but was soaked. Some of the *Titanic's* decking had broken off and was being used for impromptu oars.

Boat 13 had rowed away from the doomed ship as fast as she could. By about 2.15 a.m. it was clear that the end was near. As Lawrence Beesley watched, the *Titanic* tilted slowly up. She reached a vertical position and stayed motionless. Then the lights went out, flashed back on for a second and then went out for good. There was a loud noise, not an explosion Beesley insisted. It was instead partly a roar, partly a groan, partly a rattle, partly a smash. It went on for some seconds and Beesley assumed it was the engines breaking loose inside the ship now she was at such an unnatural angle.

Slowly but inexorably the bows dug deeper into the water. As they did so, the stern was pulled up, higher and higher, reaching a point until it was almost but not quite vertical. Some of those left on the ship could see that the end was now just moments away and had leapt off into the water rather than risk being pulled under with her. Others, driven by an instinct to hang on to every last breath of existence, clung to the deck rails or had climbed to the stern where they now hung on for grim life.

Lookout George Symons on Boat 1 saw that the stern had lifted out of the water, with the ship's propellers just showing. Nearly all the lights had gone out, and the only one left was a mast light. His boat was now about 200 yards off and rowed further away to escape the expected massive suction.

Elizabeth Shute could see that the mammoth ship was now fast disappearing. Towards the end, only a tiny light was left aboard her, a lantern at the very stern of the ship, the same view that George Symons had. She could not take her eyes off the light, the final indicator that the ship itself had any life left in her. Once it disappeared, then that would mark the end. She watched the black silhouette of the *Titanic* slowly disappear. As it did so, the crewmen onboard Boat 3 urged the rowers to make haste: 'She's gone lads, row like hell or we'll get the devil of a swell.'

To Jack Podesta, the ship had seemed to stay in the same position for a while and he wondered if the watertight compartments might save her after all. All of a sudden, the bow went under and the stern started to rise in the air. Her lights went out and there was a terrible rumbling noise. He hypothesized that it was the boilers falling as well as bulkheads collapsing.

From his grandstand position, Jack Thayer heard the rumble and roar continue to resound around the night sky. Then, as he watched, the *Titanic* split in two. A funnel split off the ship, sending a cloud of sparks into the air. It came crashing down into the water. Jack thought it was bound to hit him but fortunately it missed him by some 30 feet. The suction dragged him down. At the time he must have feared this was the end, but it was not, for as he managed to resurface he came up against an upturned collapsible.

Quartermaster Bright was in Collapsible D. They were about 50 to 100 yards away when the *Titanic* sank. He heard a noise but did not think it was an explosion, more like a clanking of chains. Seaman William Lucas, on the same boat, thought they were 100 to 150 yards away when there was an 'explosion'. Even at this late stage, he saw a faint red light about 9 miles away.

There were dozens of different views of those last moments. There was as much controversy about what happened to the ship at the end of her life as there was about any other event during her final hours. Opinions were divided about whether there were any explosions as the ship went down. There was even more dissension about whether or not she broke in two.

Colonel Gracie was certain that there was no explosion of the boilers. If there was, he is sure that he would have heard it. There was also no wave, which he believes it would have caused. Second Officer Lightoller and Third Officer Pitman also confirmed this belief. Hugh Woolner, another survivor, believed that it was the sound of crockery and loose fittings smashing as the angle of descent became steeper that could be heard. Some of the boilers and engines probably broke away from their fittings too, victims of the irresistible gravitational pull now that the ship was almost vertical.

There is conclusive evidence that the boilers did not explode and it comes from marine archaeology. Dives on the wreck of the ship have identified a number of boilers, all intact and undamaged, some still in position, others scattered loosely across the seabed, confirming that they did not blow up. The noise therefore much more likely came from the sound of collapsing bulkheads and other structural damage.

Lightoller was sure that the ship did not split in two though he confirmed that she did raise herself to the perpendicular. Third Officer Pitman thought she did not break either. Lightoller saw that the after part of the vessel then appeared to level with the water (this does not seem to make sense if she did not split). Then she reached an angle of 60 degrees and the boilers came crashing down. Finally she reached absolute perpendicular and slipped slowly under. There was no explosion whatsoever that he heard but he noticed that the water got markedly warmer.

But Third Officer Pitman heard four 'reports, like a big gun in the distance'. He assumed that this was the sound of the ship's bulkheads going. He believed that he did not hear these sounds until the ship was completely submerged, though this contradicted many other witnesses. Major Peuchen also heard 'explosions' but thought that the ship was still afloat. Fifth Officer Lowe said that he heard four 'explosions' as the ship went down. In contrast, Quartermaster Rowe heard only one sound as the ship sank, which he described as a 'rumbling' rather than an 'explosion'.

It was understandable that, given the awfulness of the situation, people heard and saw different things as the end came. Lightoller's evidence that the boat did not split in two was contradicted by a very detailed description of the end from Seaman Joseph Scarrott, in the same boat as Eva Hart. He described the sight of the last moments as something he would never forget. He had watched as she sank lower in the water with a slight list to starboard. The rate at which she went under seemed to accelerate when the water reached the bridge. When it had reached a point just past the third funnel, there were four explosions which he thought was probably the sound of boilers bursting. The ship was right up on end then.

Then she broke in two between the third and fourth funnels; this was significant as this was close to the position of the aft expansion joint, a point of natural weakness. The expansion joints (there was another further forward) were small gaps, about an inch wide, which extended down just a couple of decks. Their purpose was to allow the ship to flex when the seas were rough.

This was no problem in normal circumstances but the water that had been pouring into the ship at the rate of many tons a minute since she stuck had started to literally pull the ship apart. Again, marine archaeology is a help. The expansion joint has been identified and is now a split several feet wide, evidence of the great tension that was starting to tear the *Titanic* apart.

A piece of the *Titanic's* steel has also been raised to the surface, and part of it has been subjected to fracture tests. The steel used in the production was according to experts surprisingly strong, almost as good as modern steel would be, and perfectly adequate for the purposes for which the ship was ordinarily intended. However, as the ship started to fill with water she was put in positions she was never designed to be in. The bow of the wreck shows a number of small, hairline cracks in the superstructure, evidence of the great strains that it was exposed to.

The break-up was a slow, drawn-out process. Modern computer simulation has shown the effect of water flowing into the ship's forward compartments on the structural integrity of the *Titanic*. Incredible stresses were put on the superstructure, especially on the aft expansion joint near the third funnel. The ship would have broken from the upper decks first with the bottom of the ship failing last of all.

The incredible sight that Scarrott had witnessed was a result of the massive stresses she had been under. To make his evidence even more compelling, when the wreck of the *Titanic* was discovered decades later, the ship was found to be lying in two main parts, divided at a point between the third and fourth funnels, exactly where he said he saw the split occur.

Others had seen something very similar. Quartermaster Alfred Olliver believed that the *Titanic* broke in half and that the after-part then righted itself for a short time. Frank Osman saw exactly the same thing happening. Olliver heard several little explosions both before she sank and then when she was actually going down. Able Seaman George Moore also thought that the ship broke in half and heard two explosions.

Able Seaman Edward Buley saw the *Titanic* snap in two before she sank; he thought 'the after-part came up and stayed up five minutes before it went down'. At one stage, he thought that the after part of the ship settled horizontally and was going to float. Steward George Crowe was more specific than most. He said: 'Presently she broke in two, probably two-thirds of the length of the ship... she broke, and the after part floated back.' Frederick Scott, a greaser, saw that the ship 'broke off at the after funnel and when she broke off her stern end came up in the air and came down on a level keel and disappeared'.

Frank Evans said that she 'parted between the third and fourth funnels', leaving approximately 200 feet of *Titanic's* stern still afloat. Quartermaster Arthur Bright was categorical in his assessment of what happened at the end:

> She broke in two. All at once she seemed to go up on end, you know, and came down about half way, and then the after part righted itself again and the forepart had disappeared. A few seconds later the after part did the same thing and went down. I could distinctly see the propellers – everything – out of the water.

He did not hear an explosion as she went, more like a rattling chain.

There were then a number of reports, consistent in detail, which suggested that the ship had broken before sinking. However, despite the fact that these accounts significantly outnumbered those which asserted she did not break, the Inquiries that followed decided that the *Titanic* did not split before she sank. It is noticeable that most of those who said that she did not break were the *Titanic's* surviving officers, perhaps motivated, subconsciously or otherwise, by a residual pride in their ship. In both cases the Inquiries chose not to be led by the evidence, perhaps giving excessive weight to the minority opinion of the officers over other witnesses.

Robert Ballard, who found the wreck in 1985, gave his own explanation for what had happened, theorizing that:

> as the bow sank and the stern rose ever higher out of the water, the pressure on the keel became increasingly unbearable until it finally snapped at a weak point in the structure between the third and fourth funnels in the area of the reciprocating engine room hatch.

Given the evidence, nearly 2,000 feet between main portions of wreckage, the absence of a skid mark between the two pieces and the fact they are facing in different directions, his view was that the ship almost certainly broke in two at or near the surface. Probably the Grand Staircase had left a vast cavernous open space which created a weakness in the ship's structure.

Even more recent investigations have added a twist. These suggest that although the superstructure of the ship did split on the surface, the two pieces remained attached down at the keel. It was only when the ship began her descent to the bottom that the keel section split too. A huge and separate section of the keel has been found on the seabed lending weight to this theory.

All this is of mainly academic interest. Those who were there were not particularly concerned whether she broke in two or not. It was the human drama and its sheer horror that was the greater issue. First-class passenger Philip Mock reckoned that his boat, Number 11, was a mile away when the *Titanic* went down. He last saw her with her stern high in the air. There was a noise and he saw a huge column of black smoke slightly lighter than the sky rising high into the air and then flattening out at the top like a mushroom. This apocalyptic symbolism, coming from what was a pre-nuclear age, is perhaps one of the most haunting images of the end of the *Titanic*.

Jack Thayer tried to pull himself aboard the nearby collapsible but did not have the strength to lift his legs up. Fortunately, someone else who was already on top of what was effectively a raft rather than a boat pulled him up. The *Titanic* was still afloat, perhaps 60 feet away from him. The forward motion had stopped and it was as if she were pivoting on a point. Slowly but inexorably the stern was rising in the air. The last funnel rested on the surface of the water but Jack did not believe that it broke off.

In horror, Jack realized that he could see hordes of people still struggling towards the stern. They looked to him like a swarm of bees. As he watched, the stern lifted still higher and people began to fall off in ones and twos. She seemed to stay suspended there for minutes and slowly turned as if to hide her end from Jack's disbelieving eyes. As he looked up, he saw that he and the others gathered around the collapsible were beneath the towering propeller. But even as he thought they would come crashing down on top of them, the ship slid gently down towards the waves. *Titanic* was gone from the sight of man, not quite forever but for another seventy-three years when the world would be a very different place from the one she left.

Jack noticed that there was virtually no suction. Those in the boat watched on in horror. At the end, a sigh ascended from the collapsible, all letting out a sob as one, as if there were just one corporate soul aboard it. Margaret Brown was also watching with horrified fascination:

> Suddenly there was a rift in the water, the sea opened up and the surface foamed like giant arms and spread around the ship and the vessel disappeared from sight and not a sound was heard.

According to Charlotte Collyer, the end came with a deafening roar, an explosion. Millions of sparks shot up into the sky. Then there were two duller explosions, as if below the surface, and the ship broke in two before her eyes. The forepart sank beneath the waves and the stern reared up. It stayed in a raised position for many seconds, it seemed like minutes to her. Lookout Archie Jewell also heard several explosions. But Quartermaster Walter Wynne thought that 'she gave a kind of sudden lurch forward. He heard a couple of reports like a volley of musketry; not like an explosion at all'.

Before the lights went out, Charlotte Collyer saw hundreds of people clinging to wreckage or jumping into the water. A terrible sound shot across the waters, a guttural cry of fear and terror at the imminent doom. She tried to turn her face away but an undeniable impulse forced her to look back again. As she did so, the stern of the once great ship slipped quietly beneath the surface of the deep, as easily as if it were a pebble plopping into a pond, taking her husband with her as she went.

Mrs Lily Potter in Boat 7 had been watching from the boat for 'about two hours' (actually more like hour and a half), seeing the lights dip under the water row by row as the ship slowly settled down. The lights went out about ten minutes before the *Titanic* went down.

> She was like some great living thing who made a last superhuman effort to right her-self and then, failing, dove bow forward to the unfathomable depths below.

In lifeboat 6, Mrs Brown had not been able to take her eyes off the sinking ship, watching as the decks disappeared inexorably beneath the surface. Major Peuchen heard 'one, two, three rumbling sounds; then the lights of the ship went out'. She was about to go along with Peuchen's wallet that had been left onboard. It would be picked up from the bottom in 1987 with traveller's cheque, business card and street-car tickets still identifiable.

Now, the huge ship slowly started to rear itself up in its end. Rudder and propellers were lifted out of the water until the ship was nearly vertical. He reckoned she remained there for half a minute. Then she started to slide, slowly at first, then with increasing velocity, until she was at last out of sight, having started her journey to the seabed some 2 miles below. Someone in the boat muttered quietly 'she's gone'.

The end was also described by Mr and Mrs Dickinson Bishop in the *New York Times* of 19 April. They estimated they were a mile away when the deck began to slant slowly up. The lines of light began to point downwards at an increasing rate. Only about every quarter of an hour did they notice the difference. But then the rate increased and 'suddenly the ship seemed to shoot out of the water and stand their perpendicularly. It seemed to us that it stood upright for four full minutes'. Then it began to slide slowly downwards.

As she approached her death throes, the *Titanic* was a beautiful, mesmerizing sight to Harold Bride. Smoke and sparks started to pour out of her funnels. Then she started to turn on her nose. Bride thought she looked like a duck going down for a dive. He still heard the band playing. However, it was not 'Nearer My God to Thee' that he recalled but a tune called 'Autumn'. He was about 150 yards away when the *Titanic* rose up and then finally sank slowly beneath the waves.

Those in the boats could not avert their eyes away from the spectacle, much as they wished to. Mrs Ryerson said that as the bow went down, the lights went out. 'The stern stood up for several minutes black against the stars and then the boat went down'. Someone called out that they should row for their lives or they would all be sucked down. Several of the women, including Mrs Astor and Mrs Thayer, helped with the rowing but there was little suction.

Mrs Thayer, also in Boat 4 which was not far off, saw:

> The after part of the ship then reared in the air, with the stern upwards, until it assumed an almost vertical position. It seemed to remain in this position for many seconds (perhaps twenty) then suddenly dove out of sight. It was 2.20 a.m. when the Titanic disappeared, according to a wrist watch worn by one of the passengers in my boat.

Mrs Stephenson saw the end from the same spot. When the call came that the *Titanic* was going, a cry went up – 'she's broken'. Covering her eyes for a time, she was eventually compelled to look and saw just the stern 'almost perpendicular' in the air so that the outline of the propellers could be seen. She then took her final plunge. Third Officer Pitman took out his watch and noted that it was 2.20 a.m. exactly. As a way of confirming other events, the timing of which may be important, Pitman confirmed that this was based on the same time measurement that had operated on the *Titanic* throughout Sunday, that is it had not been changed at midnight on Sunday as planned. As Pitman pointed out, 'we had something else to think of'.

Steward Henry Etches thought:

> She seemed to rise as if she were going to take a final dive but sort of checked as though she had scooped the water up and had levelled herself. She then seemed to set-tle very, very slowly, until the last when she rose and seemed to stand twenty seconds, stern in that position and then she went down with an awful grating, like a small boat running off a shingly beach.

He detected no suction whatsoever.

An icy breeze blew up, the first noticeable one of the night. It seemed to herald the last moments of the stricken ship. As Violet Jessop watched from boat 16, *Titanic* gave an alarming lurch forward. One of the funnels went crashing into the sea as if it were a cardboard model, creating a giant roar as it hit the water. The ship then tried to right herself as if she were a wounded animal struggling to get up from a deathblow. Then she went down by the head. The noise was terrific as she rose vertically and then slid beneath the waves.

Everyone had their own way of dealing with the moment. For most, there was a hypnotic fascination in watching the terrible scene playing out before them. Much as they might have wanted to, they could not avert their eyes. For some however it was all too much. Bruce Ismay simply could not bring himself to look. The last thing he recalled of his ship was some minutes before when he had seen her green starboard light, now lost beneath the waves for eternity. He was a broken man, whose life had changed forever. The events of this particular night would haunt him to his dying day.

Of the hundreds left on the ship at the end, the blind terror that they felt as the ship reared up almost vertically was overwhelming. They stared down into a gaping chasm, into the jaws of hell itself, before sliding down into the blackness. Steward Etches said graphically that he 'saw, when the ship rose – her stern rose – a thick mass of people on the after end. I could not discern the faces of course'. Steward Crawford could also see a large number of people gathered at the stern.

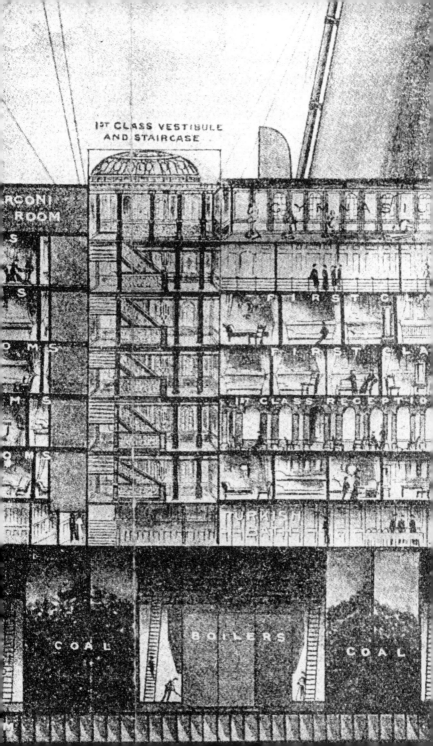

54. A cutaway illustration of the *Titanic* from *L'Illustration* magazine.

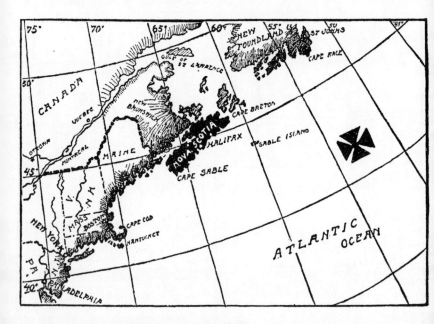

55. The position of the wreck from the Logan Marshall classic.

Previous page: 53. A plan of the inside of the *Titanic*.

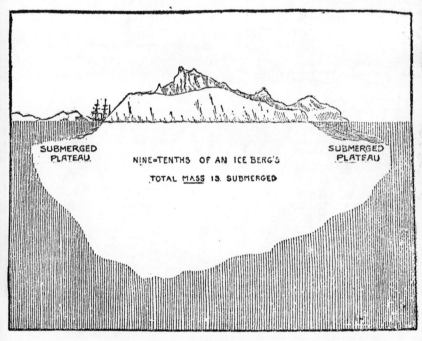

SUBMERGED PLATEAU.

NINE-TENTHS OF AN ICE BERG'S TOTAL MASS IS SUBMERGED

SUBMERGED PLATEAU

56. A diagram from Logan Marshall showing how much of an iceberg is hidden below the waterline.

57. A spiritual lesson from the disaster as shown in Logan Marshall.

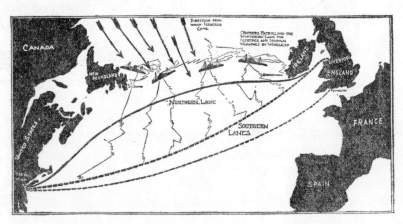

58. The North Atlantic shipping routes in 1912. These would be moved south in iceberg season.

59. Diagram showing the force of the *Titanic* hitting the iceberg.

11 45 P.M.

STRIKES STARBOARD BOW -12 ft AFT

12 05 A.M

SETTLES BY HEAD - BOATS ORDERED OUT

1 40 A.M

SETTLES TO FORWARD STACK
BREAKS BETWEEN STACKS

FORWARD END FLOATS,
THEN SINKS

1:50 A.M

STERN SECTION
PIVETS AMIDSHIPS AND
SWINGS OVER SPOT WHERE FORWARD SECTION SANK

2:00 A.M

LAST POSITION
IN WHICH "TITANIC"
STAYED 5 MINUTES BEFORE
THE FINAL PLUNGE

L.P. Skidmore
S.S. "Carpathia" Apr 15th
1912.

60, 61, 62, 63, 64 & 65. Jack Thayer was one of a number of survivors to describe the ship breaking in two as she sank. This series of illustrations drawn aboard *Carpathia* show the ship in her dying minutes and clearly show the two halves. It would be over seventy years before Thayer was proved right when the wreck was discovered resting on the seabed in two halves.

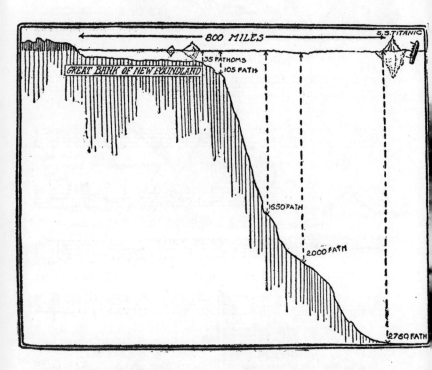

66. A diagram from Logan Marshall showing the depth of the water where the *Titanic* went down.

AUTUMN 8.7.8.7. D.   Louis von Esch, c. 1810.

God of mercy and compassion, Look with pity on my pain;

Hear a mournful, broken spirit Prostrate at Thy feet complain;

Many are my foes and mighty; Strength to conquer I have none;

Nothing can uphold my goings But Thy blessed Self alone. AMEN

Saviour, look on Thy beloved,
   Triumph over all my foes;
Turn to heavenly joy my mourning,
   Turn to gladness all my woes;
Live or die, or work or suffer,
   Let my weary soul abide,
In all changes whatsoever,
   Sure and steadfast by Thy side.

When temptations fierce assault me,
   When my enemies I find,
Sin and guilt, and death and Satan,
   All against my soul combined,
Hold me up in mighty waters,
   Keep my eyes on things above—
Righteousness, divine atonement,
   Peace and everlasting love.

67. Logan Marshall's offering for the hymn played as the ship went down, not *Nearer My God to Thee* but the tune *Autumn* as possibly suggested by Harold Bride.

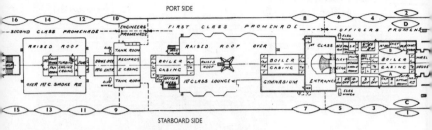

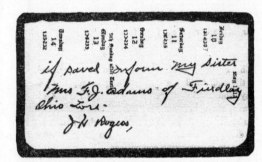

Above: 68. A plan showing the layout of the lifeboats on the upper deck of *Titanic*.

Left: 69. A copy of the hand-written note handed to a passenger leaving in a lifeboat from gambler J.H. Rogers (a.k.a. Jay Yates) who was lost.

70. A drawing from *Punch* which was dedicated to the 'brave men' who perished in the disaster. Britannia looks on as a grieving woman tries to cope with the immensity of the tragedy. In practice, nearly 50 first class male passengers survived, most controversially Bruce Ismay.

LUXURIES OF THE SEA
SWIMMING POOL
TENNIS COURTS
ELEVATORS
PALM ROOM
GYMNASIUM
GRILL ROOM
BUT
FEW
LIFE
BOATS
STEAD
STRAUS
MILLET
ASTOR
GUGGENHEIM
WIDENER
BUTT

71. *The Whited Sepulchre,* a contemporary cartoon weighing up the *Titanic's* luxuries against the lives of some of her prominent passengers.

72. A contemporary picture lionising the bravery of the men on the *Titanic*. The myth of male sacrifice developed as the world tried to make sense of the disaster. In practice, some men were much more heroic than others.

Among the few who were there on the ship at this last climactic moment and survived to tell the tale was Olaus Abelseth. He and his two companions, neither of whom could swim, were being forced back towards the stern of the ship. They watched on helplessly as the water crept up the bows of the *Titanic*. Then there was a small explosion, a 'popping and a cracking', after which the ship lurched forward. The deck on which they were standing rose inexorably into the air, becoming so steep that no one could stand. The three of them slid down into the frigid water but managed to hold on to a rope for dear life.

But they all knew that to stay where they were until the ship went under, which could now only be minutes away, would be a death sentence. They wanted to jump but waited until they were just 5 feet above the water. As they hit, they were all pulled under. Olaus had been holding on to his brother-in-laws hand but now involuntarily let go; he thought to himself as he went under 'I am a goner'.

However, his moment had not yet come though unfortunately it had for his companions; he was not after all a 'goner'. He was in the water for fifteen to twenty minutes, though he noticed little suction when the ship went down. He would eventually make his way into the swamped Collapsible A that had been washed off the ship. So too did Rosa Abbott who was thrown in the water from the stern, along with her two sons, Rossmore and Eugene, aged sixteen and fourteen respectively. She reached safety, but they were lost.

Charles Joughin was also on the ship when the end came. When the *Titanic* lurched drunkenly and decisively to port, he knew that she had just moments left. He heard the rending of metal and climbed onto the outside of the poop deck at the rear of the ship and wondered what to do next. Even at this moment when death stared him in the face the mundane intervened as he tightened his belt and moved items around from one of his pockets to another. He looked at his watch; it was a quarter past two.

Then all of a sudden he found himself in the water. He did not jump into it; the *Titanic* simply disappeared beneath his feet. He felt no suction as she went; in fact, he barely got his head wet. He, unlike many others, did not think that the ship had stood up practically perpendicularly before going under but that she had rather 'glided' beneath the waves.

A few others in the 28 degrees Fahrenheit water swam towards Collapsible A. One of the last to reach it was third-class passenger August Wennerstrom and his friend Edvard Lindell. Wennerstrom had noticed Lindell's wife Elin struggling in the water. He grabbed hold of her hand but could not pull her aboard. In the end, he had to let go. He turned to her husband only to see that he too was dead.

Colonel Gracie, pulled underwater when the *Titanic* plummeted into the abyss, thought that his end had come and mentally said goodbye again to his family, praying that they might meet once more in heaven. He said later that, at that very moment back in New York, his wife, unable to sleep, got up and turned to her prayer book. It opened at the page 'For Those at Sea' and she instantly thought that her husband was thinking of her.

He kicked upwards, driven on by a primeval urge to survive. At last, Gracie saw the increase of light at the surface. He tucked a small plank under his arm. On reaching the surface, he found a small crate which he seized; the first piece of the raft he imagined constructing. The *Titanic* had gone but just as he broke the surface he heard a slight 'gulp' as the sea closed over her.

A thin, grey vapour lay over the spot; it 'hung like a pall a few feet above the broad expanse of sea that was covered with a mass of tangled wreckage'. It reminded him of a scene out of Dante. But worse 'there arose to the sky the most horrible sounds ever heard by mortal man'.

He saw several persons clearly drowned close to him. Gracie tried to climb on top of the crate but it toppled over and threw him off. It was then that he saw one of the collapsibles, upside down, with a dozen men (believed to be all crew) desperately balanced on top of her. Gracie swam over and climbed onboard. At first no one offered to help him so he grabbed hold of one of the men already on it. Then, helped up by an unknown hand, he then assumed a reclining position on the boat. This was Collapsible B which would provide a precarious sanctuary for about thirty people in total.

Trimmer Thomas Dillon reckoned that he went down about two fathoms with the ship. He had been on deck surrounded by hundreds of people, most of them steerage. Kicking his way to the surface, he then swam for about twenty minutes. There seemed to be perhaps 1,000 people around him in the water. He saw the ship sink and then the after-part bob up again for a short time. He eventually managed to make it to Boat 4, where he fell unconscious. When he awoke, there were two dead bodies on top of him, one of whom was identified as Able Seaman William Lyons.

Storekeeper Frank Prentice was on the *Titanic* when she sank. He had been one of the many who hardly noticed the bump when the ship struck the berg. He had then stood around, casually smoking cigarettes as the ship's list got progressively worse. Seeing that she was doomed to sink, he had made his way to the stern of the ship along with hundreds of other people left aboard. He noticed the crowd singing hymns as the end approached.

He had hung from the rail, estimating that he was now about 75 feet above the water. Then he let go and fell into the water. It cut him like a knife, the intense cold chilling him to the core. Prentice had helped himself to a bottle of brandy before jumping; when he was dragged out of the water by those aboard Boat 4 the seaman in charge, Quartermaster Perkis, threw it in the water.

Prentice had not had a drop of the brandy and he thought Perkis's actions were reckless. Perkis was worried that some of the people in the boat, already nearly hysterical, would go completely over the top if they got hold of alcohol. However, Prentice later remarked that several people were pulled from the water and died of exposure and he could not help thinking that the brandy might have been the difference between life and death for these poor souls.

There were now hundreds of people in the water, fighting for their lives. The ship had gone and all that was left was the struggle to survive. There were lifebelts for all of those onboard and most people had managed to get one on. However, that was not the problem; the life-sapping cold was the issue. Most people could expect to live only for minutes in these temperatures. Their only hope was that some of the half-empty lifeboats in the vicinity might come to their rescue. For nearly all of them, these hopes were to be cruelly dashed.

15

The Survival Lottery:
02.21–04.00, 15 April 1912

There were now probably over 1,000 people in the water, though it is impossible to know how many had already gone down with the ship. Within a mile or so of the spot where the *Titanic* had slipped almost without a ripple beneath the waves into a dark lost world far below were twenty boats with a theoretical capacity for nearly 500 extra people. However, most of those empty spaces would remain unfilled.

Whether or not those lifeboats should have gone back to pick up more people became a matter of great debate. On the face of it, it was not a difficult decision to take given the situation that pertained. The failure to go back became almost the sin that dare not speak its name. There was a good deal of embarrassment evident in the explanations offered by survivors for their failure to do so, especially as so many in the lifeboats had lost relatives and friends in the disaster.

However, it was one thing to pontificate about the rights and wrongs of the actions of those in the boats from the safety of a cosy armchair in a warm front room. It was quite another to be on a small boat on the North Atlantic, having just watched the largest ship ever built disappear forever. Those in the boats were then exposed to the awful sounds of hundreds of people struggling for life in the water and fears that they themselves might be overwhelmed if they went back to help were very real.

When the stern of the *Titanic* began its long journey to the bottom of the sea and that last light had been extinguished forever, a mass of people was deposited in the freezing cold water. Life expectancy could for most of them be measured in terms of minutes. The noise that followed would sear itself into the imagination of every person that heard it. For some it would haunt their dreams for the rest of their lives. Others would have it brought to their attention in the most unexpected ways.

Nine-year-old Frankie Goldsmith was one of those in the boats. He later described the cries of those in the water as being like the sound when a home run was hit at the baseball stadium near his home in Detroit. It seemed to Jack Thayer on the other hand as if there was silence for only a minute. Then a cry went up, an individual plea for help at first, followed by another. Then the volume was turned up until there was a noise so loud that it reminded him of a thousand locusts in the woods. It went on he guessed for twenty or thirty minutes and, with a haunting *diminuendo*, faded away until at last it reached the point of nothingness.

Second Officer Lightoller was very close to where she went down. With the lights of the *Titanic* now extinguished, the scene was shrouded in darkness so Lightoller could see little, which was a relief to him. Less fortunate was the fact that the still night air magnified every sound and an alarming cacophony of noise started to build up as those stranded in the freezing water started to fight for their lives.

The noise of those struggling for survival made a life-long impression on everyone who heard it. Eva Hart heard them 'screaming and thrashing about in the water'. She later remarked that she heard 'the ghastly noise of the people thrashing about and screaming and drowning, that finally ceased'. That symphony of death always stood out for her as the most awful moment of the disaster, until her mother remarked that, bad as it was, it could not be compared to the sepulchral silence that followed. As her mother said: 'All of a sudden the ship wasn't there, the lights weren't there and the people weren't there.'

While those in the more distant lifeboats debated what to do, the only immediate hope for those fighting for their lives in the water were two collapsibles, one in danger of sinking, the other upside down. It did not offer much of a chance for anyone as the odds of getting a place in this survival lottery were stacked heavily against each individual.

Collapsible B was the nearest point of potential refuge for those who had been dumped in the middle of the freezing North Atlantic without a lifeboat. Those aboard it helped on those who swam over until they were all packed together like sardines. Now events took a harrowing turn. With no more room left, hands reaching out for help from the water had to be turned away. The stars still shone brilliantly but the sea had got rougher and started to wash over the upturned boat until all those on it were soaked and shivering.

Baker Charles Joughin who had been on the starboard side of the ship was now in the water. He doggy-paddled for a while, two hours he believed though this initially seems unlikely. However, he thought it was almost breaking daylight when he spotted a boat nearby so he might have been right. Perhaps his drop of liqueur earlier on had been a surprisingly successful survival strategy.

Then he thought he saw some wreckage and swam across to it. It was Collapsible B. There was no room for him and those aboard it would not let him on. However, he swam around to the other side, where he managed to stay near the boat with the help of another cook, John Maynard, who held out his hand to him. This was a very good time indeed to have a friend in close proximity; it could mean the difference between life and death. However, it appears that Joughin never actually got out of the water until those onboard Collapsible B were picked up by another lifeboat later on. Until that time, not only his feet but also his legs were submerged beneath the water. It was an extraordinary story of survival against the odds.

Another of those aboard Collapsible B was Colonel Archibald Gracie. When there were about thirty men on the upturned boat, the limit had been reached. There were men in the water all around. Gracie said that the crew on the collapsible would let no more aboard. However, one man, steward Thomas Whiteley, did manage to get on even though someone tried to batter him away with an oar.

Harold Bride had been deposited in the water when the ship went down. He felt the life being sucked out of him by the bitingly cold water. Then he saw a boat close by and used the last of his strength swimming over to her. It was the same collapsible that he had tried to help launch onboard the *Titanic*. There was a small opening for him on the upturned boat and he managed to half-drag himself aboard. More crowded aboard, someone crushing Bride's legs in the process. Waves began to wash over the boat and he had to grab a breath when he could.

Another crew member, Harry Senior, a fireman, swam around the other side when he was refused a hand onboard but still climbed on there, noticing Jack Thayer, Gracie and Lightoller onboard. He reckoned there were now thirty-five on the collapsible and dozens more trying to get on. Bride was there too. The men moved from side to side trying to maintain the precarious balance of the boat and paddled out of the struggling mass of humanity. Someone suggested asking for divine intervention through prayer. They did a straw poll of the religion of those aboard – Catholic, Episcopalian and Presbyterian – and opted to say the Lord's Prayer as a suitable compromise for them all to recite. In the distance, they could see lights from some of the other lifeboats in the water.

The boat had slightly raised planking on its underside (which was now, as it was capsized, its topside) and clinging on to this was all that stopped those on it from sliding into the water. Jack Thayer managed to do so in a kneeling position. In front of him was Harold Bride with his legs dangling in the water and his feet jammed against the fender which was submerged to a depth of about 2 feet. He noticed also a number of stokers aboard, scantily clad, and wondered how they could possibly survive when they were used to working in such heat. There too was Eugene Daly, the Irish bagpiper who had played the mournful 'Erin's Lament' as the *Titanic* had sailed west from Ireland. His pipes had gone forever.

Also aboard was William Mellors who was sucked down with the ship but swam clear to the upturned boat. He said that Captain Smith stood defiantly on the bridge, in tears at the terrible events being played out before him and for which he must have felt significantly responsible. There were some reports that Smith shot himself but Mellors denied this was the case. Other reports stated that he was washed overboard and refused helping hands offered to him from one of the boats. It was even said that he had rescued a baby which he had placed in the hands of someone in the boats that he had swum over to before sinking beneath the waves.

Lightoller thought that Phillips the radio operator was in the boat with him yet there is serious doubt about whether or not this was the case. The Second Officer had only believed it to be so because Harold Bride had told him. However, Bride, who would recognize Phillips far better than anyone, had not actually seen him either but thought he was there because someone else had told him. It could have been just a classic case of 'Chinese whispers'. Indeed, Bride had other things to concern him. There were a host of people, 'dozens' as he described it, trying to gain a precarious hold on the upturned boat, a matter of literally life or death for each and every one of them.

The overturned collapsible was now on the point of capsizing and just one more person could turn it over and throw every single person off into the water. As yet another person tried to get on, he was turned away. Rather than bemoan his fate, the man said: 'That is alright boys, keep cool. God bless you.' He disappeared soon afterwards, an unidentified hero whose name sadly is lost.

Olaus Abelseth floated easily in the water on his lifebelt. He had to all intents and purposes gone down with the ship but he soon bobbed up again. This appeared a temporary reprieve when a fellow passenger, flailing desperately in the water, grabbed him around the neck and pushed him under. Fighting him off, Abelseth swam around for around fifteen or twenty minutes.

Then, making the most of his lifebelt – which he thought functioned very effectively – he made his way over to a half-submerged collapsible which he had spotted. Two people on it were already dead and were thrown overboard to make way for other more needy souls some of whom were in a desperate state; Abelseth noticed a first-class passenger dressed in just his underwear.

It was Collapsible A. No one offered to help him aboard but neither did anyone try to stop him. They merely asked him to take care getting on so that the boat did not capsize. The state of some of those onboard was precarious. Some fell into the water. The others were nearly all frozen. The problem was that the sides of the boat were not properly up and could not be raised. There was a good deal of water in the boat and those in it were standing in over a foot of water during the night. Abelseth made sure he moved around regularly to keep his blood flowing.

These collapsibles were at the epicentre of the battle for survival. On the periphery of it, eighteen other boats laid off while their occupants debated what if anything they should do to help. Mrs Ryerson in Boat 4 said that the cries of the drowning seemed to go on forever. She said that some of the women in the boat protested at turning round to pick up survivors but they persisted. It seems that the boat was closer than most others to the scene; after all, several survivors had swum over to her and been picked up.

The most likely scenario is that the boat did not actively go in to pick people up but did not pull away either. They rescued six or seven men, so chilled and frozen already that they could hardly move. Two of them later died and many of the others were 'moaning and delirious'. There were no lights or compass onboard but several babies to keep the occupants busy.

The accounts of those onboard Boat 4 are similar though not identical. Mrs Thayer said that they pulled back to where the vessel had sunk and picked up six men, two of whom were drunk and gave them much trouble all of the time (possibly a less cynical interpretation is that they were, after all, delirious). The boat started to take in water and they had to start bailing. Ice cold water was up to the top of her boots all the time that they rowed – about five hours in total.

Mrs Stephenson remembered five men being picked up, whose suffering was intense. The bodies of the two who died were later taken onboard the *Carpathia* when she came to the rescue. They were given a proper burial at sea. She saw a green light shining from Boat 2. Subsequently during the night, all was quiet, there was no conversation, everyone awed by a combination of the magnitude of the disaster and the coldness of the pre-dawn hours.

Steward Walter Perkis thought that they picked up about eight people from the water. He reckoned there were about forty-two in the boat, two of whom died, whom he named as Seaman William Lyons and Steward Sidney Siebert. Samuel Hemming thought that they pulled back and picked up seven survivors. They later made for the light of another lifeboat and kept her company.

In Boat 6, the debate became quite heated. Onboard they heard 'the terrible cries and calls for help – moaning and crying'. All the women in the boat whose husbands were in the water were distraught. Gradually the noise died down. Boat 6 was about half a mile away from where the Titanic had gone down. Some of the women urged Quartermaster Hichens to return but he said it was pointless; there were 'only a lot of stiffs there'.

Hichens, in charge of the boat (capacity sixty-five, actual numbers aboard twenty-four to twenty-eight depending on whose estimate one believes) explained somewhat bizarrely: 'I did not hear any cries as regards distress. We heard a lot of crying and screaming.' Quite what he thought those cries and screams did signify if it was not distress is not immediately clear. He also explained that he could not find a compass in his boat and therefore did not know which way to head. The cries, he explained, only lasted for two minutes, a vastly shorter estimate of time than that of many other survivors.

Frederick Fleet confirmed some of this story, saying that Hichens 'would not hear of it' when asked to return. Mrs Candee remembers Hichens as being 'crazed with fear'. When the ship dipped under, Hichens refused point blank to go back, saying that their boat would be swamped. Major Peuchen, despite his superior remarks directed towards the 'Italian stowaway' earlier, seems to have allowed himself to be persuaded by Hichens that they should not go back rather too easily for some one of his supposed gallantry.

Hichens compounded the sense of terror hanging heavily over the boat by reminding those on it that they were hundreds of miles from land with no food or water. A slow death by starvation or drowning was all they could hope for. They did not even know where they were. Mrs Candee reminded him that they could see the North Star overhead so they knew exactly where they were. Hichens continued to insist he could see a light but Major Peuchen, with Fleet the only other man aboard, was sure it was a reflection. Hichens suggested that it might be a buoy. Peuchen believed that this was ludicrous, with good reason as the water was over 2 miles deep.

When the ship went down, Pitman in Boat 5 told the men onboard they would row back to look for survivors. Everyone else on the boat said it was 'a mad idea' and he allowed himself to be persuaded otherwise. Steward Etches later confirmed his evidence on this. Pitman wanted to go back to look for survivors but the rest of the boat insisted he did not do so he demurred. This was rather limp; Pitman was a senior officer on the *Titanic* and he could have insisted but he did not do so. To him, it appeared that 'there was a continual moan for about an hour'.

In Boat 9, Albert Haines said that they heard many cries from the water. After discussing with the crew onboard, the occupants decided they were already quite full and the boat would be endangered if they went back to pick more up. In fairness, this was one of the fuller boats with nearly sixty people in it; others had a much less legitimate excuse.

In Boat 2, Fourth Officer Boxhall suggested rowing back to pick up survivors but did not push the point. James Johnston, a Steward, says that they did not go back to pick up survivors because the women did not want them to and because they spotted an iceberg nearby (there are few other accounts of these being spotted before daylight so this should perhaps be treated with scepticism). Frank Osman said that they did not go back but pulled away from the wreckage so that the women aboard would not see the terrible sights and panic. He reckoned that they could only have taken in one more person. However, the evidence that has survived suggests that there was room for fifteen more people in her.

Nearly everywhere the tale was the same. Seaman Ernest Archer was in Boat 16. One of the women onboard suggested going back to look for survivors but there was no enthusiasm for the idea and the suggestion was not repeated. The suggestion just fizzled out in an embarrassed silence.

The greatest controversy surrounded the half-empty Boat 1. Under the command of lookout George Symons, the occupants heard people screaming for help but were afraid to go back lest the boat should be overturned; he was afraid, as he graphically put it, of the 'swarming of the people'. But his evidence later was contradictory, as he told the American enquiry that he did return to the wreck site. This was more than extremely unlikely, it was a downright falsification.

Charles Hendrickson, a fireman, said on the contrary that they did not go back for anybody. He implied after the event that he wanted to but the passengers aboard would not hear of it. Symons kept very quiet and all the other crew (who were in a small majority on this boat) also said little. The objection to going back, Hendrickson said later, came principally from Lady Duff Gordon, supported by her husband.

This version was supported by Fireman J. Taylor, also in the boat; he added that none of the passengers in the boat wanted to risk picking up any more survivors from the water. At the British Inquiry Taylor seemed somewhat embarrassed at Boat 1's inaction. He could not recall if the discussions about whether or not to go back were going on at the same time that cries from the water could be heard. He said that they could also not distinguish which direction these cries came from. It may be true but it may be that Fireman Taylor did not want to remember.

In addition to being terrified, Lady Duff Gordon was also violently seasick and of little use to anyone in the boat. Hendrickson insisted that he wanted to go back but he was the only person aboard to suggest that they do so; he believed that the desertion of those fighting for life in the water was 'inhuman' but he felt that he was obligated to obey orders. Sir Cosmo, with a candour which perhaps suggests he was unused to having to explain himself to anyone, said that the thought of going back never crossed his mind. He did not seem to understand, or be particularly bothered, that there were 1,000 people under sentence of death within earshot and there was room on his boat for nearly thirty of them.

Fireman Robert Pusey reckoned that they stood off the wreck site for about twenty minutes before the cries died down. When an eerie silence descended, one of the crew members muttered 'we have lost our kit'. There was an implication that Sir Cosmo would not have to suffer any financial inconvenience as a result of the disaster but that for the crew the death of the ship was a great financial burden.

Clearly there was something of an atmosphere in the boat. Perhaps embarrassed by their barbed comments, Sir Cosmo then offered to give all the crew onboard the boat money to replace it. A £5 donation for each of them would later follow, leading to a situation where Boat 1 became known as 'The Money Boat' to the crew on her.

Perhaps this was in response to Lady Duff Cooper's comment, the most unforgivable of the night, to her maid Laura Francatelli, sympathizing with her on her loss of a beautiful nightgown. The valuation of a maid's sleeping attire above 1,500 lives spoke volumes for some of the attitudes that were in evidence aboard the *Titanic* when she went down. Sir Cosmo's gesture might have been just a gesture of paternal kindness to those less financially fortunate than himself. Unfortunately, it would be all too easy for less trusting souls to infer that it was a bribe to the crew not to row back to help.

The comment from the crew aboard about the lost kit developed from a gnawing anger among the crew against their employers, the White Star Line. They knew that their employment stopped the moment that the *Titanic* slipped into the deep. This was a harsh world for the working classes, a fact underscored by the families of the lost musicians, those lauded heroes of the great ship, who received claims for uniforms supplied to them before the voyage by as yet unpaid tailors. White Star did not appear particularly interested in doing anything to help. Ordinary seaman kept books that recorded their voyages as a log for future reference when it came to being re-employed. Surviving examples record that the men on this particular trip were discharged from duty 'at sea' during the early morning of 15 April 1912.

Boat 8 was also not too far off. Mrs J. Stuart White said that, although they heard the yells of the doomed as they struggled vainly for life in the frigid waters, they could not see what was happening. All the women aboard rowed she said (an exaggeration as there appear to have been twenty-four women aboard and only sixteen rowlocks). She remembered that the crewmen were extremely rude, one of them shouting that 'if you don't stop talking through that hole in your face there will be one less in the boat'.

Mrs White was rather full of her own importance and her words should be taken with a dose of salt. She stopped several fights between the crew onboard (the crew being Seaman Jones, two stewards and a cook). She was also irritated that they were smoking pipes, a fire-risk she believed with all the woollen blankets aboard.

The man in charge, Seaman Jones, supported by the Countess of Rothes who spent the night at the tiller, wanted to return to pick up survivors from the water but everyone else, including the crew rowing, refused.

Jones made a point of saying that he wished everyone aboard to note that he had wanted to return to the wreck-site.

Apart from the efforts of Boat 4, there was only one other attempt to pick anyone up from the water. Fifth Officer Lowe was a pragmatist who 'waited until the yells and shrieks had subsided for the people to thin out'. He was in Boat 14, from which he transferred 'about fifty-three people' to the other boats. Some of the passengers thought the outspoken Welshman rude and impatient while he was organizing this.

Boat 10 was one of those nearby. Officer Lowe came over in Boat 14 and started to transfer passengers. He told the seamen in Number 10 to get into his boat so that they could row back and look for survivors in the water. Crewmen Buley and Evans hopped across, leaving the dining room steward Burke in charge of Number 10. Two men were later found in the bottom of the boat, one Japanese, the other Armenian. Burke told them to row and they eventually tied up to Boat 12.

Boat 14 was now virtually empty and could row back and pick up a boatful of survivors. Such at least was the theory. Sadly Lowe had overestimated how long someone could survive in the freezing cold water. He rowed back into the wreckage but picked up only four people alive. One of them, William Hoyt, a New Yorker, was bleeding from the mouth and nose and subsequently died. Lowe pointedly later said that he did not see the body of a single woman passenger in the water.

Joseph Scarrott was one of the crew that rowed back in to the wreck-site. Here he saw a harrowing sight, 'hundred of bodies and lifebelts'. To him, they 'seemed as if they had perished with the cold as their limbs were all cramped up'. Scarrott noticed that the bodies all appeared to be in one cluster. He saw Hoyt being brought onboard and one of the stewards trying to revive him but without success. He heard another man shouting for help but they could not reach him in time.

One of those in the water was a 'Chinese or Japanese' passenger floating on top of a sideboard or a table. Charlotte Collyer also said she saw the 'Jap' being picked up (though this is unlikely to be accurate as she would have been transferred and not in the boat that went to pick up any fortunate survivors). In her account he had tied himself to a floating door. The sea washed over him every time the impromptu raft bobbed up and down and he appeared to be lifeless and frozen. He was hauled onboard and his hands and feet were rubbed and he sprang into life.

He was seemingly without a word of English in his vocabulary. Lowe almost wished he had not bothered. He soon changed his mind. One of the oarsmen was tired and visibly slowing. The 'Japanese' man moved over and pushed him out of his seat. Then he started to row, moving the oars through the water with great vigour, which he proceeded to do until the boat reached the *Carpathia*. Lowe regretted his over-quick judgement: 'By

Jove, I'm ashamed of what I said about the little blighter. I'd save the likes o' him six times over if I got the chance.'

There was no gainsaying the horror of the sight that greeted those on Boat 14 who rowed back into the death zone. Edward Buley, who had transferred from Boat 10, recalled that of the dead 'none of them were drowned. They all looked as if frozen'. They were head and shoulders out of the water with their heads thrown back. Frank Evans, also transferred, said 'you could not hardly count the dead bodies'. He could not look in case his nerve failed him. He estimated there were 150–200 corpses in the water. However, he was also to suggest a disconnection with reality when he stated that he thought that the screams of the dying were shouts of encouragement from other boats.

As the dawn of day approached, the sea got rougher and the men perched precariously on Collapsible B had to stand up to balance the boat and keep it afloat. The cold chilled the bones and men fell off, unable to stay alive any longer. Lightoller believed that three or four men died while aboard the collapsible.

As the men talked, several spoke of Captain Smith. Harry Senior said that he had climbed aboard the boat but had not been strong enough to stay on it. Another man onboard, cook Isaac Maynard, also recalled this. Gracie asked a crew member for the loan of a hat. 'What wad oi do?' came the indignant reply. Grace also noticed one of the crew members aboard had been freely indulging in spirits before leaving the *Titanic*. Also on her with young Jack Thayer was Algernon Barkworth, a first-class passenger. They both struggled for several hours in the water hanging on to the collapsible. Barkworth was wearing a fur coat which he insisted gave him buoyancy.

Fortunately Harold Bride was one of those on the collapsible, and he could tell the others close to him of the ships with whom contact had been made. Such uplifting thoughts were needed. The boat was only kept afloat by the air that was trapped underneath and that was slowly being squeezed out so that she sank ever lower into the water. Those on the raft dared not move in case they turned her over with fatal results. A green light was later seen; however, despite their best hopes it was not the *Carpathia* coming to the rescue but the emergency light on Boxhall's Boat 2 in the distance. Boxhall in the meantime could see very little but he could hear the sound of water breaking against the ice not too far away.

Perhaps Boxhall, adrift on the vast ocean, pondered on the strange incident of the ship he saw earlier. For others though there was no time for contemplation. Sidney Daniels had been followed over to Collapsible B by a man he had seen clinging to a lifebuoy. He did not seem to understand English, so Daniels assumed he was a foreigner. He too managed to scramble aboard the collapsible but had then been overcome by the cold. Soon, he faded away.

Others clung on for dear life, hoping against hope for succour. Nerves were stretched beyond breaking point. Cursing and swearing broke out but someone suggested this was time to seek divine intervention rather than resort to vulgarities. Daniels felt tired and wanted to sleep but his neighbour warned him not to; he would never wake up again.

The boat on which Lightoller also had his precarious perch filled with more and more water hour after hour. The icy cold water crept up the legs of those on it, a fact of which they were painfully aware. Some lost their battle for survival and slipped unconscious over the side. There was nothing anyone else aboard the boat could do to help. The swell that had now blown up meant that they had to focus exclusively on their own personal salvation. Concerned that they might all be tipped into the sea, Lightoller gave orders that they should all move as one when a wave hit them in an attempt to keep the boat balanced.

Although Lightoller knew that the *Carpathia* was on its way, he was uncertain that they would survive to see her. Then, as dawn approached, the chances of salvation increased. The early, wan rays of the sun showed other boats nearby and gave a reason for hope, if only one could be summoned.

As the night went on, some boats came into contact with others. Lawrence Beesley on Boat 13 was still replaying the awful sound of those in the water when the *Titanic* sank. He had not appreciated that there were not enough boats for all aboard and the sheer volume of the noise spoke with terrifying eloquence of the number of people fighting for their lives. The cries had died away slowly, one by one. The boat did not go back, being full to something close to capacity. Someone in the boat tried to start a song to keep spirits up but it soon fizzled out.

Boat 13 later became aware of three others close at hand but too distant to do other than shout across from time to time. They started to row forward, or at least in the direction that the *Titanic's* bows had been pointing but ended up heading north (an intimation perhaps of the ship's movements after she struck the berg?). None of the boats in the vicinity had a light, which was a problem for all of them. Neither could Beesley find any food or water in the boat, though Pitman assured them later that he inspected all the lifeboats after they had been rescued and all were fully provisioned with them.

Charlotte and Madge Collyer had spent a miserable night in every sense of the word. Charlotte was frozen to the bone and someone wrapped a ship's blanket around her. The passengers were sitting with their feet in several inches of freezing water. The spray from the sea had made them thirsty but there was no fresh water and no food to sustain them. At one stage, Charlotte almost lapsed into unconsciousness and caught her hair in a rowlock, pulling out a large clump of it in the process.

Elizabeth Shute was in Boat 3. Also there were Mrs Clara Hays and Mrs Orian Davidson. They had both left their men-folk onboard the ship and kept calling out for them when they drew close to other boats. As the cold bit home, Miss Shute was starting to regret her decision to leave her thick velvet coat back in her cabin. She had felt it would impede her with her lifejacket on but now missed the warmth it would have brought her, much needed in the chilling air that seemed to freeze her to the bone. In her boat, several crewmen had been lighting cigars. The matches might be needed for signalling she thought and their actions annoyed her, so she asked them to stop.

The sky was pitch black, lit only by a thousand jewels, the tiny, distant stars. She watched fascinated as a pyrotechnic display of shooting stars streaked across the ebony backdrop, more she thought than she had ever seen before. They seemed to make the distress rockets that had been fired from the *Titanic* so infinitesimally insignificant that in retrospect they appeared absolutely futile. The other boats had drifted away now and hers seemed very, very alone. Wanting to take herself away from this dreadful place, Miss Shute allowed herself to drift off mentally, back to an adventurous holiday she had once taken in Japan. Meanwhile in Boat 7 Mrs Catherine Crosby got very cold during the night and Third Officer Pitman put a sail over her head and shoulders to keep her warm.

There were moments of light relief too. Third Officer Pitman in Boat 5 had tied up with Boat Number 7 and transferred three passengers across to them to even the numbers up. In his boat was Ruth Dodge who had forgotten to tie her shoes up when she left the ship, as a result of which her feet were now numb. One of the seamen offered her his socks, telling her that they were clean on that morning.

But the terror was never far away either. As the night went on, some of the passengers aboard the boats were transferred to others. Somehow, Eva Hart found herself alone. As dawn started to appear, she started to look around her for her mother, without success. She screamed and cried until she was later reunited with her onboard the *Carpathia*.

Some continued to pull for that illusory light. Mrs Emma Bucknell was in boat 8. She said that they steered for the distant light miles away all night. She thought it may have been a fishing vessel. Alfred Crawford was also on this boat. He saw two lights, not more than 10 miles away. They did not seem to get any nearer to them as they rowed but they did end up further away from the *Carpathia*, the rescue ship, than any other boat.

For three hours, those in Number 6 pulled for a light until it 'grew fainter and then completely disappeared'. Charles Stengel in Boat 1 said that they followed a light that was to the bow of the ship. However, they did not seem to get closer to it and in the end they decided to head instead for the green light on display from Boat 2 (these were some signals that Boxhall taken onboard with him and had lit from time to time).

In Violet Jessop's boat, Number 16, as the night wore on the light of the ship that they had been following retreated still further. For hours, it had drawn them off course. The sea got rougher and Violet began to feel both nauseous and scared. The baby in her arms started to cry; its whimpering made her pull herself together. She wrapped the eiderdown she had grabbed from her cabin tightly around it. At last, the whimpering stopped and the baby fell asleep. But as the waves grew more turbulent, and with only four people in the boat rowing, the situation grew more serious. Unable to locate any food, water or light, the morale of those aboard started to deteriorate.

Alone on a wide open sea they all waited, praying for salvation. They watched with eyes glued on the horizon for signs of a rescue ship. At one time, Lawrence Beesley saw the sky lighten so much that he thought the day was dawning but it was instead the Northern Lights putting on a dazzling pyrotechnic performance. They looked everywhere for the tell-tale sign of a ship on its way to the rescue, first a single light appearing, the masthead light, and then another lower down, the deck light. This would have told them that salvation was imminent. But it was very difficult to identify anything. Stars were rising and falling all the time and these created confusion. At other times, a single light would be seen and it would only later become apparent that they were lanterns from other lifeboats.

Ships were, unseen, on their way to help. To the west, the *Mount Temple* was making her way towards the reported SOS position. By about 3.00 a.m., she had met the ice. Captain Moore had put on extra lookouts, including one in the bow. Not long after reaching the ice, something loomed ahead out of the darkness. Suddenly they saw a schooner coming the other way – from the direction of the now submerged *Titanic* – showing her green light as she passed by. Captain Moore, on the bridge of the *Mount Temple*, could also hear the sound of her foghorn as she moved on by.

It is odd in all the debates about the *Californian* that more has not been made of this schooner. She was according to Moore coming from the direction in which the *Titanic* had recently been. At the time he spotted her, 3.00 a.m., he estimated that she was about 12½–13 miles from the *Titanic*. It is highly likely then that she was much closer, and within sight, when the great ship went down, though Moore thought that she was going at just a couple of knots.

Without wishing to get onto a pro or anti-Lord bandwagon, this surely is conclusive proof that there was at least one other vessel in the vicinity of the *Titanic* that night apart from the *Californian* though just how close she actually was must be the subject of conjecture. However, before pro-

Lordites get too excited, Fourth Officer Boxhall was convinced that he also saw a white light and that he would not expect to see one on a sailing ship such as Moore had spotted but only on a steamer.

Moore was now about 14 miles from *Titanic's* reported position. He could also see a steamer on his port bow, a 'foreign' ship he thought, going ahead of the *Mount Temple*. He thought he could see the same ship when dawn broke. By 3.25 a.m. however, Moore felt that the ice was too thick to push on through and slowed right down. This was a substantial ice-field to his east, which Moore thought was about 6 miles wide and 20 miles long.

It was at about 3.30 a.m. that someone in the *Titanic's* scattered lifeboats saw yet another light appear upon the far horizon to the south, 'a faint, faraway gleam' as it was described. However, this one got bigger until it was clear that this was a man-made beacon of some description. Then there was a dull, muffled explosion far away. One of the sailors aboard thought it was a cannon but it was not. It was a distant rocket fired from a rescue ship. Soon a single light appeared and then, shortly afterwards, another, lower, just as hoped.

There was now no doubt about it; it was help on its way. The occupants of Boat 13 looked for something to light to attract the attention of the ship. Someone found a letter in their pocket and a match was put to it to create a makeshift torch. It did not last for long before it spluttered out but by its flickering illumination Lawrence Beesley saw something for the first time that night that sent shivers coursing down his spine; tiny lumps of ice in the water, a poignant reminder of why there were sitting in a lifeboat in the North Atlantic at 4.00 a.m. on an April morning.

As the temporary light was extinguished, the rescue ship in the distance also seemed to come to a halt. At 3.16 a.m. *Carpathia* time Rostron had reckoned he had about 12 miles to go to the SOS position. At 3.30 a.m. he had gone half-speed ahead, then slow. At about 4.00 a.m. he stopped.

The *Carpathia* had come up against the ice too and had negotiated her way safely through it. For the commander of the rescue ship was not only a brave man, he was a prudent one too. Somewhere nearby another captain lay beneath the icy water, brave no doubt but certainly not prudent. Just a few miles away too was another sea-captain whose prudence was undoubted but whose judgment, many would suggest, should be under question.

While these extraordinary events were being played out, the pace of life aboard the *Californian* was as sedentary as it had been all night. Between the two of them, Stone and Gibson had watched eight rockets appear beneath the stars. At last, Stone saw the nearby ship disappearing to the south-west of the *Californian*. He had tried repeatedly to make contact with the Morse lamp but had failed utterly. Now thinking that the ship was on its way towards port, he told Gibson to report to Lord what was happening.

It was about 2.00 a.m. *Californian* time when Stone thought he saw the ship disappearing at a rate of knots. He could just see her stern light. The *Californian* had swung around considerably now and was pointing WSW. He told Gibson to tell Lord that the ship had fired eight rockets and was now out of sight. He noted to himself that the rockets seemed to have been moving in the same direction as the ship he had been watching.

As a matter of interest, Second Officer Lightoller, when later asked how many rockets had been fired from his ship that night, said 'about eight'. In the interest of balance, and also to demonstrate how murky many of the details from that night are, Third Officer Pitman recalled seeing a dozen. Boxhall, who was firing them off, recollected that he had sent up between half a dozen and a dozen.

Gibson went to pass the message on to Lord. Shortly afterwards he was back. He said to Stone that he had told Lord that they had tried to contact the other ship repeatedly and had got no answer. Lord had then asked if the signals were all white. At 2.45 a.m. ship's time Gibson then whistled down the speaking tube to confirm that no more lights had been seen and that the steamer was now completely out of sight. He confirmed that the signals were all white and had no colours in them.

These two accounts though are fraught with confusion. Gibson related an account of a conversation that Lord had no later recollection of. Lord later said that he had a vague recall of Gibson opening the chartroom door and then closing it immediately. Lord asked him what he wanted but got no reply and he certainly remembered no discussion. In his affidavit, he did not mention his conversation with Stone at 2.45 a.m. at all.

Lord's inability to remember this 2.45 a.m. conversation was very strange. He was asleep in the chart room but the speaking tube was in his cabin next door. This means that he not only slept through a conversation with Stone but also had to walk from one room to the next while asleep to have a conversation he could not subsequently remember. He then had to walk, still asleep, back to the chart room and lay back down once more.

Then there were the rockets. Several times, it had been mentioned that the rockets were white, as if there was some great significance in this. However, the regulations about distress rockets mentioned nothing about rockets other than there should explode in a star-like display; the colour did not matter. It was a point of some ambiguity; the rules said that the rockets might be any colour – some argued that white was not actually a colour.

However, the star-like appearance of what had been seen intimated a distress signal. There was though something else that did not. Rockets were supposed to make a loud noise when they went off. Neither Stone nor Gibson heard anything on a night that just about every eye-witness said was one of the quietest, calmest imaginable. This was something of a contradiction; they looked like distress rockets but they did not sound like them, having in fact no sound at all. At the very least, it suggested that the rockets must have been some way off.

This though was not the end of the rockets as far as the *Californian* was concerned. At 3.20 a.m. Gibson saw another rocket about two points before the beam to port. He reported these at once to Stone. Three minutes later another one lit up the distant sky and then another. The first was distant, 'two faint lights in the sky' as Stone described it. It was clearly a long way off. None of these later rockets was reported to Captain Lord, though seeing eleven rockets fired off in the night-time can surely not have been an everyday occurrence.

In fact, the time that the *Californian* saw this was about half an hour after the *Carpathia* had fired off its first rocket (assuming the ships' times were closely aligned to each other). At 2.40 a.m. *Carpathia* time Rostron had seen a green flare way ahead of him. It was Boxhall's signalling in the boats that attracted his attention. Rostron knew that green was the White Star Line's night signal. He also knew that he was a good 20 miles off according to the SOS position and the light seemed quite high up. It gave him hopes that the *Titanic* was still afloat. It is noticeable that although Rostron saw this green light, no one on the *Californian* did suggesting again that they must have been some way off.

Rostron had fired off his first rocket in reply to Boxhall's green flare, as a sign that his ship was steaming to the rescue. Just then, he saw the light of a star reflecting off something bright and solid ahead of him – an iceberg. Now he was entering the danger area. From them on he was darting and diving in and out of bergs and small ice. In his own words:

> More and more we were all keyed up. Icebergs loomed and fell astern; we never slackened, though sometimes we of course altered course to avoid them. It was an anxious time with the *Titanic's* fateful experience very close in our minds. There were seven hundred souls on the *Carpathia*; these lives as well as the survivors of the Titanic herself depended upon a sudden turn of the wheel.

The rockets were a ray of hope for those in the lifeboats, for they came from their rescuer. Rostron carried on firing them at intervals of a quarter of an hour. As the occupants of Boat 13 peered ahead, the *Carpathia* swung round and showed herself to be a large steamer with all her portholes alight. Beesley saw those lights and, in his own words, realized that they spelt 'deliverance'. Until now, though they thought that rescue was coming, it was believed to be from the *Olympic*. Now, much sooner than expected, they were to be saved from the chill embrace of the early-morning breeze and the threat of the ice-strewn ocean. Whispered prayers were uttered and tears freely shed as the wonderful thought of imminent rescue sank home.

The *Carpathia* had covered the 58 miles to the *Titanic's* reported position in three and a half hours, well above her top speed. This in fact gave a clue to the fact that the *Titanic's* reported position was incorrect. A double-watch of crew had been designated to act as look-outs on the *Carpathia*, hoping against hope that they would catch sight of the *Titanic* still afloat. Instead, Captain Rostron had sighted twenty large icebergs, 100 feet or more high. He dodged his ship in and out of them with a great deal of courage, for his ship might easily have slammed into one of the bergs just as the *Titanic* had.

It had not come a moment too soon for those on Collapsible B. Someone there had suggested that they should row for the light of the ship they had seen while the *Titanic* was going down. Then someone else shouted that there was a ship coming up behind them. For some reason, someone checked the numbers aboard; there were thirty people left there. As dawn broke, they saw the *Carpathia* stopped, 4–5 miles away. They also saw four lifeboats, strung together in a line, not far from them, perhaps half a mile.

Jack Thayer had found the water intensely cold. It had washed over the upturned boat constantly. Towards dawn, the wind blew up and it became increasingly difficult to keep the boat stable. Bride continued to keep spirits up with talk of the *Carpathia* coming to the rescue. Between 3.30 a.m. and 4.00 a.m. the lights of the rescue ship were spotted on the horizon (Pitman on Boat 5 saw her lights at around 3.30 a.m.). Thayer was still lying underneath another man, who was crushing his legs.

Fifth Officer Lowe had returned to his small flotilla after his game but disappointing effort to pick up more survivors. As they at last gave up their mercy mission and made their way back towards the other boat, most of them aboard were in tears. But it was now time to think of the living. With the rising of the wind before dawn, Lowe had hoisted a sail. They had been travelling along 'quite nicely' when in the distance Lowe saw the *Carpathia* coming.

Others could see this wonderful sight too. From the start, first-class passenger Mrs Margaretta Spedden in Boat 3 said that the stokers aboard urged that they row away from the ship to avoid the risk of suction. Two oars were lost early on in the haste of departure. Now that the *Carpathia* had appeared on the horizon, someone set some paper alight to act as a beacon for the rescue ship to home in on.

In Collapsible D, Number 14 had come alongside, telling them to stick together. Then ten or a dozen were transferred from Boat 14, which was now very full, to the collapsible and in return one seaman was passed from the collapsible to the lifeboat. Chief Steward Hardy who was on the collapsible had noticed that there were 'Syrians' chatting in the bottom of the boat in 'their strange language'.

Now, as the first rays of dawn signified the start of a day that many thought they would never see, there was no doubt where the focus of everyone's attention lay. Spread out over several miles, the boats inexpertly started to pull as well as they were able for the squat liner in the distance. All looked to the south. Those who had been pulling for that elusive light in the other direction gave up the battle and turned around. Maybe when day broke at last no one bothered to look but, at any event, no one subsequently reported seeing a ship to the north of them. Whatever ship might have been there in the night was now out of sight.

16

Deliverance:
04.01–08.30, 15 April 1912

From all directions, every lifeboat started to converge on the *Carpathia*. Some had managed to tie up together so that there was some sense of security for their exposed impromptu and untrained crews. Others floated singly but for these too the ship, still distant, gave hope. However, some of them still had miles to go and for many the *Carpathia* would bring pain as well as rescue. Many still hoped to see loved ones that they had left behind on the sloping decks of the *Titanic* waiting for them as they climbed aboard. For most, these hopes were to be cruelly dashed.

Some still seemed in real danger of their lives, especially on the perilously perched Collapsible B. At around dawn, those on the collapsible saw the *Carpathia* steaming up on the horizon. They gave a cheer but she seemed to come up very slowly. They could see in the distance lifeboats already pulling close to her but they were incapable of emulating them in the condition they were in. Dawn if anything made matters worse for the sea grew rougher and their situation ever more precarious. Their raft sank still lower and they began to fear that they would sink before they were rescued.

However, daylight did at least enable them to see their position and this gave them the courage to take a few more risks. One by one, they all stood up except for Bride whose feet were badly frostbitten. As the raft rolled, they continued to try to move with the swell to stop it becoming even more unstable. At last they managed to attract the attention of another lifeboat. A combination of Lightoller's whistle and the raucous shouts of those on the raft did the trick and salvation was finally at hand.

However, they were about 400 yards away and it seemed to take an eternity for them to get over. When the gap was finally closed, those aboard were loaded onto two of the other lifeboats. Gracie had been working on the body of a dead crewman in the boat but had given up, recognizing the onset of *rigor mortis*. Mrs Thayer was on one of the rescuing boats but her son Jack was so far gone that he did not even notice her. Harold Bride was in a particularly bad way and had had to be held on for the past half an hour. Now he had to be lifted into the rescuing lifeboat. In the lifeboat that they transferred to, there were perhaps seventy now onboard and it sank lower in the water with the extra weight.

The transfer came not a moment too soon. Even as they saw the boats and called them over, the collapsible slipped lower in the water with a motion that seemed to presage her doom. It was too much for one man who slipped over the side. They held his head above water but it was too late. He was gone. They took his body into the boat that rescued them (they were thirty in number according to Lightoller) and tried their best to revive him but without success. It was later suggested though not proved that this was wireless operator Jack Phillips.

Samuel Hemming was in Boat 4, one of the rescuing craft. At daybreak, they had seen another boat and tied up to her. Boat 4 had then helped Boat 12 to take off people from the sinking collapsible. Mrs Thayer thought that they took off fifteen people. With about sixty in the boat now there was no room to sit down so most aboard were standing.

Mrs Martha Stephenson said that as dawn broke a wind got up and the sea became rougher. It was just before daylight that they saw a light on the horizon that they were sure was a rescue ship. Quartermaster Perkis however argued that it was the moon. But when the others asserted that it must be a ship, Perkis said that it might be the *Carpathia*. This was interesting as there was no wireless operator aboard. It suggested that he had been briefed before leaving the doomed ship that help was on its way.

When Boat 4 approached the collapsible they took great care as they were afraid that the wash as they approached would completely sink the collapsible. The other boat, Number 12, also took on a number of people from the seriously endangered collapsible. As day came, they found themselves in a great deal of wreckage, especially deckchairs.

Collapsibles A and D were fairly close to each other. Onboard A, Abelseth was sat next to an American from New Jersey with whom he had travelled from London. He appeared to be unconscious. Abelseth shook him, telling him 'we can see a ship now' and the man stumbled into consciousness. 'Who are you?' he asked. 'Let me be.' Abelseth propped his head up with a piece of board so he could see the rescue ship but his efforts were in vain and half an hour later the man died. In the morning, they saw a boat with a sail up. They shouted for all they were worth and Boat 14 came over and picked them up.

Quartermaster Bright was in Collapsible D nearby. To him Collapsible A looked flush with the water and could not have stayed afloat for much longer. Boat A was left where it was, including three bodies that were aboard. There was a strange codicil to this tale. Nearly a month later, the boat was spotted by the White Star liner *Oceanic*. The bodies were still there and were given a proper burial at sea. The empty collapsible was taken back to New York to be returned to its rightful owners. One of the dead found in the boat was first-class passenger Thomson Beattie. The two others were an unidentified fireman and sailor.

Also in the boat was R.N. Williams' abandoned fur coat which had somehow got into Collapsible A with him even though he said he had thrown it off while in the water. Harold Wingate, an official of the White Star Line, had the coat sent to a furrier but little could be done for it except to dry it out. Nevertheless it must have come as something of a shock when the coat he thought he would never seen again turned up on Williams' doorstep.

Harold Lowe was in command of Boat 14 when he saw Collapsible D. She looked in a bad way. Mrs Irene Harris, a New Yorker, was in great pain aboard her, nursing a broken arm. Then Lowe saw Collapsible A, which was in an even worse state. He rowed across and took off about twenty men and a woman. He then took Collapsible D in tow.

As he approached the collapsibles Lowe, ever the action man, took out his revolver and fired off several shots as a warning not to rush when his boat pulled over. Most of those in the boats were too tired to think about rushing anything. Lowe at last came alongside and transferred the survivors. He left the bodies behind, reckoning that his prime duty was to the living. All those on the boat were up to their ankles in water when they were taken off. Whisky was handed around those onboard in an attempt to keep warm and perhaps also to buck spirits up.

With the arrival of a new day, an incredible sight, previously hidden, revealed itself, one such as which none of those present could ever have imagined. It was a landscape of ice mountains, of white plains that stretched out before them as far as the eye could see, seemingly going on forever. One of those who saw it recalled:

> The dawn disclosed the awful situation. There were fields of ice on which, like points on the landscape, rested innumerable pyramids of ice. Seemingly a half hour later, the sun, like a ball of molten lead, appeared in the background.

As the day grew lighter, the sea became choppy.

Major Peuchen was one of the few men in Boat 6. Towards morning, they had come close to Boat 16 and tied up to it. Given the shortage of men aboard, those in Boat 6 asked for extra help rowing and a fireman was transferred across. He was dressed in thin clothes and Mrs Brown wrapped him in a sable stole, tied around his exposed legs. She then told him to cut loose from Boat 16. Quartermaster Hichens, notionally in command, raised a 'howl' of protest. Mrs Brown threatened to throw him into the water if he continued to carry on. The fireman reprimanded Hichens, reminding him that he was talking to a lady.

Mrs Brown remembered seeing a man in Boat 16 in his white pyjamas; she thought that he looked like a 'snowman' and suggested that he row to keep warm. Of necessity, women helped with the rowing too. The two boats were kept lashed together and Hichens at this point seems to have given up and retreated to the background.

Peuchen also suggested that Hichens should help with an oar but the Quartermaster pulled rank on him and told him to continue rowing. Mrs Candee confirmed Peuchen's story about the Quartermaster. Hichens told the subsequent Inquiry that he had at one stage let one of the ladies take the tiller but she was incapable of controlling it so that he had no choice but to take it himself. He said that he suffered badly from the cold (some of those on the boat were aware of this, and they put a blanket over him to keep him warm). At one stage, Peuchen recalled, he also asked if anyone had any brandy with them. The Quartermaster agreed that this was so but he only took a tablespoonful of it to drink he insisted.

They made little progress because of the lack of oar-power. 'There were only two of us rowing a very heavy boat with a good many people in it,' they later recalled; a likely explanation for at least some of the boats failing to make much progress towards the source of the elusive light in the night-time. Mrs Brown, seeing they were short of men, decided to row and asked a young woman, Miss Norton, to assist her. Immediately she 'began to row like a galley slave' according to Mrs Candee who was there and they pulled together, as much to keep warm as anything.

As the faint streaks of dawn started to light the day it revealed the majestic shapes of icebergs, 'like fairy castles' to Violet Jessop in Boat 16, parading past them as they crept lethargically on. Whereas once these might have appeared beautiful, they now seemed like monsters of destruction to Violet. They could not see anything, not even another boat. They were deserted in the middle of a vast, ice-laden ocean. Violet felt terribly alone and desolate. She tried to think of something to take her mind off the dreadful situation they were in. She had bought a piano just before she left and now she feared that she would never have the chance to play it.

It was just at this moment, when all seemed blackest, that someone pointed a shaking finger in the direction of the horizon. There, a few miles away but definitely headed on the right course, was a ship. To some aboard, it raised false hope. One even thought that it was the *Titanic*, still afloat, and that she would soon be back on it, reunited with her husband and two sons whom she had left behind a few hours before.

Hugh Woolner, who had been in Collapsible D, noted that as morning broke he could see:

a great many icebergs of different colours, as the sun struck them. Some looked white,
some looked blue, some looked black and others were dark grey.

Charles Stengel in the under-utilized Boat 1 noticed when he boarded
the *Carpathia* later that one of the bergs looked very like the Rock of
Gibraltar, an interesting comparison as it was the same one made by
Joseph Scarrott of the berg he had seen strike the ship.

Amid all this grandeur, this dazzling array of magnificence which
portrayed equally well both nature's beauty and her power, eyes turned
towards the *Carpathia*, promising as it did deliverance. In Boat 3,
Elizabeth Shute watched as at last the stars drifted away and the pink glow
of a distantly rising sun started to tint the morning sky. Suddenly someone
shouted that they could see a light. She did not at first believe them. Such
remarks had been made before but they had only been the light shining
from another lifeboat. She did not want to build her hopes up, only to see
them cruelly dashed.

Someone lit a newspaper to attract attention and at this moment Miss
Shute looked after all. To her indescribable relief it was indeed a ship that
was on the horizon, strong and steady, brightly lit by lights. Mrs Davidson
took off her hat, suggesting that it would make a good torch as it would
burn for longer. This was not just to aid any rescue attempt but to avoid
being accidentally run down by the ship. However, the thought was
superfluous for the ship was still.

Gradually, in her poetic words, 'the ship and the dawn came together, a
living painting'. As the sun's rays provided sharper light as its golden orb
moved higher in the sky, an amazing picture was emerging. Everywhere
there was ice, white mountains, each one more fascinatingly chiselled than
its neighbour as she put it.

Captain Rostron had arrived by the first boat at around 4.00 a.m.
just as the day was dawning. He had been negotiating his way through
dangerous ice since 2.45 a.m. He was forced to swerve around an iceberg
before approaching the first *Titanic* lifeboat. He noticed – he could not
fail to do so given its extent – ice all around; perhaps twenty icebergs up
to 200 feet high and numerous smaller bergs as well as 'growlers'. He
thought that this was close to the spot where the ships went down as there
were lots of small bits of wreckage.

At around 4.00 a.m. the *Carpathia* spotted a green light just 300 yards
ahead. It was so low in the water that it must have come from a small boat.
Rostron sounded the ship's whistle to let her know she had been spotted
and then ordered 'dead slow ahead'. As they approached, a woman shouted
up that they had only one seaman in the boat and couldn't row very well.

The light came from Fourth Officer Boxhall in Boat 2. Boxhall said that
Carpathia staff told him he pulled up alongside at about 4.10 a.m. Mrs

Mahala Douglas later noted that Captain Rostron on the *Carpathia* had seen the green lights from about 10 miles away. Boxhall steered his boat as well as he was able towards the welcoming arms of salvation. The dawn was breaking and the rescue ship had stopped perhaps quarter of a mile from a berg. There was ice as far as he could see, the first time he had ever seen such a sight on the Grand Banks in his career. As the sun rose they looked white but before it did so they had a black hue; a factor perhaps in the collision. Mrs Douglas also noted that as they drew alongside the *Carpathia* they found it difficult to steer as there was only one seaman onboard.

Frank Osman, also in the boat, had looked around him when day broke and saw a berg:

> with one big point sticking on one side of it, apparently dark, like dirty ice, 100 yards away. I knew it was the one we struck. It looked as if there were a piece broken off.

Miss Elizabeth Walton Allen was on the boat. She was from Missouri and was on her way back to the States to pick up her belongings before returning to England to marry a physician, Doctor J.B. Mennell (she appears in Colonel Gracie's account of the disaster as Mrs J.B. Mennell). As the boat pulled in to the side of the *Carpathia*, a ladder was let down. Those on the boat seemed reluctant at first to climb it so Miss Allen took the lead. She was therefore first up the ladder and first aboard the *Carpathia*. Someone asked her where the *Titanic* was and she said simply that she had gone down.

Captain Rostron had been looking on closely and could see that the boat was not under full control. Rostron manoeuvred his ship as close as he could to the boat. As the sun moved higher, he could see many boats scattered over a wide area. Eventually, he spotted all of them within what he estimated to be a four-mile radius. It must have been a shocking sight for him; he had not known until now that the *Titanic* had sunk but the evidence of those lifeboats told him all he needed to know.

Other boats too started to head for the welcome sight. As they started to approach the *Carpathia*, the Cunard ship's own passengers were starting to stir, probably intrigued by the extra speed that their vessel had been making. As they came up on deck, an amazing sight met their eyes, a vast, hard, white carpet of ice with the occasional berg reaching up like a hill from a wide, flat plain. Yesterday when the sun went down they had been many miles to the south, not warm no doubt but without a hint of ice anywhere. This was an astonishing revelation.

Onboard the *Carpathia*, Mrs Wallace Bradford from San Francisco was woken by unusual noises and the smell of smoke. As she looked out of her porthole she saw a huge iceberg nearby. It was not white and at first sight she thought it was a rock but could not work out how this could be the case when the ship was nowhere near shore.

She made her way on deck when a man told her that the *Titanic* had sunk and they were picking up survivors. She saw two boats approaching; neither seemed very full. As other boats approached, she saw through her binoculars that they were making very slow progress suggesting that this was a very amateur bunch rowing.

Others did their best to chronicle the event for posterity. There were a newlywed couple onboard, James and Mabel Fenwick. Mrs Fenwick was a stocky woman who looks in photographs very much the senior partner against her more diminutive husband. They were certainly comfortably off as they were embarking on a three-month honeymoon around Europe.

Mrs Fenwick was a keen photographer. As it became clear that they were in the presence of something extraordinary, she snatched up her camera and rushed up to the deck. There, an unbelievable vista revealed itself. Across the water, little globules of ice made the surface of the sea appear like a patchwork quilt. In the distance a long, ribbon-like land of ice stretched. But there in the foreground were tiny boats, one with a sail raised, headed for the side of the ship. Mrs Fenwick then proceeded to snap some of the most extraordinary photographs in maritime history.

The early days following the disaster were marked by some journalism of a highly suspect and sensationalist variety. Logan Marshall's book, published in 1912, was an excellent example of this *genre*. He espouses some unlikely tales which tell more about the standards of journalistic editorialism at the time than they do about what really happened on the *Titanic*. One example was when he described an overheard conversation from one of the lookouts who said that the phone was ringing for three minutes or more after they spotted the iceberg before the bridge answered it. In that time, the lookouts would have had time to climb down the ladder, report to the bridge, make a cup of tea and return to their perch again before the berg was struck.

He has a particular touching tale about the lifeboats that approached the *Carpathia* which has much more to do with spinning a good yarn than it does factual accuracy. It concerns a big black dog called Rigel, a pet of First Officer Murdoch's, who swam in the water for three hours next to a lifeboat. As this approached the rescue ship, it was noticed by those onboard the liner and the boat was in danger of being run down. However, Rigel barked so loudly that the attention of those onboard the *Carpathia* was alerted. Everyone in the boat was safely picked up, including the dog who was adopted by one of the crew. Unfortunately there is no corroborating evidence for this tale which is therefore most likely a work of fiction, which explains why the story of Rigel is one of the *Titanic's* forgotten legends.

Other boats – most but not all minus dogs – pulled towards safety. One of them, Boat 3, hauled across to the rescue ship. After a big effort, they were at last by the side of the *Carpathia*. A rope had been shaped into a swing that was dangled down into the lifeboat, on which the passengers were hoisted up one-by-one. The woman in front of Elizabeth Shute was somewhat on the heavy side. On the deck of the *Carpathia*, a voice ironically told those hoisting her up to watch out; 'careful fellers, she's a lightweight'. When it was Miss Shute's turn she kept bumping against the side of the ship as she was hauled up. Her hands were so cold that she could hardly keep hold of the rope. Then, at last, safety. Gentle hands helped her aboard and a kindly doctor wrapped her in a blanket and took her to the dining room where hot drinks were liberally applied in an effort to warm her up.

As other lifeboats arrived, the scene became ever more harrowing. Onboard many of them were women who were now widows, hoping that they might find their men onboard the *Carpathia*. In nearly every case they were disappointed. In the dining room was a slightly more cheering sight though. A small boy, one of the Navratil children, was lying. His feet had become uncovered and were icy cold. Miss Shute gently applied a hot water-bottle to them and was herself warmed when a broad smile spread across his cherubic face in thanks.

Boat 13 with Lawrence Beesley aboard made for the *Carpathia*, in friendly competition with other boats to get there first. She had to be navigated around an iceberg on the way. Then the dark sky started to be tinted with pink highlights as the sun began its welcome journey across the sky from beyond the eastern horizon. On the way towards the rescue ship they saw what seemed to be sailing ships in the distance but, as the light increased, it became apparent that these too were icebergs.

Beesley was a man possessed of the talent to write purple prose. As the sun climbed in the sky, its rays shone on the ice mountains:

> they stood revealed as huge icebergs, peaked in a way that suggested a ship. When the sun rose higher, it turned them pink, and sinister as they looked towering like rugged peaks of rock out of the sea, and terrible as was the disaster one of them had caused, there was an awful beauty about them that could not be overlooked. Later, when the sun came above the horizon, they sparkled and glittered in its rays; deadly white, like frozen snow rather than translucent ice.

On drawing close, they saw that the ship was a Cunarder and then made out the name *Carpathia* boldly painted on the superstructure above them. At last, they drew in to her port side, sheltered from the breeze. Women climbed the rope ladders that had been let down first, aided by ropes tied around them. Men were next and then the crew last of all. The baby aboard was pulled up in a sack. At last, Lawrence Beesley stood on the deck of a large ship again and thanked God for his life.

Beesley was struck by the demeanour of his fellow survivors who were there with him. There was no hysteria that he could see, not even yet a sense of mourning or grief though there was certainly concern for those who the survivors had last seen onboard the *Titanic*. There was he thought more a sense of relief, joy almost, that they were still alive. The full horror of loss had not yet started to sink in.

Steward Andrew Cunningham was on Boat 4, which he thought reached the *Carpathia* at about 7.30 a.m. When first seen from the boat, the ship was 4–5 miles away. Mrs Ryerson also thought that the *Carpathia* about 5 miles away when spotted. Her recollection was that they arrived by her at about 8.00 a.m. Mrs Thayer however thought that they were nearer 3 miles away. They could not wait for the *Carpathia* to come to them as they were in danger of sinking themselves.

Mrs Stephenson thought that it was about 6.00 a.m. when they arrived at the *Carpathia*, these contradictory timings showing how difficult it was to keep an accurate track of time. She confirmed that the boat was in danger of sinking. She said that Captain Rostron suggested that the boat would have been lucky to have stayed afloat for another hour. They had been bailing her out constantly as she had been leaking badly. Two of the women onboard were very seasick but the babies had slept most of the night in their mothers' arms.

Mailbags were lowered over the side in which the children and babies were hoisted up (little Millvina Dean's mother kept hers as a souvenir for her – nearly 100 years later it was still in her possession). The passengers were told to throw off their lifebelts and were then hauled up to the open gangway in chairs. There were warm blankets and brandy for everyone. They then went to the saloon, where hot coffee and sandwiches were being served.

It is informative to note that the accounts above, all related by people in more or less the same spot, vary in small details, especially as to time and distance. In the light of arguments that were about to explode in the very near future about the actions of the nearby *Californian* this should be remembered. It is not to suggest for one moment that people are dishonest, it is merely that in the stress of a great catastrophe people can witness the same events but recall them differently. After all, when one's very life has been under threat taking a careful note of the time is hardly a priority. Nor do distances matter that much, especially when many of the observers on the spot are not anyway people skilled in or used to making such judgements.

In the meantime, the arguments aboard Boat 6 continued. When *Carpathia* hove into view, it was Mrs Candee who suggested that they row towards her and the others on the boat agreed. Mrs Candee suggested that Hichens did not even think the *Carpathia* was there to rescue them but to pick up bodies. The boat rowed towards the *Carpathia*, arriving by her at around 8.00 a.m.

She was one of the later boats to reach the rescue ship. This was partly because she was undermanned but also because she had been attempting to row off to the north. Peuchen noted that they seemed to be rowing back over the site of the wreck; he saw a barber's pole floating on the surface. This gives an important clue that, unless there was a significant rate of drift in the current – something all ships present denied – then the elusive light they had been chasing was indeed to the north of the stricken ship for, in rowing south, they were rowing over the wreck site.

The sea had grown progressively choppier and by the time that Boat 6 drew close to the *Carpathia*, it was difficult to approach her. It took several attempts to get near and each time the lifeboat bounced off the side of the ship. Those on the boat suggested that Hichens, in a final act of stubbornness and incompetence had refused to row around to the side sheltered by the *Carpathia's* profile where the sea was smoothest. A rope ladder was thrown down and gingerly, one by one those in Boat 6 climbed up to the safe haven of the *Carpathia's* deck.

Hichens recalled, in a final effort to confirm his self-delusions of heroism, that he was the last to leave the boat and scramble aboard the rescue ship. His heroism was lost on most of his passengers and indeed his grasp on matters nautical did not often ring true, as was exemplified by his later statement that he had encountered icebergs before 'up the Danube' which must have been something of a geographical rarity.

In some boats, such as Number 8 with Seaman Thomas Jones and the Countess of Rothes onboard, an unexpected respect had grown up between people who in the ordinary turn of events would never have met. It is safe to say that such a situation was definitely not the case on Boat 6. Mrs Mary Smith summed up the general view by saying that she did not believe Hichens was drunk, as some had hinted, but that he was merely 'a lazy, uncouth man, who had no respect for the ladies and was a thorough coward'.

Those who were in Boat 8, including Steward Alfred Crawford, recalled that it was near daybreak that they saw a steamer coming up, which proved to the *Carpathia*. The boat was turned round – it was furthest away from the rescue ship following its wild goose-chase after the elusive light. It would be a long haul across to the rescue ship.

Fifth Officer Lowe too described the light he had seen as being to the north at a distance of about 5 miles. The steamer he saw had been displaying a red sidelight to them. Along with Major Peuchen's evidence there was a strong, though not unanimous, view that this was the direction in which the 'mystery ship' lay. There too, somewhere, lay the *Californian*.

Boat 16 was one of the last to pull up alongside the stationary *Carpathia* (Jessop, with a smidgeon of poetic licence, later asserted that it was the last but there is evidence to the contrary). As she climbed aboard, Violet was offered a brandy which went down 'like molten fire'. As she stood there, a woman ran up and snatched the baby she was carrying from her without uttering a word. She was too shocked to react, for since arriving it had become clear that few of her boat's fellow passengers had found the loved ones they so desperately sought for on the *Carpathia*. The full, brutal horror of the disaster was starting to dawn on everyone.

One of those in shock was fifteen-year-old Edith Brown, who had been in Boat 14. Onboard the *Carpathia* Edith went to look for her father every time another lifeboat pulled in. Her mother however realized that there was little real hope and told her daughter as sensitively as she could: 'You've lost your father, you won't see your father anymore… he's gone.'

Others were suffering badly from their ordeal in the water. Sidney Daniels was given a cup of coffee – he later said it was the first he was ever tasted – and taken below to the sickbay where he stayed for a while.

There were some amazing stories of survival to relate to those onboard and indeed to the wider world. Many of them centred around people who had started the day in Collapsible B and had later been transferred to Boat 12 which was the last one to be picked up. Charles Joughin was one of them. When he saw other boats coming to the aid of the perilously submerged collapsible, he simply let go of his friend Isaac Maynard's hand and paddled across. He had been in the freezing water for two and a half hours. He later admitted that he had had a tumbler half full of whisky before being immersed. It seems to have worked wonders.

Jack Thayer was another lucky survivor. Only as the lifeboat drew close to the *Carpathia* did he dare to believe that he would be saved. The sun was at last higher in the sky and it had taken the edge off the early morning chill. As they approached the side of the rescue ship, he saw a rope ladder with wooden slats hanging down. He did not see much ice apart from four bergs in the distance. As he climbed aboard, he saw his mother, who looked in vain for his father at his side.

He told her of his adventures and as he did so someone pushed a coffee cup full of brandy into his hands. It warmed him up quickly, and he thought what a strange place this was to experience the first alcoholic drink of his life. Those experiences he had feared he would miss out on were already starting to be fulfilled. One of the *Carpathia's* passengers lent him his bunk and his pyjamas and, despite the horrors of the night, he soon fell into a short but deep sleep. He felt surprisingly well after his nap and went out on deck with his mother. They were now passing to the south of an ice-field which someone told him was more than 20 miles long and 4 miles wide.

Others had seen a similar sight. Joseph Scarrott, whose pre-sailing premonitions had proved fully justified, saw five or six bergs when Boat 14 had made her way over earlier in the morning. He also saw floes and when he finally boarded the *Carpathia* he saw an ice-field that he believed to be 25 miles long. Only from the elevated decks of a ship was it possible to appreciate the full extent of the ice-field.

Colonel Gracie was also on Boat 12 as it pulled for the *Carpathia*. When they arrived there and the Colonel climbed aboard, Gracie noticed for the first time an old acquaintance, Third Officer Pitman, who had been on the *Oceanic* which the Colonel had crossed to Europe in. Gracie climbed up a rope ladder on to the ship, tempted to get down on his knees and kiss it. He was given a hot drink and took off his wet clothes, which were taken away to be dried. He sat in a corner, huddled under blankets. A family acquaintance on the *Carpathia*, Louis Ogden, lent him some clothes. Gracie's new boat, Number 12, was one of the last to reach the *Carpathia* at 8.30 a.m.

As the survivors from Bride's boat were taken onboard the *Carpathia*, a dead body was left in it. Bride later said that it was Phillips, though others were not so sure. Bride painfully climbed the rope ladder up to the deck. He was given a shot of liquor to revive him. Then he was taken down to the hospital.

There was to be a tragic twist in the tale of Jack Phillips. After news of the disaster started to filter through back in England, his father received a reassuring telegram. It said simply: 'Making slowly for Halifax. Practically unsinkable. Don't worry.' It was initially believed to have come from Jack Phillips himself. But within an hour it had emerged that it was in fact from his uncle, and was sent as a reassurance to Phillips' father. It had exactly the opposite effect than that desired.

Second Officer Lightoller had also transferred from Collapsible B to Boat 12. As the sun rose higher in the sky and the welcome sight of the *Carpathia* was seen from the boat, so too had the sea run higher and the wind blown stronger. The boat was full to capacity and beyond and Lightoller feared that she might sink under at any moment. The roughness of the sea increased as they approached the *Carpathia* but at last they were next to her, their ordeal almost concluded.

Lightoller was the last man aboard, a neat symmetry when he had been one of the last to leave the *Titanic*; in fact he was later to tell the American Inquiry that he did not leave the ship, she had left him. His old friend, First Officer Dean of the *Carpathia*, cheerfully asked him: 'Hello Lights! Whatever are you doing here?'

Lightoller looked around him at the bedraggled band of survivors that scanned the horizon to see some sign of life. Those aboard waited, usually in vain, for other boats to bring lost loved ones in. When they did not arrive, increasingly frantic suggestions were made as to what might have happened to them. They might have been picked up by other ships. Perhaps there were more boats yet to come in? Could some not have found sanctuary atop the ice? In the end, Lightoller decided that it was best to give honest rather than evasive advice. He knew that there were no chances left.

Charles Hurd, a passenger on the *Carpathia*, saw the last boat pull alongside. Women, some with cheap shawls protecting their heads from the bitter cold, others with expensive furs performing the same function but presumably more effectively, began to weep as they climbed unsteadily up the ladders that had been swung over the side or were lifted up in slings cobbled together for the purpose.

It was not long before the legends started either, even aboard the *Carpathia*. Sensationalism became a prominent feature of newspaper accounts, making the interpretation of such accounts a matter that requires great caution. An unnamed steward on the *Carpathia* told how an English colonel among the survivors went mad when a boat containing his mother capsized next to the *Carpathia* and he spent hours looking for her. This was complete nonsense. Twenty boats left the *Titanic* and all twenty were accounted for by the *Carpathia*. None of them capsized, though at an earlier stage one or two might have been in real danger of doing so.

It was now, just as the last boat was being picked up, that another ship arrived on the scene. The *Californian* had at last come to the rescue. Onboard the *Californian*, Ernest Gill later said that the gossip was that the captain had been informed in the night by an apprentice, Gibson, of the fact that rockets had been sighted. The talk of the crew, claimed Gill, was: 'Why in the devil they didn't wake the wireless man up?' Whatever Gill's questionability as a witness, this has the ring of truth about it. Ships, especially small ones, are close-knit communities and the reports of the previous night's pyrotechnics would have been the talk of everyone below decks within a matter of hours.

Chief Officer Stewart had come on duty at 4.00 a.m. He had been briefed on the strange events of the previous watch by Second Officer Stone. Stewart picked up his binoculars and saw a ship to the south, a four-master. His immediate assumption was that it was the ship that had been nearby in the night. He said to Stone: 'She's alright, she is a four-master.' The statement that she looked alright was a strange one unless those watching her had thought that there might have been something wrong with her in the first place.

However, Stone told him that she was not the ship he had been watching. The ship he saw now was a four-master with two masthead lights; the one he had watched in the night only had one masthead light. Supporters of the theory that the *Californian* was not the ship close to the *Titanic* use the evidence of Boxhall from the *Titanic* to help their case; Boxhall said that he also saw a four-masted steamer. Stewart looked closely now at the ship to the south and thought she had a yellow funnel. She was then not the *Carpathia* whose funnel was red.

The *Mount Temple* was nearby and had a yellow funnel but it was not likely to be her. The *Californian* was to the east of the ice-field while the *Mount Temple* was on the other side to the west. Captain Lord came up on the bridge at 4.30 a.m. and also looked at the ship, which he thought was 8 miles off to the south.

Stewart now updated Lord on the events of the previous night. Stewart passed on Stone's account, including the information that Stone did not think that the rockets he had seen were distress signals. A strange conversation then followed. Lord said that he did not recollect either the visit from Gibson at around 2.00 a.m. or the call down the speaking tube from Stone around three quarters of an hour later. He would later insist that he was still only aware of one rocket being fired.

At around 5.00 a.m. they discussed their plans for their journey that day. Stewart asked if, before pushing through the ice now that they could see their way through, they were going to see if the ship to the south was alright. Lord said not, as she was not firing any rockets now. Stewart had still not told him that the ship they could see was not the ship that had been signalling in the night. Lord told him reassuringly that 'she looks alright'. With this remark, Lord was hinting at the possibility that there might be a relationship between a ship firing rockets and a ship in distress.

It was only now, Lord said, that Stewart briefed him that a number of rockets had been fired. It was also now, after talking together for half an hour, that Stewart told Lord that the ship they could see to the south was not, according to Herbert Stone, the one that had been firing rockets in the night. A terrible realization now started to dawn on the Captain. Aware now of the possibility that a ship firing a number of rockets at night in the middle of the North Atlantic near an ice-field might be regarded as a sign of distress, Lord did what any prudent sea captain should do in such a situation. He woke up the wireless operator.

Stewart went to rouse Cyril Evans at once. He strode into the operator's room which was never locked. Evans later recalled that Stewart told him: 'There is a ship that has been firing rockets in the night. Please see if there is anything the matter.' Stewart denied ever mentioning the rockets but said that he merely asked Evans to find out if he could what the ship to the south was. It was another example of that increasingly frequent phenomenon, two people from the same ship having very different recollections about the same events. It would be easy for critics of Captain

Lord to suggest that Stewart was downplaying the significance of the rockets quite deliberately after the event.

Evans jumped up and started his wireless up. A message was received back from the *Mount Temple* within about a minute. It told him that the *Titanic* had struck an iceberg and was sinking. This message was also logged by the *Mount Temple*, though the ship's wireless operator, John Durrant, recalled that he had told Evans that the ship had actually sunk. This was at 5.11 a.m., *Mount Temple* time.

The message was passed up to the bridge though for some reason the name of the ship sunk was not, so Lord sent Stewart back down to find out more (again the evidence is contradictory; other accounts have Evans coming back at once with the news that the *Titanic* had foundered). Another message was received at 6.00 a.m. from the *Virginian* which clearly did not yet have an update on the full extent of the disaster. This said: 'Titanic struck berg; want assistance; urgent; ship sinking; passengers in boats, His position 41.46, 40.16.'

Lord got his ship under way at 6.00 a.m. This is a long delay given the news that had been received. Lord later explained this away by saying that he asked Evans to make sure he had got the right position, he did not he explained 'want to go on a wild goose chase'. It contrasted markedly with the actions of Captain Rostron who, having received news of a distress call the night before, had turned his ship around and *then* asked his wireless operator if he was sure of his facts.

Lord first had to push his way through the field ice, assisted by now by the light of day. He was he later admitted nervous. He did not think that the ship he had seen was the *Titanic* which he calculated to have been 19 miles away given her reported position. He did however think that someone on his ship should have been able to see any distress flares if she had sent any up.

He made very slow progress through the ice but once he burst through to the western side of the ice-field he was soon at full speed. He steered south and at 7.30 a.m. met the *Mount Temple* who was at the *Titanic's* SOS position. There was no sign of any wreckage whatsoever. It seemed unlikely that this was the spot where the ship had sunk.

This was not just Lord's analysis. Captain Moore and the *Mount Temple* arrived at the *Titanic's* reported position but could see nothing, neither wreckage or bodies, to intimate that there had been a wreck there. This was not in the least surprising, for the position was significantly wrong and the *Titanic* had in fact sunk on the eastern side of the ice-field that the *Mount Temple* was to the west of (at least 8 miles away according to Moore). The *Californian* had also been on the eastern side and had pushed her way through for nothing.

Lord could see another steamer on the far (east) side of the ice-field so he now looked for another opening to turn back on himself. It was the

Carpathia. He made his way back east and arrived at around 8.00 a.m. There was now nothing much to do.

Rostron prepared to make his way away from this awful place with the survivors. Before leaving, he organized an impromptu religious service on deck, after confirming with Ismay that he had no objections to this idea. However, his assessment that this was the wreck-site was probably wrong and not just because the wreck of the *Titanic* was found some miles away seven decades later. Rostron only saw one body, a male, probably one of the crew. Yet the survivors had reported seeing hundreds of bodies in the water after the great ship went down.

This was a situation confirmed by Captain Lord who said there was very little wreckage when his ship arrived on the scene. To him, it seemed 'like an old fishing boat had sunk'. He stayed on the scene looking for more survivors until 11.20 a.m., when he headed towards Boston. Shortly afterwards, around 12.10 p.m., he met the German liner *Frankfurt* travelling the other way towards the scene of the disaster.

Other ships had been doing their best to help. Far away, too far as it turned out, the *Olympic* and her crew had prepared themselves to charge to the rescue. Stewards helped deckhands to make rope ladders for survivors to climb aboard when they reached *Titanic*. Cooks got hot food ready and bedroom stewards prepared for an influx of up to 2,000 extra people. Everybody was ready to do their bit, but tragically they had no chance of reaching the stricken sister in time to make any difference whatsoever.

The *Birma* too was on her way. She was used to this sort of thing, having played a starring role in rescuing those onboard the stricken liner *Republic* in 1909. She also headed for the *Titanic's* SOS position. Just like the *Mount Temple* and the *Californian* all she found was an empty sea with no sign of a wreck. They later passed this information on to the British Inquiry. The information was either overlooked or studiously ignored.

Just over 700 people, these were all that remained from over 2,000 souls on the *Titanic*. The world as yet did not know what had happened. With the technological constraints then in play, it would take a while for news of the full extent of the tragedy to emerge. When it did, it was beyond comprehension.

17

The World Waits:
15–18 April 1912, USA, Great Britain &
Elsewhere

The world of 1912 was one which was in something of a transition in many different ways. The use of technology was one of them. Signor Marconi's development of wireless (he did not in fact invent it but was the driving force behind its evolution into a practical medium of communication) was a huge step forward from the days when ships could simply disappear without trace. However, it had some way to go before it was perfected, a fact of which Marconi, always striving to improve, was well aware. It was only just over a decade since the first long-distance wireless message had been sent and it was part of an ongoing project of development.

It was not though just the technology itself that was deficient. The systems and processes around it were also in much need of improvement. The loss of the *Titanic*, and the soul-searching that followed it, would provide much needed impetus to the process. It was one thing to have this great new technology to hand, quite another to use it effectively.

What the new technology did mean was that the world was aware that something extraordinary was going on much more quickly than would have been the case in the past. However, there was considerable confusion over the details or indeed the ultimate outcome for some time to come. Ironically, rather than making the situation clearer, confusion over wireless messages was set to muddy the waters for several days.

In the early hours of Monday 15 April, a young wireless operator in Philadelphia, David Sarnoff, picked up reports that the *Titanic* was in trouble. He passed these on. By the time the morning papers were printed, stories concerning the *Titanic* were in them though many were very inaccurate. Most press accounts on 15 April said that *Titanic* was being towed to port by the *Virginian*. Only *The New York Times* reported the bare known facts: 'New Liner Titanic Hits Iceberg; Sinking by the bow at midnight; Women Put Off in lifeboats; Last wireless at 12.27 a.m. blurred.'

At 1.58 a.m. on 15 April New York time, Philip Franklin, Vice-President of International Mercantile Marine, White Star's ultimate parent company, was awoken at home by a phone call from an opportunistic reporter. The journalist wanted to know if Franklin had heard that the *Titanic* was sinking. Incredulous, Franklin quizzed him about where he had heard such a ridiculous rumour. The reporter replied that the initial source of the message was the *Virginian*, at sea in the North Atlantic. At 3.05 a.m., a further message came through that had been sent to Cape Race: 'Last signals from Titanic were heard by the *Virginian* at 1225 EST [Eastern Standard Time]. He reported them blurred and ending abruptly.' Although not identical, it was very close to the version that appeared in some of the press later that day.

This message was waiting for Franklin when he went into the IMM office early that morning. White Star's man on the spot in the North Atlantic was Captain Haddock of the *Olympic*. He was known to be going to the aid of the *Titanic* and was equipped with a powerful wireless set. Franklin sent a series of wires to Haddock to try and establish the complete picture. Several messages came in during the day, as Haddock himself did not yet have the full story and he had to transmit his information in fragments.

In the meantime, Rostron did what he could to deal with the crisis on the spot. The *Carpathia* took aboard the *Titanic's* lifeboats after all their occupants had been lifted on to the ship but the collapsibles were left where they were. The rescue ship then made a brief procession around the area to see if she could pick up any further survivors that might have climbed on top of the ice or were still floating around on wreckage. Rostron noticed that there was a stoic calmness about all the survivors who seemed to be dealing with their ordeal exceptionally bravely.

Then Rostron organized a memorial service in the saloon, over the spot where the great ship had gone down. There was not a lot of wreckage left, some deckchairs and small pieces of wood but a large volume of cork, probably from the collapsed bulkheads of the *Titanic*. Just one body was seen in the water. He looked like a crew member to Rostron and was quite obviously dead. He decided to leave the body where it was as he did not want to disturb the survivors further.

By around 8.30 a.m. on 15 April, other ships had begun to arrive on the scene. Rostron eventually decided to leave all further searching to them and concentrate on the survivors he already had onboard. He contacted the *Californian* and asked her to look around the area – he thought there was one lifeboat still unaccounted for. This was presumably the abandoned Collapsible B which had no one left in it. He asked the *Californian* to look around. It was now about 10.50 a.m.

Just what to do with his new passengers was a major problem for Rostron. The *Carpathia* was headed for Gibraltar but did not have enough provisions aboard for all her extra passengers. He would also soon pass out of wireless range with the weak apparatus he had on the ship. Halifax was the nearest port but it meant passing through the ice to reach there.

One of the first things that *Titanic's* survivors wanted to do was contact the outside world with news that they were safe. They crowded around the *Carpathia's* stewards with messages for the wireless operator to send on. All messages were to be transmitted free of charge and stewards were soon collecting them from the survivors for the wireless operator Harold Cottam to despatch. It was not until much later that they found out that many of them never arrived. Cottam was a one-man band and the pressure of work eventually wore him out, requiring Harold Bride to rise from his sick-bed and help him.

That Monday afternoon, a roll-call of the survivors was held in the saloon of the *Carpathia*. This was sent by Marconigram to the shore to notify the world of those who had been saved and who had, by implication, also been lost. However, there were mistakes in the lists causing a good deal of anxiety in some cases and raising false hopes in others. Lawrence Beesley for one was never mentioned in the official list of survivors sent from the *Carpathia*. Obituaries were published of him, assuming that he had been lost. However, the name of another man whom Beesley had got to know onboard the *Titanic* was regularly reported as saved in the official despatches. His son even travelled to New York expecting to be reunited with him there. However, the news was false and his hopes were dashed.

There were more sombre moments on the *Carpathia* that day. Four men were either dead when taken aboard or died within minutes of arriving. First-class passenger William Hoyt, third-class passenger Abraham Harmer and Steward Sidney Siebert were taken from the boats. Harmer was something of a mystery man. He was a Russian with the real name of David Livshin. They were buried at sea at 4.00 p.m. They were to be joined by Able Crewman P. Lyon. Their bodies were tied up in sacks, which had been weighted at their feet. Then they were taken to a small opening in the ship just above the waterline. Here, they were tipped into the sea off a plank suspended over the side.

On the afternoon of 15 April, Rostron carefully guided his ship around the jagged edges of the ice-field. It was so extensive that Beesley felt sure that the *Titanic's* boats could have rowed passengers onto the ice and then gone back to pick up more. The *Carpathia* steered a course just 200–300 yards off the ice, until just before nightfall to most people's relief it came at last to an end. Most sailors around at the time said that they could not recall ever seeing an ice-field this big before.

One strange, and subsequently jarring, episode was played out onboard the *Carpathia*. The crew from Boat 1 were asked to have their photograph taken by Sir Cosmo Duff Gordon and they also signed Lady Duff Gordon's lifebelt. Sir Cosmo also made a presentation of £5 to each member of the crew. The photograph suggested more of a celebration than the aftermath of a disaster where over 1,500 people had died. It all added to the perception that this was Sir Cosmo and Lady Duff Gordon's personal crew. It was an insensitive and inappropriate piece of theatre on their part which would subsequently metaphorically place both of them in rather deep water.

Onboard the *Carpathia*, Mrs Margaret Brown saw Quartermaster Hichens relating his heroic part in the events of the previous night. Logan Marshall described Mrs Brown as the woman who 'cowered the snivelling Quartermaster' and such was the case now. Gesticulating wildly to an enthralled audience, Hichens regaled them with tales of his valour. However, a look from her was enough to halt his narrative and he beat a hasty retreat.

The survivors were well looked after by the passengers on the ship. The barber's shop was raided for combs, ties, any small item that might return a semblance of normality to what must have seemed like a particularly bad dream. It soon ran out of items such as toothbrushes. Elizabeth Shute managed to purchase a cloth cap to keep her head warm. It was hardly stylish but such trivial considerations did not seem so important anymore. There were a few handkerchiefs left too, so these were also purchased. She now had some of the bare essentials required for the short journey they were about to make.

There were not enough clothes to go around though, and some survivors were forced to spend the rest of the trip dressed in their dressing-gowns and nightwear or whatever else they had on when they left the *Titanic*. Just where they would sleep was another problem. The luckiest were given cabins by those aboard the *Carpathia* but they were the fortunate few. Women slept on the floor of the library and saloons at night on makeshift straw mattresses. The men were allocated the smoking room and a stock of blankets. However, the room was so small that some opted to sleep out on deck. Lawrence Beesley for one struck lucky. One of the passengers offered him a berth in his cabin.

Captain Rostron had given his cabin to Mrs Thayer, Mrs Widener and Mrs Astor while Jack Thayer slept on the floor. There were not enough beds on the *Carpathia* for all those aboard so Violet Jessop slept on the deck, on a bench, under the stars.

Despite the kindness of the *Carpathia's* passengers, a pall of gloom and despondency hung over the ship. There were so many widows whose hopes of finding their husbands had been finally and cruelly dashed, so many children who had lost fathers. Dreams had been shattered and for many on the ship all they had to look forward to was a long, lonely life full of uncertainty.

A few hours after he came aboard the *Carpathia*, Bruce Ismay received a visit from Captain Rostron. He suggested that the Chairman might like to send a wire to the outside world which must have been hungry for information. Ismay concurred and prepared such a communication.

It was short but to the point: 'Deeply regret advise you Titanic sunk this morning after collision with iceberg, resulting in serious loss of life. Full details later.' Despite being delivered to the wireless room on that Monday, it would not reach New York until Wednesday. In the absence of firmer information, the world began to make up its own version of events.

Rostron said later that he gave clear orders about the priorities to be exercised by the wireless operator, who it will be remembered was under the captain's notional authority aboard ship, a prerogative that was often not enforced in practice but would be now. Rostron ordered that two official messages be sent first of all, one to Cunard who owned the *Carpathia* and the other to the White Star Line. This would have an approximate estimate of the number of survivors and would state that the ship was headed for New York.

A similar message was sent to the Associated Press for public consumption. Then Rostron, who had commanded that a list of all survivors be drawn up, instructed Cottam to send the names ashore. He transmitted the first and second-class lists to the *Olympic*, which had a much more powerful wireless apparatus than she did and could forward the names on to shore, but ran out of signal before the third-class list had gone.

Rostron asked Ismay what he wanted to do with the survivors. Ismay replied that he should do whatever he thought best. Rostron had already reasoned that New York was the best option. He also introduced a protocol for sending out wireless messages. He gave instructions to the overworked radio operators to first of all send out his official messages, then the names of survivors, then survivors' private messages.

The decision of where to go with his new passengers was not an easy one for Rostron. Even if he had wanted to, he did not have enough provisions or space for 700 extra mouths to continue on his journey to Europe. He considered taking the *Carpathia* to Halifax, Nova Scotia, but he was unsure if the city could cope with a disaster this big (it could; just a few years later there was huge explosion in the city which claimed even more lives than those lost on the *Titanic*, caused when a munitions ship was involved in a collision and blew up). He also had no desire to sail through ice, both for his own peace of mind and those of his new group of passengers who would probably have been terrified at the sight. So, New York it was to be.

That same evening the news started to emerge to the outside world in all its sombre detail. At 6.15 p.m., the White Star line received a message from Captain Haddock on the *Olympic*. It told all that needed to be told; if not 100 per cent accurate, it was close enough to the truth to wake the world from its wishful thinking that all was well:

Carpathia reached *Titanic's* position at daybreak. Found only boats and wreckage. *Titanic* had foundered at about 2.20 a.m. in 41.16 north, 50.14 west. All her boats accounted for. About 675 souls saved, crew and passengers, latter nearly all women and children.

The last part of the statement was materially misleading; only 353 women and children passengers were saved according to British Inquiry figures along with 20 female crew members – in other words half those saved were male. However, taken as a whole the message was close enough to the truth to alert everyone to the size of the disaster at least. As the day went on, Franklin had done his best to reassure frantic friends and relatives seeking information. He genuinely did not know what had happened himself. Now there was no place to hide.

Franklin still could not believe it. Despite the statement from Haddock that all boats were accounted for, he continued to ask whether any passengers might have been picked up on any other ships. This faint hope was finally quashed by Haddock on a message received at around 1.45 a.m. on 16 April.

That same day, Tuesday 16th, the survivors on the *Carpathia* met and decided to set up a fund to help those who would undoubtedly have suffered as a result of the disaster. A committee was appointed onboard the ship to raise funds to help the destitute reach their destinations when they arrived in America. The committee consisted of Margaret Brown, Mrs Emma Bucknell and Mrs Martha Stone. By the time that they reached New York, $15,000 had been raised. Mrs Astor donated $2,000 of this.

They also decided to club together for a loving cup to present to their saviour, Captain Rostron. More mundane matters though needed to be attended to. Beesley visited the steerage survivors that same day to take their names. It was important to find out more about the needs of those who had survived. They were grouped into classes based on nationality, English, Irish and Swedish in the main. They were asked if they had money and where they intended to go onto in America.

The Countess of Rothes won great praise for her actions in the lifeboats the night that the *Titanic* sank but she also impressed Lightoller for her unceasing ministrations to those aboard the *Carpathia* which were very necessary. Beesley noted that almost all the Irish girls in steerage were penniless. They were in the main travelling just to New York. For whatever reason, the Swedish passengers had managed to save most of their money. They were mostly travelling onwards once they landed and had railway tickets to do so.

Many initial press reports suggested that the *Titanic* was being towed to Halifax. A number said that in Halifax no one was believed lost. All passengers would be unloaded. They would then transfer them to New York by train. There were reports that other ships were helping with the rescue. One was the *Parisian*, *en route* from Glasgow to Halifax. The *Baltic*, *Virginian* and *Olympic* were also nearby but the *Carpathia* had definitely picked up a number of survivors.

Philip Franklin had initially said that although the company lacked detailed information, the survivors would reach Halifax Wednesday evening. During Monday he confirmed that he believed that there was no loss of life. A number of railway carriages were despatched from Boston on Monday night. Special arrangements were made for Customs officials to travel from Montreal to Halifax to process the passengers through the bureaucratic formalities as quickly as possible. However, with Haddock's crushing confirmation on Tuesday morning that there was no hope of finding other survivors, there was no longer any justification in continuing with this optimistic line.

In New York Franklin, who would front up the organization's press communications, now knew the truth but he could not bring himself to face it at once. When he received these tidings from a trusted White Star skipper, he knew at last how awful the situation was. He delayed making a further announcement to the press but after three quarters of an hour he had regained enough composure to face them. In that first briefing he told the world that the *Titanic* had gone down. It was another three hours though before he came back to brief everyone in more detail, virtually breaking down as he admitted that there had been a terrible loss of life.

Many of the crew came from Southampton. The news hit the city like a bombshell. An infectious panic spread rapidly as those first, garbled messages were received, and relatives frantically sought news of their loved ones who had been onboard. All too frequently those unaccounted for were the main and often the only bread-winner in the family. Women ran out of their homes and made their way as quickly as they could to the shipping offices. London newspapers, sensing the spreading shadow of catastrophe, sent their reporters to the city, just a short train journey away.

First news was posted outside the White Star offices on Monday but there were few details. The Salvation Army was on the scene, sending people into homes to watch children so mothers could go out in search of news. A large crowd gathered outside the offices, desperate for news. The Army's correspondent in its paper, *The War Cry*, captured the scene as well as any journalist when he wrote:

> None but a heart of stone would be unmoved in the presence of such anguish. Night and day that crowd of pale, anxious faces had been waiting patiently for the news that did not come. Nearly every one in the crowd had lost a relative.

Newsboys walked the streets, crying out the news. Some heard in strange ways. One Southampton woman was visited by her insurance man (door-to-door visits were the way of things back then) who casually remarked that the ship had gone down with all hands. She went white; as she explained her 'hubby' was onboard. The next news she knew was that the ship was being towed to Halifax with everyone saved. Then of course the true situation started to emerge. This lady, Mrs Lewis, was lucky; her husband Arthur Lewis was one of those who survived.

Reginald Loveless, a Junior Clerk for White Star, arrived at the offices to find the street outside in Canute Road packed with people desperate for news. A worrying message had been posted in the window of the *Southampton Times* which announced that the *Titanic* was 'probably sinking'. When the grim news started to filter through on Tuesday 16 April that she was indeed almost certainly at the bottom of the ocean, it became for Southampton the blackest day in living memory. The word '*Titanic*' seemed to be on everyone's lips.

Little further news appeared on the Tuesday, except that five of the ship's officers were safe. On Wednesday afternoon, a workman came out and nailed a blackboard to the rails outside the offices, though there were still no details posted on it. Frantic relatives sought desperately for news to confirm that their loved ones were safe, people like Arthur Paintin's wife (the couple had only been married in the previous November). She came down on the Wednesday worried out of her mind. Paintin, aged twenty-nine, who had the traditional nickname 'Tiger', was Captain Smith's personal steward (a nickname still used for Captain's Stewards today). As time went on and no news came in his wife started to realize that she was now tragically his widow.

Northam, where many of the crew lived, was worst affected of all. One resident said that nearly every house had lost a son or husband. Everywhere curtains were drawn. The log book of Northam Girls' School noted that on 16 April many girls were absent, panic-stricken at the news of the disaster and in floods of tears. When further news came through, crushing many hopes, the school and the local community did what it could to help. Clothes were distributed to many of the bereaved children and they were visited by the Lady Mayoress.

Times had already been hard in Southampton. The coal strike had meant that work had been in short supply. Families had been forced to resort to pawning their meagre possessions to gain some temporary respite from hardship. When news of the *Titanic's* imminent sailing had come, and the White Star Line had started recruiting, the local economy had picked up and there was the promise of better times ahead. Now, with so many bread-winners gone, the shadow of poverty loomed darker than ever for so many families.

The first lists of survivors were posted outside the Canute Road offices on 17 April. The lists were not complete; White Star announced that the signals across the Atlantic were 'rather weak'. Now more frantic than ever, relatives and friends whose loved ones had not been included on the initial list of survivors kept a long night vigil in the road, hoping against hope that more names would be added.

A heavy and un-seasonal dusting of snow added to the sense of gloom, though the frosty covering soon melted. Even now, people hoped that the ship's supposed 'unsinkability' would prove her salvation. In Northam, where so many men had come from, the sense of panic was stronger than anywhere, with women running out in aprons and hastening down to the shipping offices. Hours passed and no more news emerged and the crowd became ever more distressed. It became clear that the 'unsinkable' might sink after all.

Southampton became for a short time the focus of Britain's national press. White Star staff like Reginald Loveless spent a complete week at work, sleeping on the hard floor at night while they awaited firm news to pass on to the overwhelmed crowd outside. White Star staff did their best. Coffee was taken out to the mass outside. However, hard as the local staff tried they could not manufacture news that did not exist. Looking on the board for news became a ritual; several times a day relatives would make the fruitless journey to Canute Road and would eventually go home again disappointed. Women wore black even though they often did not yet know the worst. They sent their children to look at the notice-boards for news, unable to bring themselves to examine any lists of survivors themselves.

It was 7.00 a.m. on the morning of Friday 20 April that firm news at last started to arrive. A clerk came out of the offices and put up a list on a long strip of paper on the huge blackboard. The names were written up in big blue letters and the crowd of mainly women who had been there all night struggled to look at the list. Their eyes were red with tiredness and worry; they had not slept in many cases since Tuesday. They would soon be red with tears. The news was in the main as bad as it could be: of 898 crew members, only 212 had lived through the disaster and 549 Southampton residents had been lost, nearly all of them crew.

To some, there was relief; in the absence of news many had convinced themselves that their loved ones were lost and in a few cases they were wrong. For the rest, the agony continued for a while. The list, the crowd were told, was not yet complete. Some men shared a surname and in such cases there was uncertainty about which individual had survived.

Communications were difficult and there was much confusion. Sidney Daniels was a young steward on the ship. He survived but somehow was missed in the roll-call that was taken and so he did not appear on any list of those saved. When he arrived in New York, all surviving crew were permitted to send a cable to their families to reassure them. Daniels sent one to his father, which must have come as a great relief. However, as he was sailing back on the *Lapland* which had been commandeered by the White Star Line, a letter from the company was sent to his father telling him that he was lost. The tension must have been unbearable and went on until father and son were reunited in England.

A visiting journalist described Southampton as a widowed city. Flags flew at half-mast and the pillars of the Guildhall were dressed in black crepe. Many of the inhabitants were wearing black. He estimated that 500 homes had been deprived of their main bread-winner. In one Northam school, 125 children were now fatherless. The journalist noted that, for most of the widows, life had to go on. Although there was grief, it was kept firmly below the surface. The practicalities meant that it had to be.

One bereaved Southampton resident took the lead in helping her fellow sufferers. Eleanor Smith, Captain Smith's wife, released a statement in which she stated:

> My heart overflows with grief for you all and is laden with sorrow that you are weighed down with this terrible burden that has been thrust upon us.

Now, the hammer-blows started to strike home. As details of the few who had survived emerged, by implication so did details of those who did not. Mrs Ann May might have been an extreme example but her story sums up the clouds of devastation that descended on Southampton. She had lost a husband and a son, both firemen on *Titanic*. It was the first time that both had gone to sea together, forced to do so by the coal strike. The eldest (both men were named Arthur) had meant to go on another ship, the *Britannia*. The younger had gone because he needed work, with a wife and young child to keep.

Mrs May was quoted in the *Daily Mail* of 18 April 1912 as saying that she was now alone with eleven dependants. The eldest of these made a few shillings a week through any odd jobs that turned up. The youngest was a boy of six months old. To say that the future looked bleak was an understatement. Lucky relatives were in a distinct minority; the luckiest of all may have been Mrs Slade whose sons should have been on the ship but had left the *Grapes* pub late and missed it. At the time, it had seemed a piece of extreme bad luck but now the reverse was true. Mrs. Slade's explanation for their missing the ship was the bad vibes they had against it; it seems as if her sons had not been completely forthcoming with the truth.

The coal strike was held responsible for a sizable proportion of the loss of life in Southampton. One correspondent suggested that one half of the crew would have been working on other ships if it had not been for the effect of industrial action, though he admitted that others would of course have taken their place and been lost if the strike had not been on. It was a particularly cruel form of Russian roulette which had been played and the losers had paid with their lives.

Some of those onboard had previously been workless for four or five weeks and this meant that families went hungry. They left little money behind them as a result. The correspondent quoted the case of an Alderman of the city who had been trying to help some of the destitute mothers; twelve of them were responsible for sixty children between them. In one example, the wife of a steward was quoted as being penniless, in another a woman had six children and a seventh was well on the way; again she had not a farthing to call her on.

The devastation was beyond imagining. The Salvation Army's periodical, *The War Cry*, quoted an unnamed family where the father had gone down on the *Titanic* and the mother had just died in childbirth leaving six orphaned children behind. There were even those who commented that the rule of 'women and children first' might seem natural to some but it had plenty of dissidents opposed to the view in the city.

In the meantime, the rescue ship headed west back to America. As the *Carpathia* sailed steadily on towards New York, she had to contend with a whole range of weather conditions. In addition to the ice she had just left behind her, she sailed through warm sunshine, fogs, choppy seas and thunderstorms where the noises were so loud and sounded so close that some of the survivors aboard thought that more distress rockets were being fired.

It was a trying voyage for those aboard. The ship was crowded far beyond its limits. Some of the survivors continued understandably to delude themselves, thinking that they would meet loved ones left behind on the *Titanic* back in New York. They said that they may have been taken there aboard ships that were faster than the *Carpathia* or, alternatively, might have been following on in slower ships. Remarkably though, there were few reports of sickness among the survivors. The doctors on the ship reported no cases contacting them for assistance.

Harold Cottam was overwhelmed by the volume of traffic he had to deal with. When Harold Bride had been dragged aboard the *Carpathia*, he was taken to the hospital where he remained for ten hours. Then word came that Harold Cottam, the ship's regular wireless operator, was getting 'a little queer' with the sheer number of messages that he was being asked to send. Bride was asked if he could go and assist. Although he could not walk due to his extended immersion in the icy water, he went up to the wireless room on crutches and did what he could to help.

From that point on until arriving in New York, Bride never left the room. Meals were brought to the cabin and a non-stop service was provided thereafter. Bride and Cottam worked in shifts, with the *Titanic's* wireless man sometimes working from his bed. Harold Bride subsequently defended the performance of the *Carpathia's* makeshift wireless team, saying that he positively refused to send press messages while there were so many personal messages to send from survivors (though the suspicion must remain that he had arranged for some kind of exclusive with the *New York Times* in which he gave his interview on 19 April).

Bride castigated the wireless operators onboard the US Cruiser *Chester*, which had been trying to get news on Archie Butt, a prominent *Titanic* passenger, for President Taft, for their lack of competence. The main problem, he said, was that they knew American Morse but not Continental Morse. Their lack of capability taxed the endurance of the *Carpathia's* wireless room to the limit.

In the end, Bride suggested that they stopped bothering to try and correspond with them. The volume of personal messages was turning into a major headache, with 119 messages sent out on 19 April. Bride was extremely condescending towards the navy operators he had been forced to communicate with, describing them as 'as slow as Christmas coming'. Even as he left the *Carpathia* at the start of a new life that would never be the same as the old, a pile of 100 unsent messages lay unprocessed on the desk.

Captain Rostron was adamant about one thing; there were no attempts at censorship on his ship, a line of investigation that Senator Smith would subsequently follow rigorously at the American Inquiry. Rostron regretted the fact that there had been a great deal of confusion due to the lack of information immediately after the disaster. However, the ship only had a short-range wireless set, its one operator had been overwhelmed and even the help of Harold Bride had not managed to make sufficient inroads into the huge number of messages that needed to be sent. Of course, his radio operator had only picked up the distress call from the *Titanic* by a sheer fluke.

Wireless Operator Harold Cottam was so busy that he had reached the point of exhaustion and beyond. He did not sleep at all on Sunday or Monday and only fell asleep, involuntarily, late Tuesday night. He did not remember receiving a message from the President of the United States but then he was so overwhelmed that he was not really looking at received messages. He knew that the *Chester* had asked for a list of survivors but was also aware that a list of first and second-class survivors plus the crew had already gone off.

No less a person than Marconi himself was asked to give evidence on the issue of wireless at the American Inquiry. He said that at one stage someone (not Marconi) had suggested that Jack Binns, the hero of the *Republic* rescue a few years before, should be transferred to the *Carpathia* to help catch up with the backlog of messages. It was estimated that the ship had sent 400 to 500 messages on her way back to New York.

Cottam denied categorically ever sending a message saying that the *Titanic* was being towed to Halifax; indeed, it is difficult to understand why he could possibly have a reason for doing so when he would have known better than most that such a statement was blatantly untrue and would be proven to be so. However, such a message did appear from some speculative source, though its provenance was never proved despite Senator Smith's later perseverance at the American Inquiry to discover where it had come from.

The message that had erroneously come from somewhere said: '*Titanic* proceeding to Halifax. Passengers will probably land there Wednesday. All safe.' It purported to come from the White Star Line, though it was never traced back to any individual in particular. It was dated 15 April 1912, the very day that *Titanic* disappeared beneath the waves.

As the *Carpathia* moved sedately back towards New York, the thoughts of Bruce Ismay were on getting home as quickly as possible. At 5.35 p.m. on 17 April the following message was received by Franklin:

> Most desirable *Titanic* crew aboard *Carpathia* should be returned home earliest moment possible. Suggest you hold Cedric, sailing her daylight Friday unless you see any reason contrary. Propose returning in her myself. Please send outfit of clothes, including shoes, for me to Cedric. Have nothing of my own. Please reply. YAMSI [Ismay's call-sign].

The *Cedric* was another White Star ship in New York. She was due to be gone by the time the *Carpathia* arrived, hence Ismay's request to delay her departure. Franklin was reluctant to postpone her departure though and replied that they would instead return the crew later on another ship, the *Lapland*. Ismay continued to persist, allegedly at the behest of Second Officer Lightoller, but Franklin could not be persuaded to change his mind. In the end, *Cedric* sailed at noon on Thursday, 18 April, just nine and a half hours before *Carpathia* docked. However, by then the situation had changed completely anyway, as the US Senate had authorized an investigation into a disaster that had deprived many Americans of their lives.

On the afternoon that the *Carpathia* approached New York, the ship's doctor asked Jack Thayer to speak to Bruce Ismay who had not set foot outside his cabin since coming aboard. He made his way to his room and knocked on the door but there was no answer so Jack went in. Ismay was sat on his bunk, dressed in his pyjamas. He stared straight ahead as if glaring into oblivion. He was shaking like a leaf. Jack tried to converse with him, telling him that he should not be blamed for taking the last boat but it was as if Ismay was lost in some other faraway world. Jack left the room quietly, realizing that at this moment Ismay was unreachable. He could have sworn that Ismay's hair had been almost black a few days before but had now turned silver-white.

This is fully in keeping with what Ismay himself later said. He appears to have been a man in shock. When questioned at the American Inquiry shortly after landing at New York, he confirmed that he had not talked with the accident with anyone except Second Officer Lightoller. In fact, Lightoller was the only one of the four surviving officers whose name he knew. It was as if it was simply too much to take in.

The world now waited to see the survivors of this awful ordeal for the first time. President Taft of the USA and King George V of Great Britain had exchanged telegrams of condolence in the aftermath. The House of Representatives went into recess for twenty-four hours and flags across Washington were lowered to half-mast. The disaster had shaken the world to the core in a way that few other disasters, before or since, have managed to do. Now the world waited, eager to find out the truth concerning this apocalyptic catastrophe.

18

Honouring the Dead:
April – May 1912, North Atlantic & its Periphery

The extent of the tragedy was staggering. Somewhere in the North Atlantic were 1,500 corpses (exact figures are a matter of debate but all casualty lists approximate to this figure), floating like ghostly flotsam and jetsam on the surface of the sea. Some no doubt had gone down with the ship, trapped in the labyrinth of corridors and passageways. Their grave would be the hulk of the great ship, broken-backed and fallen. There they would decay along with the rusting hulk of the once-proud queen of the oceans. Saltwater does not preserve bones well and none would be found when the ship was later located, unlike for example the *Empress of Ireland* where the fresh water has preserved the remains of some of the lost of that particular tragedy.

There were many others though probably floating on the surface of the North Atlantic, at the mercy of the currents which could take them many miles away from where they perished. There had been life preservers for everyone aboard and most people seemed to have put one on so many of the dead should still be visible. The life preservers appeared to have been one of the few things that worked properly that night. Those who had gone back with Officer Lowe to look for survivors had seen hundreds of bodies at the wreck-site so it was likely there were many of the dead that could be recovered.

White Star's agents in Halifax, A.G. Jones and Company, were contacted to arrange for a ship to visit the last reported location of the *Titanic* and search for them. The *Mackay-Bennett*, a cable-laying ship, was requisitioned for the task. The largest undertaker in Nova Scotia, John Snow and Company, was hired to oversee the collection and preservation of the bodies. A number of embalmers were to make the trip. One of them, Annie O'Neill, was to be responsible for the bodies of any women and children found.

Tons of ice was poured in the hold, ice to preserve rather than this time to destroy. Over 100 coffins were loaded. The crew were all volunteers, to be paid double the going rate to compensate them for the horrible sights that inevitably awaited. They left on 17 April. As the *Mackay-Bennett* drew near the wreck-site, the ship's wireless operator contacted all other vessels in the vicinity asking for details of any bodies or wreckage seen floating in the water. Messages began to come in, one from the steamship *Rhein* on 20 April saying that she had spotted wreckage and bodies as well as three icebergs.

Bruce Ismay announced that the *Mackay-Bennett* would radio reports in every morning, which would then be published as soon as possible in White Star offices. This would at least allow some people to have a form of closure and give them the small compensation of being able to bury their dead with dignity. On 22 April, the first list was published with twenty-seven names on it. The next day, a note was published saying that the ship had picked up a further seventy-seven bodies. Some of these were embalmed and would be returned to port, the rest were to be buried at sea.

The German liner *Bremen* had meanwhile reported when she reached New York sighting more than 100 bodies when she passed through the area. The *Mackay-Bennet* had been close by at the time. One passenger aboard was reported to have seen the body of a woman floating with a baby in her arms. More bizarrely, another female body was reported to be clasping the corpse of a shaggy dog.

When the *Mackay-Bennett* duly arrived on the spot, one of those aboard her, John Snow Junior, described how dozens of bodies could be seen floating in the water. The watches of all those recovered had stopped at 2.10, which was interesting as it was ten minutes before the ship was supposed to have sunk so maybe some of the corpses were of people who had jumped off before the ship went down. As the doleful process of recovery began, the sea grew choppy and pulling the bodies from the water was a hard and harrowing task.

Each body that was hauled aboard was tagged with a piece of canvas with a number engraved on it. The accounting then began in a ledger of death, in which the physical characteristics and any other identifying features of the corpse were marked against the relevant number in the book. It was not easy; days of immersion had often made those who had died look older than they actually were.

Fifty-one bodies were picked up on the first day. Every one wore a lifebelt and floated high in the water. Twenty-seven of the bodies were embalmed and the other twenty-four were buried at sea. The next day, another twenty-seven were picked up, of which fifteen were returned to the deep with all the dignity that could be mustered. The crew members spoke of horrible sights, of terrible disfigurements, of corpses that could not be recognized as human anymore. However, sometimes even those awfully battered could be identified; J.J. Astor was recognized by the initials on his shirt collar. He of course was taken back for burial; there was no chance that his body would be consigned to the deep. Even in death there would be class discrimination. Neither was it the last example of such a phenomenon. Mrs Astor presented Captain Lardner with a cheque for the crew of $2,000 in appreciation.

More messages of bodies in the water were received by the *Mackay-Bennet* from passing ships. Captain Lardner continued his diligent search, determined to do his best in his disconcerting task. However, without proper refrigeration equipment onboard the bodies recovered were now starting to decompose. A second ship, the *Minia*, was called into service, though she was delayed for practical reasons; the local undertakers had run out of coffins so more had to be made. On 22 April she too set out, with tons of ice and 150 coffins aboard. She arrived on site on Friday 26 April.

By 25 April, a revised list had been put up by White Star as the *Mackay-Bennet* continued her thankless task. The after deck was crowded with piles of coffins. A total of 190 bodies would be brought back and another 116 had been buried at sea; in other words 306 had been recovered in total. The *Minia* arrived at the wreck-site on 26 April, picking up a further fourteen corpses. Among those identified were John Jacob Astor, Isidor Straus and Hudson Allison, all prominent first-class passengers.

Class distinction continued; first-class passengers were placed in coffins, while other passengers were put in canvas bags. Bodies of crew members were simply placed on deck, smothered in ice and then covered over with tarpaulins. This did not go unremarked at the time. On 8 May 1912, the *Elizabeth Daily Journal* reported that the body of Mail Clerk John March had reached Newark and been delivered into the hands of local undertakers Smith & Smith. March's body had been picked up by the *Mackay-Bennett*. To quote the paper:

> The undertakers were surprised at the condition in which the body was shipped, as they allege that no effort had been made to embalm it and that the body was in a cheap pine box.

The *Mackay-Bennett* arrived back in Halifax on 30 April. A pall of gloom hung over the port, where every flag was at half-mast, including that of the ship itself. The church bells began to strike their haunting knells. The after-deck of the ship as she hove into port was piled high with coffins, now each bearing a tragic, terrible burden. Sailors carried each one down the gangplank, handing them over to undertakers. Hearses started to take the bodies to a makeshift morgue. A tight cordon was thrown round the scene, making it virtually impossible for any intrusive press photographer to snap a photograph of these intensely painful moments.

The *Minia* was back a week later, though she only carried seventeen bodies. The most prominent of these was Charles Hays, President of the

Grand Trunk Railroad, whose remains were taken back to Montreal by train. One of those onboard the *Minia* when she picked up the bodies provided further evidence that the *Titanic* had broken up when she sank. He noticed that much of the wreckage, especially chunks of the Grand Staircase, came from below decks so he reasoned that the great ship had not been intact when she went down.

The ship's physician, Dr Mosher, conducted a post mortem on these bodies. Of the seventeen corpses, only one had water in the lungs, showing that the remainder had died of exposure. Some said (though it was not clear that this information had come from the doctor) that they had been alive for at least four hours before dying which sounds highly unlikely given the temperature of the water.

This was not quite the last attempt at recovery. A fisheries ship, the *Montmorency*, left port on 3 May and found four bodies, one of which was buried at sea. A second attempt by her soon after came across only wreckage. On 15 May, the *Algerine* made one last attempt and came across one more body, that of Steward James McGrady. These attempts had collectively recovered 328 bodies, 209 of which were brought ashore.

Halifax was not a pleasant sight. The *Nova Scotian Evening Mail* reported:

> The first bodies taken ashore were those of the crew. These bodies had not been embalmed or even sewn up in canvas and presented a gruesome sight that it would be impossible to picture. The bodies were carried on stretchers by members of the Mackay-Bennett crew and at times as many as 30–40 bodies were in a heap on the deck where they had been taken from the ice-filled hold.

Only first-class passengers, the last to be brought off, were in coffins. The rest were deprived of this mark of respect. It was an undignified scene but very much in keeping with the superficial attitude of White Star towards all but her most prominent passengers. In a particularly jarring note, the company proposed to charge 'cargo rates' for shipping any bodies back to England. The company that had been responsible for the deaths of over 1,500 people did not even have the decency to ship their bodies back for free. It is too easy to ascribe this shoddy behaviour to the mores of the time because not everyone acted in this way. For example, it was a marked contrast to the attitude of Cunard who refused to take any payment from White Star for *Carpathia's* part in the rescue efforts.

At the morgue in Halifax, normally a curling rink, the bodies were each examined by a coroner. Cause of death was invariably listed as 'accidental drowning' though many of the deceased must have been frozen to death or even crushed as parts of the *Titanic* fell on them as the ship broke up. They were then put in private cubicles where they could be identified. This could be a harrowing process; one of the undertakers came across the body of his uncle who had been onboard.

To some, the shock went beyond that of identifying a lost loved one. Catherine Harbeck from Ohio went to pick up the body of her husband, William, a cinematographer travelling second-class. It was only when she arrived that she found out he had been travelling with another woman who had been registered as Mrs Harbeck, who was in fact really Henriette Yvois. Harbeck had been found clutching Henriette's purse, in which his wedding ring had been placed. The real Mrs Harbeck took the body back home for burial. However, it was perhaps understandable that she did not arrange for a headstone to be placed over his grave.

Even more bizarrely, one woman, Lydia Fox, impersonated her sister Cora. She claimed to be the widow of Stanley Fox (in fact, she was of course his sister-in-law), who lay in the morgue. Only a telegram from the real Cora stopped the body from being abducted. It is not certain why Lydia took this extreme course of action, though Stanley was carrying personal effects worth more than $2,000 with him which might well have had something to do with this extraordinary deception.

The process of identification was carried out with well-organized precision, in stark contrast to most events concerning the loss of the *Titanic* it must be said. Once a body had been identified, it could be transported home by train for the payment of a first-class rail fare. The first to be released in this manner was the body of J.J. Astor. Photographs were taken of those who could not be identified to aid identification in the future; some of these gruesome snapshots, macabre evidence of the catastrophic events of the disaster, have survived the passing of time.

Fifty-nine bodies were reclaimed and taken away for burial, the rest were to be interred in Halifax; again, money talked and those with none could not afford to ship the remains of their loved ones home. Three local cemeteries were to be used, Fairview which was non-sectarian, Mount Olivet (Catholic) and Baron de Hirsch (Jewish). There was an unseemly wrangle when some bodies were claimed by Rabbi Jacob Walter which had been believed to be non-Jewish and some had to be taken to other cemeteries instead; in this undignified squabbling some of the coffins were damaged and had to be replaced.

A number of memorial services were held at St Mary's Cathedral in the city before the bodies were taken away for burial. Fifty-nine were buried in one day at Fairview, on a slope overlooking the sea. As the last of them was interred, the band of the Royal Canadian Regiment played 'Nearer My God to Thee'. The day following this mass internment, a single burial took place, that of an unidentified male child just over a year old. Despite many attempts to trace his family, none could be found. Many people wanted to pay for this burial but the honour was eventually given to Captain Lardner and the crew of the *Mackay-Bennett*.

There is an amazing postscript to this story which brings us right up to the modern day. Developments in DNA technology would bring fresh hope that the secrets of this unidentified child might at last be revealed. It had long been assumed in the absence of positive evidence that the body of this tragic victim was that of Gösta Pälsson from Sweden, aged two. Then, in 2001, an astonishing revelation; further testing had at last proved the identity of the unknown boy. He was Eino Panula, thirteen-months old.

This was incredible news but there was yet one more twist to come. DNA as a science continued to advance and scientists expressed doubts over the reliability of the identification. In 2007, another bombshell was dropped. The identification had been revised. Further tests now revealed that the body was that of one-year old Sidney Goodwin.

Despite the unwelcome confusion over the identification, there was a certain telling symmetry between the three cases involved which helped to explain why their relatives had not been around to identify them when the heart-wrenching sight of the tiny corpse was revealed in the morgue in 1912. Gösta was travelling with his mother and three siblings, Eino with his mother and four siblings, Sidney with his parents and five siblings. In total, these three families represented nineteen lives. They shared two things in common. Firstly, they were all third-class passengers. Secondly, every single one of them died.

This very human story brings home the awfulness of the tragedy. Closer examination also reveals how fallacious the images of 'women and children first' onboard the *Titanic* are. Of the nineteen lives lost, fourteen were women or children under fourteen years of age. By the rules supposedly in operation on the *Titanic* that night, none of them should have died. They prove that the maxim of 'women and children first' was applied far more scrupulously to first and second-class passengers than it was to third-class.

Young Sidney's identification also shed some indirect light on what had happened to some at least of the third-class passengers. He was a babe in arms, so it is reasonable to assume that he would be with the rest of his family when he died. His body had been found and therefore had presumably not gone down with the ship. Therefore, it may be inferred that neither did his family. They at least had apparently not then been trapped below decks but had reached the upper decks far too late to get to a boat.

In all, 121 *Titanic* victims were laid to rest at Fairview, 19 in Mount Olivet and 10 in Baron de Hirsch. A simple slab marked most of the graves, except for where families paid for something more. The most elaborate headstone was that of Chief Steward Ernest Freeman. It read:

'He Remained at his Post of Duty, Seeking to Save Others, Regardless of His Own Life and Went Down With the Ship.' It was paid for by none other than Bruce Ismay. Surely cynics cannot have failed to comment on the irony of it all when the end of Ernest Freeman contrasted so jarringly with the escape of his generous post-mortem benefactor.

These were not however the last bodies to be recovered. Well into May, a liner was sailing across the North Atlantic when she came across Collapsible A, still afloat. Onboard the abandoned boat were three bodies, first-class passenger Thomson Beattie and two unidentified crewmen. A lifeboat was lowered from the ship with an officer and a doctor. Passengers watching from the deck noted that the passenger was still wearing full evening dress. All the bodies were sewn up in weighted canvas bags and committed to the deep. Collapsible A was picked up and taken back to New York to be returned to the White Star Line, her rightful owners (the *Titanic's* lifeboats incidentally were never used again. Souvenir hunters stripped them of anything portable and the boats rotted away in a Brooklyn boatyard).

The newspapers reported a grisly tale in connection to the discovery of these corpses, more likely reflective of the sensationalist reporting of the time than based on any fact. Papers like the *St Pauls Daily News* told that the three men in the boat all had pieces of cork in their mouth and that there was evidence of the cork and the wood in the boat being chewed. They surmised that this proved that they had not been dead at all and had resorted to all kinds of desperate measures in an attempt to avoid a long, lingering death from starvation.

There was a final irony to these last rites of the disaster. The passing ship flew the pennant of a white star proudly over her decks. Just five years before, this ship, the *Oceanic*, had been the pride of the White Star fleet, 'the queen of the seas'. The new *Olympic*-class ships had seemingly relegated her to a much humbler level, yet here she was, making her way across the oceans that her larger successor had failed to negotiate even once.

She could perform one final service for her lost stable-mate, that of giving three of her passengers and crew a dignified farewell. It perhaps did not mean too much to those who had survived the terrible ordeal of 14/15 April 1912, save possibly one, Charles Lightoller, Second Officer of the *Titanic*, the same Charles Lightoller who had previously been First Officer of the *Oceanic* (Frederick Fleet had also served as a lookout on her).

This twist in the tail had not yet quite finished. The year after the loss of the *Titanic*, Lightoller would be back on the *Oceanic*. He was still there when World War I broke out and the ship was requisitioned for naval service. In September 1914, Lightoller had retired to his cabin when a sudden shudder shook the *Oceanic*. She had run aground and

Lightoller once more found himself in charge of lowering the lifeboats. She eventually broke up three weeks later. Neither accident could be attributed to Lightoller but those who believed in the concept of 'jonahs' aboard ships might have done well to stay away from him, a suspicion that would surely have hardened when the torpedo-destroyer that he was in charge of in 1918 was struck by a trawler and sank six hours later.

Of all the funeral services held for the *Titanic* victims whose bodies were recovered, none matched that of bandmaster Wallace Hartley (though J.J. Astor was also interred with a great deal of pomp). Hartley's corpse was recovered on 30 April and was brought back to Halifax. It was battered beyond recognition but the violin case strapped to his back reputedly served to identify him (though the case never arrived back with his family). It was shipped back to England onboard the *Arabic*, which was sailing to Liverpool. Here, his body was collected by his father, Albion.

In a scene that might have come straight from a Victorian melodrama, Wallace Hartley's remains were brought by a horse-drawn hearse, travelling at night to avoid inquisitive spectators which can only have added to the sombre atmosphere overlaying the procession. On arrival, his coffin lay in state in the Bethel Chapel in Colne, where the Hartley family emanated from (though Wallace had not lived there for some years).

The interment took place on Sunday 18 May in Colne Cemetery. The procession to the graveside was led by five brass bands. They were followed by a Battalion of the East Lancashire Regiment and representatives of various other bodies, including council members. The gates of the cemetery were kept shut and only the procession with the immediate family was let in while the huge crowds were kept outside until family and close friends had made their way to the grave.

The chapel was packed to overflowing during the service (it normally held 600 people but there were 1,000 inside that day). It was estimated that 40,000 people lined the streets; this in a town with a population just over half that. The procession stretched for half a mile and took an hour to reach the cemetery from the chapel. As the coffin was lowered into the ground, a choir sang 'Nearer My God to Thee' which was now enshrined in *Titanic* legend. Then a party of buglers played the Last Post.

Of all the places that are connected to the *Titanic*, Wallace Hartley's grave is perhaps the most moving. It lies towards the bottom of a hill that angles crazily from the entrance at the top down to the graves down in the valley. The angle of the slope is as steep as that of the ship on which Bandmaster Hartley was standing as she started her final plunge to the bottom. Windswept it may be but the view across the valley and over to the hills on the far side is one of rare grandeur. It is a fitting place for a hero to spend eternity.

The town resolved to remember Wallace, whose bust was duly erected in a prominent public place. His place in the legend was firmly assured for as long as people remembered the disaster. The vicarious mourning of the wider citizenry could not however disguise the fact that this was a personal tragedy for the family. Albion, his father, was visibly close to collapse when he collected his son's corpse at Liverpool. His fiancée, to whom he had only been engaged for a short time, must have been distraught. He had considered not going on the trip so that he could be close to her and had only decided to go because of the money he could make to help towards their future together.

On his grave were inscribed some notes from the hymn 'Nearer, My God, To Thee'. His father had said it was Wallace's favourite hymn and that he had always said he wanted it played at his funeral. However, there were three well known settings of the hymn. One, by Sir Arthur Sullivan of Gilbert and Sullivan and *Onward Christian Soldiers* fame, was called *Propior Dio*. This was Hartley's personal favourite and it is from this, now the least well-known of the trio, that the notes that adorn his grave are taken.

There were two other tunes, one called *Horbury* and the other *Bethany*, which are better known, partly because later film versions of the *Titanic* disaster would use them and thereby prolong their fame. One of these, *Horbury*, is used on the musician's memorial that was later erected to honour the ship's band in Southampton. The myth of 'Nearer My God to Thee' is so confused that no one is even sure which melody to use when remembering the *Titanic's* dead. But it was established almost from Day 1. In 1912, a musical tribute called 'The Band Played Nearer My God to Thee as the Ship Went Down' had soon appeared.

A memorial concert at the Albert Hall on 24 May 1912 – 'Empire Day' in Great Britain – was held in honour of the lost musicians (at the time, those who were owed money for their uniforms were still pressuring the families of these heroes for payment with White Star seemingly uninterested in getting involved; there were some interesting double standards in play). Sir Henry Wood, founder of the famous 'Proms' had orchestrated an arrangement of 'Nearer My God to Thee' for the occasion. Here, an enormous orchestra, in fact an amalgamation of seven London orchestras that had been conducted on the night by such luminaries as Sir Edward Elgar and Sir Thomas Beecham, raised the roof with a capacity audience singing the hymn in remembrance of the lost.

In fact, it was not the first time that the hymn was connected to a disaster. In a much less remembered wreck, the steamship *Valencia* struck a reef near Vancouver on 22 January 1906. A small group of survivors managed to make it ashore. Here, they watched:

> the brave faces looking at them over the broken rail of a wreck and of the echo of that great hymn sung by the women who, looking death smilingly in the face, were able in the fog and mist and flying spray to remember: Nearer, My God, to thee.

Only 37 survived out of 173 souls aboard. Every single woman and child was lost.

Therefore, perhaps the mythology of the *Titanic* was inspired by this tale. Mythology seeks to make sense of senseless loss by draping it in trappings of heroism and, in the context of the early twentieth century, religious sensibility and acceptance of fate. It is all part of the pathos of the tragedy. And yet that is perhaps too cynical. A number of survivors said they heard the hymn. The band would certainly have known at least one version of it, and there are some musical similarities between all three versions of the hymn so it would be easy to confuse one with another.

Like many things concerning the *Titanic*, there is evidence that the hymn was played and evidence that it was not. It is more a matter of faith than one of history. Even at the time, Logan Marshall's book opined that the last tune played was an Episcopal hymn, 'Autumn', although 'Nearer My God to Thee' had been played shortly before. And yet myth becomes history, both distorting it but making it live on, and the story of the disaster would not be complete without the strains of one version of the hymn carried by the gentlest of sea breezes across an ice-adorned ocean. Charlotte Collyer said she heard it, Mrs Vera Dick, a first-class passenger, was equally certain she did but Colonel Gracie was sure he didn't. Violet Jessop heard it played but thought it was long before the ship went down as she was waiting to get into a boat. It is hard to be sure who was right and who was not.

The parts played by some of the key players in the disaster created some difficulties as far as remembrance was concerned. First Officer Murdoch was honoured with a small plaque in his home town of Dalbeattie, close to the Scottish borders. He was a much respected man locally, so much so that when the Hollywood epic *Titanic* appeared and suggested that he committed suicide – something which there was very little evidence to support – there was an absolute furore about it. The moviemakers made a charitable donation and tried to defuse the debate, but the controversial scene stayed in. If nothing else, it was an interesting insight as to how the disaster still touched a nerve eighty-five years after it happened.

Captain Smith's position was even more invidious as far back as 1912. The stories that went about that he had died a hero, inspiring his passengers and crew to 'Be British' in the face of imminent death touched something deep in the national psyche of his home country. A statue was planned to commemorate him. Yet his home town in Hanley, Stoke-on-Trent, felt uncomfortable about this. After all, ultimate responsibility for the disaster rested with him. He it was that had led his ship into a known ice-field at something not far off her top speed and then had been ultimately responsible for the disastrous loading of the boats.

Accordingly, the burghers of the town decided that they did not really want the statue on their patch though they did put up a plaque in the town hall. Lichfield, some miles away, picked up the baton and the statue was placed there. It was a fine work, showing an imperious and confident Captain Smith, peering out, not over the ice-fields and stormy seas of the North Atlantic but across the rather less dangerous expanses of the municipal gardens and their cultured flowerbeds in the heart of a small town in Middle England.

There was some poignancy about the identity of the sculptor. The commission was executed by Kathleen Scott, widow of the famous but tragic British Antarctic explorer, Captain Robert Falcon Scott, whose icy sepulchre had been found in 1912. In fact, although the exact date of Scott's death is unknown, from his diary it appears to have been around 30 March of that year, just a fortnight before Captain Smith himself met his end. Some of the last words in Scott's diary surely echo the *Titanic* Captain's sentiments as he surveyed the North Atlantic from his doomed leviathan: 'Great God, this is an awful place!'

Scott's end was heroic and tragic, as Captain Smith's had to be. The inscription beneath Captain Smith's statue reads:

Born January 27 1850, Died 15 April 1912. Bequeathing to his countrymen the memory and example of a great heart, a brave life and a heroic death. Be British.

Finding glory in heroic failure from time to time appears to be a particular feature of the British psyche, a trait evidenced by such spectacular examples as the Charge of the Light Brigade, the death of Captain Scott and, indeed, the loss of the *Titanic*.

Captain Smith's beloved daughter Helen unveiled the bronze-cast statue in 1914 and Lichfield jealously protected its adopted son. However, in more recent times the *Titanic* has become a strong commercial draw and Hanley decided that it wanted the statue they had previously rejected back. But they were unsuccessful in the attempt though the battle still goes on. Captain Smith even made the famous Madame Tussaud's wax museum but unfortunately his effigy did not survive a fire in the 1920s.

Premonitions and presentiments of doom became part of the mythology too. One of Bruce Ismay's grandchildren later told the story of how Bruce's brother had been ill and in a coma at the time of the tragedy. On the night of the disaster, he had suddenly come out of it and said: 'Bruce is in trouble. Bruce is in trouble.' The *Daily Mirror* of 19 April 1912 quoted the tale of Mrs Gatti, wife of the Restaurant Manager on the *Titanic*. The night she went down she had 'a strange presentiment of danger and throughout the night she was unable to sleep'.

Then there was Joseph Scarrott's feeling that something was very wrong with the feel of the ship or Chief Officer Wilde's discomfort with the ship, with his 'queer feeling' about her. There was also the woman on the dockside at Southampton who, to the contempt of her neighbours, had said: 'That ship will not reach New York.' Another account describes how Jack Marshall and his family were watching the *Titanic* as she sailed past the Isle of Wight. Suddenly, Mrs Marshall grabbed her husband's arm and screamed: 'It's going to sink! That ship is going to sink before she reaches America!'

Some such stories are clearly untrue. The *Guardian* on 6 January 1966 told of an auctioneer in Poole, England who tried to sell a violin in an auction. It was known as the 'Phantom Violin' because a former owner of the instrument kept returning to play it after death. The auctioneer, also the owner of the instrument, said that his wife could not live in the same house as the violin, which had survived the sinking of the *Titanic*. It was allegedly played by one of the band. However, and this is where fiction definitely moves away from fact even if the rest was true, the violinist had survived but was a broken man and could not play the instrument again so he sold it for £20. It is a good yarn but one that sadly cannot be true as none of the ship's band made it to safety.

These stories are not offered up as points of historical fact. They mirror accounts that often appear at the time of a great disaster and many of them are after the event in nature. Nevertheless, stories such as those of the *Titanic* live on through their mythology as much as, if not more than, the truth. They too have their place in sustaining the legend and fostering a continuing interest in the truth. Not for the first or the last time in the annals of history, the story of the *Titanic* is one where perception and reality merge, with perplexing results, into one homogeneous whole.

19

Searching for the Truth:
April – May 1912, New York &
Washington

At the time that it happened, the *Titanic* disaster was the greatest maritime disaster ever known. It was not just the number of lives lost, huge though that figure was. It was also the fact that the ship was considered to be a technological marvel and, if not exactly unsinkable, as near to it as it was possible to make her. It was a matter of moments before the soul-searching began as everyone tried to make sense of something that was to most people senseless.

Lawrence Beesley put pen to paper with a common sense that could not be bettered. He wrote:

> Two-thousand-odd passengers went aboard thinking that they were on an absolutely safe ship, and all the time there were many people – designers, builders, experts, government officials – who knew there were insufficient boats onboard, that the *Titanic* had no right to go fast in iceberg regions – who knew these things and took no steps and enacted no laws to prevent their happening.

The disaster, as Beesley observed, shook the world from its complacency. With ships getting larger and larger, everyone presumed that they were also getting safer and safer. This was a complete fallacy, as the world now knew only too well. Even the ship's builders knew that a disaster needed to be considered when they designed it with davits capable of launching sixty-four lifeboats. But they had reasoned that this was an unnecessary and superfluous waste of money – it was after all not required by law – so they sent it across the Atlantic with just sixteen lifeboats and four collapsibles. It was a mistake they never repeated again – in part because they would not be allowed to, either by law or by public opinion.

Lawrence Beesley came up with a number of practical suggestions to improve safety including the following:

– To allow the interception of racing vessels by international police vessels.

– To allow the same police vessels to report the location of ice or consider the use of cruising lightships to discover and report the location of ice.

– For governments to legislate to enforce lifeboats for all onboard ship. Beesley was particularly harsh on the American government who had laws more stringent than those of Britain but failed to apply them [his British nationality might have had something to do with this rather debatable conclusion].

– That each passenger should be allocated a numbered seat in a lifeboat on boarding.

– That boat drills should be held as soon as possible after leaving port.

– That a full-time boat-master should be appointed to be given responsibility for lifeboats onboard large ships.

– For some lifeboats to be fitted with engines. These boats could be used for towing others.

– For members of the crew to be properly trained in rowing.

– To consider the use of pontoons on ships which could float off if the ship sank.

– For searchlights to be fitted to all ships [Major Peuchen also thought this was a good idea but maritime experts were undecided as to the wisdom of this].

– For better bulkhead construction, both lateral and higher [similar in fact to the arrangements that the *Mauretania* and *Lusitania* already had].

– To provide 24-hour cover for the wireless.

– For submarine-bell communication allowing ships in distress to communicate their position to other ships [but the range was only 10–15 miles for a large ship and less for a small one]. These were already being used for lighthouses to communicate to ships offshore.

– To move shipping lanes south to reduce the likelihood of meeting icebergs [though this would make journeys longer and more expensive].

All this was well and good and indeed mostly very sensible. However, there was great momentum for more formal proceedings to be held to ensure that such changes took place. There was much criticism in Britain of outdated Board of Trade regulations. T. Moore, Secretary of the Merchant Service Guild, said: 'The Titanic disaster is an example, on a colossal scale, of the pernicious and supine system of officials, as represented by the Board of Trade.' It was well known that there were not enough boats aboard modern ships, largely he suspected for economic reasons on the part of the ship operators. He noted that the Guild had been pressing for twenty years for seamen to be consulted on the numbers of boats required onboard ships.

President Sidney Buxton of the Board of Trade promised a full Inquiry in Britain on 18 April in the House of Commons. He noted that a committee had recently recommended substantial changes to the regulations but that some concerns about the recommendations had led to them not being adopted. Now, with tragic hindsight to call upon as a guide, he admitted that there could be no delay in implementing revised provisions. He however pointed out that the Board could not force ships to slow down in any circumstances, nor could they force ships to adopt a more southerly route in winter. This was somewhat limp, as if a ship wished to sail under a British flag then her owners would have to accept the conditions imposed when they chose to do so.

There was also much pressure to hold an Inquiry in the United States given the large number of American lives lost. It was to be held under the auspices of Senator William Alden Smith in the Chair. It began on 19 April and would go on until 25 May. Some crew members were subpoenaed to appear before it but the rest left on the *Lapland*. However, the enquiry wished to interview some of these too and a tug chased after the ship to return with five of them.

Smith was a Senator from Michigan, a state which was a long way from the sea though as supporters of his would fairly point out the Great Lakes are fairly large stretches of water (as their name suggests) and matters nautical were certainly locally relevant. However, his knowledge of maritime affairs was, based on some of his questions at the Inquiry he was about to chair, pretty limited.

But perhaps that is not what he was chosen for. Flamboyant and talkative he certainly was (verbose might be a more appropriate adjective) and he loved the sound of his own voice. But he was as tenacious as a dog with a bone when he picked up a scent of something contradictory, which in itself is not a bad qualification for heading up an Inquiry.

Whatever his qualifications, however, he became the butt of some cruel barbs from a hostile British press and the British crew he interviewed seemed no better disposed towards him either. Lightoller for one found the proceedings in Washington a farce. The crew were housed in what he called a second-rate boarding house. Eventually, they were so incensed at the nature of proceedings that they decided to stop cooperating with the authorities, an attitude that came across forcefully in some of the discussions held with the Senatorial Committee. The British Ambassador, Lord Percy, had to work overtime with all his diplomatic skills to calm choppy waters down.

That there were pressures being exerted on the Inquiry from somewhere was apparent. On the fifth day, Senator Smith suddenly made an announcement. He complimented those called as witnesses for their cooperation but then said:

> From the beginning until now there has been a voluntary, gratuitous, meddlesome attempt upon the part of certain persons to influence the course of the committee and to shape its procedure.

Smith went on to make it crystal clear that this person or persons unknown would not succeed in any such attempt. It is just a pity that it was never established who these persons were, as there was clearly a hidden sub-plot being played out in the shadows as far as Smith was concerned.

The American Inquiry was a sub-committee appointed by the US Senate to investigate the disaster. It would interview eighty-two witnesses, fifty-three of them British (mainly crew). It opened on 19 April in the Waldorf Astoria Hotel in New York, built under the auspices of the late J.J. Astor, with the first witness being Bruce Ismay. Smith was in the Chair assisted by Senator Francis Newlands. Their terms of reference required them, *inter alia*, to examine the number of lifeboats aboard, whether adequate inspections were made concerning the ship and also to look at the possibility of international regulation to examine such matters as the size of ships and the routes that such ships sailed on.

The crew on the whole appear to have been reasonably looked after while in America with expenses provided and sight-seeing laid on, though Lightoller's reservations already mentioned suggest that some were not impressed with them. Some of the crew even appeared in performances at the Imperial Theatre where they recounted their experiences, in return for which they received a share of the proceeds.

They found various ways of making a small amount of money from their involvement in the catastrophe. Souvenir hunters were prepared to pay for their kit; Jack Podesta sold his belt for a dollar. Others were invited to attend a new Woolworths that had just opened in New York. They were told to serve behind the counter and pocket all the money that they took. Frederick Fleet, who was required to attend the Inquiry for eight days, complained that he missed out on his share of the proceeds.

Bruce Ismay was first to take the stand when the Inquiry began in New York (on the third day it moved to Washington DC). Within the first few questions Senator Smith set the scene for what was to come. After asking Ismay where he boarded the ship (answer: Southampton) he then enjoined him four questions later to tell him the circumstances of the voyage 'beginning with your going aboard the vessel at Liverpool'. Smith's questioning was often repetitious and he seemed to struggle to grasp some very basic concepts. Sometimes the questions were so obvious that it is tempting to think there must have been some ulterior motive behind them (a classic example being when he asked if it would be more difficult to spot icebergs if it was foggy).

Bruce Ismay came under very close scrutiny during both inquiries. He was the senior official aboard the *Titanic* and also he had had the bad taste to survive, not at all what was required of him. He was asked questions such as how many times he had dined with Captain Smith on the voyage (answer, once), clearly as a way of probing how cosy relationships were between the two and how likely the captain would be to be influenced by any attempts by Ismay to keep a good speed up. Ismay was quick to admit that he was well aware of what speed the *Titanic* was going, as he offered the information that Captain Smith planned to drive the ship for the first time at full speed on Monday and Tuesday (by which time she was, of course, entombed beneath 12,000 feet of water).

Ismay appeared uncomfortable when asked about the lifeboats. He did not directly indicate whether there were enough aboard or not, but merely that they complied with current regulations – in fact, 'she may have exceeded the Board of Trade regulations for all I know'. She did, which suggests that he knew full well that this was the case. He was also quick to point out that the British Board of Trade regulations were accepted unequivocally by the American authorities. It could not disguise the fact that the regulations were patently inadequate.

The question of the contracts the Post Office had with White Star came up too, again as a way of seeing if there were any commercial reasons why a ship would not want to slow down even if it were approaching a danger area. Ismay told the American Inquiry that the UK contract was worth £70,000 (about US $350,000 then) a year for all White Star ships. There was no mention in the contract of deadlines, though White Star was required to provide ships that could travel at least 16 knots. The American contract for the mail was structured very differently, with the company paid $4 for every mile travelled.

The thoughts of Bruce Ismay as regards possible lessons to be learned were important for pragmatic reasons; as a senior official of IMM he was in the perfect position to implement them. When asked for his views at the US Inquiry, he said that he thought the bulkheads built into ships should be extended (in future White Star ships they were). He also came up with the rather obvious statement that it would be 'very desirable to increase the boatage capacity', though rather than having more boats he felt having rafts that would float off the deck if a ship sank would help. Suffice to say, ships like the *Olympic* would be provided with boats for all at once, before any change to the law might be made. Disasters at sea were not good for business.

Second Officer Lightoller, when quizzed on the subject of emergency equipment said that there was sufficient life-saving apparatus for everyone onboard. To be generous, that is being economical with the truth. There were enough lifebelts to go around for sure but it was obvious to everyone that there was insufficient boat space. A lifebelt was not much good at saving lives when water temperatures had dropped below freezing, as this catastrophe tragically demonstrated.

When the subject turned to access to the boats, Lightoller nearly put his foot in it. The question was asked about allowing steerage passengers' access to the Boat Deck. The Second Officer testily replied that they had no right to be there, before realizing that this might not be the most suitable answer given the circumstances. He qualified the statement by saying that there was of course no restraint on this occasion. However, his first reaction gave a clue as to the attitudes widely held onboard that night. Discrimination might have been unconscious and unsystematic but it was there nonetheless.

Lightoller, despite his heroic image – and indeed heroic actions – does not come across as a particularly convincing witness at either Inquiry. He does not even appear to understand why anybody would wish to question a seaman about the loss of a ship, as if it were an accident of nature so freakish that it could not have been avoided and that no 'landsman' could possibly understand all the factors involved. Many of his answers were evasive; some were untrue. When asked for example how many people a collapsible boat would carry, he reckoned about twenty. In fairness, it was a slightly moot point as no one genuinely seemed to know. Yet Collapsible C had nearly forty people in it and the official capacity it turned out was forty-seven.

Lightoller was also irritated by Smith's lack of seafaring knowledge in particular. It is true that the Senator pulled out all the stops to get at the truth, a laudable and indeed vital attribute. However, his questioning was often repetitive and he had, to judge from the Inquiry transcripts, a truly infuriating ability to jump around from one line of questioning to another without any obvious mental connection between the elements. Some of his questions were downright nonsensical. His most famous supposed gaff was when he asked Fifth Officer Lowe what an iceberg was made of; 'ice, I suppose, sir' came the withering reply.

It was not quite as silly a question as it sounds as icebergs do indeed carry around large lumps of rock. Far more ridiculous was Smith's question about whether or not any of the passengers had tried to survive by hiding themselves away in the watertight compartments. The Senator subsequently explained that he deliberately asked this seemingly obtuse question to quash a rumour he had heard yet his attempts to defuse the situation bear all the hallmarks of a man who has asked a plainly silly question and wishes to absolve himself of any subsequent embarrassment. Within hours, the Senator had earned the ironic sobriquet of 'Watertight Smith'.

The session between Smith and Lowe was one of extreme verbal jousting. At one stage the Senator said to the Fifth Officer: 'I am not having a very easy time with you, because you do not seem to be willing to answer my questions.' It seemed as if there was an unofficial policy of revealing as little as possible to the American Inquiry in place. There was a moment of light relief though when Smith quizzed Lowe about suggestions from a passenger that he had been drinking the night the ship went down. Lowe picked up a glass of water and told the Senator that that was the strongest drink he ever touched.

There was a lengthy exchange between Smith and Lowe on the subject of the lowering and manning of the boats where the Senator, rightly, was like a bloodhound picking up the scent of prey. Lowe may have been naturally verbose but his answers also smacked of using diversionary tactics. Smith wondered why Lowe thought it safe to lower a boat with fifty people in it when Lightoller was doing it with only twenty-five; it was a matter of a man's approach to risk explained the officer.

Why, Smith wondered, did men not know their boat stations when they had been drilled at Southampton; a good point but one that Lowe could not answer because the tests were flawed; only sixteen men had rowed the boats at Southampton, less than one per boat and totally inadequate – Lowe himself acknowledged as much. The matter was even worse when it was recognized by Lowe that eight to ten men were needed to fill and lower each boat suggesting that a minimum 160 crewmen were needed to man all the boats. Smith could not see the point of having state of the art lifeboats when there were insufficient men to use them properly – and it is not difficult to see why he didn't think this was a very sensible policy. It highlighted the appalling slackness in the matter of boat drill.

With other *Titanic* witnesses, it is difficult to tell from a dry transcript whether they were being uncooperative or were just overwhelmed by events. Frederick Fleet professed himself to be an appalling judge of times and distances and provided plenty of evidence to back his view up. He had no idea how high up the crow's nest was; he had no idea of how long it was between spotting the iceberg and hitting it; he had no idea how far away it was when he spotted it; he had no idea how big it was. Frederick Fleet does not, reading the transcripts, come across as a confidence-inspiring lookout unless one is content to accept that he does not need any feel for the detail of what he is looking at. Unless, of course, he too thought that the Inquiry was in itself something of a liberty.

The main news story was of course the loss of the *Titanic* itself but another sub-plot was about to emerge, that of the *Californian*. When Captain Lord's ship steamed away from the wreck-site on 15 April, it appeared destined to be just a minor detail, a bit-part player, in the drama. The main source of notoriety on the day of the disaster, 15 April, was wireless operator Cyril Evans. Ironically for a man who had nothing to say during the night, it was now almost impossible to keep him quiet. Inspector Balfour in the *Baltic* on his way to the wreck-site eventually admonished him for his incessant chitchat, telling him in a very formal way to keep quiet and stop jamming the airwaves.

The *Californian* then resumed its journey to Boston. What happened over the course of those next few days had something of the appearance of an automobile accident happening in slow motion. Whatever Captain Lord did, the crash he was about to be involved in appeared with hindsight to be totally unavoidable. The rest of the journey to Boston would mostly be completed in fog; it was an appropriate analogy for the story that was about to overwhelm the *Californian.*

As the *Californian* steamed onwards to Boston, stories were starting to travel across the airwaves. Ironically, they were inaccurate at first and the initial storyline led to a dead-end. Onboard the *Olympic* was a man named Roy Howard, a news manager with the United Press. Taking advantage of the *Olympic's* powerful apparatus, he sent a message to the USA suggesting that the *Californian* might have picked up some bodies. It was not true but it got the attention of the press.

There was then something of a snowball effect. Despite the fact that the ship had no bodies aboard, it was not long before other enterprising reporters started to work out that the *Californian* was not far off the *Titanic* when she sank. By 18 April, the Leyland Line was messaging to Lord, asking for his report. The captain began to scent trouble ahead.

That day he spoke privately with Stone and Gibson about their surreal few hours on the bridge the night that the *Titanic* sank. Then he asked them to commit their thoughts to written statements. What he read cannot have made him altogether happy, for they did not see the light of day for fifty years. Combined they told a story that might be quite hard to explain away; of rockets being seen, possibly from the ship they had been watching, and of that same ship disappearing at about the same time that the *Titanic* went down.

By 19 April, the *Californian* was waiting outside of Boston Harbour. Lord sent ahead news that he did not have any bodies onboard but he was happy to speak to the press and tell them what little he knew. And so he did. Onboard his ship he held a press conference when he at last tied up at the dockside. He appeared confident in his answers to the pressmen. He told them how his ship had arrived too late to be of any assistance and had found only wreckage. He said that he had never seen so much ice (which must have been true because he had never been in any before) and that he had only been able to help by cruising around the wreck-site in a vain search for bodies or survivors.

Generally he made a good impression. The only piece of his conference that jarred was his refusal to divulge his position which he said was regarded as a 'state secret'. Then, however, ship's Carpenter McGregor decided to write a letter back to England expressing his dissatisfaction with the conduct of the *Californian* on 14/15 April. He also discussed the same topic with his relatives in Clinton and that is how the *Clinton Daily Item* got to break the story. It was only a small local paper but it was the start of a quite massive story.

The news item told how the *Californian* had been within 10 miles of the *Titanic* when the berg was struck, of how her lights could be seen plainly and of how a number of rockets had been sighted. However, nothing had been done in response. By the time that the *Californian* did move, it was far too late to make a difference. Other papers picked up the story and Captain Lord began to accelerate out of control towards the accident that was waiting for him.

Ernest Gill then picked up the scent of money and told his rather confused story involving ships that moved at a rate of knots twenty minutes after the *Titanic* had been involved in a rather serious collision with an iceberg, and of rockets that were seen even when ships were no longer in view contrary to what the *Californian's* officers of the watch were looking at. She was to him clearly a 'vessel in distress' but he did not think it was his job to report it to anyone else.

The deficiencies of his tale notwithstanding, it was a story that the press greedily ran with. Lord found himself on the defensive and started to dig himself some rather big holes. He went to the press with his own version of events. Unfortunately, this had some oversized distortions of the truth in it. For example, he used Chief Officer Stewart to hide behind, saying that Stewart had been on watch when the rockets were allegedly seen but had not spied anything. This was hardly surprising as he was fast asleep at the time.

No one had seen any rockets, he said, a falsehood of titanic proportions. Then he had woken up the wireless operator to find out anything about the extent of the ice field they were in. Evans distinctly remembered a mention of rockets in his evidence which now seems to have slipped Lord's memory. Lord himself said that he knew that once Gill went to the press with his report then further investigations were inevitable. Unfortunately, he did not make it any easier for himself by the blatantly incorrect statements he made to the press. At any event, his appearance before Senator Smith was now certain.

It was on the eighth day, Friday 29 April, that this new storyline began to unfold in the Inquiry. This was the day that 'donkey-man' Ernest Gill took the stand. It began with Gill's affidavit being read out; of how it had been just about midnight when he had stepped out on deck and seen what looked like 'a big German' steaming past, of how half an hour later he had gone out again and seen two rockets, of how she must be a vessel in distress and of how he chose to do nothing about it.

The story was full of holes; no one else had mentioned seeing 'a big German', he saw her sailing quickly along when everyone else had been watching a stationary ship and to cap it all he had seen rockets but no ship while those on the bridge had quite clearly seen both. Over time, Gill's position would become even more confusing, as by the time he reached

London several key details would change. He was not, in short, the most convincing of witnesses.

There was also a distinct impression that he was making things up as he went along and could change his mind mid-question. Senator Fletcher asked him what colour the rockets he saw were. Gill replied: 'It would be apt to be a very clear blue; I would catch it when it was dying. I did not catch the exact tint, but I reckon it was white.' An answer that was as clear as the murkiest mud (though interestingly Quartermaster Hichens in his London evidence noted that the rockets he saw from the lifeboats were of different colours, including white, but also some were blue).

Then Gill was asked if he saw any stars in the rockets (the present author is no legal expert but believes this is known in legal circles as 'leading the witness'). He replied: 'Yes sir, the stars spangled out. I could not say about the stars. I say, I caught the tail end of the rocket.' Which begs the question did he see any stars or didn't he, for if he did not then he could not have seen them spangle.

He reckoned he saw two rows of lights (this on a ship, if it was the *Titanic* he was looking at, with six decks with accommodation, all lit up). An examination of the transcript suggests that the Inquiry's questioning of Gill was cursory in the extreme; either the evidence he had presented was felt to be conclusive or he was not regarded as a credible witness; to be frank, either interpretation is possible. But he had just set the scene for the main attraction of the day; Captain Stanley Lord of the *Californian*.

The questioning started gently with Lord talking the Committee through the entries concerning ice in the ship's log. He told how he had tried to pass an ice warning on to the *Titanic* but how his operator in return had been told to 'shut up'. Then he was asked the key question; how far away was the *Californian* from the *Titanic*. In reply, Lord said that his calculations suggested a gap of just under 20 miles. There was some gentle probing around this but no serious attempt to see how reliable a calculation it was.

Understandably there was much discussion about the wireless operator and the fact that his apparatus was turned off overnight. Further questions were asked about the use of binoculars by the lookouts and the need to post extra lookouts when in bad weather conditions. Then, to the heart of the matter – those rockets.

It was Senator Smith who asked whether or not Lord had seen any distress signals, either rockets or flashes from a Morse lamp. Lord attempted to swat the question away as if it were a troublesome fly; he said: 'The officer on watch saw some signals but he said they were not distress signals.' Smith asked Lord to expand. Lord took a deep breath and launched himself into his explanation.

He told how he had first seen a light at about 10.30 p.m. Thinking it was a ship (though Third Officer Groves who was on watch thought it was a star) he went to check with Evans, the wireless operator, to see if he had been in communication with any other vessels. Only the *Titanic*, Evans replied. The ship he could see, Lord asserted, was definitely not her.

Then came the story of the failed attempts to Morse the nearby stationary ship, the report of a 'rocket' (singular) and Lord then dropping off to sleep. When questioned more on whether or not the rocket was of the distress variety, Lord confidently replied: 'You never mistake a distress rocket.' However, he thought that given the distance between the two ships it was unlikely that they would be able to see any such signals from the *Titanic* (he would suggest differently in London). And that was pretty much it, as far as the rockets at least were concerned.

The only other witness called from the *Californian* was wireless operator Cyril Evans. This was a bit strange; there would be no interrogation of Second Officer Stone who had reported that these rockets were not distress signals, none of Apprentice Gibson who was by his side while many of the extraordinary events of that night were unfolding nor of Third Officer Groves who was sure that he had been able to see a passenger steamer nearby.

However, Evans still had a story to tell. He was first of all quizzed about his brush-off by Jack Phillips of the *Titanic*, something he made light of as being part of the job. It was the story of his awakening in the morning though that started to unravel Lord's storyline. He told how Chief Officer Stewart had come into his room between 3.00 a.m. and 4.00 a.m. (this is New York time, about two hours behind ship's time) and how he told him that 'there is a ship that has been firing rockets in the night' and could he see what if anything was the matter with her. Within five minutes the terrible news about the *Titanic* had been received.

It was like gunpowder being lit with a slow-burning fuse. No one on the Committee seemed to realize the significance of this at first, for it intimated that there were people in high places aboard the ship who were not convinced that what had been seen were not distress signals. The fuse though was burning more brightly by the time Evans was asked what he thought of Gill's story.

It then emerged that practically the whole ship had been talking about the rockets. Again, the point was not followed up at once. In best rambling Inquiry tradition, the Committee then asked questions about the strength of the ship's wireless apparatus, completely unconnected to the previous conversation (something of a trait) before walking all the way around the mulberry bush and ending up back at the rockets again.

Evans was coaxed to tell what he knew but when he was about to start he was told not to spread idle gossip. However, he had had a conversation with Apprentice Gibson, who told him that Captain Lord had been called three times in the night but had shown little, or effectively no, response. The cat was now starting to poke its whiskers out of the bag.

Evans said he had no further specifics to offer but that the rockets were the talk of the ship. Smith then asked whether Gibson had had any joy in his attempts to Morse the *Titanic*. Evans was awake to this and said that the ship they had Morsed did not reply but of course they were not sure this was the *Titanic*. However, it was a tell-tale sign of the way that the Senator's mind was working.

Evans seems to have detected what was happening. He threw in a story (true, as it happened) that there was an oil tanker that had run out of fuel and was being towed; he believed that the Chief Officer thought it might have been her (probably less likely to be true). Then, a few more questions, in particular did Evans know if Gill was being paid for his story (the answer was yes, $500). And that was that.

It was Evans, a man who did not claim to have seen any rockets, who unwittingly started to tighten a noose around Lord's neck. It was he who told of a captain called three times who did not respond (though if the Senators had probed more they would have found out that the last two occasions were far too late to make a difference). It was he who said that the rockets were the talk of the ship and that even officers thought they might have been distress rockets. Lord had left the court earlier thinking that that perhaps was the end of it all, which might have been a tactical error on his part. Evans made sure that his story began to look suspect but in the light of what he had said the decision not to call Gibson or Stone to the witness stand was incredible.

Captain Moore of the *Mount Temple* was also interviewed by the Committee. He told them about the schooner he had seen coming from the direction of the *Titanic* wreck-site.

He also gave some interesting information on the *Californian*. He saw her headed west through the ice-field presumably headed for the *Titanic's* last (erroneously reported) position. On Captain Lord's evidence this was between 6.00 a.m. and 6.30 a.m. Moore estimated that he was about 6 miles away from the *Carpathia* but he could see both her and the *Californian* from the bridge of his own vessel. In his view the *Californian* was about the same distance to the north of the *Carpathia* as his *Mount Temple* was to the west of the latter ship.

This puts the *Californian* only 6 miles away from the *Carpathia* who was presumably not far off the spot that the *Titanic* went down. Given the fact that in passing from east to west Lord had been travelling cautiously, this makes it highly unlikely that his ship was as much as 20 miles away from the *Titanic* when she sank. Senator Smith certainly thought not. He interviewed the famous wireless operator Jack Binns, hero of the *Republic* sinking, on 8 May and during this session he let slip his belief that the *Californian* was only 14 miles distant. He confirmed this soon after when questioning wireless inspector Gilbert Balfour, telling him that the *Californian* was 'within 15 miles'.

Captain Knapp of the US Hydrographic Office was also called as a witness. He testified that this had been a bad winter, with his office 'constantly receiving reports of ice in the North Atlantic'. Interestingly, daily reports in April 1912 showed a steady movement south but no one seemed to have joined up the dots and concluded that this was part of an ongoing process, otherwise the shipping lanes could have been moved further south. On 15 April, later on the very day of the disaster, ice had been reported 19 miles to the south of where the *Titanic* had been reported sunk. By May it was at the 39th degree of latitude and even below that, more than 2 degrees south of where the disaster occurred.

Knapp introduced some physics into the proceedings, calculating that the force with which the doomed ship had struck the ice was equivalent to 1,173,200 tons or enough to lift fourteen structures the size of the Washington Monument. He also introduced an element of controversy into them. He produced an ice chart on which the known position of ships in the area that night was marked. He put on a mark which showed the 'hypothetical' position of the *Californian*; that is where she must have been if she was indeed the 'mystery ship'. He relied in particular on the rather dubious evidence of Ernest Gill. By so doing of course he gave his estimate of the *Californian's* hypothetical position an authenticity that supporters of Captain Lord's cause understandably criticised. Certainly, it assumed the appearance of something of an established fact.

The use of wireless was another key line of enquiry for Smith's investigation. The Senator asked Philip Franklin if there had been any attempt by IMM to contact Captain Smith while he was at sea; the reason for this line of questioning being to establish whether or not there had been any pressure on the *Titanic's* captain to keep up a high speed and arrive in New York on time. Franklin assured him that there had been none and that the captain was the sole decision-maker on such matters when he was at sea.

To support his case, he quoted White Star regulation 101, which stated: 'No supposed gaining of expedition or saving of time on the voyage is to be purchased at the risk of accidents.' Such were after all bad publicity and not good for future business. Anyway, said Franklin, there was never any attempt on a record. As he said, *Titanic* ran 3–4 knots slower that her Cunard rivals, the *Mauretania* and *Lusitania*. He went on to state: 'It was never thought by anybody that the *Titanic* would anything like equal the speed of the *Mauretania* and *Lusitania*.' That is a statement of fact, though it has not stopped a number of myths developing that the *Titanic* was after a speed record which was, for her, an impossibility.

Marconi was one of the witnesses who appeared on several occasions. He thought that two wireless operators onboard each ship would be a good idea, though he tactfully but correctly pointed out that ship owners would baulk at the cost involved. Currently smaller ships either had one or none at all. However, Marconi insisted that the operators were under the command of the captain of the ship once they were onboard. He also stressed that the Berlin Convention, a recently agreed regulatory framework for international wireless communication, required that precedence should be given to distress signals over all other messages.

The *Titanic* disaster exposed a number of underlying problems with maritime regulation. Some of the issues revolved around the way seamen handled their ships but others made it clear that the still new wireless system needed a radical overhaul. One issue in particular emerged at the Inquiry that left a nasty taste in the mouth.

After the *Republic* incident a few years before, wireless operator Jack Binns who had successfully summoned help to the stricken ship became something of a national hero. However, he had also sold his story to the press, a precedent that it now transpired operators Cottam from the *Carpathia* and Harold Bride from the *Titanic* had sought to emulate.

What made this particularly problematic was the information, or lack of it, that had come out of the *Carpathia* when she was headed for New York. Coming on top of the initial messages that had appeared suggesting that the *Titanic* was safe and being towed back to Halifax, it created a suspicion that there had been a deliberate hushing-up of information so that the operators could sell their stories as an exclusive when they arrived back. Perhaps the greatest problem was that a message from President Taft, no less, had been ignored. In reality, the truth probably was that the wireless operators were just overwhelmed by the volume of traffic but there was a unpleasant whiff in the air and Senator Smith was determined to cleanse it.

Various representatives of the Marconi Company, including Guglielmo Marconi himself, were put through the mill on several occasions at the New York hearings. Senator Smith soon smelt a rat when a wire emerged saying that Cottam should 'keep his mouth shut' until he returned to New York and that arrangements had been made to sell his story for a 'four-figure sum'. Several messages were produced, including one from Frederick Sammis, a senior Marconi official, and another ostensibly from Marconi himself, though he denied any personal knowledge of it.

Even the wireless operators seemed unclear about how much they were paid for their information, with Bride at one stage in the American

Inquiry saying he had been paid $500 for it and at another time saying it was $1,000. Apart from anything else, what emerged in particular were the unsatisfactory employer-employee relationships around the wireless operators. They were all employed by the Marconi Company, and various overseas derivatives of it, but were answerable to the captain once they were onboard.

Shipping companies were at liberty to reject particular operators if they so wished but the reality was that, unless there was an emergency, captains rarely took a lot of interest in what their wireless operators were up to – Captain Rostron for example did not know the name of his wireless operator, Harold Cottam.

One of the major causes of the huge loss of life was the fact that just about 20 miles away (depending on whose version you believe) from the floundering *Titanic* operator, Cyril Evans was dozing off in bed. Operators tended to decide their own hours, which were regulated only by the volume of traffic (in the main private messages, which were the money-earners) that they needed to send. Of course, operators needed to sleep some time and on 'one-man ships' that would normally be at night when the volume of traffic was low. But of course the hours of darkness were also the time when the risk of accident was greatest. It was a dichotomy that needed to be addressed.

One of the witnesses interviewed at the American Inquiry who came out of it particularly badly was Frederick Sammis, Chief Engineer of the Marconi Company. Reading through the transcripts of the Inquiry, he comes across as arrogant and slippery, a man who seemed to feel that the Inquiry was lucky to have him there when he could be off making huge commercial deals back in the office instead.

Here was a man who, if not an out and out liar, was certainly economical with the truth. Senator Smith was particularly irked that messages from the President of the United States of America went unanswered and, given stories (true as it happened) of exclusive deals with the media, suspected some dodgy dealing. Sammis was understandably defensive about the deals made with the operators. He stated that he had nothing to do with them but he certainly acted as a conduit between the journalists and men who were, to all intents and purposes, his employees or something close to it.

A considerable amount of time at the Inquiry was taken up with Smith trying to chase down the true story behind the actions of the wireless operators and, in the event, he never really succeeded. Smith and Sammis spent some time sparring about whether or not the operators should be making money out of an international tragedy, with the Senator convinced in his own mind that they should not. Sammis on the other hand seemed to find little wrong with the idea of supplementing what he seemed to suggest were inadequate wages – this despite the fact he was a senior official of the company responsible for paying them.

Signor Marconi's reputation was on the line too. Sammis suggested that his boss was well aware of the deal and there were cables with his name on suggesting this was so. Marconi however denied all knowledge of them and, perhaps as a result of both his international reputation and Marconi's general amenability as a witness – he was not subpoenaed and appeared voluntarily on a number of occasions – Senator Smith did not push the point.

Sammis felt that too much was being made of the deal with the operators as he believed that this was the only occasion, apart from that of Jack Binns and the *Republic*, where such a transaction had taken place. When the Senator's questioning began to run on, Sammis asked if he could be excused; he had to go and sign a $100,000 contract. It was pretty obvious where his priorities lay.

Other suggestive snippets of information emerged at the Inquiry. First-class passenger Norman Chambers opined that some at least of the watertight doors that needed to be closed manually remained open. He recalled his steward telling him early on in the voyage that most of the stewards were new and no one would show them where anything was, an unfamiliarity that may have been a factor in any inefficiencies experienced in shutting the doors (which required the removal of a special cover plate before they could be closed).

Mrs Mahala Douglas told of friction between the crew and passengers onboard Boat 6 (this was hearsay, as she herself was on Boat 2). She said that her friends in that boat had told her that the crew had 'been picked up from the London unemployed'. They had allegedly remarked on the fact that because of the disaster they were enjoying a night off and would soon be returning to the ranks of the unemployed from which they had come. All the women, said Mrs Douglas, had remarked on the generally unsatisfactory nature of the crew and in particular their inability to row a boat. However, she wished it to be clear that this criticism did not apply to the officers and that Lightoller and Boxhall were in particular worthy of praise.

The American Inquiry concluded that no one could be blamed solely for the disaster. But, the Committee affirmed that the *Californian* and the *Titanic* had seen each other's lights while the catastrophe was unfolding. Captain Lord of the *Californian* was censured for his role in the events and the Inquiry suggested that ships could be equipped with searchlights in the future. Senator Smith, in his summing up, accused Captain Smith of being over-confident and careless and the *Titanic's* officers for leaving the sinking ship too early.

The American Inquiry interviewed all told eighty-two witnesses, fifty-three British and twenty-nine American (Signor Marconi counting as an honorary 'Brit' in this case). It delivered a series of findings and a list of recommendations. It began its findings by making an entirely merited commendation of Captain Rostron's actions, saying:

> The committee deems the course followed by Captain Rostron of the *Carpathia* as deserving of the highest praise and worthy of especial recognition.

They noted the lack of bodies found *in situ* by either the *Carpathia* or the *Californian*. They deduced that 'the supposedly watertight doors were NOT watertight' (which could presumably have been worked out without an Inquiry being needed). There was 'no general alarm sounded, no whistle blown and no systematic warning was given to the passengers'.

They also commented on the *Frankfurt*. Although the ship was actually 153 miles to the south-west when in communication with Phillips, the *Titanic's* wireless operator, could not have known this and his cavalier dismissal of her was foolish in the extreme. As the report politely put it (Phillips was after all not alive to defend himself and he was something of a hero, in many ways a justified accolade):

> In view of the fact that no position had been given by the *Frankfurt* and her exact distance from the *Titanic* was unknown at that time, the answer of the operator of the *Titanic* was scarcely such as prudence would have dictated.

Nevertheless, the report erred seriously in its interpretation of the *Californian* incident. It was not that the *Californian* was not on the surface a reasonable suspect as the source of those mysterious lights. There were indeed searching questions to be asked and answered. However, Senator Smith and the committee made a serious error in not considering the evidence much more carefully. They ignored well-attested information that showed, for example, that *Titanic* did not sink at the spot quoted in its SOS message or anywhere near it or that the ship that was seen from the *Titanic* appeared to some to be moving significantly whereas all the *Californian* witnesses confirmed they did not move, other than a slow drift, all night.

They also ignored the irrefutable evidence that there were other ships in the vicinity, admittedly often unidentified but confirmed by witnesses as definitively not the *Californian*. With no evidence to back it up, the report asserted that the position quoted by the *Californian* was wrong. There was only one ship categorically quoting their position incorrectly that night, the doomed *Titanic* which was much further away than she said she was.

Lord was, regardless of this, castigated for his actions (or perceived inactions might be more accurate), with a concluding statement that 'such conduct... is most reprehensible, and places upon the commander of the

Californian a grave responsibility'. Unfair? Certainly; Lord was not on trial so he could not defend himself and yet here he was guilty as (not) charged, without a chance of a cross-examination to destroy the deeply-suspect story of Ernest Gill, now $500 better off for his dedication to the truth.

It was also, on the basis of what had been heard, unjustified, as it was not supported by the evidence that the Committee had chosen to hear (though there was plenty they did not hear that would have filled in a number of the gaps). The problem lay not necessarily in the conclusion they had arrived at but in the path they had travelled down to get there. That said and done, Lord came off lightly compared to the vilification the British Inquiry would aim at him.

The Inquiry further noted: 'there was no system adopted for lowering the boats', there was no guidance as to where to load them from, there was no idea of how many crew were needed to man them or how many passengers to load. In other words, the loading of the boats was an utter, amateur shambles. Captain Smith, for all his popularity with his passengers, had let them down. Here at least the report got it right, though it stopped short of criticising *Titanic's* captain. It would not do to criticise a man who many thought had gone down with his ship.

The Inquiry also ignored the evidence it had heard when it came to the question of discrimination again third-class passengers. Both Abelseth and Buckley said it existed but it did not stop the Committee coming up with the conclusion that there was 'no discrimination against any class'. This is odd; there is no evidence of first-class passengers being forced to climb up cranes onto the Boat Deck so that they can avoid the gates that would otherwise keep them out, which is what some of the third-class passengers had been forced to do.

The report also noted that the ship 'sank intact' despite the fact that the large number of people who said that it didn't far outnumbered those who said it did. As most of those saying she was intact were officers, with perhaps an unmerited sense of pride in their ship uppermost in their minds, there seems to have been a strong bias towards them as being somehow more reliable than the rest of the hoi-polloi.

Senator Smith and his colleagues were also unimpressed at the organization and ethics of wireless operators and believed that more regulation was needed. The report noted:

> The Committee does not believe that the wireless operator [referring specifically to Cottam on the *Carpathia*] showed proper vigilance in handling the important work confided to his care after the accident.

The Marconi Company was also criticised specifically for allowing its operators to sell their stories to the press. This seems a trifle harsh on Cottam who may have sold his story but had also spent three days without sleep in an attempt to keep up with his messages.

Finally, there were a series of recommendations, which were prefaced with a comment that perhaps nearly everybody could agree with that 'this accident clearly indicates the necessity of additional legislation to secure safety of life at sea'. Most of the recommendations were non-contentious too, briefly summarized they were:

– Terminate reciprocal inspection arrangements with other countries. Up until now, the arrangement had been that British ships sailing to the USA could rely on inspections held in Britain without having to go through the same process on the western side of the Atlantic and vice-versa. No longer would the American authorities accept this arrangement, an unmistakable sign that they considered British regulation as being too lax.

– Make sure there were sufficient lifeboats for everyone, passengers and crew, onboard.

– Ensure that there were at least four crew members, skilled in handling boats, assigned to each lifeboat. These should be drilled at least twice a month.

– Ensure the assignment of passengers and crew to lifeboats before sailing.

– Provide ships having more than 100 passengers with two searchlights. The Committee felt that if these had been provided on the *Titanic* then the iceberg may have been spotted earlier. Nautical opinion was divided on this; many seafarers felt that the bright lights could dazzle other ships if not used properly and as a result cause more accidents rather than help prevent them.

– Introduce tighter regulation of radiotelegraphy, with an operator to be on duty at all times.

– Not fire rockets except as a signal of distress, thereby eliminating the possibility of a Second Officer Stone mistaking them for company signals in the future.

– Extend the watertight skin inside ships higher up the inside of the outer plating.

– Extend watertight bulkheads higher up the ship; clearly a good idea but no such thing as an unsinkable ship could be built. (The *Lusitania* had more extensive bulkheads than *Titanic* but sank in less than twenty minutes when hit by a German torpedo in 1915.)

Yet there were things not mentioned that contributed importantly to the loss of life on the *Titanic*. There were no recommendations about captains slowing down their ships in areas where ice was known to be, a dangerous practice which was widespread among all mariners. The evacuation procedures, heavily criticised in the report, did not get a mention in the recommendations other than in a roundabout way with the reference to the need for more drills. Nothing was said either about the use of lookouts, despite the fact that a number of captains had put extra lookout on the bows of the ship to spot ice earlier, a practice not adopted by Captain Smith on his 900-foot long leviathan.

The Inquiry had not been very well organized and some of the questions revealed the limitations of those sitting on the Committee. British sensibilities were irritated by the temerity of a foreign nation subpoenaing British citizens for events that had taken place in international waters and resentment positively jumped out of the headlines of some leading newspapers in the country.

Despite all this however the broad spectrum of conclusions was not far wide of the mark. Some were obvious, such as the need to have boat space for every single person onboard. Few were innovative or eye catching. But they did not need to be; ship owners had been ignoring the blindingly obvious for far too long. A wide range of people had been interviewed, giving among other things an invaluable library of information to future generations of historians. As noted though the limited range of witnesses called concerning the *Californian* was a real opportunity missed to get at the truth; even though the final conclusion might have been the same it was a shame that more care was not taken in arriving at it.

The findings concerning the lack of discrimination against third-class passengers were also suspect and did not accord with all the evidence. Still, to balance any sense of innate superiority that supporters of the British Inquiry might possess, at least the American Senators took the trouble to speak to some third-class passengers which was not the case in London.

And so the focus moved east across the waters to the Old Country to a very different Inquiry, where most of the investigating committee were nautical men and all the witnesses bar a handful in a very special category were either crewmen or those involved in some way in the shipping industry. London prepared itself for the British Inquiry, with a proud maritime nation jealously protective of its reputation eager to find the truth. It would in many ways be quite a different kettle of fish from the American Inquiry as Captain Stanley Lord of the *Californian* was about to find out to his own great personal discomfiture. But at the end of it all, its conclusions would not be very different from those of 'landlubber' William Alden Smith.

20

The British Perspective:
May – June 1912, London

The British Inquiry began on Tuesday 2 May 1912 in the Scottish Drill Hall, Buckingham Gate. The silent star of the show was a 20-foot model of the *Titanic*, a presence that cast a giant shadow over the proceedings. In one photograph, Bruce Ismay appears in front of it, as if she were a towering phantom creeping up behind him. The Inquiry would conclude its proceedings on 21 June. Before they began, there were several disagreements about whose interests should be represented there, as several unions wanted to take part in the proceedings. Lord Mersey, chairman of the Inquiry, initially refused to remit this but eventually relented and allowed some of them at least to take part.

On 6 May, Lord Mersey and his fellow assessors took a day away from London and visited the *Olympic* in Southampton. Harold Sanderson, Managing Director of the White Star Line, met the delegation at Southampton West station and took them down to the White Star dock. Onboard the ship, they saw the watertight doors being closed and a lifeboat being launched. The ship was so similar to the her lost sister in so many respects that it was a perfect way for the assessors to get a better idea of the events they were about to investigate.

Lord Mersey would make a name for himself (for future historians at least, for he was already a famous contemporary name when he started the *Titanic* Inquiry but his place in history is due to his maritime Inquiries) as a man who investigated shipwrecks. After the *Titanic,* there would be the *Empress of Ireland* and the *Lusitania* Inquiries and also the lesser known but at the time politically significant investigation into the loss of the *Falaba*, which was sunk by a U-Boat in the First World War, an act which cost the life of an American citizen and nearly brought the USA into the conflict.

Unlike Senator Smith, his American counterpart, Mersey at least could claim a maritime city as his point of origin, having been born in Liverpool in 1840. He came from the rising class of merchants in Victorian England; ignoring the traditional route into the law via Oxford or Cambridge he studied at the Liverpool Institute and the University of London. He was called to the Bar at the age of thirty, and gained a reputation as a man with a keen mind but also as someone who cut to the point without caring too much for the sensibilities of those who entered his presence; in short, a man who did not suffer fools gladly. He was not an impressive speaker and he was not a dominating presence physically either but he did have an ambience about him which made it clear that he was completely in charge of his court-room.

He was assisted during the Inquiry by a team of assessors: John Biles a naval architect and a professor at the University of Glasgow, Captain Arthur Clarke, a brother of Trinity House which maintained the lighthouses of Britain, once a seaman but now retired from the sea, Rear Admiral Somerset Gough-Calthorpe, at forty-two years of age young to be in his exalted naval position, Commander F.C.A. Lyon, a former P&O Commander and Edward Chaston, a Technical Engineer. Those who do not rate the Inquiry's conduct very highly point out that there were no serving merchant seamen on the panel. Nevertheless there were a wide range of maritime skills represented on it and there were none of the laymen who composed the panel of the American Inquiry.

When the Inquiry began on 2 May, there was none of the widespread interest seen at its American equivalent, at least not in terms of those who attended it. The drill hall of the Scottish Regiment in Buckingham Gate was in a very 'English' part of London, close to Whitehall and its corridors of power and near the sylvan fields of St James Park. However, it was not at all suited for the events that were about to take place as the acoustics were terrible and Lord Mersey was not possessed of a very powerful voice. A number of questions had to be repeated and some witnesses asked to speak up. Mersey was a man in his seventies and clearly had trouble even hearing some of the evidence that was being presented.

Another curious aspect of the proceedings was the number of lawyers appearing representing various parties. Several unions tried to gain access for their respective members, a number of people tried to represent different groups of third-class passengers and other lawyers tried to put themselves forward as representatives of other parties. Lord Mersey had a difficult time of it keeping all those would-be interest groups at arms length, otherwise his hearings could quickly have descended into farce. With a number of people asking to represent various small groups of passengers, Mersey compromised by allowing one representative to appear on behalf of each class. Mr W.D. Harbinson for example appearing for all third-class passengers.

On the first day, events began with some of those overtones of disorganized amateurism with which some would say too many British civil servants have been associated over the years; the regimental band of the Scots Guards did not realize that the Hall, where they practised their military marches and patriotic suites, had been commandeered by the Inquiry and turned up complete with their instruments. Unfortunately, their band practice would have to be rearranged for another location; if Lord Mersey could not hear when the Hall contained merely witnesses and lawyers, he was unlikely to have much luck with a military band playing.

Mersey had been appointed Wreck Commissioner just for the duration of the Inquiry; it was not a permanent position as the British authorities did not take kindly to shipwrecks and major examples of them did not occur very frequently. The very first words uttered at the Inquiry told something of the need for some redemptive resolution to emerge from its results. Both the Attorney-General, Sir Rufus Isaacs, and the Right Honourable Sir Robert Finlay, appearing on behalf of the White Star Line, referred glowingly to the heroism that had been shown by so many on the *Titanic*. The power of the legend was already taking hold.

Mersey's Inquiry was to address twenty-six pre-defined questions (to which one important extra sub-question would be added during the course of the proceedings – it concerned whether or not any other ships were close enough to help; its answer – the *Californian*).

These covered a wide range of topics. Some were a matter of simple fact. These included confirmation of the track that the ship followed, whether the lookouts were provided with binoculars, where and at what time the *Titanic* sank, how many she had onboard and how many were saved (including an analysis by class). There were also questions that required more subjective conclusions, including ones examining the design of the ship, the discipline of those aboard after the berg was struck, the precautions taken before the collision, the suitability of the speed she was going at, the adequacy of the lifeboats and the use of wireless communication. Not, in fact, too very different from the American Inquiry.

However, the tone of the proceedings would be quite different, much more legalistic than Senator Smith's Inquiry. The first day was one of those opening sessions so typical of many a legal process, crucial in terms of the conduct of the Inquiry but lacking in much drama for the neutral observer. This covered such matters as who was to be represented during the Inquiry and how. Mersey turned down applications from various Unions to be represented although Thomas Scanlan was allowed to appear for the National Sailors and Firemen's Union. Crucially it would become clear that although the interests of categories such as third-class passengers were to be represented, hardly any passengers were to be called as witnesses (two, if one excludes Bruce Ismay who was hardly a passenger in the conventional sense of the word).

The Attorney-General's opening address mentioned a number of ships; the *Titanic* of course, the *Carpathia* which had charged to the rescue, the *Baltic* and *Caronia* who had both sent ice warnings to the doomed leviathan. There was not a word though of the *Californian*, a situation that would change dramatically partway through events.

Lookout Archie Jewell was the first witness to appear. He was asked a number of questions, most of which replicated what had been asked at the American Inquiry. At the conclusion of his examination, Lord Mersey told him: 'I think you have given your evidence very well indeed.' The Inquiry was underway, and Jewell was the first of many to give his version of events. Early on in proceedings Mersey and the Inquiry members took some time out to make their visit to the *Olympic* in Southampton so that they could better understand the layout of the *Titanic*.

Not everyone was as non-contentious as Archie Jewell. Joseph Scarrott, the next witness after him, admitted that first and second-class passengers had a much better chance of surviving than third-class because boats were located in 'their' areas. He then admitted that there was ample time to bring all women and children from third-class up to the Boat Deck but was not pushed as to his opinion as to why, if this was the case, so many of them perished. Scarrott was also examined as to the number of seaman in Boat 14 when she was lowered. He answered that there were two including Officer Lowe and that this was simply not enough; in his view eight to row plus one at the tiller was necessary to control a boat properly.

Able Seaman William Lucas was also asked about third-class passengers. When questioned about their access to the Boat Deck, he offered the view: 'I do not think those people had time to go there without directions from somebody; I hardly knew my way there myself.' Most of the passengers he saw on the Boat Deck he believed were first-class. He also noted that some of the boats at least were not filled, 'because there were no women knocking about', and confirmed the view that boats were being effectively filled with women and children only on one side of the ship.

Able Seaman John Poingdestre saw a number of third-class passengers milling around as the ship started to sink, unsure of what to do. He confirmed that in normal circumstances they would not be allowed up onto the Boat Deck and that this remained the case even in this dangerous situation. It was in areas such as this that the limitations of Mersey as a Wreck Assessor unfortunately came through. His questioning, from the surviving transcripts, often comes across as being aggressive and, for members of the crew who were presumably already apprehensive about appearing as witnesses, this cannot have helped. A sensitive Chairman would have followed up such hints of problems to bring out more, possibly crucial, information but Mersey was not such an individual.

It is hard to avoid the impression that some traditional class prejudices revealed themselves in Mersey's attitude throughout the Inquiry; his questioning of some of the crew (for example that of Fireman Alfred

Shiers) was arrogant, patronizing, supercilious and intimidating. In fact, it is difficult to read through the Inquiry transcripts without an increasing sense of anger at his off-hand attitude. Perhaps that explains why, with regard to the third-class passengers in particular, not everyone on the *Titanic* received a fair deal from the Inquiry. There was plenty of evidence that little effort was made to get all but a couple of groups of third-class passengers up to the Boat Deck but this was not robustly followed up.

The first few days of the Inquiry were somewhat low-key. Most of the prominent witnesses were still in America, in the main tied up with the Inquiry there. However, on the seventh day there was the first sign of controversy looming. First of all, this was the day on which the Duff Gordons were mentioned as potential witnesses. They were still making their way back on the *Lusitania* but, because of their involvement in the so-called 'money boat', they were the first and only 'real' passengers to appear at the British Inquiry.

Also the crew of the *Californian* were on the list to appear that day; there would be many more of them than had appeared in the USA. In recognition of their involvement, Mr C. Robertson Dunlop was to watch the Inquiry on behalf of the ship and her owners, the Leyland Line. However, he was not formally allowed to represent either the crew or the owners as neither was officially on trial; this was to have important repercussions at a later stage.

And so, on Day 7, 14 May 1912, a sense of drama at last descended on the Inquiry when Captain Stanley Lord of the *Californian* took the stand. The first questions were innocuous enough; how many people could his ship carry – 102 – and what lifeboat capacity did his vessel have – 218. Then a quick discussion on the wireless messages he had had sent out but, before very long, they got to the point in the story where Lord had stopped for ice, ice that stretched 'as far as I can see to the northward and southward'.

Then Lord moved on to the heart of his story, of the ship he had seen (now close on 11.00 p.m.) about six or seven miles away from the *Californian* which he confirmed, in case any of the Committee was in doubt, he believed was not the *Titanic*. He proceeded to tell his story, of how he had sent an ice warning to the *Titanic* – which she had rebuffed – of how he had briefed the Second Officer and then of how he had taken himself down to the Chart Room to rest, thereby hopefully removing himself from any further responsibility.

The crux of the story was of course the rockets seen by his officer of the watch and gradually Lord moved towards this key point. Lord said that 'a white rocket' had been seen by Stone, a fact that had been reported to him at 1.15 a.m. Mersey's ears pricked up and he immediately inserted a suggestion that the direction where the rocket was seen was where the

Titanic was. Lord replied with the rather unbelievable suggestion that no one had ever told him what direction the rocket was seen in. Mersey seemed amazed that he had not checked it out with his Second Officer as to the source of this unusual signal; he had every right to be so one might think.

It soon led to Mersey having a conversation in the courtroom with the Attorney-General about the lights of another ship that had been seen from the floundering *Titanic*. Mersey revealed at once what he was thinking about the *Californian*: 'What is in my brain at the present time is this; that what they saw was the Titanic.' It is hard to be exact from just reading a transcript but this must have been within an hour of the questioning beginning. From now on, Lord was on the back foot.

Mersey and Isaacs had already done their homework. They then asked Lord how many masthead lights the ship he saw had; he said one. Mersey commented that this was different from the number given by Third Officer Groves (whom they had not even interviewed yet) and that the *Titanic* had two lights (in fact, it is not clear that this was the case and it has been suggested by some writers that she only had one so this snippet of evidence is inconclusive). However, there was no doubt that the Commissioners seemed to want to believe Groves' version because they thought the *Titanic* did indeed have two masthead lights; Lord was again a marked man.

Lord admitted that he queried Groves about this later. He said he was curious to establish the identity of the ship *between* him and the *Titanic*. Here the basis of his defence was appearing; the ship he saw was *not* the *Titanic* but another interposed between the two. He denied emphatically ever having a conversation with his Third Officer about Groves' belief that the ship he was looking at was a passenger steamer.

Mersey quickly started to exhaust his stores of patience, which do not appear to have been very high. When the interchange about the identity of the nearby ship was in progress, he remarked to Lord: 'You do not give me answers that please me at present.' His faith in Lord was not about to be restored when they got onto the subject of the rockets in more detail. Lord affirmed that he had no recollection of his 2.00 a.m. conversation with Gibson save that he had a very vague remembrance of the Apprentice opening the door and shutting it again. He was tired. Excessive sleepiness was to be his second line of defence.

Lord said he returned to the bridge after his deep sleep at 4.30 a.m. still unaware that more than one rocket had been seen and with no memory either of Stone's call down the speaking tube at 2.45 a.m. to say that the ship he had been watching had now disappeared. It was only subsequently that he found out there had been more than one rocket. Up until now, all the *Californian's* other witnesses had been sitting in the hall, listening to all this before it came to their turn to appear. The Attorney General, Sir

Rufus Isaacs, suggested that they should now leave. Mersey was quick to agree. Something contentious was clearly in the offing.

Everyone there realized that the rockets and Lord's actions in response to them were the heart of the matter. Isaacs was directing the questioning and now attempted to move in for the kill. He asked Lord if Gibson had reported eight rockets to him. Lord said he had no recollection of such a situation. Isaacs then asked what he thought a ship might be firing rockets for. Why had he remained in the chart room, Isaacs asked? Especially when he knew there was ice in the vicinity. The implication was clear but Lord sought to rebut it; why should he worry about the danger of ice when the ship he could see had stopped?

Lord then threw up a smokescreen. He introduced his theory that the 'rockets' might be company recognition signals. He had suggested as much to Stone but his Second Officer had replied that he did not know. Then, the decisive moment. Isaacs asked Lord if the answer satisfied him, to which Lord replied that it did not. She might though, he suggested, have been responding to his Morse signals which she had up until then been ignoring. Such a suggestion does not appear convincing on the pages of a transcript and it certainly did not convince Isaacs. Lord explained that he asked Stone to carry on Morsing the ship and send Gibson down with further information. That further information never arrived. Yet Lord stayed wrapped up in his Chart Room even though he was not sure whether the signals were for recognition purposes or for something more sinister. Isaacs was so disbelieving of the answer that he asked the same simple question more than once, as if he could not comprehend what he was hearing in reply.

The nub of the questioning, and the moment that Lord in hindsight lost his battle, was found in a very simple exchange:

> Isaacs: 'You did not think it was a company's signal?'
> Lord: 'I inquired, was it a company's signal?'
> Isaacs: 'But you had been told he [Stone] did not know?'
> Lord: 'He said he did not know.'
> Isaacs: 'Very well, that did not satisfy you?'
> Lord: 'It did not satisfy me.'
> Isaacs: 'Then if it was not that, it might have been a distress signal?'
> Lord: 'It might have been.'
> Isaacs: 'And you remained in the chart room?'
> Lord: 'I remained in the chart room.'

This was a crucial confession; the rockets at the least might have been distress signals and yet Lord did not bother to go and look for himself. It was not difficult to see that Lord was not going to come out of this Inquiry very well. The Captain of the *Californian* attempted to extricate himself from the hole he had dug; he did not think they were distress signals coming from the nearby ship because they made no noise and, at a five mile distance, someone was bound to have heard them. But the damage had been done.

Isaacs reviewed Lord's evidence so far and asked him if he was happy in retrospect with his actions. Lord replied that the only thing that was bothering him was that, if the *Titanic* was nineteen miles away, then they ought to have seen any distress rockets she sent up. Yet of course if she was nineteen miles away, then she could not be the ship that they could see five miles off. She was clearly not the *Titanic* as far as Lord was concerned because 'a ship like the Titanic at sea is an utter impossibility for anyone to mistake'. He would not misidentify her from five miles distance.

When pushed on why he did not wake the wireless operator, Cyril Evans, Lord first of all seemed incredulous that anyone could contemplate taking such action at 1.00 a.m. He then said that he was not worried about the situation because he thought that the rockets had been company recognition signals; yet of course Stone had admitted to no such thing so it was at the very least a reckless approach to take. But Lord told the Inquiry he was awaiting further information, for 'I had a responsible officer on the bridge who was finding things out for me'.

This was another line of defence for Lord (for, if he was not in legal terms on trial, in the court of public opinion he certainly was). In summary, his explanations for his inaction were that the ship he saw was not the *Titanic*, it was not clear that the rockets were distress signals, he was excessively sleepy and the events of the night were the responsibility of the officer on the watch. It was not a convincing set of arguments and it did not convince a number of people at the time. Mr Roche, representing the Marine Engineers' Association, was the first to make the suggestion during the Inquiry that the presence of ice might have led to Lord's reluctance to respond to any distress signals in case, by responding, he had exposed his own ship to danger. Lord of course denied it but it was a suggestion that, to some, hit the mark.

Towards the end of Lord's evidence, something extraordinary emerged. On 15 April, the day after the night the great ship went down, Chief Officer Stewart was responsible for writing up the log of the *Californian*. He used the ship's scrap log to do this. The amazing thing was that nowhere in the log was there any mention of the eleven rockets – eight (presumably) from the *Titanic* and three from the *Carpathia* – that had been seen by the ship's officers of the watch. It was as if the *Californian's* officers believed that watching eleven rockets lighting up the night sky while the greatest ship ever built sank nearby was just an everyday event, worthy of no further note.

Lord was followed in the witness box by Apprentice James Gibson. Gibson repeated his story of how he could see a ship, stopped but indistinct, about four to seven miles off. He could see a light flickering and at first thought it was a Morse lamp. However, picking up binoculars he could see that he was mistaken. Stone had seen five rockets while he had been below and he had then seen three more himself. Then at about 1.20 a.m. Stone had told Gibson that the ship was steaming slowly away to the south-west (where, incidentally, there was supposedly an enormous ice-field).

Gibson then told the Inquiry about Stone's comment that the other ship looked 'queer'. Not surprisingly, Mersey's ears pricked up again. They were positively antenna-like when Gibson proceeded to tell everyone that, on looking at her with binoculars, she appeared to be listing to starboard. When Gibson then told an incredulous audience of Stone's comment that a ship would not be firing rockets at night for nothing, Lord's fate was already sealed.

Mersey was intrigued by the comment Gibson made that the ship had 'disappeared' just after 2.00 a.m. Subtlety was not his Lordship's strong point; he suggested point blank that a ship disappeared when she went to the bottom. It was difficult not to associate the nearby ship with the *Titanic* especially when Gibson said how he thought that the list he saw was explained by the red port sidelight rising higher out of the water while the other side was dropping.

The Inquiry dwelt on this particular aspect of Gibson's evidence for some time. It was indeed a strange picture he painted; of he and Stone watching through binoculars, wondering why the ship looked so strange, attempting to explain to themselves why her lights seemed higher out of the water, trying to fathom out why she had been throwing up rockets, looking for reasons as to why she might be listing. Yet, save to stand there, watch and wonder, they did nothing. Given the fact that 1,500 lives had been lost somewhere within twenty miles of them, it seemed a stunning lack of proactivity by just about everyone aboard the *Californian*.

Gibson was followed by Stone and the impression of lethargic inertia that the Apprentice had portrayed was amply reinforced by the Second Officer's evidence. Those questioning him were incredulous at how an officer on the watch could see five rockets fired up in quick succession and not realize that there was something wrong. Stone was asked on a number of occasions what he thought the rockets were for but merely said that he had passed on the information to Captain Lord to judge for himself. He refused to accept the idea that at any time he thought they might have been distress signals. Mersey soon gave him the cold shoulder too with the remark: 'You know, you do not make a good impression on me at present.'

The *Californian* crew were having a much tougher time of it in London than they had in Washington. By now, the cat was not only out of the bag but was running around wildly resisting all attempts at control. Herbert Stone in particular received a grilling, especially over those rockets. One of those cross-examining him, Thomas Scanlon, who was representing the National Sailors' and Firemen's Union, asked him some especially awkward questions. Again, a dusty transcript can relate the words spoken but not the tone in which they were uttered but the following should perhaps be read with an overtone of incredulity in the voice:

> Do you mean to tell his Lordship that you did not know that the throwing up 'of rock-
> ets or shells, throwing stars of any colour or description, fired one at a time at short
> intervals' is the proper method for signalling distress at night.

Stone confirmed that he knew full well that such was indeed the case and Mersey moved in for the kill, asking 'and is not that exactly what was happening?' It was a question with only one possible answer, which might explain why Stone never said a word in response. When pushed however Stone eventually confirmed that what he saw looked like distress signals but he could not understand how a vessel that was in trouble could steam away.

One of the possible explanations appeared in his answers, for Stone appeared to be a man far too much in awe of his Captain. When asked whether he was worried about the ship he could see, he said he was not. 'If there had been any grounds for supposing the ship would have been in distress the Captain would have expressed it to me,' he said. Yet Lord of course had not even seen this ship since the rockets had started to light up the starlit sky.

The real farce of the *Californian* incident is that Lord effectively blamed Stone for not telling him anything was wrong and Stone effectively told the Inquiry that it was Lord's job to tell him if anything was amiss. Both men were waiting for the other to do something. Removed from its tragic context, it would have been like a scene out of a Keystone Cops movie set at sea. Whether or not the *Californian* might have got across to the *Titanic* in time – and it is by no means certain that she could if Lord had not known of the distress rockets until 1.15 a.m. – there was something badly wrong with the management of the ship that night.

The impression was reinforced on Day 8 when *Californian's* Third Officer Charles Victor Groves took the stand. He was of course the man on watch on the bridge when the mystery steamer was first seen. He had spied a ship with two masthead lights steaming from the east. As she got closer, he reported her presence, as ordered, to Lord, going down to the chart room, knocking on the Venetian doors and telling the captain of the new arrival on the scene (though if we believe Lord's account he of course knew she was there already).

There was no doubt in Groves' mind that he was looking at a passenger steamer. He went back to the bridge and tried to Morse her but without success. At one stage he thought he saw a Morse flash in response but picking up his binoculars he could see that he was mistaken. Lord came up on the bridge shortly after and did not agree that the ship was a passenger steamer. He also remarked that the only passenger steamer near them was the *Titanic*.

Groves departed the bridge at 12.15 a.m. and, apart from his unsuccessful foray into the Marconi room, played no further part in the drama until after 6.00 a.m. the next morning when he was awoken and asked to report to the captain as the *Titanic* had sunk. He had at once gone to see Stone, whose room was just across the corridor from him. Stone told him of the rockets that he had seen. Groves had got dressed at once and returned to the bridge. It was coming up for 7.00 a.m. now and he could see another steamer on their port bow. It was the *Carpathia* with her flags at half mast. Mersey asked why, to which Groves responded that she was 'half-masted for death my Lord'.

Groves left the witness box after confirming that, if he had been on the watch, the rockets would certainly have been mentioned in the log. Completing the log was the task of Chief Officer George Frederick Stewart who was next to appear. He was quizzed on the log which he had written up. He confirmed that he would ordinarily have mentioned rockets in the log but that there were none in the scrap log he used to write the official version up from (this would have been prepared by the Officer on the Watch, Stone, during his shift and the omission of any mention of rockets was down to him). Groves confirmed he saw a ship to the south when he came on watch at 4.00 a.m. She had one funnel and four masts like the *Carpathia*. However, he did not think it was her because she had a yellow funnel.

Wireless Operator Cyril Evans was then called as a witness. He was quizzed as to his communications with the *Titanic* and then the activity aboard the *Californian* when he was awoken on the morning of 15 April. He completed for the time being the evidence of those aboard the *Californian*. His tale mirrored in essence that he had already told in America. The story had made a great impression on those present in the hall and it was safe to say that that impression was far from positive as far as Captain Stanley Lord and his staff of officers was concerned.

Ernest Gill appeared later, regarded as a 'deserter' by Captain Lord after leaving the *Californian* in Boston. Mr Rowlatt, interviewing him, considered that there was no longer any doubt about the veracity of his story as it had broadly been confirmed by other witnesses heard by the Inquiry (though had he dug deeper he would have found important differences in the detail). Gill claimed that he had never deserted at all but had missed the ship when subpoenaed by the American Inquiry. This was somewhat strange; Captain Lord had been interviewed in America on the same day as Gill and had no trouble at all coming back to England on his ship, the one that Gill was too late to catch; yet another example of someone from the *Californian* who seemed to have trouble getting his story straight.

The Inquiry then returned to witnesses from the *Titanic*. Steward John Hart was interesting in that his passengers were in steerage and so he was able to give their perspective. He had fifty-eight of them to look after altogether and insisted that he roused them all when the ship struck. He then supervised them as they put on their lifebelts though some refused to do so. Then as they waited for further orders, his passengers – who were housed at the rear of the ship – were joined by male steerage passengers coming back from further forward.

After a while, orders arrived. The stewards were to get their women and children passengers up to the Boat Deck. Some, Hart insisted, did not go, believing that they were safer where they were. However, he himself took a number up, using his knowledge of the ship to pick out the best way for the journey through the labyrinth of corridors and stairways. He insisted that there were no barriers to their progress and that he took his party up the Boat Deck, where he left them and returned to pick up another group. On his way back, he saw a colleague, William Cox, leading another party up by the same route.

One item of Hart evidence that did help shed light on the situation was his statement that it was only women and children that were being allowed up onto the Boat Deck. He found it a struggle to return back to steerage quarters 'owing to the males wanting to get to the boat deck'. The male steerage passengers in other words appear to have been kept far away from the boats, an impression confirmed later in the questioning of Hart when he stated that stewards stopped the male passengers from moving up.

There was a formality about the proceedings as a whole which was in keeping with the spirit of the times. The British Inquiry exhibited the stiff upper lip for which the nation was famous in abundance as well as the class consciousness of the era. Crew members were normally referred to by their surnames only, as if they were servants from below stairs. Yet even among this rigorous decorum, the human tragedy sometimes shone through. Steward Samuel Rule it turned out had had his nerves shattered by the tragedy and had been a regular visitor to his doctor since coming back home.

Another witness, George Symons, had returned home to family in Weymouth when one Saturday evening he heard a knock on the door. It was two gentlemen who had come down to get a statement from him on behalf of Sir Cosmo and Lady Duff Gordon (though it was suggested during the Inquiry when the issue came up that this was without the Duff Gordons' knowledge). In the course of that conversation, Symons admitted to being 'master of the situation' in the boat, something which Sir Cosmo was no doubt anxious to hear as a number of accusations about him had started to circulate. It was very much in his interests to deny any part in stopping the heavily under-filled Boat 1 from going back to pick up any more survivors.

Fireman James Taylor was also interviewed by this supposedly self-appointed representative of the Duff Gordons and gave evidence at the Inquiry. Most other crew members in Boat 1 were also questioned by Mersey's Committee before, at last, Sir Cosmo himself entered the witness box. He said that, by the time he was lowered away in Boat 1, he believed that the *Titanic* was in serious trouble. He insisted that when he got off in the boat, there were no more passengers to be seen but it was not the fact of his survival that was the greatest cause of controversy.

That was Boat 1's failure to go back for more survivors. Sir Cosmo admitted that, when the ship went down, he heard a dreadful wailing which he knew must be the sound of people drowning. However, he insisted that there was never any discussion about whether or not they should row back. But he was busy looking after his wife and at no time did it cross his mind that they should do so. He also did not think it was possible, for in the dark they did not know where those in the water were. He heard no discussion, he said, in which his wife had insisted they should not return and more or less suggested that crew members like Hendrickson who had said so to the Inquiry were lying.

He did admit though that he made the offer of a £5 present for each crew member while he was in the boat with them. But he insisted that this was nearly half an hour after the ship went down and also after the cries of the drowning victims of the disaster had stopped; in other words, it was not a bribe to stop the boat from going back to help. However, not everyone, including Mr Harbinson representing third-class passengers, was convinced.

Sir Cosmo's explanations were not at all convincing. The suggestion that he thought it quite natural not to go back and try and save survivors made him come across as someone interested in saving his own skin (and his wife's of course) regardless of anyone else's. Such suggestions had already appeared in the press. Sir Cosmo referred to the large number of stories that had already appeared in America, which he said were 'all inventions'. Interviews with Lady Duff Gordon were reported which he insisted had never taken place.

Sir Cosmo's evidence completed, it was his wife's turn to take the stand. This was done of her own volition. So many stories had appeared about her that she wanted to take the opportunity to clear her name. She was generally treated deferentially by the interviewers at the Inquiry. However, her claim that she did not hear any cries from the water after the *Titanic* sank left her in a minority of about one. Robert Pusey, a Fireman, was in the boat – he heard them. Trimmer Frederick Sheath was there; he heard them too. Able Seaman Albert Horswill was yet another Boat 1 witness to the cries. One can only assume that either Lady Duff Gordon's seasickness had had an effect on her hearing or that she had had an unfortunate loss of memory.

She also insisted that no conversation took place about whether or not Boat 1 should go back to pick up survivors. In fairness to her, most other Boat 1 witnesses confirmed this. In fact, Hendrickson's confident assertion was not backed up by others in the boat. George Symons, supposedly in charge of the boat, stated: 'I never heard anybody of any description, passengers or crew, say anything as regards going back.' Either Hendrickson had not made any such suggestion or the other occupants of Boat 1 collectively did not wish to admit that he had.

When the *Titanic's* surviving officers returned from America, they were quickly put in front of the Inquiry. Second Officer Lightoller made his debut on the tenth day of the Inquiry, on 17 May. Lightoller had more time for the British Inquiry than he did its American counterpart; at least he felt that the man chairing the former had some knowledge of the sea. But his own comments after the event provide an interesting insight into the prevailing paradigms that were in evidence. His view was that 'a washing of dirty linen would help no one' and that 'in London it was very necessary to keep one's hands on the whitewash brush'.

To him, it seemed pointless to argue whether or not the lifesaving appliances were unsatisfactory; the mere fact there had already been a root-and-branch change in processes straight after the disaster proved that they were. Neither did he see any reason to think that the *Titanic* should have slowed down after entering the ice region. Lightoller was a frustrating witness, determined to give away no more than he had to. As a result, it was hard to determine what he genuinely believed in and how much he said because he felt obligated to say it.

In the British Inquiry, Second Office Lightoller was asked to answer 1,600 questions, making it an exhausting experience for him. Lightoller was anxious that no one should take the rap for the disaster, including the White Star Line and the Board of Trade. He found a particularly dogged adversary in Mr Scanlon, representing the Sailors' and Firemen's Union. By the time he had finished, Lightoller said he felt more like a legal doormat than a Mail Boat Officer.

Frederick Fleet was also called before the Inquiry. It was not an experience he enjoyed; one of his interrogators later referred to him as 'the suspicious man' who 'looked at us all'. In all probability, Fred Fleet was probably just an individual overwhelmed by events and struggling to find the right words to say to the intimidating convocation before him. Interestingly, he now suggested that there was a haze on the night in question, though it did not amount to much. Lee had been much more definitive there was such a haze in his evidence but Mersey was not inclined to believe him, thinking it was an excuse for not spotting the berg.

Fleet got rattled at various points in his testimony; he had witnessed a lot – the sighting (too late) of the iceberg, the mystery light, the events in Boat 6. The last straw was when Mr Harbinson started his questioning; Fleet snapped back at him: 'Is there any more likes to have a go at me?' Mersey relieved him soon afterwards after a long interrogation, saying: 'I think you have given your evidence very well, even though you seem to distrust us all.'

Bruce Ismay found himself on the defensive on two counts, firstly as the leading representative of the White Star Line and secondly as a male passenger who had had the temerity to survive. He was understandably anxious to emphasize that he was there as just another passenger (something that was difficult to defend when he was not paying for his ticket) and that in particular he had nothing whatever to do with the navigational decision-making on the *Titanic*.

Yet he seemed remarkably well informed on the number of revolutions the *Titanic's* engines made at various stages of the voyage. And he quickly alienated some of the Committee; when asked whether or not the ship might have considered slowing down because of the imminent danger of ice, he replied that he was not a navigator. It was a remark that earned a rebuke from the Attorney-General. Bizarrely, when pushed he suggested that it might actually be safer to steam more quickly through ice-fields so that they could get through them more speedily, a suggestion that has as little connection with logic as the *Titanic's* maiden voyage had with successful journeys across the Atlantic.

Ismay was inevitably asked about his survival when he got off in one of the last boats to leave the sinking ship. Yet perhaps his most interesting statement was that he saw a clear white light but he did not think it was from the *Californian* – whose lights had been seen off the port side of the *Titanic* – because this light was to starboard. Lord Mersey seemed disappointed as it cast some doubt on his conclusion – not yet definitively stated but surely in his mind by now – that the *Californian* was indeed the mystery ship whose lights could be seen.

In general terms, Ismay appeared to be a man who, given his exalted position, knew surprisingly little about his organization. He did not know whether the number of crew onboard his company's ships had been increased to take account of the extra lifeboat capacity they now had after the disaster, he did not know if it was true, as claimed, that his company had contract conditions which limited their liability in the case of accident caused through negligence on the part of their officers, he did not know how significantly the routes his ships were taking had shifted as a result of a decision to adopt more southerly routes after the sinking. These were all questions that a man in his position might be expected to know the answers to but Ismay claimed he did not.

Most incredibly of all, Ismay suggested that, even though the *Olympic*-class ships were a quantum leap in terms of size from existing vessels, no one in White Star had considered the need for more lifeboat capacity. But he trotted out the stock response that these ships were 'practically unsinkable' and were their own best lifeboats. It was an irony born of hubris.

The impression of a disconnect from reality was further reinforced when Ismay suggested that these ships only carried lifeboats at all so that they could pick up survivors from other ships in the event of an accident or to row the odd passenger to shore on an excursion. He quickly revised his view when his interviewer suggested that, in the event of a fire, they might be quite useful in getting the passengers off a burning ship. The fact that Ismay had not thought of this without being prompted perhaps gives an insight into contemporary views towards safety considerations. And anyway the fact that the *Titanic* had sunk, with not enough room for over half the people onboard, barely seemed to have registered.

Eventually, the inevitable question was asked about the circumstances in which Ismay left the ship. He admitted that, at the time he did so, he was aware that there were hundreds of people left on her who were destined to drown. However, he did not consider it his responsibility to give up his own life too. Judged by the morals of the time, not everyone considered this right. Mr Edwards, who asked the question, felt that it 'was his duty to remain on that ship until she went to the bottom'.

The Right Honourable Alexander Montgomery Carlisle was another to be faced with the difficult question of lifeboats, or rather lack of them. He had been a member of the Shipping Advisory Committee in 1911. This august body had been tasked with assessing the number of lifeboats aboard the new super-liners in that year. Equally pertinently, if not more so, he had been involved in the design of the *Olympic* and *Titanic* when working for Harland & Wolff, though he had now left the company. He had been responsible for asking the lifeboat davit designers, Welin's Quadrant Davit Company, to design equipment that would enable these vessels to carry over forty lifeboats.

This had been done as a safeguard. It was known at the time that the Board of Trade were considering revising the lifeboat regulations in the light of the ever-increasing size of ships and the davit design was considered in case they demanded that more lifeboats be carried; by considering such things in advance White Star hoped to avoid unnecessary expense if such changes came about.

The designs were submitted to White Star and to Bruce Ismay in particular. Carlisle remembered having a detailed design discussion with Ismay and Harold Sanderson, the Managing Director of the company, which lasted for about four hours. This was about a variety of issues and the discussions about the lifeboats lasted for five or ten minutes. Carlisle admitted that he did not argue the case for more lifeboats very strongly but said he felt at the time more should be provided – he believed forty-eight, three on each set of davits, was the optimum.

Although the davits were designed to carry four boats, they never did on the *Titanic*. Carlisle left Harland & Wolff two years before she was launched but carried on a campaign to increase lifeboat capacity aboard such ships as part of his new role with the Advisory Committee. But the Advisory Committee had produced a Report which did recommend that there might be changes to existing regulations – it suggested that lifeboat capacity could be reduced. Carlisle did not agree with this conclusion but signed the report anyway. He was clearly not a man possessed of great conviction or strength of character. Under pressure from the Inquiry, Carlisle admitted: 'I was very soft when I signed that.' Such softness might have contributed to the loss of 1,500 lives save for the fact that the Report's findings had not been implemented. There was no question now that they ever would be.

The Inquiry eventually came to a close after asking 25,622 questions and interviewing ninety-seven witnesses. For lovers of trivia, the last witness interviewed was Captain Arthur Tride, skipper of the *Manitou*. He was asked whether his ship would slow down if warned of ice ahead. In common with most other skippers asked the question, he said no, unless it was hazy. Then it was time for the lawyers, their discussions and their summing up, a process that took several more days.

Attorney-General Sir Rufus Isaacs, in his summing-up at the British Inquiry hit the nail on the head when he said:

> No doubt if there had been proper organisation [of the boat-loading] there would have been a greater possibility of saving more passengers. What struck one was that no one seemed to have known what his duty was or how many persons were to be placed in the boat before it was lowered.

Sir Rufus, in the polite language of the day, wondered why the officers were so risk-averse in their policy towards the loading of the boats. He was more outspoken in his criticism of some seamen for not going back to pick up more survivors out of the water but seemed reluctant to be too critical of the officers, whose 'heroic' conduct was already starting to become part of the *Titanic* legend, especially in Britain. It made it even more difficult to do so when some of the key players in the drama, especially in this instance Captain Smith and First Officer Murdoch, were dead.

After the event Lightoller recognized that there had been a great deal of slackness about in the shipping industry generally before the *Titanic* went down. Change was needed. As he put it:

> No longer is the Boat-Deck almost wholly set aside as a recreation ground for passengers, with the smallest number of boats relegated to the least possible space.

It was a tacit recognition that the reduction of the boats planned on the *Titanic* from sixty-four to sixteen was, with the luminous benefit of hindsight, a disastrous error.

The British enquiry cost £20,231 including a salary of £1,050 for Lord Mersey. The largest payments, cynics might say inevitably, were made to solicitors – £2,500. Altogether different categories of lawyers netted a very nice £13,000 from the enquiry. The *British Seafarer*, the journal of the British Seafaring Union, did not pull any punches when commenting on the 'whitewashing enquiry':

> The ruling classes rob and plunder the people all the time, and the Inquiry has shown that they have no scruples in taking advantage of death and disaster. Who said sharks?

Lord Mersey reported back on 30 July 1912. Captain Smith did not escape criticism, though Mersey exonerated him to some extent because he was only acting in the same way that most other sea captains of the day did. Mariners generally did not slow down for ice unless visibility was bad. The *Titanic* experience had shown that to be poor practice, which now had to change. Mersey rejected any suggestion that a record attempt was being made or that Ismay had influenced Captain Smith's attitude with regard to the speed of the ship. However, Mersey warned, if another captain in the future ignored the message given by the disaster and did not slow down for ice, then any accident resulting would have been caused by his negligence.

Ignoring the evidence of a number of witnesses, Mersey decided that the ship did not break in two before she sank. More correctly, in line with the evidence, he stated that there had been no proper boat drill. The organization, he said, should have been better and if it had been then more lives might have been saved. More lives could have been saved too if boats had gone back to pick up people out of the water; Boat 1 was understandably picked out for particular criticism. However, he rejected the suggestion that Sir Cosmo Duff Gordon had attempted to control the crew through any bribe and also felt that Bruce Ismay deserved no criticism for getting into a boat and saving himself. Had he not done so, he would merely have added one more life to the roll-call of the lost.

Captain Rostron was again singled out for praise. Mersey said: 'The Court desires to record its great admiration of Captain Rostron's conduct. He did the very best that could be done.' In contrast, Captain Lord of the *Californian* was castigated more than anyone else, with Lord Mersey suggesting that most lives might have been saved if his ship had reacted as it should have done. He thought that the *Californian* was only five miles away from the *Titanic* on the night. He was convinced that the doomed leviathan was the ship that was seen from the *Californian*.

Despite all the evidence Lord Mersey found that there had been no discrimination against third-class passengers. Perhaps it was because he had not seen fit to call any to give witness to his Inquiry. Few however made much of a fuss about it at the time, or at least if they did no one in a position of authority opted to pick up the issue and run with it. Union journals like the *British Seafarer* were expected to stick up for 'their kind' but the rest of the population did not seem unduly interested in the problem.

Mersey attributed the large proportion of third-class lost to their reluctance to abandon their baggage and their location on the ship. Nevertheless, the figures do take some explaining away; first-class passengers saved 62.5 per cent (203 out of 325), second-class 41.4 per cent (118 out of 285) and third-class 25.2 per cent (178 out of 706). 89 third-class women were lost (out of 165) and 52 children (out of 79). Women and children first? Not for everyone it seemed.

A poet Harvey Thew commemorated the actions of the men aboard with the words 'no stone or wreath from human hands will ever mark the spot where fifteen hundred men went down but manhood perished not', implying that every life lost was of a man. This is not to decry the heroism of many men, who did perish in far greater numbers than anyone else but a higher proportion of first-class men was saved than of third-class children so it does not quite tell the whole story.

Logan Marshall, whose book was in its way a classic of its type (high on drama, not always so on fact) dedicated his book to:

> the 1,635 [sic] passengers who were lost with the ill-fated Titanic, and especially to those heroic men, who, instead of trying to save themselves, stood aside that women and children might have their chance; of each of them let it be written, as it was written of a Greater One – He Died That Others Might Live.

'There was no debate,' the same source asserted, 'as to whether the life of a financier, a master of business, was rated higher in the scales than that of an ignorant peasant mother.' This was melodramatic, sentimental hogwash. If there was no debate it was because all too often the 'ignorant peasant mother' was nowhere in the vicinity of the Boat Deck to have one.

Nevertheless, the legend of male sacrifice became quickly established. And indeed there were those who did give their lives for others so that women and children could get in to the boats and find safety. However, it was not universally so, as on one side of the ship men freely entered the boats. And, it might reasonably be asked, why should they not do so when those boats were half empty anyway? However, legends develop for a purpose and something good needed to come of this awful and avoidable tragedy. So an ideal developed, one which demonstrated both the virtues of male chivalry and also, *inter alia*, Anglo Saxon stoicism (and by implication superiority) when faced with death.

On 18 April 1912, an American spiritual commentator, the Reverend Henry van Dyke of Princeton, delivered a message of spiritual consolation to those bereaved in the tragedy. Among other things in his text, so resonant of the era, he said:

> There is a great ideal. It is clearly outlined and set before the mind and heart of the modern world, to approve and to follow, or to despise and reject. It is 'women and children first!'

Much of the rest of his text was an encomium to the men onboard which he felt epitomized the Christian faith that they espoused. Even then though there were dissenting voices speaking against those who held these rather lofty views of what the disaster had to teach the world of all that was good in human nature. Alma White published a book in 1912 called *God Speaking to the Nations*. Rather than speaking highly of Christian virtues, White's view was that the disaster was a judgment by God on a world cursed with sin.

George Bernard Shaw and Arthur Conan Doyle had a very public bust-up over the merits or otherwise of the lessons to be learned from the disaster. Doyle, that pillar of the British establishment, felt that the catastrophe showed courage 'in the highest form'. Shaw, closely connected to Irish nationalist sentiments and no friend of British attitudes, felt completely the opposite; his reaction to the disaster was one of 'profound disgust, almost national dishonour'. A most entertaining letter exchange then took place in full view of a fascinated world.

But White and Shaw were in a distinct minority and supporters of the establishment like Mersey seemed reluctant to challenge public perceptions of heroism and male sacrifice. For Mersey to have challenged these ideals as being merely mirages would have gone against the grain and he was no such individual; the heroic self-sacrifice of men to save the women and children was already an established part of the legend and it would not do to rock the boat, so to speak.

The conclusions of the Inquiry were summed up in the findings at the end of the Report. A number of them referred to facts and figures e.g. how many passengers were carried (1,316) and crew (885 plus 8 bandsmen recorded as second-class passengers). More interesting were those requiring the expression of an opinion, such as the fact that in the Inquiry's view the arrangements for manning and launching the lifeboats was inadequate, as was the lookout provision (an extra man should have been posted at the forecastle according to Mersey). The Inquiry concluded that binoculars were not essential for lookouts to keep a proper watch. The speed of the *Titanic* at the time of collision – 22 knots – was excessive.

A series of twenty-one recommendations was made at the end of the Report, the most important element as collectively they encouraged the development of safer shipping in the future. Post-*Titanic* many of them were obvious but they cannot have been that obvious for they would surely then have been implemented beforehand. The disaster had shaken the world of the trans-Atlantic liners out of its complacency.

The Inquiry suggested that urgent research be undertaken into more extensive watertight compartments to be designed for the ships of the future. Most obviously, lifeboat accommodation should be based on the number of people ships could carry and not their size. The general rule should be a place for everyone onboard. There should also be at least one lifeboat fitted with an engine. The boats must also be fully supplied with all their equipment and supplies before the ships they were on left harbour.

In terms of manning the lifeboats, crew members were to be specifically trained in the task. More frequent boat drills were to be held and Board of Trade Inspectors were to satisfy themselves about the adequacy of arrangements before ships left port. More general recommendations included a suggestion that there should be what Mersey described as a 'police force' on ships to maintain order in times of emergency. There should also be a wireless operator on duty at all times. Ships should slow down when ice was reported ahead and captains should be advised that it was a misdemeanour not to go to the aid of a vessel in distress under the terms of the Maritime Conventions Act, 1911.

And so the Inquiry came to a close and life returned to a sort of normality. However, for the 711 (or so) survivors normality perhaps would never come again. They had witnessed the death of the greatest ship the world had ever known at close quarters, had seen her plummet to the ocean depths, had heard the cries of the freezing mass as the sea and the cold night air sucked the life out of them. For them nothing would ever be the same again. But life still had to go on.

21

Post Mortem: The World After the Titanic

Even before the Inquiries delivered their verdicts, the *Titanic* had already radically changed the maritime world. The *Olympic* was meant to sail from Southampton to New York on 24 April. However, the crew refused to go anywhere, unhappy at the lifeboats that had been provided after the disaster that had befallen the ship's younger sister. These had been collapsibles taken from the navy, which some of the crew alleged were in poor condition and were not in fact seaworthy. The dissent spread like wildfire and the men refused to go anywhere unless wooden lifeboats were laid on.

Captain Clarke, the Inspector who had signed off the *Titanic* as fit for duty, felt that the collapsibles provided were perfectly acceptable. However, the men were not having it. They had inspected the boats and found some of them to be rotting. White Star's original plan was to replace the strikers with a more pliant crew. However, the next day some of the collapsibles were tested and found to be mostly seaworthy and the strikers offered to go back to work if the one that had been found to be unsatisfactory was replaced.

But then a hitch arose. The strikers refused to sail unless the crew who had broken the strike were dismissed. White Star refused to do so. Fifty-four strikers went ashore and were arrested for mutiny. On 4 May 1912 they were tried and found guilty by magistrates in Plymouth but were not imprisoned or fined because of the circumstances of the case; in other words the magistrates could not ignore the letter of the law but they took account of the spirit too. The strikers eventually returned to work and *Olympic* at last set out nearly a month late on 15 May.

More radical surgery was needed as far as the ship itself was concerned. On 9 October 1912, the *Olympic* went back to Belfast for a major refit. Sixty-four wooden lifeboats were put aboard her, exactly the number that Alexander Carlisle had originally allowed for in his davit design. An inner watertight skin was added and some of the watertight bulkheads extended upwards. As a result of all the changes, she had a gross tonnage of 46,359 tons, 31 tons more than her tragic sister. *Olympic* stayed the largest ship officially afloat until June 1913 when the *Imperator* formally entered service.

At the time, the loss of the *Titanic* was a shattering event, unsurpassed in its pathos or tragedy even expressed in simple terms of how many lives had been lost. There had been no other shipping disaster to rival it. It was the first of three major maritime catastrophes in the space of four years, to be followed in 1914 by the loss of the *Empress of Ireland* which sank after being hit by another ship in a fog-bound St Lawrence River and then the *Lusitania* in 1915. In both of these, over 1,000 lives were lost.

The *Lusitania* tragedy had a minor and distant connection to the *Titanic*. Those who had lost both loved ones and possessions on the latter had been pushing for substantial amounts of compensation. On the *Lusitania* were a number of letters summoning British *Titanic* claimants to hearings in New York. The loss of the Cunard liner in 1915 caused the postponement of these hearings until all claimants could be properly notified.

Another connection was that, just a few days before, on 30 April 1915, Captain William Turner of the *Lusitania* had appeared at some preliminary compensation hearings in New York about the loss of the *Titanic*. He was asked if he would have acted any differently than Captain Smith did and answered that he would have steered a more southerly course. He left New York for Britain the next day and his ship was torpedoed on 7 May. Now he would have his own Inquiry to worry about.

It took three years of pre-trial manoeuvring for the *Titanic's* claimants to get their day in court. White Star naturally enough employed a top firm of lawyers – Burlingham, Montgomery and Beecher – to represent them. There was a wide range of claims. Irene Harris, widow of Henry Harris, a theatre magnate, filed one for $1 million for the loss of her husband's life. William Carter claimed $5,000 for his red Renault and Emilio Portaluppi $3,000 for a photograph of the great Italian, Garibaldi, personally signed. Eugene Daly wanted $50 for his lost bagpipes while Edwina Troutt claimed for her marmalade-making machine. Harry Anderson wanted $50 for his lost Chow dog.

Lord Mersey had cleared anyone of negligence for the disaster but the British courts were less keen to do so. The father of a lost third-class passenger, Patrick Ryan, had already brought a negligence claim against the *Titanic's* ultimate owners. The court found for the plaintiff, who was awarded £100 for his loss. White Star appealed but lost. The company was therefore officially guilty of negligence regardless of the outcome of the British Inquiry.

This no doubt encouraged others to file their claims against the company. Although further hearings were held in America, British law was applied to them. The total claims amounted to a staggering $16.8 million, over twice as much as the ship cost to build. This move was important as under American law any claims would be limited to the salvage value of the ship, just $97,000. However, the final amount awarded was far less than that claimed, just $663,000.

The *Lusitania* differed from the other two disasters just mentioned in that it was the result of a deliberate act rather than an accident. The outbreak of World War I changed the world far more than the *Titanic* disaster did. It introduced killing and death on an industrial scale. No doubt the loss of a ship with 1,500 lives was an awful tragedy but how did it measure up in Britain for example against a casualty list of 60,000 men on one morning, 1 July 1916, during the Battle of the Somme? Other personal tragedies emerged, hitting communities across the country, and in the process helping to deaden the impact of the loss of the *Titanic* on most save those who were directly affected by it, for whom of course the sense of personal loss would never completely go.

Even those who had survived the catastrophe were not immune from the war. Having managed to escape against the odds, Daniel Buckley joined up with the forces of his new country when they entered the war in 1917. Buckley, he who had managed to survive when so many of his fellow third-class passengers had perished, had only enjoyed a temporary reprieve and died on 15 October 1918.

For those who lost loved ones during the disaster, the events of 14/15 April 1912 remained a nightmare, to be lived out every day of their lives. Charlotte Collyer was one such, a woman who clearly loved her husband very much. She was determined to stay on in America to live out the dreams she and her beloved Harvey had planned for themselves along with little Madge. On 21 April 1912, Charlotte had written to her mother that 'some want me to go back to England but I can't, I could never at least yet go over the ground where my all is sleeping'.

It was a tragic, and no doubt, sincere wish that Charlotte expressed but it was not long before reality began to impinge. With her husband dead, all that she had gone to America for had vanished and it was not long before she decided that she was better off going back to England. She did and shortly after was married again, reality once more perhaps breaking in. However, whatever happiness she might have found in this new relationship was brief indeed for she died of tuberculosis in 1914. Charlotte had received funds from the relief efforts that had been set up to help those bereaved by the disaster and money had been provided to help the family return to England but for them tragedy continued unabated.

Other survivors had died even earlier. Colonel Gracie's survival had been an incredible tale but he had spent hours semi-immersed in ice-cold water and for a man in his mid-fifties, even one who tried to keep fit, it had been a debilitating ordeal. He had enthusiastically committed his experiences to print but by the end of 1912 he was gone, having entered into a diabetic coma which he never came out of and passing away on 4 December in New York. A number of *Titanic* survivors were at the graveside when he was interred. His great friend 'Clinch' Smith had gone on before him. On reaching New York, Gracie had attended a memorial service for him. There, the congregation had sung 'Oh God, Our Help in Ages Past', just as Gracie and Smith had done during the morning service on the *Titanic* on Sunday 14 April.

Gracie was not even the first to go. Maria Nackid had died on 30 July and Eugenie Baclini on 30 August 1912. Eugenie, a third-class passenger, was three at the time of the sinking and had escaped with two sisters and her mother in Collapsible C. Maria was only a baby, who had got off with her father and mother, herself still a teenager, also in Collapsible C. Surviving the *Titanic* was no guarantee of happiness in later life.

When World War I broke out, millions of tons of shipping was sunk. Associates of the *Titanic* were heavily affected. Her younger sister, the *Britannic* (the name *Gigantic* had hurriedly been dropped), was put into action as a hospital ship. She was sunk after hitting a mine in 1916 while travelling to the eastern Aegean to pick up casualties to ship back to Britain. She was however luckier than her sister, as she was only manned by crew and staff but no other passengers; there were some losses but they were in double figures. If she had sunk on the way back, the losses could have dwarfed those on the *Titanic*. But despite all the improvements made to her design after her sister sank, she went down in less than an hour.

One of those onboard the *Britannic* was Violet Jessop. She had a lucky escape. She was sucked under the water and struck her head on the keel of the doomed ship but her luxuriant auburn hair cushioned the blow. Years later, she suffered from bad headaches and went to a doctor who told her that at some time she had sustained a fractured skull. In the thirties, she married but the relationship was a disaster of an altogether different sort and it did not last long. She later wrote her memoirs, a sprightly offering full of life and fun, as one suspects Violet was.

Edith Russell lived in a very different world than Violet Jessop. She came from a rich Jewish family, yet she did her bit in the War too. She spent time in the trenches with the troops as one of the first female war correspondents. She later travelled extensively, survived tornadoes, car accidents, even another shipwreck. Edith never married and in later life became a reclusive and not altogether friendly figure, living her last years in squalor in a London hotel. A maid commented on her that 'Old Edy was the contrariest old hag who ever crossed my path'.

The War claimed several other notable participants in the *Titanic* drama too. During the conflict, the British government took over control of the *Californian*. She was torpedoed by a German submarine off the coast of

Cape Matapan, Greece, on 9 November 1915, though fortunately just one life was lost in the process. Captain Lord was not onboard. After his appearance at the British Inquiry and the question marks against his conduct, he was asked to resign from the Leyland Line which he did.

Carpathia survived for longer but met a similar fate. On 17 July 1918, she was part of a convoy which was attacked by a German submarine, U-55. She was hit, listed to port and sank bow first, with some of her crew killed by the explosions (two torpedoes hit her) but 157 passengers were rescued along with the remainder of the crew. She sank at 2.45 a.m. Her wreck was found in 1999, still in good condition and in one piece, at a depth of 500 feet.

As a result of the vast losses of the First World War, with millions losing their lives, the effect of the disaster became less profound. While the *Titanic* was never truly forgotten, it began to fade into the pages of history, a story known well enough but not one of truly legendary status. Over time it began to disappear from public consciousness and it might have become just a footnote of history if several key events had not happened to restore it to the minds of the public.

However, those involved directly never forgot it. Despite being cleared of any impropriety by the British Inquiry, Bruce Ismay never got over the *Titanic* disaster. The newspaper men had their knives sharpened for Ismay and never let him escape the slur of living while so many of his passengers died; the famous William Randolph Hearst was especially vocal in his criticisms. Ismay resigned as chairman of the White Star Line and president of IMM on 30 June 1913.

Despite hostility towards him, Ismay made generous charitable contributions towards various funds for distressed seamen. However, he lived out most of the rest of his life in a reclusive way, far from the public eye, in Ireland where he could indulge in his favourite pastimes such as fishing. He suffered from diabetes in the 1930s and lost part of a leg to amputation. He died in Mayfair, London, in 1937 of a cerebral thrombosis at the age of seventy-four.

Second Officer Lightoller never got the captaincy he perhaps expected in return for his loyalty to White Star. Frustrated and no doubt disgusted, he retired from the White Star Line and took up odd jobs such as an innkeeper and a chicken farmer. In the 1930s, he wrote up his experiences in *Titanic and Other Ships* and also recorded his memories for posterity. However, he courted controversy in the process and the Marconi Company threatened to sue him for comments he had made in the book.

Lightoller remained in love with the sea and bought a small yacht, the *Sundowner*. He and his wife were both keen sailors; Sylvia would later claim that she was on a boat that was nearly run down by the *Titanic* when it was off Southampton. And it was in this yacht that Lightoller, never a man to live a quiet life, had his last glorious moment. In 1940, the British army was trapped on the beaches of Dunkirk, surrounded by the enemy. The British Government cobbled together a flotilla of small boats to help larger craft evacuate these men. The *Sundowner*, with Lightoller at the helm, was one of them. He later ran a small boatyard and died of heart disease on 8 December 1952.

Joseph Boxhall also never got his captaincy, though he did make First Officer on the *Aquitania* when Cunard and White Star merged. He died on 25 April 1967. At his request, his ashes were scattered at sea at 41 degrees, 46 minutes North, 50 degrees, 14 minutes West. It was a final gesture; this was what Boxhall had calculated as the *Titanic's* last position and he was sure that he was right. Pitman never made captain either though he was not helped by his deteriorating eyesight which caused him to be transferred to the Purser's department. He served in this position in the Second World War, being awarded an MBE (Member of the Order of the British Empire) in 1946. He died on 7 November 1961.

Harold Lowe was another *Titanic* survivor not to get his own ship. He served in the Royal Navy during World War I and eventually made the rank of Commander in the Royal Naval Reserve. He died on 12 May 1944 of hypertension. He had acted gallantly, if outspokenly, on the night of the disaster and had been little rewarded for it, in common with his fellow officer survivors.

The rest of the surviving crew lived out their lives normally in anonymity. Sidney Daniels died in Portsmouth, his home town, in 1983 at the age of ninety, the last surviving crew member. Other long-lived survivors included Charles Joughin, who had good reason to be thankful for his large tumbler of whisky. He was later involved in another wreck, that of the *SS Oregon* which sank in Boston Harbour, and he served in troop transports in World War II. He died in New York in 1956.

Only one seaman could claim with justification that his career had benefited from his involvement with the disaster. Captain Arthur Rostron found himself moving on to greater things after his rescue efforts. He commanded several prominent Cunard ships, including the *Lusitania*. When World War I broke out, he was in charge of the *Aulania* which was turned into a troopship. In this capacity, he took part in the Allied operations at Gallipoli. He then took over the *Mauretania*. He received several public honours in Britain for his achievements and in 1928 took command of the *Berengaria* and became Commodore of Cunard, the highest position he could rise to in the company.

Retiring in 1931, he was in Southampton when the *Mauretania* began her last journey to the breaker's yard in Scotland. He was meant to go aboard as the start of her final voyage but, overcome with emotion, he had to leave. Maybe too he had seen a ghost for, sharing a last berth in

Southampton before her own journey to oblivion was another great ship, relic of a bygone era, none other than the *Olympic*.

The *Titanic's* older sister had enjoyed a long and mainly distinguished career. She became known as 'Old Reliable' having journeyed countless times to and fro across the Atlantic. And she had her own moments of glory. On 27 October 1914, she went to the rescue of a stricken warship, *HMS Audacious*, struck by a mine off the coast of Ireland and taking on water fast. She took off 250 of her crew, though the warship later blew up.

Later, *Olympic* was requisitioned as a troop transport. On 12 May 1918, *Olympic* sighted a U-Boat. Her then captain, Bertram Fox Hayes, put his ship full speed ahead towards the submarine and rammed her. The U-Boat's captain ordered his vessel to be abandoned; it turned out that he was planning to torpedo the *Olympic* when sighted. This was the only instance in the entire War that a U-Boat was sunk by anything other than a naval vessel.

During the War it was calculated that *Olympic* carried over 200,000 troops and travelled 184,000 miles, a colossal achievement compared to her younger sisters. She returned afterwards to civilian duty and her boilers were changed from coal-firing to oil-firing. However, the depression did for her. She was also not helped by an accident in 1934 when, travelling in heavy fog, she hit and sank the Nantucket Lightship. It was decided to mothball her in 1935. She was eventually scrapped in 1937.

The *Titanic* faded into oblivion, a fascinating but increasingly irrelevant part of history, or so it seemed but then there was a resurgence of interest in her. Not for the first, nor surely for the last, time Hollywood played its part in perpetuating and developing a legend. So too did a writer by the name of Walter Lord who published a book on the disaster called *A Night To Remember* in 1956. This in itself almost assumed legendary status in the *Titanic* corpus but it was not quite the bolt from the blue that some devotees might suggest it is. In 1953, Barbara Stanwyck had appeared in a movie about the disaster which at least kept the tale alive in the public consciousness.

Nevertheless there is no doubt that Lord's book was a seminal event, leading as it did to a movie of the same name which came out in 1958 in which Kenneth More starred as Second Officer Charles Lightoller. The movie mined the myths and the pathos well. The band played on as the ship began to sink beneath the waves and a small child is protected by an old man as well as he is able as the ship begins her death dive, a hauntingly moving scene that sums up as eloquently as it possibly could the feeling of hopelessness that must have descended upon the hundreds of people left to face eternity with no chance to escape their fate.

Several people connected to the *Titanic* showed a close interest in the movie, Lawrence Beesley looked over the ship used in the film and was famously reluctant to get off the model as it was sinking. Helen Smith, daughter of Captain Smith, was there too. Life had not been especially kind to her. Her mother Eleanor had been killed when run over by a taxi in London in April 1931. Helen married several times. Her first husband, a sea captain by the name of John Gilbertson died at sea of black water fever.

Helen then married Sidney Russell-Cooke in 1922. They had twins, Simon and Priscilla. Sidney died in 1930 in a hunting accident, Simon was killed in action in World War II, aged twenty-one, and Priscilla died of polio in 1947. It was a tragic sequence of events for a woman for whom premature death had been a constant companion yet she lived life to the full, driving sports cars and becoming a pilot. It was as if she cocked a snook to adversity and determined to treat death as an irrelevance. She herself died in Oxfordshire in 1973.

The movie had an interesting and unexpected side-effect. Shortly after its release, an eighty-one year-old man appeared in the offices of the Mercantile Marine Services Association (MMSA) in Liverpool. He announced simply that he was Lord of the *Californian*. Captain Stanley Lord had largely disappeared from the public view after the British Inquiry. In fact, although the events of that fated night did his career no good, they did him little harm either.

After the Inquiry, for a short time discussions were held with a view to prosecuting him. However, it was decided that any such action was unlikely to succeed. Lord had appeared as a witness and had revealed significant parts of his story when he had not been formally charged. It was felt that this put him at an unfair disadvantage and the discussions got nowhere.

Lord soon found himself another ship working for the Lawther Latta and Company Ltd. It was not a glamorous command, involved in more merchant shipping, but whatever else might be said of him he did not seem to be an excessively ambitious man. He would be on £20 a month and a monthly bonus of £5. During World War I, Lord successfully evaded all attempts to torpedo him. In the late twenties, his eyesight deteriorated and he retired early. He received a glowing reference from his employers who described him as 'one of the most capable commanders we have ever had'.

Because of the lack of any crippling impact on his career from his association with the *Titanic*, Lord had ignored rather than accepted the findings from the British Inquiry. However, he was not positively presented in the film version of *A Night to Remember* and therefore felt that he should now fight to clear his name, so he launched himself into an attempt to do so along with the MMSA. In some ways, it is a battle that is still being fought.

The book and the film of *A Night to Remember* stoked an interest in the *Titanic* story, and this served a real purpose as the band of survivors continued to diminish with the passing of time. One by one they slipped away, none more tragically than lookout Frederick Fleet. He had finished with the sea in 1936 and returned to Southampton where he became a newspaper seller. He was devoted to his wife who died on 28 December 1964. There followed an unfortunate domestic dispute which ended with Fleet homeless. Unable to face a future full of so many uncertainties, Frederick Fleet hanged himself, a tragic end to a troubled existence.

Interest in the *Titanic* lived on and was from time to time fired up anew. There had for many years been ideas about how the ship might be raised but it was first necessary to discover her. Despite her size, this turned out to be like looking for a needle in a haystack and the searchers were not helped by the fact that her position had been quoted incorrectly (with all due respect to Fourth Officer Boxhall).

In 1985 an expedition set out led by Dr Robert Ballard to find the wreck. It looked as if it would be a frustrating expedition, with hour after hour and day after day of fruitless viewing of a video monitor. During the early hours of 1 September, most of the crew were wrapped up asleep. It was just about 12.48 a.m. when the monotony of the ocean-floor mud was broken by something different. At first, it was not clear that this was anything but a false alarm but then unmistakable signs of wreckage emerged. A few minutes later, the suspicion that this was the site of *Titanic's* resting place was confirmed when a huge cylinder, a boiler, emerged out of the murky depths.

The rest, as they say, was history but Dr Ballard did not forget that he was on the scene of an immense human tragedy. At 2.20 a.m. that morning, the exact time that the great ship had slipped beneath the waves, he held a short but poignant memorial service on the fantail of the ship he was on, the *Knorr*. The flag of Harland & Wolff was raised over the spot in honour of one of her fallen children.

The pictures of the bow of the ship still apparently slicing through the water though in reality completely motionless over 2 miles down on the seabed became iconic, but the discovery did shatter a few dreams. The *Titanic* was far from intact, her bow section and stern about half a mile apart and a debris field littering the seabed in between the two segments. She was covered in rusticles (the features created by iron-eating bacteria, which look like rusted icicles or ferrous stalactites) and her fabric was being slowly eaten away; since being discovered, she has noticeably deteriorated significantly. It has been estimated that this strange bacteria eats away 0.1 tons of her remains every day. At the time, not everyone was completely euphoric about the discovery. The British newspaper, the *Times*, opined:

For our part, at the risk of appearing to be enemies of progress, we feel a tinge of regret that the marvels of underwater photography have already disturbed a legendary tale.

But the find both generated renewed interest and also offered invaluable evidence to historians as to how *Titanic* had met her end. However, that interest was exceeded by that generated when another Hollywood epic appeared in 1997. Simply entitled *Titanic* – no fancy titles were needed – James Cameron's movie created an impact almost as great as that generated by the original disaster. It won an amazing eleven Oscars, including Best Picture and became the highest grossing film of all time with worldwide takings of $1.8 billion. Incidentally, for lovers of trivia this made the film the joint highest Oscar winner of all time along with *Ben Hur* and *Lord of the Rings – The Return of the King*.

Of course, film critics might argue that it was the glamour of the leading actors and actresses that accounted for the success, or the stunning special effects, the evocative music score or indeed a combination of these and other factors. However, for those who have been exposed to the *Titanic* story it is the tale of those on the ship itself that makes it such an epic and gripping saga. But it is worth reminding ourselves that this story was not one of Hollywood glamour and romance but rather of nightmarish horror for all those involved in it. The passing of a hundred years has done nothing to lessen its impact. It is highly likely that the next hundred will be similarly unsuccessful in driving the *Titanic* into the fathomless depths of forgotten memory.

There is a postscript which provides a fitting end to this account of the *Titanic* disaster. In 1990, it was decided to review the case of 'Lord of the *Californian*'. A British government agency, the Marine Accident Investigation Branch, was requested to do so. It pored over the evidence for two years and still there was no sign of a report being published. It soon emerged why. It appeared that those investigating the circumstances could not agree on a conclusion.

Eventually, on 2 April 1992 a report was at least released, signed off by the Deputy Chief Inspector James de Coverly. Its findings were brief but contentious. The assessment was that the *Californian* was between seventeen and twenty miles away from the *Titanic*, that she may have been seen but only if the light was unusual (an effect known as 'refraction') and it was therefore more likely than not that the two ships could not see each other. However, the report concluded that distress signals were seen and proper action was not taken by those onboard the *Californian*.

Both sides in the dispute claimed a victory; 'pro-Lordites' asserting that their ship was too far away to help the doomed *Titanic*, anti-Lordites declaring that they had been right all along to castigate the *Californian* for ignoring distress rockets. In reality, the findings pleased nobody. To further muddy the waters, it appeared that a previous version of the report, prepared by Captain Thomas Barnett, a recently retired officer of great experience, had thought that the ships were much closer together, no more than ten miles apart.

The contradictory messages from this latest assessment by experts was a fitting 'conclusion' to a debate that can have no real conclusion, based as it is on contradictory and unreliable evidence. There is no black and white end to the *Californian* incident as indeed there is no possibility of providing definitive answers to so many other great mysteries of the sea. It is destined to live on as long as the story of another, much greater ship survives, the *Titanic*, fated to meet a terrible end before even completing one voyage. Even now, as the rust eats away at her corpse bit by inevitable bit, the legend of the 'ship of dreams' remains as real and as hypnotic as ever.

Select Bibliography

There have been hundreds of publications on the *Titanic* and I do not intend to provide a complete list of them here. Those I refer to in this select bibliography are publications that have been of particular use in writing this book. They may be broadly be divided into primary source eye witness accounts and secondary sources.

Primary Sources

The main source of eye witness material are the transcripts and reports of the American and British Inquiries. These may be accessed via the internet on www.titanicinquiry.org. In addition, an invaluable aid, and one that has in the main been relied on in this book, are the Paperless Archives of the *Titanic Historical Document Archive* (see www.paperlessarchives. com). Two CD-ROMs of information from these have been reproduced which contain both the Inquiry transcripts plus a range of various other useful and interesting documents.

Eye witness accounts appeared in 1912 in the classic early account by Logan Marshall. This has been re-released in *On board the Titanic – The Complete Story in Eyewitness Accounts* (Dover Publications, Mineola, New York, 2006). It has also been published as *The Sinking of the Titanic – 1912 Survivor Accounts* (Seattle Miracle Press, Washington, 10th reprinting June 2003). The book needs to be used with some caution, as some of the comments are plainly sensationalist: a particularly fine example being the caption against a photograph of an iceberg, which records how Lady Duff Gordon had seen such an object a few minutes before they ran into it. But it does capture the spirit of the times with regard to the disaster well.

A number of extensive eye-witness accounts can be found in *The Story of the Titanic as told by its survivors* (edited by Jack Winocour, Dover Publications, Mineola, New York, 1960). This has the eye-witness accounts of Lawrence Beesley, Archibald Gracie, Charles Lightoller and

Harold Bride. These accounts can also be found in other modern prints such as Beesley in *The Loss of the Titanic by one of the survivors* (Mariner Books, Boston/New York, 2000) or Gracie in *Titanic – A Survivor's Story* (Chicago, 1998) which also contains a short account written by Jack Thayer.

The disaster was particularly hard on Southampton and a large number of extracts from survivors accounts along with many fascinating photographs can be found in *Titanic Voices – Memories from the Fateful Voyage* (written, compiled and edited by Donald Hyslop, Alastair Forsyth and Sheila Jemima, Sutton Publishing, Stroud, 1997 reprint, 1994 original). A number of short eye-witness extracts with the survivors themselves speaking has also been produced by Kingfisher Productions in liaison with Southampton City Council in DVD format. An interesting and lively account was also written by Violet Jessop in *Titanic Survivor – The Memoirs of Violet Jessop Stewardess* (Sutton Publishing, edited and annotated by John Maxtone-Graham, 1998, republished 2007).

There was of course a mountain of press commentary on the disaster at the time and some of it can be seen in *The Titanic Disaster – As reported in the British National Press April – July 1912* (Dave Bryceson, Patrick Stephens Limited, Yeovil, 1997).

Secondary Sources

There are many of these in circulation but it is worth emphasizing that in the main points of reference for this book are to be found in the primary sources referred to above. However, useful additional details have also been accessed in the books referred to below. It would also be wrong not to acknowledge the huge amount of information available on the Internet, in particular at www.encylopedia-titanica.org, which is an absolutely invaluable gold mine of facts and opinions about the *Titanic*.

The classic account of the sinking is *A Night to Remember* by Walter Lord (first published in 1956, the version I have used here is the Penguin Books illustrated edition, Harmondsworth etc. 1978). Lord also produced a book called *The Night Lives On* (Penguin Books, Harmondsworth etc. 1986) which is more of a discussion of various aspects of the sinking.

Another popular account, with many illustrations is *Titanic: Triumph and Tragedy – A Chronicle in Words and Pictures* (John P. Eaton and Charles A. Haas, Patrick Stephens Limited, Yeovil, Somerset, 1995 reprint). In addition, various aspects of the tragedy are also examined in *The Complete Titanic – From the Ship's Earliest Blueprints to the Epic Film* (Stephen J. Spignesi, Birch Lane Press, Secaucus, New Jersey, 1998), something of a miscellany but with some interesting background information.

A fascinating and unusual insight into the disaster from an academic historian's perspective is *Titanic – A Night Remembered* by Professor Stephanie Barczewski (Hambledon Continuum, London and New York, 2006 edition). This gives good insights into the legends of the ship and the impact of the disaster on various cities in the UK that were affected by it.

Wyn Craig Wade gives an excellent insight into the conduct of the American Inquiry in *The Titanic – End of a dream* (Weidenfeld and Nicholson, London, 1980 edition).

The discovery of the wreck has been examined in a number of publications and in particular *The Discovery of the Titanic* by Dr Robert D. Ballard (Guild Publishing, London, 1988 edition).

The story of the *Californian* and the *Titanic* has developed a literature all of its own. Those preparing to delve into the story in more detail would be best armed with large pots of coffee as the confusing and contradictory evidence requires careful analysis. A number of books take the part of Captain Lord; these include *The Titanic and the Californian* by Peter Padfield (Hodder and Stoughton, London, 1965), *The Titanic and the Mystery Ship* by Senan Molony (Tempus, Stroud, 2006) and *Titanic and the Californian* by Thomas B. Williams, edited and revised by Rob Kamps, Tempus, Stroud, 2007). The contrary argument is presented in particular in *The Ship That Stood Still* by Leslie Reade, edited and updated by Edward P. De Groot (Patrick Stephens Limited, Yeovil, 1993).

List of Illustrations

of the escape from the sinking *Titanic*. The boats start to move away to avoid the expected suction. However, the iceberg in this picture was not seen when the ship was sinking. © J & C McCutcheon Collection. 29. Slowly but surely, *Titanic* settled bow first into the water, being dragged inexorably down into the deep. Her lights blazed till almost the end, it was a surreal sight for those in the lifeboats to see the portholes descent into the depths. © J & C McCutcheon Collection. 30. To the amazement of the awed watchers in the lifeboats, the doomed vessel remained in the upright position for a time estimated at five minutes. Many witnesses claim the ship broke in two near the end. © J & C McCutcheon Collection. 31. A collapsible Englehardt boat approaches the Cunard Line's *RMS Carpathia*, which had steamed at 17 knots to get to the survivors. The women in some boats were in nightgowns and bare feet and the wealthiest woman mingled with the poorest immigrants. © J & C McCutcheon Collection. 32. A lifeboat by the side of the *Carpathia* with its occupants waiting to be rescued. There were no scenes of panic from amongst the exhausted and traumatised survivors. © W.B. Bartlett. 33. A *Titanic* lifeboat pulls close to the *Carpathia*. The sail hoisted shows this to be the boat under the command of Fifth Officer Lowe. © W.B. Bartlett. 34. *Titanic* lifeboat alongside the *Carpathia*. The gangway doors are open to facilitate access. © J & C McCutcheon Collection. 35. *Titanic* survivors aboard the *Carpathia*. © W.B. Bartlett. 36. The survivors reached the *Carpathia* early next morning and were hauled aboard the small Cunarder. © J & C McCutcheon Collection. 37. Mr and Mrs George Harder, a young honeymoon couple, on the deck of *Carpathia* after surviving the disaster. © J & C McCutcheon Collection. 38. Harold Bride, the second Radio Operator was carried off the *Carpathia* as he had injured his feet badly in the frozen waters. His survival story was one of the most remarkable of the night. © J & C McCutcheon Collection. 39. Photograph taken before the 'orphans' of the *Titanic* were correctly identified and returned to their mother. The boys are French brothers Michel (age 4) and Edmond Navratil (age 2). To board the ship, their father assumed the name Louis Hoffman and used their nicknames, Lolo and Mamon. Their father died in the disaster. They arrived in New York in the care of Miss Hays, a fluent French speaking survivor. Amberley Archive. 40. A front page headline from *The World* describing the sinking to a hungry audience. Note the exaggerated number of women and children claimed saved. © W.B. Bartlett. 41. The indomitable Margaret Brown, *Titanic* survivor. © W.B. Bartlett. 42. Captain E.J. Smith's statue, Lichfield. A long way from the icy North Atlantic to municipal gardens in Middle England. © W.B. Bartlett. 43. Captain Rostron of the *Carpathia* who was praised for his heroic rescue efforts. © W.B. Bartlett. 44. William Stead, a famous reformer and editor who went down with the ship. A fortune teller had told him to 'beware of water'. © W.B. Bartlett. 45. Mrs Eloise Smith, one of the first-class passengers who was widowed on the *Titanic*. © W.B. Bartlett. 46. Guglielmo Marconi whose wireless operators helped saved 700 lives in the disaster. © W.B. Bartlett. 47. Mrs Widener, who left here husband behind on the sinking ship. © W.B. Bartlett. 48. George Widener, who was lost in the sinking with his son. © W.B. Bartlett. 49. Isidor Straus, owner of the famous New York department store Macys, who was lost with his wife Ida who refused to enter a boat. © W.B. Bartlett. 50. Crowds wait in New York for news of those who have been saved and who have been lost on the *Titanic*. Firm news took several days to come through. © W.B. Bartlett. 51. A photograph of Mrs Benjamin Guggenheim leaving the White Star offices in New York after trying to get news of her husband. He had dressed in his best before going down with the ship. © W.B. Bartlett. 52. Crowds await the arrival of the *Carpathia* with *Titanic* survivors in New York. © W.B. Bartlett. 53. A plan of the inside of the *Titanic*. © W.B. Bartlett. 54. A cutaway illustration of the *Titanic* from *L'Illustration* magazine. © J & C McCutcheon Collection. 55. The position of the wreck from the Logan Marshall classic. © W.B. Bartlett. 56. A diagram from Logan Marshall showing how much of an iceberg is hidden below the waterline. © W.B. Bartlett. 57. A spiritual lesson from the disaster as shown in Logan Marshall. © W.B. Bartlett. 58. The North Atlantic shipping routes in 1912. These would be moved south in iceberg season. © W.B. Bartlett. 59. Diagram showing the force of the *Titanic* hitting the iceberg. © W.B. Bartlett. 60, 61, 62, 63, 64 & 65. Jack Thayer was one of a number of survivors to describe the ship breaking in two as she sank. This series of illustrations drawn aboard *Carpathia* show the ship in her dying minutes and clearly show the two halves. It would be over seventy years before Thayer was proved right when the wreck was discovered resting on the seabed in two halves. © W.B. Bartlett. 66. A diagram from Logan Marshall showing the depth of the water where the *Titanic* went down. © W.B. Bartlett. 67. Logan Marshall's offering for the hymn played as the ship went down, not *Nearer My God to Thee* but the tune *Autumn* as possibly suggested by Harold Bride. © W.B. Bartlett. 68. A plan showing the layout of the lifeboats on the upper deck of *Titanic*. © W.B. Bartlett. 69. A copy of the hand-written note handed to a passenger leaving in a lifeboat from gambler J.H. Rogers (a.k.a. Jay Yates) who was lost. © W.B. Bartlett. 70. A drawing from *Punch* which was dedicated to the 'brave men' who perished in the disaster. Britannia looks on as a grieving woman tries to cope with the immensity of the tragedy. In practice, nearly 50 first class male passengers survived, most controversially Bruce Ismay. © W.B. Bartlett. 71. *The Whited Sepulchre*, a contemporary cartoon weighing up the *Titanic's* luxuries against the lives of some of her prominent passengers. © W.B. Bartlett. 72. A contemporary picture lionising the bravery of the men on the *Titanic*. The myth of male sacrifice developed as the world tried to make sense of the disaster. In practice, some men were much more heroic than others. © W.B. Bartlett.

Available from December 2011 from Amberley Publishing

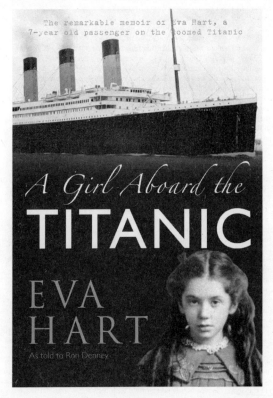

The remarkable memoir of Eva Hart, a 7-year old passenger on the doomed Titanic

'I saw that ship sink, I never closed my eyes. I saw it, I heard it, and nobody could possibly forget it. I can remember the colours, the sounds, everything. The worst thing I can remember are the screams'. This is the amazing story of how Eva survived the sinking of the *Titanic* and the affect it had on her life following the tragedy. The events of a few hours in her childhood remained with her so vividly throughout her life that it took Eva nearly forty years before she could talk openly about the tragedy.

£16.99 Hardback
60 illustrations
192 pages
978-1-4456-0089-5

Available from December 2011 from all good bookshops or to order direct
Please call **01453-847-800**
www.amberleybooks.com

Available from September 2011 from Amberley Publishing

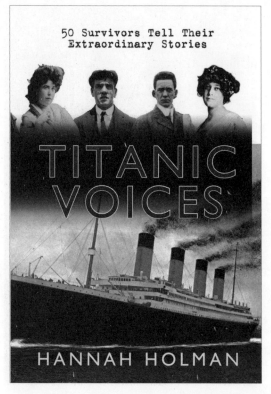

The sinking of the Titanic *in the words of the survivors*

There were 712 survivors of the *Titanic* disaster and their horrific experience has captivated readers and movie goers for almost 100 years. But what was it actually like for a woman to say goodbye to her husband? For a mother to leave her teenage sons? For the unlucky many who found themselves in the freezing Atlantic waters? *Titanic Voices* is the most comprehensive collection of *Titanic* survivors' accounts ever published and includes many unpublished, and long forgotten accounts, unabridged, together with an authoritative editorial commentary. It is also the first book to include substantial accounts from women survivors - most of the previously well known accounts were written by men.

£20 Hardback
120 illustrations (20 colour)
512 pages
978-1-4456-0222-6

Available from September 2011 from all good bookshops or to order direct
Please call **01453-847-800**
www.amberleybooks.com

Available from October 2011 from Amberley Publishing

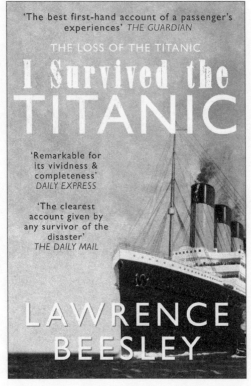

The first-hand account of the sinking of the Titanic *by second class passenger and Englishman, Lawrence Beesley, the longest and most detailed memoir of the sinking*

'The best first-hand account of a passenger's experiences... a first-rate piece of descriptive writing'
THE GUARDIAN

'Remarkable for its vividness and completeness' THE DAILY EXPRESS

'The clearest account given by any survivor of the disaster' THE DAILY MAIL

'Thrilling' THE SPECTATOR

'As authoritative and comprehensive an account of the greatest marine disaster of modern times as will ever be written' NEW YORK TIMES

£16.99 Hardback
100 illustrations
192 pages
978-1-4456-0443-5

Available from October 2011 from all good bookshops or to order direct
Please call **01453-847-800**
www.amberleybooks.com

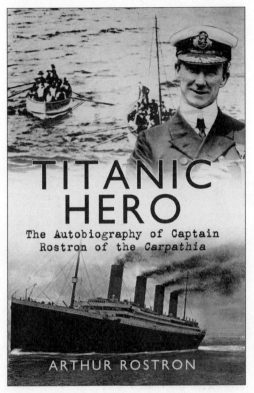

Index